Global Gifts

This anthology explores the role that art and material goods played in diplomatic relations and political exchanges between Asia, Africa, and Europe in the early modern world. The authors challenge the idea that there was a European primacy in the practice of gift giving through a wide panoramic review of diplomatic encounters between Europeans (including the Portuguese, French, Dutch, and English) and Asian empires (including Ottoman, Persian, Mughal, Sri Lankan, Chinese, and Japanese cases). They examine how those exchanges influenced the global production and circulation of art and material culture, and explore the types of gifts exchanged, the chosen materials, and the manner of their presentation. *Global Gifts* establishes new parameters for the study of the material and aesthetic culture of Eurasian relations before 1800, exploring the meaning of artistic objects in global diplomacy and the existence of economic and aesthetic values mutually intelligible across cultural boundaries.

Zoltán Biedermann is Associate Professor and Head of Spanish, Portuguese, and Latin American Studies at University College London.

Anne Gerritsen is Professor of History and directs the Global History and Culture Centre at the University of Warwick.

Giorgio Riello is Professor of Global History and Culture at the University of Warwick.

Studies in Comparative World History

Editors

Other Books in the Series

Michael Adas, *Prophets of Rebellion: Millenarian Protest Movements against the European Colonial Order (1979)*

Philip D. Curtin, *Cross-Cultural Trade in World History (1984)*

Leo Spitzer, *Lives in Between: Assimilation and Marginality in Austria, Brazil, and West Africa, 1780–1945 (1989)*

Marshall G. S. Hodgson, Edmund Burke III (eds.), *Rethinking World History: Essays on Europe, Islam and World History (1993)*

Philip D. Curtin, *The Rise and Fall of the Plantation Complex: Essays in Atlantic History (1990; second edition, 1998)*

John Thornton, *Africa and Africans in the Making of the Atlantic World, 1400–1800 (1992; second edition, 1998)*

David Northrup, *Indentured Labor in the Age of Imperialism, 1834–1922 (1995)*

Lauren Benton, *Law and Colonial Cultures: Legal Regimes in World History, 1400–1900 (2002)*

Victor Lieberman, *Strange Parallels: Southeast Asia in Global Context, c. 800–1830, vol. 1: Integration on the Mainland (2003)*

Kerry Ward, *Networks of Empire: Forced Migration in the Dutch East India Company (2009)*

Victor Lieberman, *Strange Parallels: Southeast Asia in Global Context, c. 800–1830, vol. 2: Mainland Mirrors: Europe, Japan, China, South Asia, and the Islands (2010)*

Ulbe Bosma, *The Sugar Plantation in India and Indonesia: Industrial Production, 1770–2010 (2013)*

Karin Hofmeester and Bernd-Stefan Grewe, *Luxury in Global Perspective: Objects and Practices, 1600–2000 (2016)*

Global Gifts

The Material Culture of Diplomacy in Early Modern Eurasia

Edited by
ZOLTÁN BIEDERMANN
University College London

ANNE GERRITSEN
University of Warwick

GIORGIO RIELLO
University of Warwick

CAMBRIDGE
UNIVERSITY PRESS

University Printing House, Cambridge CB2 8BS, United Kingdom

One Liberty Plaza, 20th Floor, New York, NY 10006, USA

477 Williamstown Road, Port Melbourne, VIC 3207, Australia

314-321, 3rd Floor, Plot 3, Splendor Forum, Jasola District Centre, New Delhi - 110025, India

79 Anson Road, #06-04/06, Singapore 079906

Cambridge University Press is part of the University of Cambridge.

It furthers the University's mission by disseminating knowledge in the pursuit of education, learning and research at the highest international levels of excellence.

www.cambridge.org
Information on this title: www.cambridge.org/9781108401500
DOI: 10.1017/9781108233880

First published 2018
First paperback edition 2019

A catalogue record for this publication is available from the British Library

Library of Congress Cataloging in Publication data
NAMES: Riello, Giorgio, editor. | Gerritson, Anne, 1967– editor. | Biedermann, Zoltan, editor.
TITLE: Global gifts : the material culture of diplomacy in early modern Eurasia / edited by Giorgio Riello, University of Warwick; Anne Gerritson, University of Warwick; Zoltan Biedermann, University College London.
DESCRIPTION: Cambridge ; New York : Cambridge University Press, 2018. | Series: Studies in comparative world history | Includes bibliographical references and index.
IDENTIFIERS: LCCN 2017041311 | ISBN 9781108415507 (hardback : alk. paper) | ISBN 9781108401500 (pbk. : alk. paper)
SUBJECTS: LCSH: Diplomatic gifts–Europe–History. | Diplomatic gifts–Asia–History. | Material culture–Political aspects–Europe–History. | Material culture–Political aspects–Asia–History. | World politics–To 1900.
CLASSIFICATION: LCC D397 .G56 2018 | DDC 327.5009/031–dc23
LC record available at https://lccn.loc.gov/2017041311

ISBN 978-1-108-41550-7 Hardback
ISBN 978-1-108-40150-0 Paperback

Contents

Figures

Tables

Contributors

Zoltán Biedermann is Associate Professor and Head of Spanish, Portuguese and Latin American Studies at University College London. He is the author of three books and numerous articles and book chapters on the history of European expansion and knowledge exchange in the Indian Ocean. He is currently finishing his fourth book, *Island Empire*, a study of the Portuguese involvement in Sri Lanka before 1600.

Adam Clulow teaches East Asian History at Monash University, Melbourne, Australia. His first book, *The Company and the Shogun: The Dutch Encounter with Tokugawa Japan*, was published in 2014 and he is currently working on a project focused on early modern diplomacy.

Natasha Eaton is Reader in the History of Art at University College London. Her research focuses primarily on cross-cultural encounters between India and Britain in the eighteenth and nineteenth centuries and contemporary art in South Asia. She is author of *Mimesis across Empires: Artworks and Networks in India, 1765–1860* (2013) and *Colour, Art and Empire: The Nomadism of Visual Representation* (2013).

Antonia Gatward Cevizli is a Lecturer and Course Leader in Art History at Sotheby's Institute of Art, London. Her research focuses on cultural exchange between the Italian city-states and the Ottomans in the fifteenth and early sixteenth century.

Anne Gerritsen is Professor of History at the University of Warwick, UK. From 2013 to 2018, she also holds the Kikkoman Chair for the study of Asia-Europe Intercultural Dynamics at the University of Leiden in the

Netherlands. She has published on the domestication of global commodities in the early modern Netherlands and on the history of porcelain. She is currently completing a manuscript on global and local interactions in the sites of porcelain manufacture in China.

Barbara Karl is director of the Textile Museum St. Gallen, Switzerland. Her main areas of expertise are Indian textile production for the Portuguese during the sixteenth and seventeenth centuries, cultural and material exchange between Europe and the Islamic World during the early modern period and the history of collecting.

Mary Laven is Professor of Early Modern History at the University of Cambridge and has published widely on the cultural history of religion. Her publications include *Virgins of Venice: Enclosed Lives and Broken Vows in the Renaissance Convent* (2002) and *Mission to China: Matteo Ricci and the Jesuit Encounter with the East* (2011).

Luca Molà is Professor of Early Modern Europe, History of the Renaissance and the Mediterranean in a World Perspective at the European University Institute in Florence, Italy, and a member of staff of the Department of History, University of Warwick, UK. He has written on the history of the silk industry and on the history of innovation and patents in Renaissance Italy.

Carla Alferes Pinto is Postdoctoral Fellow at the Portuguese Centre for Global History (CHAM) of the Faculty of Social and Human Sciences at Nova University of Lisbon and University of the Azores, Portugal. She has researched and published on the artistic relations between Portugal and India and on the study of demand, production and appropriation of material culture and artistic objects in the sixteenth and seventeenth centuries.

Giorgio Riello is Professor in Global History and Culture at the Department of History at the University of Warwick, UK. He has written on the history of trade, material culture, textile and fashion and is the author of *Cotton: The Fabric that Made the Modern World* (2013) and coauthor of *Luxury: A Rich History* (2016, with Peter McNeil).

Claudia Swan is Associate Professor of Art History at Northwestern University, Evanston, Illinois. She has published on early modern Dutch art and science, the history of collecting and the history of the imagination; her forthcoming book is entitled *Rarities of These Lands: Encounters with the Exotic in Golden Age Holland.*

Preface

Precious objects and valued commodities did not merely "move" from one place to another, they were purposefully exchanged across cultural and political boundaries. While such exchanges may often have had commercial aspects, we focus here on their political and especially diplomatic dimensions. The giving and receiving of diplomatic gifts constitute a crucial element in the formation of early modern connections and provide us with a powerful analytical tool for enhancing our understanding of that formation. The exchange of material goods as gifts, in the pressured context of diplomatic exchange, inevitably involved the movement and realignment of power. The manner in which they were selected, presented, received and understood tells us something about how the agents of the exchange saw that power and dealt with this realignment. Gifts, and the processes by which they were transacted, thus allow us to explore the multiple modes of exchange that were available in the early modern world.

Diplomacy was – as recent research suggests – pervasive in the interactions between Europe, Africa and Asia, and the display and transaction of material goods (treasured objects, objets d'art) during diplomatic acts are one of the keys for understanding the growth of global connections. Anthropology has taught us about the reciprocity of gifting in many human societies, the principle of *do ut des*: one rarely gives anything away without expecting something in return. But gifts are not passive objects in the diplomatic game. They can contribute to the destabilization of relations or help in the consolidation of power hierarchies. They play a crucial role in the processes of negotiation and, in fact, are often the only testimonies that survive of past encounters between dignitaries of European, African and Asian societies. *Global Gifts* thus endeavors to highlight the role of visual and material goods in diplomatic contexts and, inversely, enrich our understanding of diplomatic exchanges by emphasizing the presence of art and material culture. The two approaches are, by all means, complementary and work well together to throw new light on the emerging field of connected global history.

Based on a series of innovative papers presented at conferences held at the University of Warwick and the University of London, this book explores a variety of subjects relating to the study of global visual culture in the early modern period. Among other questions, it examines why ivories from Sri Lanka were valued in Renaissance Europe, what Italian Jesuits found to be the most adequate gifts at the imperial court of China, what French and Dutch diplomats carried to Japan and Siam, how Muslims and Christians exchanged artifacts in the Mediterranean and the Indian Ocean in a time of religious strife and why paintings offered as gifts by the British were not particularly appreciated in eighteenth-century India. Through such a variety of subjects, we explore how aesthetic and commercial value worked across cultural borders and how objects contributed to the making of early "globalized" visual cultures. More importantly, this book seeks to challenge the widespread emphasis on economic exchange that has characterized the study of global connections, and shift the focus to the political exchange of power across cultural boundaries. The exchange of diplomatic gifts played a key part in the growth of early modern global connections.

The present volume brings together a diverse but coherent body of case studies into the making and unmaking of gifts between European and Asian powers during the early modern period. In this sense, this is a pioneering volume with all the advantages and disadvantages that such a status entails. We are grateful not just to the authors who worked with us but also to many other colleagues and friends who helped shape our ideas. Our thanks in particular go to Maxine Berg, Leah Clark, Dana Leibsohn and Beverly Lemire. We are aware that many of the statements made over the course of the following pages may require qualification in a nearby future. But we are also confident that our collection will transmit our enthusiasm for what bears all the signs of emerging as a new field of historical inquiry.

Introduction

Global Gifts and the Material Culture of Diplomacy in Early Modern Eurasia

Zoltán Biedermann, Anne Gerritsen and Giorgio Riello

Gifts played a key role in the making of the early modern world. They were an indispensable ingredient of global diplomacy and were central to the establishment and development of global connections. This much is clear from the wealth of scholarship on early modern gift exchange and diplomacy. This volume builds on the existing literature, but takes the field in new directions. First, it explores the question of what exactly a diplomatic gift is. The question is not new, but demands new answers in light of the emergence of global history and the insight that material culture provides a key complement to textual sources for historical research. Second, this volume argues that global gifts were an important vehicle for the establishment of shared values and material and visual experiences. We seek to show that gifts were key agents of social cohesion and transcultural systems of value in the emergence of a global political community in the early modern world. And third, we argue that gifts were agents in the unfolding of political rivalries and asymmetries of power.

This introductory chapter begins with an exploration of the diplomatic gift itself, followed by a consideration of recent developments in the fields of material culture studies and global history and their impact on our understanding of what makes a diplomatic gift. We then move on to a consideration of the agency of gifts in the establishment of power relations in the early modern world. Here we see gifts both creating cohesion and facilitating shared regimes of value, while at the same time highlighting differences in meaning and value, to the point of creating and

We would like to thank Antonia Gatward, Leah Clark, Dana Leibsohn, Beverly Lemire, Luca Molà and Claudia Swan for their valuable comments on this introduction.

exacerbating political rivalries and asymmetries of power in the early modern world.

THE MAKING OF A DIPLOMATIC GIFT

Ambassadors without appropriate gifts had little hope of being successful. Take the case of the embassy sent in 1657 by Charles X Gustav of Sweden (r. 1654–60) to the Ottoman sultan Mehmet IV (r. 1648–87). Having to travel incognito, Claes Brorson Rålamb, the chief Swedish ambassador, reached Constantinople without any suitable gift for either the sultan or the grand vizier. He was received by the Porte, but the embassy was ultimately a failure.[1] He was not the only ambassador to face difficulties with gifting. A century and a half earlier, Vasco da Gama had arrived in the kingdom of Calicut in India and faced a similar challenge. The meager gifts he presented to the Samudri Raja in 1498 were simply not in line with what was expected from a merchant, let alone an ambassador. Gama's successors, the governors residing in Goa, had to learn swiftly the art of gifting in order to survive in the Asian political arena. Their apprenticeship set the tone for centuries of diplomatic exchange to come.[2]

Gifts were, along with the letters sent by foreign rulers, at the heart of the ceremonies that accompanied the formal reception of ambassadors in Asia and in Europe. Two pages from the *Akbarnama* or Book of Akbar (Figure I.1a, b) show the reception of an embassy from Safavid Persia by the Mughal emperor in 1562. While the envoy of Shah Tamasp (r. 1524–76), Sayyid Beg, is shown in the company of Akbar (r. 1556–1605) on the right sheet, gifts are depicted ostentatiously as they were prepared for delivery on the left.[3] Another image, in many ways similar, shows us Louis XIV of France (r. 1643–1715) receiving an ambassador from Persia in 1715 (Figure I.2). Mohammed Reza Beg, the envoy of Sultan Husayn (r. 1694–1722), appears presenting a letter

[1] Rålamb was aware that the lack of suitable gifts would have been perceived as an affront. Yet his travel incognito did not allow the carrying of precious gifts. Sten Westberg, "Claes Rålamb: Statesman, Scholar and Ambassador," in *The Sultan's Procession: The Swedish Embassy to Sultan Mehmed IV in 1657–1658 and the Rålamb Paintings*, ed. Karin Ådah (Constantinople: Swedish Research Institute in Constantinople, 2007), 26–57, esp. 43–44.

[2] Zoltán Biedermann, "Portuguese Diplomacy in Asia in the Sixteenth Century: A Preliminary Overview," *Itinerario* 29, no. 2 (2005): 13–37; a revised version is available in id., *The Portuguese in Sri Lanka and South India: Studies in the History of Empire, Diplomacy and Trade* (Wiesbaden: Harrassowitz, 2014), 7–32.

[3] Susan Stronge, *Painting for the Mughal Emperor: The Art of the Book 1560–1650* (London: V&A Publications, 2002), 23 and 38.

FIGURE I.1A Painting from the *Akbarnama*: "Akbar receives Iranian ambassador Sayyid Beg" (folio 1). Outline by La'l and painting by Ibrahim Kahar. Opaque watercolor and gold on paper, Mughal, c. 1586–89. Victoria and Albert Museum IS.2:27-1896.

FIGURE I.1B Painting from the *Akbarnama*: "Akbar receives Iranian ambassador Sayyid Beg" (folio 2). Outline by La'l and painting by Ibrahim Kahar. Opaque watercolor and gold on paper, Mughal, c. 1586–89. Victoria and Albert Museum IS.2:28-1896.

FIGURE 1.2 “L’audiance donné par le roy Louis XIV à l’ambassadeur de Perse . . . 19 février 1715” (Hearing given by King Louis XIV to the ambassador of Persia . . . 19 February 1715). Engraving, 44.5 cm × 56.0 cm.

from his master to Louis XIV, followed by his coadjutants carrying a sample of gifts. The cartouche reports the speech made by the ambassador to renew the friendship between the two rulers, and then gives a detailed list of the objects not shown in the image. These included "a sabre encrusted with diamonds, emeralds and stones of all colors and the encasing covered in pearls; a rose made of rubies; 280 turquoises; 100 oriental pearls; 7 garnets weighing 250 grains; 12 pieces of gold cloth and 12 of silver cloth."[4]

In Versailles or Agra, as in other European and Asian courts, the arrival of ambassadors tended to create material expectations. Ambassadors might spend months preparing for the reception and negotiating what objects were to be displayed in what manner. In hostile environments, gifts paved the way for dialogues or generated disputes. They might be stolen or lost. They could be put on display for courtiers to see, and at times be disposed among nobles as part of the munificence of the receiving king. All these acts would ideally be recorded and commemorated in additional artifacts such as reports, paintings and engravings – and of course amply talked about among the elite. Under such circumstances, diplomatic gifts created desire as much as they satiated it. Shah Abbas II of Persia (r. 1642–66) sent textiles with his diplomatic missions to promote the consumption of Iranian fabrics.[5] On arriving in Moscow in 1650, an ambassador of Abbas had with him over 300 pieces of velvet, damask, satin and taffeta, as well as sashes and 15 carpets. Such a stock would in other circumstances have passed him for a merchant. In this case, however, there was no doubt that he should be welcomed as a diplomat.[6]

What does exactly make a "diplomatic gift" a gift as opposed to just being an object of trade? As a point of departure, what we have chosen to

[4] See *La Perse et la France: Relation diplomatiques et culturelles du XVIIe au XIXe siècle*, catalogue of the exhibition held at the Musée Cernuschi, January–March 1972 (Paris: Musée Cernuschi, 1972).

[5] On diplomacy and the use of textiles by the Iranian court, see Sinem Arcak Casale, "The Persian Madonna and Child: Commodified Gifts between Diplomacy and Armed Struggle," *Art History* 38, no. 4 (2015): 636–51; and Maria João Ferreira, "Embroidered Flowers and Birds for Shah Abbas I: Chinese Silks in Portuguese Diplomatic Missions in the Early Modern World," *Textile History*, forthcoming (2018).

[6] Elena Yurievne Gagarina, ed., *The Tsars and the East: Gifts from Turkey and Iran in the Moscow Kremlin* (Washington, DC: Freer Gallery of Art and Arthur M. Sackler Gallery, 2009), 4. Russia received also enormous quantities of silk from Chinese embassies as for instance the 700 bolts of patterned and embroidered silk sent by the Shunzhi Emperor (r. 1644–62) to Russia as part of the 1649 embassy. Maria Menshikova, "Chinese Silk in Imperial Russia in the 17th–18th Centuries," in *The Silk Road: A Road of Silk*, ed. Zhao Feng (Shanghai: Donghua University Press, 2016), 234–36.

engage with in the present volume are things given away in the context of diplomatic negotiations without a direct pecuniary payment in exchange. To borrow Zemon Davis's words, the "'gift mode' ... exists along with [and is thus distinct from] the mode of sales ... and the mode of coercion."[7] This said, such categories are most useful if they can also, at one point or another, be fine-tuned or overcome. The deeper we go into the history of diplomatic gifts, the more difficult it becomes to establish exactly where the boundaries between gifts, luxury commodities, tribute and booty can be drawn. Most theories of gift-giving emphasize – as indeed common sense would suggest – that gifts tend to be made with a past or a potential future benefit in mind. In other words, gifts tend to come with strings attached, they generally imply some sort of reciprocity, though they are part of a wider economic logic pervading all social relations. As Marcel Mauss stipulated in what is still the most frequently cited work on the subject, gifts served to form and express commitments to "services and counter-services," and they helped create a web of obligations following the logic of "*prestation totale.*"[8]

Gifts played a key role in the symbolic economy and the social relations of the people handling them, which takes us into difficult terrain because it lays bare the ambiguities involved in the very notion of the economic. As the literary scholar David Hawkes put it, economic analysis "can be called 'materialist' only on the supposition that the economy is a material phenomenon" – which of course it is not.[9] If we are to take Mauss seriously today, then we have to acknowledge how his entire theory of reciprocity was grounded in a critique of mechanistic economic theory, pointing to the importance of reciprocal gifting as the glue that holds societies together, a point to which we return below.[10]

7 Natalie Zemon Davis, *The Gift in Sixteenth-Century France* (Madison and London: University of Wisconsin Press, 2000), 9.

8 Marcel Mauss, *The Gift: The Form and Reason for Exchange in Archaic Societies*, transl. W. D. Halls, foreword Mary Douglas (New York: Norton and Company, 1990), 5.

9 David Hawkes, "Materialism and Reification in Renaissance Studies. Review Article," *Journal for Early Modern Cultural Studies* 4, no. 2 (2004): 114.

10 For an illuminating analysis of Mauss's theory and how it has been misread over the decades, see Patrick J. Geary, "Gift Exchange and Social Science Modeling: The Limitations of a Construct," in *Negotiating the Gift: Pre-Modern Figurations of Exchange*, ed. Gadi Algazi, Valentin Groebner and Bernhard Jussen (Göttingen: Vandenhoeck and Ruprecht, 2003), 129–40. See also Beate Wagner-Hasel, "Egoistic Exchange and Altruistic Gift. On the Roots of Marcel Mauss's Theory of the Gift," in ibid., 141–71, and Harry Liebersohn, *The Return of the Gift: European History of a Global Idea* (Cambridge and New York: Cambridge University Press, 2011).

Our understanding of diplomatic gifts, then, is shaped by several further questions. How did gifted artifacts work (or sometimes fail to work) in the context of early modern diplomatic exchanges across cultural boundaries? What can the history of things tell us about the making of the early modern world that other histories do not? The main objective of the present volume is to address these and other questions through a series of case studies from the Eurasian context. But first we offer a reflection on gifts in academic fields of study, at the intersection of three different but related fields: the resurgent history of diplomacy, material culture studies and the discipline of global history.

NEW APPROACHES TO DIPLOMACY IN THE EARLY MODERN WORLD

Our contribution to the historical understanding of the relationship between material culture and diplomacy is part of a wider shift in how diplomatic history is interpreted today. "Diplomatic history is back," wrote an enthused reviewer for the *Renaissance Quarterly* in 2011.[11] The discipline has undergone a significant transformation over the past fifteen years. In marked distance from the older tradition grounded in legal and political theory, a new brand of diplomatic history inspired by the cultural turn of the 1990s has emerged. The New Diplomatic History is not primarily about the formal (legal, institutional, political-philosophical) precepts of diplomacy anymore.[12] It aims instead to complement our understanding of those traditional core themes by studying the wider cultural and social foundations of diplomatic action. Some of the most important and paradigm-shifting work on the early modern period has come from continental European scholars working on early modern Europe. In Italy, Riccardo Fubini and Daniela Frigo have pioneered the study of diplomacy as a tool not only of "external" affairs but also "internal" state formation.[13] French and German historians have

[11] Paul M. Dover, "Review of Robyn Adams and Rosanna Cox, eds., *Diplomacy and Early Modern Culture*," *Renaissance Quarterly* 64, no. 4 (2011): 1279–81.

[12] The term first appeared in John Watkins, "Toward a New Diplomatic History of Medieval and Early Modern Europe," *Journal of Medieval and Early Modern Studies* 38, no. 1 (2008): 1–14.

[13] Riccardo Fubini, *Italia quattrocentesca: Politica e diplomazia al tempo di Lorenzo il Magnifico* (Milan: Franco Angeli, 1994); Daniela Frigo, ed., *Principi, Ambasciatori e "Jus Gentium": L'amministrazione della Politica Estera nel Piemonte del Settecento* (Rome: Bulzoni, 1991), trans. as *Politics and Diplomacy in Early Modern Italy: The Structure of*

developed the notion of a "cultural history of politics" (*histoire culturelle du politique*, *Kulturgeschichte des Politischen*), where early modern state building is examined as a cultural process.[14] Most historians of early modern Europe thus agree that it is important to inquire into what Nicholas Dirks, a historian of India, called the "cultural foundations of power."[15]

Diplomacy emerges almost naturally as a central topic of inquiry especially with regard to our understanding of the making of early modern dynastic states and empires. Ironically, however, the very historiography that is thus embracing notions of performance, theatricality and display borrowed from cultural anthropologists and from historians of the non-Western world is also being timid in its ventures beyond the boundaries of Europe. There are practical reasons for this, given what is still generally a wide gap between the historiographies of early modern Europe, of European expansion and of other regions of the world. Under such conditions, it already counted as a bold move when, as happened in 2008 with a landmark special issue on diplomacy of the *Journal of Medieval and Early Modern History*, the boundaries of the continent were pushed to include Byzantium and Muscovy.[16] Only recently have we seen a widening of horizons with remarkable thematic issues in *Art History* and in *Journal of Early Modern History* (on diplomacy in the Mediterranean in 2015, and on diplomacy and visual and material culture and on diplomacy and cultural translation in 2016).[17]

Diplomatic Practice, 1450–1800 (Cambridge: Cambridge University Press, 1999). Also see Christopher Storrs, *War, Diplomacy, and the Rise of Savoy, 1690–1720* (New York: Cambridge University Press, 1999).

14 Barbara Stollberg-Rilinger, ed., *Was heißt Kulturgeschichte des Politischen?* (Berlin: Duncker & Humblot, 2005); Ronald Asch and Dagmar Freist, eds., *Staatsbildung als kultureller Prozess. Strukturwandel und Legitimation von Herrschaft in der Frühen Neuzeit* (Cologne: Böhlau, 2005).

15 Nicholas B. Dirks, *The Hollow Crown: Ethnohistory of an Indian Kingdom* (Cambridge: Cambridge University Press, 1987), 5.

16 "Towards a New Diplomatic History", *Journal of Medieval and Early Modern Studies* 38, no. 1 (2008).

17 Maartje van Gelder and Tijana Krstić, eds., "Cross-Confessional Diplomacy and Diplomatic Intermediaries in the Early Modern Mediterranean," *Journal of Early Modern History* 19, nos. 2–3 (2015); Meredith Martin and Daniela Bleichmar, eds., Objects in Motion in the Early Modern World, *Art History* 38, no. 4 (2015); Nancy Um and Leah R. Clark, eds., "The Art of Embassy: Objects and Images of Early Modern Diplomacy," *Journal of Early Modern History* 20, no. 1 (2016); Toby Osborne and Joan-Pau Rubiés, eds., "Diplomacy and Cultural Translation in the Early Modern World," *Journal of Early Modern History* 20, no. 4 (2016).

One problem certainly is that some historians might still struggle to overcome the notion of European exceptionalism.[18] Scholars of early modern diplomacy in Europe in particular may find it difficult to liberate themselves from the perception that there is a heartland – in and around northern and central Italy – from which early modern diplomacy as we know it ultimately emerged. It was, after all, in Venice, Florence and Rome that so many of the fundamental characteristics of diplomatic practice were developed during the fifteenth and sixteenth centuries – or so we believe. Like historians of Renaissance art, historians of Renaissance diplomacy often find it challenging to accept that comparable processes may have occurred in other parts of the world. Even more daunting is the prospect that certain innovations may have originated outside the borders of Europe and influenced the course of history in those imaginary heartlands, rather than vice versa.[19]

Even more disconcerting than this reticence among diplomatic historians of Europe to engage with global history is the hesitation of global historians to embrace diplomacy as a core subject. Between Jack Wills's *Embassies and Illusions* published in 1984 and Sanjay Subrahmanyam's *Courtly Encounters*, a collection of talks published in 2012, very few monograph-length studies resulting from the global history boom have tackled early modern diplomatic culture as a topic in itself.[20] In contrast with the modern period, for which books on diplomacy abound, early modernists have tended to make more disjointed incursions into the field. Some of the most auspicious recent explorations are those in Markus Vink's *Encounter on the Opposite*

[18] Jerry Bentley, "Europeanization of the World or Globalization of Europe?," *Religions* 3 (2012): 441–54.

[19] See namely D. Goffman, "Negotiating with the Renaissance State: The Ottoman Empire and the New Diplomacy," in *The Early Modern Ottomans: Remapping the Empire*, ed. Virginia H. Aksan and Daniel Goffman (Cambridge: Cambridge University Press, 2007), 61–74. Also see, for art and science, Valérie Gonzalez, *Beauty and Islam: Aesthetics in Islamic Art and Architecture* (London and New York: I. B. Tauris and The Institute of Ismaili Studies, 2001); and Hans Belting, *Florence and Baghdad: Renaissance Art and Arab Science* (Cambridge, MA: Harvard University Press, 2011).

[20] John E. Wills Jr., *Embassies and Illusions: Dutch and Portuguese Envoys to K'ang-hsi, 1666–1687* (Cambridge, MA: Harvard University Press, 1984); Sanjay Subrahmanyam, *Courtly Encounters: Translating Courtliness and Violence in Early Modern Eurasia* (Cambridge, MA: Harvard University Press, 2012). Also see Wills's earlier study, *Pepper, Guns, and Parleys: The Dutch East India Company and China, 1622–1681* (Cambridge, MA: Harvard University Press, 1974). At the tail end of our period, mention must be made of James L. Hevia's *Cherishing Men from Afar: Qing Guest Ritual and the Macartney Embassy of 1793* (Durham, NC, and London: Duke University Press, 1995), and Christian Windler's *La diplomatie comme expérience de l'Autre. Consuls français au Maghreb (1700–1840)* (Genève: Librairie Droz, 2002).

Coast (2015) and Adam Clulow's *The Company and the Shogun* (2014) along with some important work on European-Ottoman diplomacy.[21]

Literary historians have begun to successfully unravel the diplomatic narratives of English envoys to Asian courts, and a case has been made for placing such texts at the heart of the making of early modern European literature.[22] Attempts have been made to summarize the main features of Portuguese diplomacy in the East, a particularly complex subfield given the precociousness of Lusitanian expansion and its extreme exposure to Asian political cultures.[23] And two recent volumes of collected essays in German have brought to the fore the intercultural logics of diplomatic reception ceremonies in transcultural contexts, especially in the Middle East.[24]

This book argues that what is needed is a diplomatic history capable of engaging with its topic in a global setting. The stage that we will be observing is not, of course, stable. The globe as such was in the process of being invented by the various sides involved in early modern transcontinental encounters. So was the diplomatic playing field on which representatives of political formations as diverse as the Venetian Signoria, the

21 Adam Clulow, *The Company and the Shogun: The Dutch Encounter with Tokugawa Japan* (New York: Columbia University Press, 2014), esp. 25–58; Markus P. M. Vink, *Encounters on the Opposite Coast: The Dutch East India Company and the Nayaka State of Madurai in the Seventeenth Century* (Leiden: Brill, 2015). Also see Bhawan Ruangsilp, *Dutch East India Company Merchants at the Court of Ayutthaya: Dutch Perceptions of the Thai Kingdom, c.1604–1765* (Leiden: Brill, 2007). On the Ottoman case, see among others Palmira Brummett, "A Kiss Is Just a Kiss: Rituals of Submission along the East-West Divide," in *Cultural Encounters between East and West, 1493–1699*, ed. Matthew Birchwood and Matthew Dimmock (Newcastle: Cambridge Scholars, 2005), 107–31.

22 Richmond Barbour, "Power and Distant Display: Early English 'Ambassadors' in Moghul India," *Huntington Library Quarterly* 61, nos. 3–4 (1998): 343–68; id., *Before Orientalism: London's Theatre of the East, 1576–1626* (Cambridge: Cambridge University Press, 2003), esp. 146–93; Miles Ogborn, *Indian Ink: Script and Print in the Making of the English East India Company* (Chicago: University of Chicago Press, 2007); Douglas Biow, *Doctors, Ambassadors, Secretaries: Humanism and Professions in Renaissance Italy* (Chicago: University of Chicago Press, 2002); Timothy Hampton, *Fictions of Embassy: Literature and Diplomacy in Early Modern Europe* (Ithaca, NY, and London: Cornell University Press, 2009).

23 Stefan Halikowski-Smith, "'The Friendship of Kings Was in the Ambassadors': Portuguese Diplomatic Embassies in Asia and Africa during the Sixteenth and Seventeenth Centuries," *Portuguese Studies* 22, no. 1 (2006): 101–34; Biedermann, "Portuguese Diplomacy in Asia in the Sixteenth Century."

24 Peter Burschel and Christine Vogel, eds., *Die Audienz: Ritualisierter Kulturkontakt in der Frühen Neuzeit* (Cologne: Böhlau, 2014). The introduction by Burschel contains further references especially to work in German. Ralph Kauz, Giorgio Rota and Jan Paul Niederkorn, eds., *Diplomatisches Zeremoniell in Europa und im mittleren Osten in der frühen Neuzeit* (Vienna: OeAW, 2009).

Ottoman Porte, the Portuguese Estado da Índia, the Empire of the Mughals, the English East India Company or the *daimyo* of Japan began to interact. Needless to say, even at the level of these polities, much was in motion. Power structures were in the making while others unraveled. Rulers attempted to establish their credentials through warfare and diplomacy, but their authority was often brittle and open to internal challenges. Whoever could get hold of diplomatic moments and channel the symbolic capital they generated to consolidate his or her own authority was more likely to thrive than others who could not. The instability of diplomatic relations before the establishment of a solidly structured system of resident ambassadors and formalized interstate relations is thus an opportunity as much as it is a challenge to historians.

The sheer amount of intercontinental diplomatic interactions that unfolded from the late fifteenth century is staggering. While we are far from seeing the whole picture and certainly no quantitative assessment exists so far, it should be sufficient to consider the following: when the Portuguese began to build up a power network in the Indian Ocean region in the early sixteenth century – in other words, when they began to create the structures of what would become known as the Estado or Portuguese Empire in the East – they went from a handful of face-to-face encounters with minor rulers of coastal towns and kingdoms to a complex network of diplomatic relations within a few years. Crucially, this was due not to Portuguese planning but to the necessities of doing business in and interacting with the Asian political landscape. In places such as Malacca or Hormuz, diplomatic exchanges propelled by Siam and Persia, respectively, quickly imposed their own pace and practices on the newcomers.[25]

In Goa, the Portuguese governors would soon dedicate a substantial part of their time to the management of extensive diplomatic relations with dozens of states ranging from small port cities on the Malabar Coast to the Empires of Vijayanagara and the Mughals. The exposure to practices of gift-giving especially from the Islamic diplomatic tradition was very considerable and is yet barely understood by historians. Once other Europeans made their appearance in Asia – either through the Cape Route or by moving overland through the Ottoman sphere into Safavid Persia and other regions – the web of diplomatic relations gained additional complexity. We are nowhere near to even just estimating how many diplomatic missions occurred in those contexts over the early modern period, let alone getting to grips with the amount of gifts exchanged. But it is clear already that the

[25] Biedermann, *Portuguese in Sri Lanka and South India*, 7–32.

study of such a vast and poorly known system of diplomatic exchanges will require coordinated efforts not only at the level of archival exploration, but also with regard to the formulation of questions and lines of inquiry. A single method may not suffice in the face of the complexities of the field, yet some sort of common ground is clearly needed.[26]

MATERIAL CULTURE AND THE DIPLOMATIC GIFT

The analysis of gift-giving practices in early modern diplomatic relations has greatly benefited from developments in the field of material culture studies. Written texts, central to the understanding of diplomacy, are increasingly interpreted alongside a variety of other historical materials, including artifacts.[27] Diplomacy in particular – with its great theatricality often mediated by luxurious props and detailed written narratives – lends itself to complex interpretations through multiple sources, and here objects can be of great help to scholars, students and the general public. The material objects that served as diplomatic gifts in some of the most spectacular embassies of the early modern period have been at the heart of several recent exhibitions, including "The Tsars and the East: Gifts from Turkey and Iran in the Moscow Kremlin" (originally held at the Arthur M. Sackler Gallery in 2009), "Gifts of the Sultan: The Arts of Giving at the Islamic Courts" (originally held at LACMA in Los Angeles in 2011), and "Treasures of the Royal Courts: Tudors, Stuarts and the Russian Tsars" (at the Victoria and Albert Museum in 2013).[28] These shows were the outcome of, and at the same time resulted in, new opportunities for

[26] See for instance the thought-provoking introductory piece to the special issue edited by Toby Osborne and Joan-Pau Rubiés, "Introduction: Diplomacy and Cultural Translation," *Journal of Early Modern History* 20, no. 4 (2016): 313–30.

[27] Anne Gerritsen and Giorgio Riello, "Introduction: Writing Material Culture History," in *Writing Material Culture History*, ed. Anne Gerritsen and Giorgio Riello (London: Bloomsbury, 2015), 1–13; id., "The Global Lives of Things: The Material Culture of Connections in the Early Modern World," in *The Global Lives of Things: The Material Culture of Connections in the First Global Age*, ed. Anne Gerritsen and Giorgio Riello (London: Routledge, 2015), 1–27. See also Karen Harvey, ed., *History and Material Culture: A Student's Guide to Approaching Alternative Sources* (London: Routledge 2009), and Leora Auslander, "Beyond Words," *American Historical Review* 110, no. 4 (2006): 1015–44. For the early modern period, see Paula Findlen, "Introduction: Early Modern Things," in *Early Modern Things: Objects and Their Histories, 1500–1800*, ed. Paula Findlen (Basingstoke: Routledge, 2013), 3–27.

[28] Yurievne Gagarina, ed., *Tsars and the East*; Linda Komaroff, ed., *Gifts of the Sultan: The Arts of Giving at the Islamic Courts* (New Haven: Yale University Press, 2011); Tessa Murdoch, ed., *Treasures of the Royal Courts: Tudors, Stuarts and the Russian Tsars* (London: V&A Publications, 2013).

curators and academics to collaborate, as well as a development we might refer to as a "material turn" in several academic disciplines.

Diplomatic gifts illustrate the history of political encounters, but they can also trigger deeper considerations about the interweaving of words, acts and things at the heart of key historical processes such as the building of early modern state power and the making of transcontinental political, economic and cultural connections. They may even open doors to the telling of the material conditions of diplomacy, taking us straight into a world made of perilous travels, seasickness and infectious diseases, broken plates and rotting carpets, robberies, falsifications and penny-pinching. Material culture can thus contribute to the way recent diplomatic history has recovered the importance of individual agency and rehabilitated the figure of the ambassador beyond a mere implementer of higher political aims.[29] The letter case and comb (Figure I.3) that belonged to the Dutch ambassador Thomas Hees in Algiers provide us with such an intimate – albeit still very narrow – glimpse into ambassadorial life. Hees was sent to Algiers in 1675 as a plenipotentiary of the States-General to conduct negotiations for the purchase of the freedom of Dutch slaves.[30] On a contemporary portrait we see him in a relaxed pose, smoking, and surrounded by his nephews, his servant "Thomas the negro, 17 years old," and some artifacts acquired in North Africa. One of those is the comb case lying on the table (Figure I.4).

Focusing on the materiality of the gift helps us create narratives in which political and economic motives, including personal acts, institutional ambitions and technological innovation are seen as interwoven aspects of a single story. The procurement of suitable gifts, for example, was no trivial matter. It could consist of a shopping spree on the local market, the recycling of items that were already part of a collection, or the systematic purchasing of exceptional things in distant places. It might also involve more unexpected operations including the fabrication of novel objects following precise specifications given by the receiver himself.[31]

[29] Nancy Um and Leah R. Clark, "Introduction: The Art of Embassy: Objects and Images of Early Modern Diplomacy," *Journal of Early Modern History*, 20, no. 1 (2016): 7.

[30] Alexander H. de Groot, "Ottoman North Africa and the Dutch Republic in the Seventeenth and Eighteenth Centuries," *Revue de l'Occident musulman et de la Méditerranée* 39 (1985): 139–40; Ton J. Broos, "Travelers and Travel Liars in Eighteenth-Century Dutch Literature," in *History in Dutch Studies*, ed. Robert Howell and Jolands Vanderwal Taylor (Lanham, MA: University Press of America, 2004), 32–37.

[31] The Dutch factors in Asia, for example, compiled detailed lists of the gifts considered suitable on the basis of enquiries with the rulers and trade officials, as Cynthia Viallé has shown.

FIGURE I.3 This letter case and comb belonged to Ambassador Thomas Hees when he was in Algiers. Under the flap of the case is an embroidered inscription: "His Excellency Sir Thomas Hees Ambassador of the States General of the United Netherlands 1676." On loan from the Koninklijk Kabinet van Schilderijen Mauritshuis, Rijksmuseum SK-C-1216.

The demands made by the Ottoman elite, for instance, posed spectacular challenges to Venetian artisans, which in turn contributed to technological innovation.[32] When no information was available about which kind of objects a foreign prince might like to receive, a network of informers had to be mobilized. This was in all probability the case with the chandelier that the Habsburg ambassador Walter Count Leslie presented to Sultan Mehmet IV. Although the chandelier has long been lost, we still have a life-size drawing (c. 60 cm × 100 cm). According to the description, the chandelier weighed 22 kilos and was adorned by 303 rock crystals (Figure I.5).[33] Looking at the precision of this and other drawings of clocks and candelabra in the Vienna archives, it is clear that Dutch artisans were put to work to produce high-quality artifacts that perfectly matched the taste and expectations of the Ottoman receiver.

See Cynthia Viallé, "'To Capture Their Favor': On Gift-Giving by the VOC," in *Mediating Netherlandish Art and Material Culture in Asia*, ed. Thomas DaCosta Kaufmann and Michael North (Amsterdam: Amsterdam University Press, 2014), 291–319, esp. 296.

32 See Luca Molà's chapter in this volume.

33 Peter Noever, ed., *Global:Lab. Kunst Als Botschaft Asien und Europa, 1500–1700* (Vienna: MAK, 2009), 208–9. See also Barbara Karl and Claudia Swan's chapters in this volume considering the receptions of gifts from the Habsburgs to the Ottoman Court.

FIGURE I.4 "Portrait of Thomas Hees, resident and commissioner of the States General to the governments of Algiers, Tunis and Tripoli, with his nephews Jan and Andries Hees and a servant." Rijksmuseum SK-C-1215.

We do not know what the Sultan made of the chandelier. Metals – especially precious metals – were often melted down once an object was no longer considered worth keeping. This specific object, which we only know because a two-dimensional representation survives, shared a common destiny with the majority of diplomatic gifts: they were lost in the course of time. Indeed, in some cases gifts were not supposed to remain as tangible evidence of a diplomatic encounter at all. This was the case of the food and *materia medica* that embassies sometimes carried with them: for instance, a shipload of Italian cheese that the Ottoman

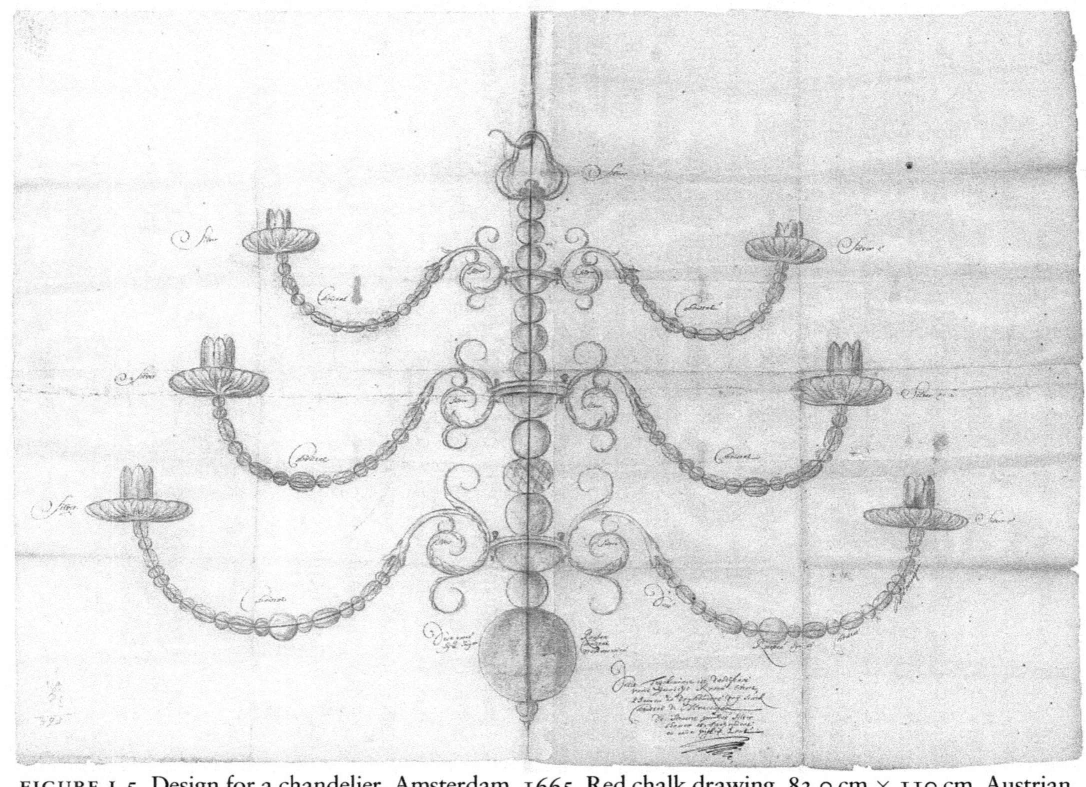

FIGURE 1.5 Design for a chandelier, Amsterdam, 1665. Red chalk drawing, 82.0 cm × 110 cm. Austrian State Archives, Financial and Aulic Chancellery Archives, Collection of Plans and Maps, inv. No. S 62/1.

Sultan Bayezid received with great pleasure from the ruler of Mantua in 1491.[34] Among the most appreciated gifts were animals. In the early fifteenth century, Bengali envoys presented a giraffe to the emperor of Ming China. Unknown in China, the giraffe was interpreted as a highly propitious *qilin*, an auspicious beast seen only when a true sage was on the throne.[35] In Europe, the most celebrated of these animals was the rhinoceros that reached Lisbon in 1515 as a gift from Sultan Muzaffar II of Cambay (r. 1511–26) to King Manuel I (r. 1495–1521) of Portugal. The Catholic king of Portugal later presented it to Pope Leo X. The unfortunate animal never arrived in Rome as the ship that carried it sank in the Mediterranean, but it was immortalized by Albrecht Dürer in one of his best-known prints – yet another example of how the ephemeral nature of certain gifts could be counterbalanced by pictorial and textual representations and the formation of collective memories.[36]

The fact that most diplomatic gifts have disappeared creates multiple challenges to historians. Early modern objects surviving today are only rarely connectable to a specific diplomatic event. Inversely, whenever textual descriptions of embassies mention gifts, it has been generally very difficult, if not altogether impossible, to identify them in collections. Some objects, including a series of ivory caskets sent from Sri Lanka to Portugal in the sixteenth century, have been successfully identified and contextualized – but they are the exception confirming the rule.[37] There is something deeply counterintuitive to this fact, given the very high status and monetary value that such objects tended to possess when they first circulated. The study of the disappearance or decontextualization of objects is certainly worth developing alongside interrogations about knowledge loss, serving as a valuable complement to the histories of collecting and science in the early modern period.[38]

[34] See Antonia Gatward Cevizli's chapter in this volume.

[35] See figure 192 in the catalogue of the recent British Museum exhibition, entitled *Ming: 50 Years That Changed China* (London: British Museum Press, 2014), 224. For a further study, see Sally K. Church, "The Giraffe of Bengal: A Medieval Encounter in Ming China," *Medieval History Journal* 7, no. 1 (2004): 1–36.

[36] T. H. Clarke, *The Rhinoceros from Dürer to Stubbs: 1515–1799* (London: Sotheby's Publication, 1986). See also Pamela Smith and Paula Findlen, eds., *Merchants and Marvels: Commerce, Science and Art in Early Modern Europe* (New York: Routledge, 2001); Hedda Reindl-Kiel, "Dogs, Elephants, Lions, a Ram and a Rhino on Diplomatic Mission: Animals as Gifts to the Ottoman Court," in *Animals and People in the Ottoman Empire*, ed. Suraiya Faroqhi (Constantinople: Eren, 2010), 271–85.

[37] See Zoltán Biedermann's chapter in this volume.

[38] On collecting, see the work of Paula Findlen, *Possessing Nature: Museums, Collecting and Scientific Culture in Early Modern Italy* (Berkeley: University of California Press, 1994); Daniela Bleichman and Peter C. Mancall, eds., *Collecting across Cultures: Material Exchanges in the Early Modern Atlantic World* (Philadelphia: University of

Another problem with diplomatic gifts is that, spectacular as they often were and are, they do not necessarily tell us much about how they were seen and received. Only rarely do we have access to as much information as in the following case pertaining to English-Ottoman diplomacy under Elizabeth I and Mehmed III. Shortly before the defeat of the Spanish Armada, Elizabeth sent an ambassador to Constantinople with the aim of fostering diplomatic ties with the Ottoman Empire, Spain's archenemy. The monarch decided to send gifts to Safiye, queen-mother of Mehmed III. Items sent included pieces of gold cloth and a jeweled miniature portrait. On reception, it was communicated to the English representatives that Safiye "so gratefully accepted [the gifts sent in her majesty's name], as that she sent to know of the ambassador what present he thought she might return that would most delight her majesty." The English envoy sent word that "a suit of princely attire being after the Turkish fashion would for the rareness thereof be acceptable in England."[39] As a result, "an upper gowne of cloth of gold very rich, and under gowne of cloth of silver, and girdle of Turkish worke, rich and faire" were sent.[40] We are even allowed to conjecture, as recently argued by Jerry Brotton, that while Elizabeth enjoyed wearing the Turkish gown, seeing it as a potent reminder of her new anti-Spanish ally, this very act was seen in Constantinople as a confirmation of England's status as a vassal state of the Empire.[41] Such relatively thick interpretations are, however, again only rarely possible with diplomatic gifts – or at least this is where we stand at present, at a time when the systematic study of this category of object is still in its beginnings.

THE GIFT IN GLOBAL HISTORY

While many early modern diplomatic encounters on the global stage still have to be read through European sources with the widely known biases, silences and plain prejudice that this presents, it does make a difference if we read the sources with an awareness of the connections and interactions that began to

Pennsylvania Press, 2011); Peter N. Miller, *Peiresc's Orient: Antiquarianism as Cultural History in the Seventeenth Century* (Aldershot: Ashgate, 2012). See also the now classic essays in Oliver Impey and A. MacGregor, eds., *The Origins of Museums: The Cabinet of Curiosities in Sixteenth- and Seventeenth-Century Europe* (Oxford: Clarendon Press, 1985). On the loss of knowledge, see Peter Burke, *A Social History of Knowledge*, vol. 2: *From the* Encyclopédie *to Wikipedia* (Cambridge: Polity Press, 2010), 139–59.

39 Both cited in Jerry Brotton, *This Orient Isle: Elizabethan England and the Islamic World* (London: Allen Lane, 2016), 189.

40 Cited in Gerald MacLean and Nabil Matar, *Britain and the Islamic World, 1558–1713* (Oxford: Oxford University Press, 2011), 47–48.

41 Brotton, *This Orient Isle*, 190.

shape so many parts of the world from the fifteenth century onward. Without aspiring to complete global coverage – our focus here is on Asia–Europe interactions – most of the contributors to this volume see the incentive to challenge national boundaries and Eurocentrism as central to their work.

Global history, then, serves here to provide a methodological framework within which gifts can be conceptualized.[42] Rather than seeing the gift in isolation, as the means by which an individual relationship between two entities is established, with one of two generally located in Europe, we propose here to situate both in global context. In practice, this means not so much that both might be located anywhere in the world, but that the relationship can be fully understood only when taking into consideration that both are part of complex networks of connections that extend beyond their immediate location.[43] The full implications of the movements of gifts can be grasped only when all these connections are also made visible.

Figure I.6 provides an exemplary glimpse of a network of relationships within which early modern gifts were exchanged. The painting, made in 1757 by the Jesuit Giuseppe Castiglione (1688–1766), depicts the offering of a set of horses. On the right-hand side of this detail of the handscroll, which is over 2.5 meters long, we see the emperor of China (Qianlong, r. 1735–96) seated on a carved seat in front of a painted screen. Standing by his side on the raised platform are two courtiers, looking toward the scene in front of them. A white horse stands in the in the left-hand of the detail, next to the hunched figure of a man prostrating himself before the emperor. Two more horses, one a deep brown color, the other skewbald (with brown and white patches) stand on the left of the white horse (not included in this image). The three horse grooms, possibly Kazakhs, all have a distinctive red, pointy hat, which marks them as visitors to the Qing Empire (1644–1911). Even without any knowledge of the ways in which the Chinese court dealt with foreign emissaries during the Qing dynasty, the viewer immediately sees a particular power relationship playing out in front of their eyes – a powerful

42 For some recent overviews of the methodologies and themes of global and world history, see Maxine Berg, ed., *Writing the Global: Challenges for the 21st Century* (Oxford: British Academy and Oxford University Press, 2013); Jerry Bentley, ed., *The Oxford Handbook of World History* (Oxford: Oxford University Press, 2013); Douglas Northrup, ed., *A Companion to World History* (London: Wiley-Blackwell, 2014).

43 See, from the vast literature on connections and their historiographical potential, Michael North, ed., *Artistic and Cultural Exchanges between Europe and Asia, 1400–1900* (Farnham and Burlington: Ashgate Publishing, 2010); Michael Werner and Bénédicte Zimmermann, "Beyond Comparison: Histoire Croisée and the Challenge of Reflexivity," *History and Theory*, 45, no. 1 (2006): 30–50.

FIGURE I.6 Detail of "Kazaks Offering Horses in Tribute to the Emperor Qianlong," by Giuseppe Castiglione (1688–1766). Hanging scroll; ink and light colors on paper, eighteenth century. 45.5 cm × 269 cm. Former Frey collection. Now in Musée Guimet, inv. nr. MG 17033.

reminder of the fact, to be explored further below, that gifting is far from being as "mutual" an affair as Western theory often likes to have it.[44] The humble and submissive posture of the gift-giver, in stark contrast to the proudly raised head of the white horse, enforces the position of power from which the emperor receives this precious gift.

The formal exchange of gifts between the Chinese Empire and the political entities the Chinese considered submissive to them formed part of the so-called tribute system and played a central role in the foreign relations of the various Chinese dynasties. The form and frequency of the tribute missions to the Chinese imperial court, the geopolitical entities that were invited to be part of the system, its representations and meanings all changed so dramatically over the centuries that the term "tribute system" has now largely become regarded as misleading. Nonetheless, the giving of gifts, both from visitors from afar to the Chinese court and from the emperor to the visiting emissaries, runs like a red thread throughout the history of early modern China. To make sense of tributary gift circulation, we need to look beyond the suggestion of a single, linear connection between for example the Kazakhs and the Chinese, toward the military campaigns and territorial expansion of the Qianlong emperor into Central Asia of the mid-eighteenth century. The nomadic Kazakhs hailed from a territory beyond the contested Central Asian region that the Qianlong emperor had set his sights on, but of course he accepted their gift of horses as a welcome sign of the extension of his power. Meanwhile, the Jesuit

[44] See Geary, "Gift Exchange," 129–40.

painter Giuseppe Castiglione, who created this record of the exchange, will have had his own perspective on it as a representative of a European religious order that sought to extend the reach of Christianity in the Qing Empire. The newly conquered Central Asian territories and the Europeans vying for influence at the imperial court all have their part to play in this offering of horses and the way its representation has come down to us.

This also was and remains a matter of complex, often shifting desires for material goods and the potential they carried to consolidate or transform hierarchies. In 1757, the chief of the Kazakhs in Figure I.6 wanted to do more than please the emperor of China.[45] In exchange for horses, he wanted textiles and tea from the Qing, a move that would doubtless have strengthened his own position and probably augmented his wealth, while at the same time increasing the circulation of certain goods among his people, in turn triggering cultural change. In 1758, the Qing emperor officially approved of a trading relationship; the Kazakhs provided horses at reasonable prices, and the Chinese shipped vast quantities of satins, silks and tea from the interior of China to the Kazakhs in Inner Asia.[46] Global history has, for some of its practitioners, close connections to economic history and the history of material connections between different parts of the world. That aspect of global history is useful in this context, too. For example, large numbers of traders accompanied any mission to the Chinese imperial court, stopping frequently en route to the palace, to sell the goods they had brought from home and buy others to sell at home. The expectation was also that the expensive gifts the emperor bestowed on the visitors would be sold at home. In that sense, then, the formal exchange of gifts that featured at the Qing court might have been little more than the thin veil hiding an extensive trade mission, as were the vast majority of the ambassadorial missions that the European

[45] As Nicola di Cosmo has shown, the facade of gift exchange on the Qing-Kirghiz nomadic frontier confirmed an unequal relationship of vassal to sovereign, while allowing all partners to maintain their status. The Qing court officials and their local representatives could represent the nomads as inferior, covering up the economic dependency of the Qing court, while the gift-bearing nomads could maintain their aristocratic status to their local audiences. Nicola Di Cosmo, "Kirghiz Nomads on the Qing Frontier: Tribute, Trade, or Gift Exchange?," in *Political Frontiers, Ethnic Boundaries, and Human Geographies in Chinese History*, ed. Nicola Di Cosmo and Don J. Wyatt (London: Routledge Curzon, 2003), 351–72.

[46] James A. Millward, "Qing Silk-Horse Trade with the Qazaqs in Yili and Tarbaghatai, 1758–1853," *Central and Inner Asian Studies* 7 (1992): 1–42. See also Peter Perdue, *China Marches West: The Qing Conquest of Central Eurasia* (Cambridge, MA: Harvard University Press, 2005), 400–402.

courts and trade companies embarked on. The exchange of gifts has its own history, undoubtedly, but the history of diplomatic gifts is in many ways the history of the desire for economic expansion.[47]

This approach reflects a recent trend in the practice of global history. The aim of world and global historians has always been to see the wider picture, to draw out comparisons and connections between different parts of the world and to challenge the assumed preeminence of the nation-state. If it seemed at one stage that this required a "macro" approach, looking at the economic convergences and divergences of the planet as a whole; more recently, scholars have become interested in the roles of individuals, especially those who negotiated individual pathways through the entanglements of the early modern world.[48] Mobile individuals like the sixteenth-century al-Hasan al-Wazzan, born a Muslim in Fez, later baptized as Giovanni Leone, who entered the history records as Leo Africanus, or the eighteenth-century Elizabeth Marsh, who passed through the West Indies, Europe, Africa and India in the course of her life, provide profound challenges to historians.[49] What remains of their records is scattered all over the world, and in a variety of languages. Yet their individual stories matter and, like the stories of individual objects, shed important light on the complex entanglements that shaped early global connections.[50] A study of the exchange of gifts, then, requires the entire repertoire of approaches, from the level of the individual and his/her artifacts – such as the things that al-Hasan al-Wazzan selected as gifts in his early years as he moved between the different courts in places like Tunis, Cairo and Timbuktu – to the offering of gifts by the representatives of the Dutch and English East India Companies, and the role of gifts in the mediation of larger geopolitical relationships.[51]

[47] See Giorgio Riello's contribution in this volume.

[48] Amy Stanley, "Maidservants' Tales: Narrating Domestic and Global History in Eurasia, 1600–1900," *American Historical Review*, 121, no. 2 (2016): 437–60, esp. 438–40.

[49] Natalie Zemon Davis, *Trickster Travels: A Sixteenth-Century Muslim between Worlds* (New York: Hill and Wang, 2006); Linda Colley, *The Ordeal of Elizabeth Marsh: A Woman in World History* (London: HarperPress, 2007). See also Miles Ogborn, *Global Lives: Britain and the World, 1550–1800* (Cambridge: Cambridge University Press, 2008).

[50] Nicholas Thomas has proposed the concept of "entangled objects," a tool through which people across the known world could make sense of one another. See his *Entangled Objects: Exchange, Material Culture and Colonialism in the Pacific* (Cambridge, MA: Harvard University Press, 1991). Also see Ian Hodder, *Entangled: An Archaeology of the Relationships between Humans and Things* (Malden, MA: Wiley-Blackwell, 2012).

[51] Zemon Davis, *Trickster Travels*, 48–49.

Instead of reducing the political relationships of the early modern world to a function of abstract state interactions, the global-historical study of diplomacy and gifts thus allows us to explore the complexities and nuances arising from a combination of individual and organizational agency and culture in an open-ended, fast-evolving system. In such a context, diplomatic gifts could build on, and hence reinforce, similarities between distant societies. In other words, global gifts afford us a glimpse into the "commensurability" of shared diplomatic practices across large parts of Eurasia.[52]

DIPLOMATIC GIFTS AND GLOBAL POWER RELATIONS

When we study the cultural construction of power across cultural borders in the early modern world, gifts emerge as connectors and carriers of complex messages about imperial ambitions, and as vehicles in the negotiation of a global regime of values. We argue that gifting is not a kind of archaic economy of exchange, but a pervasive, symbolically laden agent of cohesion for any society. In the studies in this volume, gifts emerge as a part of the social glue that made the formation of a global political community possible. There has been a relatively abundant production of studies on diplomatic gifts in Europe, grounded in part in a wider literature on gift-giving in France, England, Italy and other regions. Along with Natalie Zemon Davis's seminal work on *The Gift in Sixteenth-Century France*, numerous studies of medieval and early modern societies have emerged to emphasize the pervasiveness of gifting.[53] As Felicity Heal recently put it, "the mode of giving, as well as what was given, was crucial

[52] On the concepts of incommensurability and its opposite, see Sanjay Subrahmanyam, "Par-delà l'incommensurabilité: pour une histoire connectée des empires aux temps modernes," *Revue d'Histoire Moderne et Contemporaine* 54, no. 4-bis (2007): 34–53; and id., *Courtly Encounters*. See also Mathieu Grenet, "Muslim Missions to Early Modern France, c. 1610–c. 1780: Notes for a Social History of Cross-Cultural Diplomacy," *Journal of Early Modern History* 19, no. 1 (2015): 223–44, and the introduction to the special issue by Maartje van Gelder and Tijana Krstić, "Introduction: Cross-Confessional Diplomacy and Diplomatic Intermediaries in the Early Modern Mediterranean," *Journal of Early Modern History* 19, no. 1 (2015): 93–105.

[53] Zemon Davis, *Gift in Sixteenth-Century France*. Some other titles illustrating the broad range of topics at stake include Jane Fair Bestor, "Marriage Transactions in Renaissance Italy and Mauss's Essay on the Gift," *Past & Present* 164 (1999): 6–46; Rob C. Wegman, "Musical Offerings in the Renaissance," *Early Music* 33, no. 3 (2005): 425–37; Piers Baker-Bates, "Beyond Rome: Sebastiano Del Piombo as a Painter of Diplomatic Gifts," *Renaissance Studies* 27, no. 1 (2011): 51–72.

to social bonding and political success."[54] The exchange of gifts and benefits had wide social and political implications, thus serving as a paradigmatic example of how cultural practices contribute to the making, the consolidating, and at times the breaking of power relations in early modern societies.

If gifts played a crucial role between individuals within certain realms such as convents, towns, lordships or kingdoms, then they must be assumed to have been similarly important in the management of relations between rulers. In a world of dynastic states ranging from large terrestrial empires through a variety of composite, often geographically disjointed monarchies to a range of smaller formations including "little kingdoms," city-states, and of course some precursors of modern nation-states, personal relations between sovereigns served to express power relations on a larger, multisocietal scale. It is in this context that gifts gained the potential to shape not only the Asian or European, but also the emerging global political landscape. They did so not only in the context of dowries used to cement dynastic agreements in key moments of the lives of rulers, but also – and perhaps increasingly so – as objects or groups of objects offered on the occasion of theatrical receptions structuring diplomatic negotiations. Much came to be expected of gifts especially on the occasion of ambassadorial visits, and even more when the said ambassadors originated in a distant part of the world. With diplomats serving not only as political, but also cultural mediators, the gifts they brought along served to express the possibilities of cross-cultural communication as much as the primary political ambitions of the rulers involved.

Reciprocity and mutuality are aspects that certainly deserve emphasis in connection with the gesturing of global historians to a level playing field in the early modern period. In the battle against Eurocentrism, it has been important to underline how European, Asian and indeed African rulers engaged in diplomatic conversations without assuming that Europe was in some way predestined to global domination. To counterbalance older Eurocentric narratives, we need to keep highlighting non-Western agency in early modern encounters, including the Asian perspective on Europeans (who were often diplomats carrying gifts) and the imperial ambitions non-Western rulers hoped to pursue against, or with the assistance of, people from the West. The recent historiography of Portuguese expansion has, perhaps more than any other, pointed out how the

54 Felicity Heal, *The Power of Gifts: Gift Exchange in Early Modern England* (Oxford: Oxford University Press, 2015).

political, cultural and economic power of Asian policy-makers humbled their counterparts in Lisbon and Goa. As one observer at the Portuguese royal court put it in the early sixteenth century, it was "them" – the peoples of the continent to which a direct sea route was found in 1498 – who "discovered us."[55] In this sense, then, it is important in principle to link up global history's newly gained interest in mutuality with what is perhaps the most quintessentially mutual thing in our imagination: gifts.

However, it is equally vital not to romanticize early modern diplomacy and diplomatic gift-giving as an unhierarchical, fundamentally positive, naturally cosmopolitan stage for negotiations between equals. One risk involved in the proliferation of individual case studies on gifts – often engaging with very limited sets of objects – is that we may lose sight precisely of those aspects of gift giving that, while they imply reciprocity and mutuality, also serve to establish difference and imbalance. It is certainly legitimate to revel in the beauty of the objects involved and explore the sophistication of the exchanges they were involved in. But diplomacy is, in its very essence, about expressing ambitions, establishing differences and managing hierarchies of influence and power. Early modern European-Asian diplomacy may yet have been void of the specter of British imperialism (although Portuguese, Spanish and Dutch imperialism left their imprints over the centuries), but frictions and clashes were an essential part of the game. From petty differences in the allocation of trading privileges, prices and taxes to the clash of empires with declared and conflicting universal ambitions, diplomatic encounters carried the seeds of peace and of war at the same time. Gifts were only very rarely moved around on a perfectly horizontal plane. For most of the time, they traveled up and down complex hierarchical ladders, expressing political moods ranging from submissive prostration through more or less overt challenge to dismissal or even disdain. Gifts can thus help us understand the unfolding of political rivalries and the constant shifting of power balances, rather than just illustrating a static world of conspicuously communicating sovereigns.

Gifts were exposed to and handled by numerous agents involved in the construction of power relations. They were subject to intense scrutiny, receiving criticism as well as praise. The various people whose paths they

[55] Jorge M. Flores, "'They Have Discovered Us': The Portuguese and the Trading World of the Indian Ocean," in *Encompassing the Globe: Portugal and the World in the 16th and 17th Centuries Jay*, ed. Jay A. Levenson, 2 vols. (Washington, DC: Freer and Sackler, 2007), 2: 185–93.

crossed viewed gifts in very different ways. What might appear valuable to some might be perceived as trivial by others. Gifts carried, as they still do for all of us, the possibility of countless mutual understandings and misunderstandings. What their history suggests, however, is that because diplomatic gifts were expected to complement the performance of ambassadors and because the objective of most participants was, in essence, to make deals rather than break them, in a majority of cases they were the object of a search for common ground rather than radical dissent.[56] If at times the opposite was the case, then this only adds to their appeal as historical sources. Because their qualities, and above all their value, received attention from all sides involved in diplomatic negotiations, they can be made to serve today as indicators of how far early modern societies were capable of establishing common, transcultural systems of value.

Value itself is, as we know, no absolute quality. Theories of value abound, taking into account a wide range of social, cultural and economic factors.[57] A gift could be valuable on grounds of the materials used to produce it (which, of course, had different values in different places), but also of the quantity and quality of labor that went into it, or the symbolic charge it received in certain political or even religious contexts. Again, it seems important that we do not get fixated on rigid typologies. Pitching "material" against "symbolic" value will not take us far. Even if we do not wish to dismiss theories that affirm the existence of objective value completely (on grounds, for example, of the labor that goes into the making of an object or the relative rarity of a material – not an altogether unreasonable assumption), we need to be aware of all the other aspects that then contribute to the valuation of objects in circulation by a variety of subjective observers. In general, it is when an object changes hands that different ideas about their value form a web tight enough to bring those objective and subjective values into a meaningful, if tension-ridden dialogue. The negotiation is bound up with the display of the object, which in turn is what allows the latter to fully function as a cross-cultural

56 Cf. Johannes Fabian, "You Meet and You Talk: Anthropological Reflections on Encounters and Discourses," in *The Fuzzy Logic of Encounter: New Perspectives on Cultural Contact*, ed. Sünne Juterczenka and Gesa Mackenthun (Münster: Waxmann Verlag, 2009), 23–34.

57 David Graeber, *Toward an Anthropological Theory of Value: The False Coin of Our Own Dreams* (New York: Palgrave, 2001). Also see John K. Papadopoulos and Gary Urton, *The Construction of Value in the Ancient World* (Los Angeles: The Cotsen Institute of Archaeology Press, 2012).

signifier.[58] And that is, of course, the moment that historians interested in diplomatic gifts will find to be most abundantly documented, by both written accounts and the objects themselves.

In fact, we can consider gifts – like most other objects – to have their own biographies as proposed by Arjun Appadurai in *The Social Life of Things*.[59] The biographies of gifts are not just lists of the hands through which they went. Daniela Frigo has insisted quite rightly on the fact that "diplomacy" as such did not exist in the early modern period and that diplomatic activities are better seen as a "role" or an "office" practiced by a key actor, the "ambassador," than anything else.[60] By extension, we might argue that diplomatic gifts sometimes served as ambassadors in their own right, fulfilling a function – the "gift function" – rather than just figuring as a rigid category of object. True, gifts cannot usually talk, move on their own two feet, or perform theatrical gestures (though the occasional gifted parrot and mobile automaton may be mentioned here to complicate the picture). But their limitations are also a virtue. They can remain silent, endure humiliations in a quiet corner of a palace hall, only to reemerge later in full splendor, once the air is cleared of discord. They can stand as reminders of key moments in the life of a dynasty or a state when ambassadors have long vanished. They may be de- and recontextualized and end their lives in a museum vitrine, but if we listen to them carefully, their diplomatic past is a powerful reminder of how the world we live in results, in significant part, from endless, thoroughly ritualized negotiations (sometimes improvised) involving cross-cultural dialogues about beauty and value.

It is thus an important subfield of historical research that is currently emerging around diplomatic gifts, and we are in the fortunate position to present our findings at this precise moment. Some recent studies indicate that gift-giving may be the one aspect of early modern diplomacy that is particularly likely to contribute to a breakdown of barriers between

[58] Cf. Anthony Cutler, "Significant Gifts: Patterns of Exchange in Late Antique, Byzantine, and Early Islamic Diplomacy," *Journal of Medieval and Early Modern Studies* 38, no. 1 (2008): 79–101.

[59] Arjun Appadurai, "Introduction: Commodities and the Politics of Value," in *The Social Life of Things. Commodities in Cultural Perspective*, ed. Arjun Appadurai (Cambridge: Cambridge University Press, 1986), 3–63. Also see the excellent review of this book in James Ferguson, "Cultural Exchange: New Developments in the Anthropology of Commodities," *Cultural Anthropology* 3, no. 4 (1988): 488–513.

[60] Daniela Frigo, "Prudence and Experience: Ambassadors and Political Culture in Early Modern Italy," *Journal of Medieval and Early Modern Studies* 38, no. 1 (2008): 16.

European and global history. It is also a field that has seen some promising attempts at establishing a research agenda. Cynthia Viallé's meticulous work on diplomacy and Dutch gift giving in Asia, for instance, drafts a catalogue of key points that historians will find themselves addressing almost inevitably when engaging with European-Asian diplomacy. It points out the importance of gift giving for Dutch diplomacy from Arabia to Japan, the existence of correlations between gift value and the political status of the Company's interlocutors, the pecuniary conundrum thus created for an organization that was expected to generate shareholder profit, the curious matter of how gifts were often ordered, with very precise instructions, by those who were to receive them, the extraordinary range of items gifted, the occasional need to "test the market" with new kinds of gifts, the difficult management of expectations especially in settings that were thousands of miles away from European political centers, the complicated negotiation of value at foreign courts, the risk of disappointment, the possibility of shifts in appreciation even in the very short term, the fact that some gifts proved inappropriate and might be refused and the problem of what to do with gifts received (would they remain with the VOC servants or revert to the Company, how might this create conflicts of interest or even contribute to corruption?).[61] This list of topics is likely to grow further in the near future and keep us busy for some time. It already looms large over the chapters in this book and the ongoing research of our contributors.

THE CONTENTS OF THIS VOLUME

The contributors to this volume work in a variety of fields, including global history, area studies, and art history; all are concerned with mapping a series of relationships across time and space that involve more than the ambassadorial exchanges between two nations or empires. All have taken seriously the wider contexts in which diplomatic gifting relationships emerged and developed. The chapters appear here more or less in chronological order, without imposing geographical structures. In the first chapter, Antonia Gatward Cevizli explores the period of intense diplomatic activity between Francesco II Gonzaga, the Marquis of

[61] Viallé, "'To Capture Their Favor.'" See also id., "Zingen voor de Shogun: VOC-Dienaren aan het Japanse Hof," in *Aan de Overkant: Ontmoetingen in Dienst van de VOC en WIC (1600–1800)*, ed. Lodewijk Wagenaar (Leiden: Sidestone Press, 2015), 35–54.

Mantua, and the Ottoman Sultan Bayezid II of the 1490s. On the surface these relations appear to have been motivated by Francesco's enthusiasm for importing horses. However, such connections saw the exchange of far more than animals: from Francesco, robes made from *palio* banners, a portrait of the Sultan's brother Prince Cem – possibly by Mantegna – and a portrait of the Marquis himself; and from Bayezid, a turban and a robe of honor according to the custom of *hil'at*. The success of these exchanges depended on the knowledge, the understanding, the diplomatic skill and the technological know-how of individuals crossing borders.

Luca Molà follows the Italian-Ottoman relations into a later period, analyzing the diplomatic gifts that the Republic of Venice sent to the Ottoman Empire during the sixteenth and early seventeenth centuries. Based on a tradition going back to the early expansion of the Turks in the Mediterranean and the Balkans, the Venetian shipments of highly prized luxury goods produced by the city's industries went through a progressive acceleration in the second half of the sixteenth century. Silk fabrics soon took the lead as the most appreciated gifts, followed by glass, mirrors, woolen cloth, clocks and a range of other items, frequently mixed together. At the center of this diplomatic exchange was not only the court of the Sultan and his relatives and Vizirs in Constantinople, but also a complex network of high- and medium-ranking officers throughout the various regions of the Empire, to the point that by the end of the century these gifts almost became a disguised form of Venetian tribute. To satisfy the continuous requests for original objects coming from the Ottoman court, from the 1580s onward the government of Venice launched public competitions among skilled craftsmen with the request of inventing procedures that would allow the production of new goods, thus pushing forward the technical boundaries of the Venetian artisans. Molà's paper shows how diplomatic gifts not only cemented political connections, but acted as a driving force for technological innovation.

Innovation could be technological, but it also involved the appropriation and adaptation of new forms and artistic norms. Zoltán Biedermann discusses the Sri Lankan ivories that played a pivotal role in the making of early diplomatic exchanges with Portugal. In 1541, the Sinhalese monarch Bhuvanekabahu VII sent an ivory casket of exceptional quality to John III in Lisbon. This masterpiece, now in Munich, inaugurated a long series of objects dispatched from various Sri Lankan courts to the Portuguese monarch and his wife Catherine of Habsburg. Like many ivories from Africa, these objects integrate motifs taken from European art into an iconography anchored in other traditions. Biedermann asks what drove the invention of such combinations in the local political context, and how they achieved at distant courts what they intended. This allows us to address how aesthetic, commercial and political values could be read across cultural boundaries and how the imperfections of such readings contributed (or not) to the making of unequal power relations on the global stage.

Barbara Karl's chapter, too, focuses on the diplomatic gift-giving impulses reaching the West, in this case during the later sixteenth and early seventeenth centuries. It explores diplomatic and artistic exchanges between the Ottoman Empire and Habsburg Austria, when Ottoman power in Europe was at its apex. Inimical encounters apart, diplomatic contacts between the two powers occurred on various different levels and regularly involved the exchange of very valuable gifts – including not only top-end textiles, weapons and precious stones, but also large amounts of cash understood by the Ottomans to signal the diplomatic inferiority of the Habsburgs. The so-called Long War, begun in 1593 and leading up to the peace of Zsitvatorok signed in 1606, was in part about eliminating discrepancies and demanding a more balanced regime of diplomatic gifting. One particularity in this case regards the way many Ottoman objects survived in Vienna thanks to the collecting activities of the Habsburgs. The long border that the two empires shared combined with a powerful courtly culture of appropriating and inventorying Oriental artifacts to form one of the greatest collections of diplomatic gifts in the world.

Carla Alferes Pinto's chapter explores the gifting and collecting activities of Dom Aleixo de Meneses, the Augustinian archbishop of Goa and governor of the Portuguese Empire in the East around the turn of the seventeenth century. Soon after his arrival in Goa in 1595, Meneses began to send gifts from Asia to Fabio Biondi, the Legate of the Holy Siege in Lisbon. At the same time, he maintained diplomatic relations and commercial transactions across Asia, contributing to the circulation of a substantial number of high-end objects of art from Persia through India to China. The article focuses on some surviving objects related to the period of Meneses, exploring the complex geography of gifting, the matching of provenance and destination, the expectations involved and the results achieved. The chapter shows how diplomatic gifts contributed to the circulation of forms, techniques, materials and connoisseurship across the continents.

In Adam Clulow's chapter, we see how Dutch East India Company merchants in Japan were prolific gift-givers, handing over annual presents to the shogun and the most important Tokugawa officials for more than two centuries. The first gifts, presented in the years immediately following the establishment of a Dutch factory in Japan in 1609, were strikingly unimpressive in comparison to other cases explored in this volume. Yet over time the Company's employees became far more skilled and effective gift-givers. This chapter traces the evolution of the Company's gifts from the first, shoddy experiments to a military phase in which cannon and other weapons were presented to the shogun, before examining a shift to prestige objects that took place in the 1630s. It argues that the Company did not rely simply on importing luxury objects from Europe but also developed a highly sophisticated intra-Asian network of prestige items, which underpinned the success of its gift-giving efforts in Japan.

In 1612, the first Dutch ambassador to the Sublime Porte in Constantinople presented numerous diplomatic gifts to Sultan Ahmed I. This gift forms the subject of Claudia Swan's chapter. Over ninety crates of Dutch-made furniture, pewter work, textiles, cheese, butter, and gin were presented along with many other curiosities (*rariteyten*) in the context of securing trade capitulations on behalf of the republic in formation. Among the *rariteyten* were eight birds of paradise, which the Sultan is said to have regarded with great admiration, and close to 900 pieces of Chinese porcelain. Such exotica caused a stir in the burgeoning market in global commodities at home in Amsterdam, and were presented in the hope of representing Dutch trading power at a critical moment. Swan's chapter situates the exchange of exotica in the context of early seventeenth-century Dutch trade and the development of the commodities market in Amsterdam, and places particular emphasis on the role of awe in the production of new political affiliations by way of gift exchange in precious commodities.

Mary Laven's chapter focuses on an avowedly spiritual mission: the proposed embassy of the Pope to the Emperor of China, conceived by the Jesuits in the 1580s. That mission never took place, but the Jesuits in East Asia drew up a detailed list of (overwhelmingly secular) ambassadorial gifts. One of the most striking aspects of this list is the diverse provenance of the proposed presents: musical instruments from the Low Countries, Venetian glass, Roman marquetry, and a number of pieces modeled on Asian designs but produced in Europe. Laven's chapter underlines the importance of geographical range for many early modern gift-givers. It shows not only the global circulation of objects, materials and designs, but the power that specifically local goods were thought to have on the global stage if they could be combined into an all-encompassing corpus reflecting sheer geographical amplitude.

Giorgio Riello's contribution explores a series of diplomatic exchanges that took place in the 1680s between King Narai of Siam and Louis XIV of France. Several embassies were exchanged between the two kingdoms that brought gifts from Asia to Europe and vice versa, but only the 1685–87 Thai embassy, led by the charismatic Siamese ambassador Kosa Pan, became a major public event. The foreign ambassadors were welcomed by enormous crowds from the port of Brest where they landed in July 1686, to Paris where they were received by the king in September that year, and again in January 1687. Almanacs and the press disseminated the news of such an "exotic" embassy. The gifts received by the French king and those that in turn he sent to Siam with two large embassies allow us to consider this episode in French history as a key cross-cultural encounter. They show how the motivations and expectations that surrounded these embassies lay as much in Siam as they did in France. In an inversion of classic narratives, the chapter shows how the Asian kingdom was well aware of its strategic importance in the commercial and religious ambitions of France. The gifts convey how the understanding of geopolitics and ultimately the power of the Siamese king might have surpassed that of the French Sun King.

In the final chapter, Natasha Eaton looks at gifting in the context of the relationship between the English East India Company and Indian rulers. Two forms of gifts had prominence in Indian culture: jewels and artworks. Jewels, such as the giant Timurid ruby of Uleg Beg, featured in critical diplomatic encounters between Indian, Persian, Ottoman and Chinese rulers, and jewels became innovative and wondrous artworks. European attempts to participate in this high-stake, jewel-laden, mimetic network were, Eaton shows, mostly farcical. Eaton's chapter suggests that the English East India Company wanted and perhaps had to disrupt this regime of value. The chapter then turns to painted likenesses, which were a rare and even suspicious type of gift among Asian rulers. They were materially "cheap" and yet still carried the mimetic charge of the presence of the "giver." The colonial giver by 1778 began to expect Indian rulers to pay for these likenesses and to endure the tedium of sitting for European artists. Eaton's chapter shows how fraught the mediating role of gifts could be amid the political interactions of the end of the early modern era.

Like those gifts that never quite settled as they kept moving through the early modern world, encountering successive new audiences with different tastes and sensibilities, this book refrains from setting anything in stone – anything, that is, other than our wish to ignite new discussions around the diverse, volatile and complex material culture of Eurasia before 1800.

1

Portraits, Turbans and Cuirasses

*Material Exchange between Mantua and the Ottomans at the End of the Fifteenth Century**

Antonia Gatward Cevizli

In September 1492 Sultan Bayezid II (r. 1481–1512) described Francesco II Gonzaga, ruler of the city-state of Mantua in Northern Italy (r. 1484–1519), as a "very dear friend" of the Ottoman empire.[1] The intense diplomatic relationship between the two rulers during the 1490s naturally necessitated the exchange of gifts.[2] In recent years, a number of studies drawing on Mauss-inspired gift theory have emphasized the role played by gift exchange in social relations and explored the loaded meanings and expectations that accompanied the giving of gifts. Diplomatic gifts could facilitate a connection between two powers that was maintained by the need to reciprocate; the choice of gifts could communicate how the giver regarded the receiver, and, at the same time, the giving of particularly lavish gifts could send messages about the giver's power and wealth. An analysis of the gifts that were exchanged between Mantua and the

* The research for this chapter was carried out as part of my doctoral thesis, completed in 2011, Antonia Gatward Cevizli, "Beyond Bellini: Aspects of Italian-Ottoman Cultural Exchange," PhD thesis, University of Warwick, 2011. I am very grateful to the Francis Haskell Memorial Fund for sponsoring my research visit to the Archivio di Stato in Mantua and to the University of Warwick for funding my PhD through a Postgraduate Research Scholarship.

1 Archivio di Stato di Mantova, Archivio Gonzaga (hereafter ASMn, AG), b. 86, fasc. 16, fol. 46r: "honorandissimo, clarissimo et amicissimo caro amico del Nostro Imperio Francesco da Gonzaga . . ." See also Hans Joachim Kissling, *Sultan Bajezid's II. Beziehungen zu Markgraf Francesco II. von Gonzaga* (Munich: Max Hueber, 1965), 15.

2 Pietro Ferrato, *Il marchesato di Mantova e l'impero ottomano alla fine del secolo XV: documenti inediti tratti dall'Archivio storico dei Gonzaga* (Mantua: Mondovì, 1876); Kissling, *Sultan Bajezid's II*; for a summary in Italian, see Hans Joachim Kissling, *Francesco II Gonzaga ed il Sultano Bayezid II* (Florence: L. S. Olschki, 1967).

Ottomans reveals much about the nature of their relationship and provides us with a more nuanced picture of the interaction between the Italian city-states and the Ottoman Empire in the second half of the fifteenth century.

Mario Equicola (c. 1470–1525), the Gonzaga secretary and humanist, extolled Francesco's magnificence in his *Chronica di Mantua* (1521), describing him as one "born only for giving" and claiming that Francesco did not allow the sultan, or anybody else, to surpass him in liberality and therefore sent Bayezid gifts of great value.[3] This study will consider the choice and status of the gifts that were exchanged, which included the customary textiles alongside the rather more unusual gifts of portraits, a turban and cuirasses. Attention will also be paid to the ways in which gifts may have been understood by their receivers as the objects passed from one culture to another. Unfortunately, none of the gifts is known to have survived and their only trace is in correspondence held in the Mantuan State Archive. The lack of surviving objects combined with Bayezid II's comparatively minor role in Ottoman historiography has resulted in Mantua's low profile in the analysis of the relationship between Renaissance Italy and the Ottoman Empire.[4]

Following the conquest of Constantinople in 1453, the Ottomans began to regard themselves as a world power and their rapid expansion into Southeast Europe brought them geographically closer to their European neighbors. Venice and Genoa had longstanding diplomatic and commercial relations with the Ottomans, extending back to the mid-fourteenth century to the early years of the Ottoman dynasty. The second half of the fifteenth century is a particularly important period for Italo-Ottoman diplomacy since it saw other Italian states, including smaller courts such as Rimini and Mantua, forming diplomatic relationships with the Ottomans despite the backdrop of crusading rhetoric from the popes of the time. Many regarded the Ottomans with pragmatism, preferring the benefits of trade and perceiving opportunities to enhance their own importance in the delicate balance of power within the peninsula.[5]

[3] Mario Equicola, *Chronica di Mantua* (Mantua: n.p., 1521), section V (unpaginated): "disse, il Marchese di Mantua di esser nato per dar solo"; "Tacciomi al gran Turco Octomanno doni di gran valore mandati: non lasciandosi ne a lui ne ad altri di liberalita superare."

[4] For an assessment of Bayezid's reign, see Selahattin Tansel, *Sultan Bâyezit'in Siyasî Hayatî* (Constantinople: M.E.B. Devlet Kitapları Müdürlügü, 1966); V. J. Parry, "Bāyazīd II," in *Encyclopaedia of Islam*, 2nd ed., ed. P. Bearman, T. Bianquis, C. E. Bosworth, E. van Donzel, and W. P. Heinrichs (Leiden: Brill, 1960–2005), 1: 1119–21.

[5] For an overview of diplomacy in this period, see Daniel Goffman, "Negotiating with the Renaissance State: The Ottoman Empire and the New Diplomacy," in *The Early Modern*

THE DIPLOMATIC RELATIONSHIP BETWEEN THE MANTUAN COURT AND THE OTTOMAN EMPIRE

The subject of diplomatic exchange between Italy and the Ottomans in the fifteenth century is far more likely to call Venice to mind – as detailed in Luca Molà's chapter – than the small, landlocked North Italian state of Mantua. We must, therefore, begin by considering what motivated this diplomatic relationship and the pattern of needs that it could fulfill. The 1490s were the years when Francesco was asserting his authority as Marquis of Mantua and consolidating his growing power. Francesco was shrewdly searching for allies for his small marquisate. Friendship with the Ottoman sultan was a considerable asset on the chessboard of European politics. In March 1494 and again in April 1496 the Ottoman envoy Kasım Bey wrote to Francesco informing him that they were ready to give whatever services he may require.[6] Bayezid's power was secure as long as Prince Cem, his exiled half-brother and rival for the Ottoman throne, remained a papal hostage. The Ottomans did not follow the principle of primogeniture and, following his final defeat by Bayezid in 1482, Cem had fled to Rhodes in search of refuge with the Knights of Saint John. The Knights, however, reached an agreement with Bayezid to keep Cem in their custody in return for a lucrative annual payment. Cem was taken first to their castles in France, and then, from 1489, he became a papal hostage until he was forcibly surrendered to the French King Charles VIII in 1494.[7]

The intensity of Ottoman diplomatic engagement with Mantua must be understood in the light of Cem's captivity and the attempts to retrieve his body after his death in French custody in February 1495. Bayezid's diplomacy was initially motivated by the need for regular and up-to-date information regarding the whereabouts and health of Cem and the pattern of alliances between the European states. A number of documents attest to the information-gathering aspect of Bayezid's relations with

Ottomans: Remapping the Empire, ed. Virginia Aksan and Daniel Goffman (Cambridge: Cambridge University Press, 2007), 61–74.

6 ASMn, AG, b. 795, fasc. 15, fol. 46; ASMn, AG, b. 795, fasc. 17, fol. 66. See also Ferrato, *Il marchesato di Mantova*, 5–6; Kissling, *Sultan Bajezid's II*, 59.

7 For further discussion of Cem's imprisonment, see Nicolas Vatin, *Sultan Djem: un prince ottoman dans l'Europe du XVe siècle d'après deux sources contemporaines, Vakiat-i Sultan Cem, Oeuvres de Guillaume Caoursin* (Ankara: Imprimerie de la Société turque d'histoire, 1997).

Mantua.[8] Cem remained central to Bayezid's diplomacy even after his death. The sultan, apart from reputedly wishing to provide Cem with an Islamic burial, needed to obtain his brother's body as definitive assurance that his rival was indeed dead.[9] Cem died shortly after his transferral into French custody and his body was moved to the French-controlled citadel of Gaeta, near Naples. Following the French surrender of Gaeta in November 1496 Cem's body was handed over to Federico I of Aragon, King of Naples in exchange for French prisoners.[10] The desire to know the whereabouts of Cem's body prompted Bayezid to seek assistance from Venice in May 1495, and in February 1496 Mustafa Bey, *sancakbeyi* (governor of a subprovince) of Vlorë, sent an agent to Naples and also to Mantua.[11] Francesco promised diligently to seek "the truth out of [his] love for the sultan" ("per amore de Vostra Signoria").[12] In February 1497 Francesco was still seeking information about Cem's remains.[13] Bayezid eventually received the body in the summer of 1499, apparently hastened by his ultimatum to the King of Naples that unless the body was handed over in eight days he would attack his kingdom.[14]

It was not only developments in Italy that Bayezid was eager to monitor. The sultan was aware of France's emergence as the preeminent European power and feared that a French army could cross the Adriatic.[15] Fourteenth-century prophecies that had announced the coming of a "second Charlemagne" were widely interpreted as a reference to Charles VIII in late fifteenth-century France and the French king had declared his intentions to launch a crusade against the Ottomans from Naples and also planned to conquer Albania and Greece.[16]

During the 1490s, a critical period for both Bayezid and Francesco, there was frequent contact between the two powers. Between 1491 and

8 ASMn, AG, b. 86, fasc. 16, fol. 34r and 94r; ASMn, AG, b. 2962, lib. 5, fols 2r–3r. See also Kissling, *Sultan Bajezid's II*, 46 and 50.

9 Ahmed Aşıkpaşazade, *Osmanoğullarının tarihi: Tevârîh-i Âl-i Osmân*, ed. Kemal Yavuz and M. A. Yekta Saraç (Constantinople: Gökkubbe, 2007), 498.

10 See Nicolas Vatin, *Les ottomans et l'Occident (XVe –XVIe siècles)*, Analecta Isisiana, 51 (Constantinople: Isis, 2001), 77–91.

11 Ibid., pp. 79 and 81 and ASMn, AG, b. 2962, lib. 5, fol. 25r.

12 ASMn, AG, b. 2962, lib. 5, fol. 25r-v: "volessimo fare ogni inquisitione per saperlo ad che per amore de Vostra Signoria non siamo manchati de ogni diligentia per ritrovarne la verita ..."

13 See the letters published in Alessandro Luzio, *Isabella d'Este e i Borgia, con nuovi documenti e quattro tavole di facsimile* (Milan: Cogliati, 1915), 179–80.

14 Vatin, *Les ottomans*, 83–86. 15 Ibid., 86–88.

16 Paul Durrieu, "La délivrance de la Grèce projetée en France à la fin du quinzième siècle," *Revue d'histoire diplomatique* 26 (1912): 333–51.

1500 at least one Mantuan envoy was sent to the Ottoman court every year.[17] This continued with slightly less frequency in the following decade. The Ottoman envoy Kasım Bey stayed in Mantua for a week in 1493 and was received with great pomp and pageantry.[18] He stayed a second time in 1494 and an Ottoman envoy named Davud visited the city in 1495.[19] The Mantuan envoys to the Ottoman court reported that they were received with great honor and one noted that he had been honored more than the ambassadors from Naples or Florence.[20] The friendship with Mantua is all the more significant given that during these years Venice had lost the right to have a *bailo* (resident consul and ambassador) in the Ottoman capital.[21]

HORSES

Fine horses, luxurious trappings and equestrian pursuits were important status symbols for rulers and the elites in both Europe and Asia. One of the first imports to have been brought to Mantua from Ottoman lands during this period of diplomatic exchange was horses. The ruling family's equine enthusiasm is readily apparent in the Palazzo Te, the residence built by Francesco's son Federico II, where frescoes of the Gonzaga horses by sixteenth-century artist Giulio Romano adorn one of the principal ceremonial rooms. The acquisition of horses played a prominent role in Francesco's dealings with the Ottomans from the outset. His interest seems to have been prompted by the visit in 1488 of a certain Bernardino who had requested an audience with the marquis in order to present him with some horses that he had bought in Turkey.[22]

Horse trading was an important part of the Mantuan court's revenue alongside Francesco's employment as a mercenary captain or *condottiere*.

[17] The year 1499 is a possible exception. Kissling, *Sultan Bajezid's II*, 80.

[18] Documents describing the visit are published in Ferrato, *Il marchesato di Mantova*, 8–13, and Kissling, *Sultan Bajezid's II*, 19–25. For a summary of Kasım Bey's career, see Barbara Flemming, "Zwei türkische Herren von Avlona," *Der Islam* 45 (1969): 310–16 (312–15).

[19] For Kasım Bey's visit of 1494 and Davud's visit of 1495, see Kissling, *Sultan Bajezid's II*, 41 and 46.

[20] ASMn, AG, b. 795, fasc. 12, fol. 35. See also Kissling, *Sultan Bajezid's II*, 7.

[21] For the dismissal of the bailo, see Carla Coco and Flora Manzonetto, *Baili veneziani alla sublime porta: storia e caratteristiche dell'ambasciata veneta a Costantinopoli* (Venice: Stamperia di Venezia, 1985), 26–27.

[22] Kissling, *Sultan Bajezid's II*, 5. Kissling convincingly argued that this man was not the same Bernardino who acted as a Mantuan envoy to the Ottomans.

Francesco is believed to have owned between 650 and 1000 horses.[23] The most sought-after breeds came from the Ottoman Empire and Hafsid North Africa. The importing of horses from Ottoman territory required permission from the sultan given the military importance of horses.[24] In his first visit to the Ottoman Porte in 1491, Francesco's emissary Bernardino Missaglia obtained the necessary permission.[25] In addition to those horses that were purchased in Ottoman lands by Francesco's envoys, others were received as gifts.

Francesco's access to horses via the Ottoman market provided him with valuable bloodlines to introduce into his breeding program since Turkish horses were good runners (Figure 1.1). The superiority of the horses bred in Mantua not only offered opportunities for direct commercial gain but provided Francesco with an advantage in his gift exchange with other powers. The recently crowned King Henry VIII of England received four horses from Francesco in 1514, and according to the Mantuan emissary Giovanni Ratto, Henry had remarked that he could not have been more pleased had he been presented with another kingdom and claimed that they were the best horses he had ever ridden.[26] In his letter of thanks Henry declared that he counted Francesco and his sons among his dearest friends.[27]

Francesco reaped the benefits of his gift-giving not only in effusive words of thanks but also in reciprocal gifts and access to purchase horses and hounds from the recipient. As a sign of his gratitude Henry sent Francesco some English horses with precious caparisons and trappings. Francesco described these gifts in a letter to his wife, Isabella d'Este, claiming that she would never have seen such sumptuous trappings.[28] Francesco wrote to Henry declaring that nothing conferred on him by

[23] Federico Amadei cited in Galeazzo Nosari and Franco Canova, *Il palio del Rinascimento: i cavalli di razza dei Gonzaga nell'età di Francesco II Gonzaga, 1484–1519* (Reggiolo: E. Lui, 2003), 62. Amedei did not think this an exaggeration. A more conservative estimate of around 650 is given by Ann Hyland, *The Horse in the Middle Ages* (Stroud: Sutton, 1999), 20.

[24] Horses were included among the *memnu eşya*, goods prohibited for export from Ottoman lands to Christian states. See Gábor Ágoston, "Merces Prohibitae: The Anglo-Ottoman Trade in War Materials and the Dependence Theory," *Oriente Moderno* 20 (2001): 177–92.

[25] ASMn, AG, b. 795, fasc.12, fols. 33r–34r. See also Kissling, *Sultan Bajezid's II*, 6–7.

[26] David Chambers and Jane Martineau, eds., *Splendours of the Gonzaga: Exhibition Catalogue, Victoria & Albert Museum, London, 4 November 1981 – 31 January 1982* (London: Victoria and Albert Museum, 1981), 148.

[27] Ibid., 148. [28] ibid., 149.

FIGURE 1.1 Filippo Orso, *A Turkish Horse Caparisoned in the Turkish Style*, 1554, pen and ink, 41.9 cm × 28 cm, Victoria and Albert Museum, London © Victoria and Albert Museum, London.

nature, fortune or military skill had so raised his esteem in Italy as this.[29] Notwithstanding the rhetoric of such letters of thanks, it is clear that the improvement of the Mantuan breed provided Francesco with the possibility of giving impressive gifts that raised him in the esteem of kings and

[29] Ibid., 149.

earned him powerful friends. Indeed, horses were also sent to King Louis XII of France.[30] In 1517 Francesco wrote that his race of horses was "praised and desired … by the kings of France, Spain, England, Turkey, Hungary and by many most Reverend Cardinals, illustrious gentlemen, and finally by anybody who knows of them."[31]

In addition to their commercial benefits and their role as high-status gifts, possession of superior horses had its own intrinsic value and courts competed with each other for ownership of the finest animals. The status that fine horses bestowed on their owner is clearly exemplified in Baldessare Castiglione's (c. 1478–1529) *The Book of the Courtier*, a discussion of the virtues and conduct of the ideal courtier, written between 1508 and 1518. Castiglione had previously been a courtier at Mantua and in his book he commented on the splendors of the Mantuan court, of which he listed "a great many fine horses," and proclaimed that Francesco seemed "king of Italy rather than lord of a city."[32] The rivalry between courts was most explicitly manifested in *palios* in which horses were set to race against each other to prove the prestige and status of the court that they represented. Within a span of thirty years, Francesco's horses won 280 victories in various cities, more than any other lords of Italy.[33] The Palio of Siena in July 1494 was a particularly prized triumph for Mantua since the Gonzaga horse came 300 meters ahead of the runner-up, a Medici horse.[34] Mantua's *cavalli di razza* were held in such acclaim that they were much in demand to participate in various *palios*.[35] Francesco instigated the creation of a book, the *Libro dei palii*, recording the outstanding successes of his horses for posterity; one page was dedicated to "El Turcho de la raza."[36]

30 Stefano Gionta, *Il fioretto delle cronache di Mantova raccolto da Stefano Gionta* (Mantua: Antonio Mainardi, 1844; reprint, Mantua: Istituto Carlo d'Arco per la storia di Mantova, 1972), 105.

31 Giancarlo Malacarne, *Il mito dei cavalli gonzagheschi: alle origini del purosangue* (Verona: Promoprint, 1995), 86: "che è laudata et desiderata per una de le singulari, dal re di Franza, re Catholico [re di Spagna], d'Inghilterra, de Turchia, de Ungaria et da multi Reverendissimi Cardinali Illustrissimi Signori, et finalmente da qualunque altro che n'habbia cognitione."

32 Baldesar Castiglione, *The Book of the Courtier*, trans. Charles S. Singleton, ed. Edgar de N. Mayhew (Garden City, NY: Doubleday, 1959), 320.

33 Nosari and Canova, *Il palio del Rinascimento*, 70 and 74.

34 Ibid., 66.

35 Ibid., 67 and 325.

36 For further discusssion of the *Libro dei palii*, see Malacarne, *Il mito dei cavalli gonzagheschi*, 88–95; Nosari and Canova, *Il palio del Rinascimento*, 328–32.

According to the seventeenth-century chronicle of Mantua by Federico Amadei, in return for horses Francesco sent Bayezid a ship fully loaded with the best Mantuan cheese, which pleased the sultan greatly.[37] The quantity of cheese appears to have been exaggerated over time, although there is no doubt that cheese – most probably a wheel of grana padano – was indeed sent as a gift to the sultan. In July 1491 instructions were given to deliver twenty-five pieces of cheese to the envoy Bernardino Missaglia in preparation for his forthcoming mission.[38] Cheese was not an uncommon gift from an Italian state and was often requested by Ottoman officials who had developed a taste for Italian cheese.[39]

PORTRAITS

One of the more richly documented missions was that of the Mantuan envoy Alessio Beccaguto, who in late 1492 sent Francesco a detailed account of his journey and reception at the Ottoman court.[40] The letter informs us of a gift that Francesco sent to Bayezid: a portrait of himself. Beccaguto recounted how he had explained to Bayezid's courtiers that since Francesco could not come in person to show reverence to the sultan he wanted to be brought there in the form of a picture so that Bayezid could "see and know him" in this way.[41] The language used by Beccaguto is particularly revealing; it implies that the gift was not simply intended to present Francesco's features to the sultan but emphasizes the portrait's function in the marquis's eyes as a means for him to be vicariously present at the Ottoman court through the portrait.

The portrait is now lost and unfortunately we do not know how it was received by Bayezid. Beccaguto's letter reveals that the viziers expressed

[37] Federico Amadei, *Cronaca universale della città di Mantova*, ed. Giuseppe Amadei, Ercolano Marani and Giovanni Praticò (Mantua: C.I.T.E.M, 1955), 2: 331.

[38] ASMn, AG, b. 2904, lib. 137, fol. 79r.

[39] For Venetian examples of cheese being sent as a gift, see Maria Pia Pedani, *In nome del Gran Signore: inviati ottomani a Venezia dalla caduta di Costantinopoli alla guerra di Candia* (Venice: Deputazione Editrice, 1994), 61.

[40] British Library, London, MS Harley 3462, fols. 23r–27r (old pagination) or fols. 14r–18r (new pagination); subsequent citations will follow the new pagination. The letter is partially cited in Gülru Necipoğlu, *Architecture, Ceremonial, and Power: The Topkapı Palace in the Fifteenth and Sixteenth Centuries* (New York: Architectural History Foundation, MIT Press, 1991), 278.

[41] British Library, London, MS Harley 3462, fol. 16v: "non havendo in persona potuto venire a fare reverentia alla sua Maesta ha voluto essergli in pictura portato, accio che sua Maesta lo vegia, et conosca."

interest and admiration. As was expected of him, Beccaguto had handed over his gifts to officials who would parade them before a ceremonial window from which the sultan could watch.[42] It is a measure of the curiosity aroused by Francesco's portrait that the viziers had it brought back and took it in their hands and highly praised the face of Francesco.[43]

The court portraitist Francesco Bonsignori is a possible candidate to have made the likeness of the marquis. Vasari praised Bonsignori highly for his talent in portraiture and recorded that he made many portraits of Francesco Gonzaga and other members of the Gonzaga family, which were sent as gifts to various princes in France and Germany.[44] The portrait Bayezid received may have been similar to the drawing of Francesco II Gonzaga in the National Gallery of Ireland, attributed to Andrea Mantegna, court artist of the Gonzaga, and previously assigned to Bonsignori (Figure 1.2).

Bayezid II, unlike his father Mehmed II, is known to have disapproved of figural painting. Giovanni Maria Angiolello, an Italian captive who was a member of Mehmed's court, wrote that when Bayezid came to the throne he sold all of his father's pictures that had been made by Gentile Bellini.[45] Nevertheless, even for a conservative such as Bayezid, the gift of a portrait would not necessarily have been unacceptable in these diplomatic circumstances. Firdausi's Persian epic, the *Shahname* (The Book of Kings), recounts a legendary situation in which a portrait was not simply decorative but had the practical purpose of presenting the features of one who was absent: Queen Qaydafe of the Maghreb was able to recognize Iskender (Alexander the Great) when he attended her court in disguise because she was already familiar with his appearance through a portrait (Figure 1.3). Perhaps the similarly functional nature of Francesco's portrait, allowing Bayezid to see with whom he was dealing, would have made it more palatable.

The portrait of Francesco was not the only portrait that was sent to Bayezid from the Mantuan court. Owing to Isabella d'Este's absence from

42 For a description of the ceremonial of the presentation of the gifts, see Necipoğlu, *Architecture, Ceremonial, and Power*, 98.

43 British Library, London, MS Harley 3462, fol. 16v.

44 Giorgio Vasari, *Le vite de' più eccellenti pittori, scultori e architettori nelle redazioni del 1550 e 1568*, ed. Rosanna Bettarini and Paola Barocchi, 6 vols. (Florence: Sansoni, 1966–87), 4: 579. Vasari refers to him as Francesco Monsignori.

45 Donado da Lezze, *Historia turchesca 1300–1514*, ed. I. Ursu (Bucharest: C. Göbl, 1909), 121. Ursu maintained that the *Historia turchesca* was by Donado da Lezze; it is generally attributed to Giovanni Maria Angiolello.

FIGURE 1.2 Attributed to Andrea Mantegna, *Portrait of Francesco II Gonzaga, 4th Marquis of Mantua, (1466–1519)*, c. 1495, black chalk and gray wash on paper, 34.8 cm × 23.8 cm, National Gallery of Ireland Collection, Dublin, NGI.2019,
Photo © National Gallery of Ireland.

FIGURE 1.3 Attributed to Nakkas Osman, *Queen Qayafe Recognizes Iskender by his Portrait*, Tercume-i Sehname-i fIrdersî, c. 1560–70. Illumination, 38 × 25 cm, Topkapı Palace Library, Constantinople, MS H1522, fol. 410a.
© Topkapı Palace Museum.

Mantua at the time of Kasım Bey's visit, there are a number of detailed reports documenting what she had missed. A letter of July 1493 to Isabella from the Gonzaga secretary, Antimaco, listed a rather unusual gift: "Item a picture of the figure of the Turk who is in Rome, and of the ambassador of the *soldano*."[46] The portraits have not survived. "The Turk who is in Rome" must refer to Prince Cem and the other figure is most likely to have been the Mamluk ambassador, since the term *soldano* was commonly reserved for the Mamluk sultan while the Ottoman sultan tended to be referred to as "Signore Gran Turco," as indeed he is in this very letter.[47]

For many years this gift was misunderstood because Pietro Ferrato's transcription of the letter had omitted the heading at the top of the list of gifts that reads "To the ambassador of the Grand Turk."[48] Hans Joachim Kissling had interpreted the list as gifts sent from Bayezid – rather than received by him – and, given the sultan's orthodox views toward figural painting, had concluded that the portraits were perhaps a sort of "wanted poster" for a murder plot against Cem in which Francesco was involved.[49] Instead, the portraits of Cem and the Mamluk ambassador probably accompanied a report on Cem's situation which was a significant aspect of the Ottoman-Mantuan relationship.

The pictures were described as having been formerly in the possession of the celebrated painter Mantegna ("che haveva Andrea Mantinea").[50] Mantegna (c. 1431–1506) had been in Rome in 1488–90 working for Pope Innocent VIII. During that time he had seen the pope's hostage and

46 ASMn, AG, b. 2443, fasc. 2, fol. 88r and ASMn, AG, b. 2190, fasc. 18, fol. 648: "Item uno quadro de la figura del Turco che è a Roma, e de l'ambasciatore dil soldano ..." See also Ferrato, *Il marchesato di Mantova*, 11–13.

47 Kissling, *Sultan Bajezid's II*, 35. Hedda Reindl-Kiel interpreted the document as referring to a portrait of the Ottoman envoy Kasım, although she noted that the term *soldano* usually denoted the Mamluk sultan; see Hedda Reindl-Kiel, "Ottoman Diplomatic Gifts to the Christian West," in *The Ottoman Orient in Renaissance Culture: Papers from the International Conference at the National Museum in Krakow, June 26–27, 2015*, ed. Robert Born and Michal Dziewulski (Krakow: National Museum in Krakow, 2015), 99.

48 ASMn, AG, b. 2190, fasc. 18, fol. 648: "Al Ambasciatore del Signore Gran Turco." The missing heading radically changes our understanding of the portraits as noted simultaneously by Molly Bourne, "The Turban'd Turk in Renaissance Mantua Francesco II Gonzaga's Interest in Ottoman Fashion," in *Mantova e il Rinascimento italiano: studi in onore di David S. Chambers*, ed. Philippa Jackson and Guido Rebecchini (Mantua: Sometti, 2011), 56, and Gatward Cevizli, "Beyond Bellini," 244.

49 Kissling, *Sultan Bajezid's II*, 35–36.

50 Ferrato, *Il marchesato di Mantova*, 13. A mistranslation in the Italian summary of Kissling's research complicated matters further by stating that the pictures were later to be found in the possession of Andrea Mantegna. Kissling, *Sultan Bajezid's II*, 41.

had written to Francesco Gonzaga describing Cem in lively detail, referring to his elephant-like walk and wildly exaggerating the size of his turban; Mantegna had promised to sketch him.[51] The Mamluks supported Cem's claims to the throne, and in 1489 – in the middle of Mantegna's stay – a Mamluk ambassador had visited Rome, lending credence to the theory that the portrait depicted a Mamluk diplomat.[52] This raises the tantalizing possibility that Francesco may have presented Bayezid with portraits by Mantegna that originated from the artist's Roman sojourn.

CLOTH, CLOTHING AND ARMOR

Antimaco's letter not only listed the gifts given to Bayezid, but also informed Isabella of their value: a gold necklace worth 550 ducats, a belt with a value of 50 ducats, 200 ducats in coins ("*testoni*") – another way in which Francesco's features could be presented to the Ottoman court – and 10 ducats for each member of the party.[53] He did not itemize the cost of the many textiles given. We do know, however, that the marquis had some difficulty in purchasing textiles of the quality he desired. Another courtier wrote to Isabella informing her how Francesco had wished to have six robes ("*casaghe*") "*alla turchesca*" made as gifts for the ambassador and how, not succeeding in finding a sufficient brocade or damask in the merchants' shops, he had ordered that the *palii* (banners) from his own collection should be used for the tunics.[54] One *palio* to be used was that of San Leonardo, the horse race run in Mantua in honor of that saint. *Palio* banners were made of the most luxurious fabrics and were expressions of a city's prestige and wealth. In the 1490s they could easily cost

[51] ASMn, AG, Autografi, b. 7, fol. 123r-v. See also Filippo Trevisani, ed., *Andrea Mantegna e i Gonzaga: Rinascimento nel Castello di San Giorgio. Exhibition Catalogue, Palazzo Ducale, Mantua, 16 September 2006–14 January 2007* (Milan: Electa, 2006), 173.

[52] Vladimir Lamansky, *Secrets d'état de Venise: documents, extraits, notices et études servant a éclaircir les rapports de la Seigneurie avec les Grecs, les Slaves et la Porte ottomane à la fin du XVe et au XVIe siècle*, 2 vols. (New York: Franklin, 1968), vol. 1 : 230–32; Stefano Infessura, *Diario della città di Roma di Stefano Infessura scribasenato*, ed. Oreste Tommasini (Rome: Forzani, 1890), 241–42.

[53] Ferrato, *Il marchesato di Mantova*, 12–13. These figures are further corroborated by the courtier Francesco Cusastro's letter to Isabella, ASMn, AG, b. 2443, fasc. 1, fol. 29r. See also Giancarlo Malacarne, *I signori del cielo: la falconeria a Mantova al tempo dei Gonzaga* (Mantua: Artiglio, 2003), 285, and an unpublished letter to Isabella from the courtier Federico de Casalmaggiore. ASMn, AG, b. 2443, fol. 317.

[54] For Francesco Cusastro's letter, see ASMn, AG, b. 2443, fasc. 1, fol. 29r. See also Malacarne, *I signori del cielo*, 285.

between 100 and 200 ducats.[55] Francesco handed over to the tailor twelve *braccie* of brocade, the *palio* of San Leonardo, and another *palio* measuring twenty-five *braccie* of crimson damask from his own collection.[56] These were transformed into two brocade robes, one lined with satin, the other with damask; a robe of crimson velvet; and three others of damask, all for the ambassador.[57]

The courtier Federico de Casalmaggiore wrote a description for Isabella of Kasım Bey on horseback clothed with the gold necklace, the two brocade robes and the belt and declared that it was "a magnificent thing to see him with that turban."[58] Given the estimations above, Kasım's attire should probably be valued conservatively at around 700 ducats – equivalent to seven altarpieces of the caliber of Mantegna's *La Madonna della Vittoria* of c. 1495.[59] This sum does not include the other four robes, the 200 ducats presented in coins, the three "very beautiful" crossbows, the mail shirt, the stomach armor, the portrait(s), the seven silk garments for the ambassador's attendants and 10 ducats for each person.[60] Francesco's gifts compare favorably with those given by the pope to Cem on his arrival in Rome in 1489: 700 ducats, brocade robes and the use of a horse.[61] For a small state such as Mantua to clothe the Ottoman envoy in such splendor demonstrates Francesco's efforts to impress both Bayezid and his Italian contemporaries with his wealth and liberality.

The gifts that Bayezid sent to Francesco on the same occasion are recorded in the running commentary of correspondence sent to Isabella. The sultan sent sixteen different types of fabric: cloth of gold (*serâser*, the most luxurious Ottoman textile), velvet, damask and camlet along with

[55] Elizabeth MacKenzie Tobey, "The Palio in Italian Renaissance Art, Thought and Culture," PhD thesis, University of Maryland, 2005), 139–40; see also her appendix 2 for a table of the money spent on *palio* banners, unfortunately not including Mantua, 312–16.

[56] ASMn, AG, b. 2443, fasc. 1, fol. 29r. See also Malacarne, *I signori del cielo*, 285.

[57] Ibid.: "Una casagha de brochador fodrata de raso, una casagha de brochador teneto fodrata de damascho, una casagha de velù cremesino piano, tre altre casaghe de damascho, tute per la persona del Ambasiator."

[58] ASMn, AG, b. 2443, fol. 317: "et lo prefato ambasiatore era ornato cum quella colana et cum le due veste di brocato et lo cinto che era una superba cosa vederlo cum quello turbante."

[59] For documentation of the cost of Mantegna's altarpiece, see Molly Bourne, "Mantegna's *Madonna della Vittoria* and the Rewriting of Gonzaga History," in *The Patron's Payoff: Conspicuous Commissions in Italian Renaissance Art*, ed. Jonathan K. Nelson and Richard J. Zeckhauser (Princeton and Oxford: Princeton University Press, 2008), 181.

[60] Ferrato, *Il marchesato di Mantova*, 12–13. Other sources refer to five silk garments for the rest of the party.

[61] Infessura, *Diario della città di Roma*, 241.

two Turkish bows and two bridles of Turkish stamped leather.[62] Francesco hoped to receive a precious textile of another kind from the sultan and sent Beccaguto to meet Kasım Bey in Venice in 1494 to request a relic in Bayezid's possession that was believed to be the shirt of Christ, along with forty good horses.[63] Mantua already housed a number of impressive relics, the most important being the Precious Blood of Christ. The pope had recently received part of the Holy Lance as a gift from Bayezid and perhaps this prompted Francesco's attempt to add Christ's shirt to Mantua's collection. No further evidence has come to light about Francesco's request and it was presumably not met. The contemporary Roman historian Sigismondo De' Conti claimed that there was no hope of Christ's shirt being obtained since Bayezid, like his father before him, wore Christ's shirt for protection in battle.[64]

In November 1495, two kaftans of gold brocade ("*brocati doro*") and a horse sent by Bayezid successfully reached their destination – the previous year Kasım Bey had been robbed of the gifts he was carrying.[65] What is the most interesting about the gift of kaftans are the accompanying letters explaining that they were given as a sign of friendship to reward Francesco's valor and stating that "we have done this according to the custom of our land."[66] We learn from a letter from Kasım Bey that Francesco's victory against the French at Fornovo in July 1495 had earned him much praise at the Ottoman court.[67] Francesco later wrote to the Ottoman envoy that his troop's battle cry had been "Turco! Turco!" and with it their enemies had been routed, which he went on to say was no small praise for the sultan.[68] A letter from the vizier Hersekoğlu Ahmed Pasha to Francesco states that robes and a horse were customarily given by the sultan to reward his brave men.[69] This explanation differentiates these robes from the previous gifts of garments since it refers to the practice of *hil'at* (Arabic: *Khil'at*): the sultan's presentation of

[62] Documented in letters from Francesco Gonzaga and Cusastro published in Malacarne, *I signori del cielo*, 280–81 and 285.

[63] Kissling, *Sultan Bajezid's II*, 33.

[64] Sigismondo De' Conti, *Le storie de' suoi tempi dal 1475 al 1510*, 2 vols. (Rome: G. Barberà, 1883), 2: 27.

[65] For the robbery, see Kissling, *Sultan Bajezid's II*, 41.

[66] ASMn, AG, b.86, fasc. 16, fol. 93v: "Secondo usanza del paese nostro così havemo fatto." See also Kissling, *Sultan Bajezid's II*, 56.

[67] ASMn, AG, b. 795, fol. 58r. See also Ferrato, *Il marchesato di Mantova*, 6–7. Francesco's victory was in fact ambiguous; see Bourne, "Mantegna's *Madonna della Vittoria.*"

[68] Bourne "The Turban'd Turk," 55.

[69] ASMn, AG, b. 795, fol. 83. See also Kissling, *Sultan Bajezid's II*, 73.

robes of honor to subjects whom he wished to reward or single out for distinction. The practice has been compared to the presentation of medals by Western rulers.[70] The bestowing of a robe of honor on Francesco for his success at Fornovo implied that the marquis was an Ottoman vassal but Francesco was probably unaware of such nuances.

The perceived status of the recipient was expressed in the choice of fabric for the *hil'at*. Unfortunately, no kaftans or items subsequently fashioned from them can be identified from the dispersed Gonzaga collections. We are, therefore, reliant on the textual evidence that the robes were made of gold brocade (*brocati doro*). Another limitation is that the document is in Italian and, therefore, we do not know the Ottoman terminology that would identify the grade of textile and enable us to gain a better understanding of Francesco's importance in the sultan's eyes. Nevertheless, to be presented with a pair of kaftans was a significant mark of honor, and, given the circumstances for which Francesco was being rewarded, they are likely to have been made from a precious fabric.

Another item of Ottoman dress is recorded to have been sent to Francesco by Bayezid: a turban. It was listed in an inventory of Gonzaga property drawn up in 1540–42.[71] It was rather an unusual choice of gift since turbans were synonymous with Islam. Indeed, the expression "to take the turban" meant to convert. Another example of turbans being sent as gifts to a Christian ruler is the case of 1650 when fifty turbans were sent to the court of Vienna, which has been interpreted as a possible invitation to convert.[72] Francesco acquired at least fourteen turbans in this period as a result of active procurement on his part.[73] These turbans were in the Ottoman style rather than the genuine article since they were fashioned in Italy. They were presumably to have been worn in the carnival season or in theatrical

70 For further discussion of *hil'at*, see Nurhan Atasoy, *Ipek: The Crescent and the Rose: Imperial Ottoman Silks and Velvets*, ed. Julian Raby and Alison Effeny (London: Azimuth, 2001), 32–34.

71 For the turban sent by Bayezid, see Daniela Ferrari, *Le collezioni Gonzaga: L'inventario dei beni del 1540–1542* (Cinisello Balsamo: Silvana, 2003), 277–78. A turban is also listed in another inventory of 1543 cited in James Mann, "The Lost Armoury of the Gonzagas, Part II. The Libro d'Aquila," *Archaeological Journal* 100 (1943): 16–127, at p. 50.

72 Hedda Reindl-Kiel, "East Is East and West Is West and Sometimes the Twain Did Meet: Diplomatic Exchange in the Ottoman Empire," in *Frontiers of Ottoman Studies*, ed. Colin Imber, Keiko Kiyotaki and Rhoads Murphey, 2 vols. (London; New York: Tauris, 2005), 2: 119.

73 See Bourne, "The Turban'd Turk," for discussion of Francesco's attempts to acquire turbans from Venice.

performances.[74] Bayezid's gift of a turban would certainly have been well received by the turcophile Francesco, who was even attempting to learn some Turkish.[75] However, there would probably have been considerable divergence in the way in which it was perceived by the giver and the receiver.

The sultan had been greatly pleased with Francesco's gift of some *corazzine* (a type of cuirass for the protection of the chest and back) in 1491 that were sent in defiance of a papal ban on the export of war materials to the infidel.[76] Bayezid had asked to be sent more cuirasses and six or eight mules (used in this period to carry artillery and provisions) along with a cuirass and two *panciere* (armor that protected the stomach) for each of the pashas.[77] This was not an isolated case. A letter of 26 October 1492 from the armorer Micheleto delle Corazzine to Francesco gives a hint at the quantities of armor being made for the Ottomans; Micheleto informed the marquis that he had done "a lot of work for Your Lordship and especially those works for the Grand Turk."[78] It was not only Bayezid who enjoyed access to such goods: both the sancakbeyis of Vlorë and Shkodër bought custom-made armor through their contact with Francesco.[79]

The requests were mostly for cuirasses and stomach armor. While it has been known for some time that Francesco sent armor to the Ottomans, the specific items that were requested have not been examined. A *corazzina* was made up of individual metal pieces riveted together with large curved steel plates across the breast and back for greater protection before being covered with fabric (Figure 1.4). The significance of the requests for cuirasses and stomach armor becomes clearer when one considers Ottoman armor of the time. The Military Museum in Constantinople holds a mail shirt that belonged to Behram Pasha, the Beylerbeyi (governor general of a province) of Rumelia, the southern Balkans, who died in 1532 (Figure 1.5). A man of his standing would have had some of the most protective armor available. Unlike the simple mail shirts worn by cavalrymen, Behram Pasha's mail shirt was fitted over the chest and back with small individual strengthening plates held by mail. An Italian *corazzina* with its large curved

[74] Ibid., 57–58.

[75] ASMn, AG, b. 2443, fasc.18, fol. 515. See also Kissling, *Sultan Bajezid's II*, 26, and Molly Bourne, *Francesco II Gonzaga: The Soldier-Prince as Patron* (Rome: Bulzoni, 2008), 243–44.

[76] ASMn, AG, b. 2904, fasc. 141, fols. 15v–16v. See also Kissling, *Sultan Bajezid's II*, 7. For further discussion of *merces prohibitae*, the goods banned for export to Islamic countries by papal bull, including metals, timber, ships and horses, see Ágoston, "Merces Prohibitae."

[77] ASMn, AG, b. 2904, fasc. 141, fols. 15v–16v. See also Kissling, *Sultan Bajezid's II*, 7.

[78] ASMn, AG, b.2441, fol. 250: "havendo facto lavorerii assai per Vostra Signoria et maxime quelli lavorerii del grando turcho . . ."

[79] Kissling, *Sultan Bajezid's II*, 38 and 61–62.

FIGURE 1.4 Milanese, *Corazzina*, 1380–1410, steel mail and plates and hemp cloth, 66.5 × 58 cm, Raccolta d'Arte Applicata, Castello Sforzesco, Milan,

FIGURE 1.5 Ottoman, mail shirt of Behram Pasha, Beylerbeyi of Rumelia (d. 1532), Askeri Müze, Constantinople. Author's photograph. Reproduced with permission from the Askeri Müze, Constantinople.

plates of steel across the chest and back offered superior protection and explains the Ottomans' eagerness to obtain armor from Mantua.

Envoys themselves often remain obscure figures with scholars concentrating on the content of the letters that they delivered, the gifts exchanged and the reports that they wrote. Francesco's choice of Bernardino Missaglia as envoy to the Ottomans was a significant one. Whereas most Mantuan diplomats in the fifteenth and sixteenth centuries tended to be chancellery secretaries, alternating between work in the central administration of government and missions abroad, Missaglia had been in charge of the

Mantuan armory for some time.[80] In fact, in the field of armor, the name Missaglia is a familiar one since the Milanese Missaglia family was known for producing the most renowned armorers of the time. Vannozzo Posio drew the analogy: "saying Missaglia at that time was like saying Krupp at the beginning of the twentieth century."[81] Mantegna's *La Madonna della Vittoria* depicts Francesco in what is most probably Missaglia armor (Figure 1.6). However, Bernardino Missaglia's background has not previously been discussed in relation to his role as envoy to the Ottomans. Kissling even stated that there was nothing detailed to be said about him.[82] Access to Northern Italian armor played a major role in Francesco's sustained relations with Bayezid and his sancakbeyis, throwing into sharp relief the significance of the choice of Missaglia as Mantuan emissary. Coming from this prominent family of armorers, Missaglia would himself have been a repository of knowledge on the subject.[83]

A letter to Francesco in 1504 from the Bolognese humanist Floriano Dolfo reveals that contemporaries were aware of the marquis's illicit gifts of armor to the Ottomans. Dolfo recounted the scathing things that Cristoforo del Poggio, secretary to the ruling Bentivoglio family in Bologna, had said about Francesco and his court:

> And furthermore, that against all reason and justice you have maintained and continue to maintain friendship and confederacy with the Grand Turk, the enemy of the Christian faith, and have sent him presents of arms that, according to our law are prohibited, and there is no other Lord who would undertake nor dare to commit such a flagrant act, and he said many other things that were sharper and more serious than the things above.[84]

80 Daniela Frigo "'Small States' and Diplomacy: Mantua and Modena," in *Politics and Diplomacy in Early Modern Italy: The Structure of Diplomatic Practice, 1450–1800*, ed. Daniela Frigo (Cambridge: Cambridge University Press, 2000), 147–75; diplomatic relations with the Ottomans are not discussed in this study. On Missaglia's role at the Mantuan court, see Vannozzo Posio, *Le armature delle Grazie tra storia e leggenda* (Modena: Mucchi, 1991), 24 and 29.

81 Posio, *Le armature*, 24.

82 Kissling, *Sultan Bajezid's II*, 5.

83 For discussion of the backgrounds of both Bernardino Missaglia and Alessio Beccaguto in relation to their missions to the Ottomans, see Antonia Gatward Cevizli, "More Than a Messenger: Embodied Expertise in Mantuan Envoys to the Ottomans in the 1490s," *Mediterranean Studies* 22, no. 2 (2014): 166–89. On the Missaglia family, see Posio, *Le armature*, 25, and Jacopo Gelli and Gaetano Moretti, *Gli armaroli milanesi: i Missaglia e la loro casa* (Milan: Hoepli, 1903), 56–58.

84 Floriano Dolfo, *Lettere ai Gonzaga*, ed. Marzia Minutelli (Rome: Edizioni di storia e letteratura, 2002), 196: "et più, che contra ogni rasone et equitate haveti mantenuto et manteneti amicitia et confederatione cum lo Gran Turcho, nimico de la fede Christiana, et mandatili presenti de arme che, secondo la lege nostra, sono prohibite, et non è altro Signore che usi nè ardisca operare tale flagitioso acto, et dicto molte altre parole più brusche et grave de le cose soprascripte."

FIGURE 1.6 Andrea Mantegna, *The Madonna and Child* or *La Madonna della Vittoria*, 1495, oil on canvas, 280 cm × 166 cm, Musée du Louvre Paris, Inv. 369, © RMN-Grand Palais (Musée du Louvre)/Jean-Gilles Berizzi.

In 1494 Bayezid had gathered troops and artillery in Albania in anticipation of a crusade led by the French. The armor that Mantua was providing could have been used to protect the Ottomans from the French in such an eventuality and highlights the potential seriousness of Francesco's contravention of the papal ban. It also demonstrates that concerns for the delicate balance of power within the Italian peninsula could trump religious ideological preoccupations. Friendship with Bayezid bolstered Francesco's power and influence and the giving and selling of superior Italian armor was part of the currency of that relationship.

CONCLUSION

The intense period of diplomatic exchange between Francesco Gonzaga and Bayezid II was arguably much more fruitful in terms of the resulting material exchange than any political outcomes. Francesco was able to enjoy the prestige of his friendship with the sultan but such contacts did not prevent him from being imprisoned in Venice in 1509 for his participation in the anti-Venetian League of Cambrai nor did Isabella's pleas for the intervention of the sultan and one of his sancakbeyis seem to have been much of an asset.[85] Bayezid eventually succeeded in obtaining the body of Prince Cem but Francesco does not ultimately seem to have been instrumental despite his efforts.

There is no doubt that the Ottoman-Mantuan relationship was mutually beneficial in terms of material goods. Permission to purchase horses from Ottoman markets contributed to Francesco's improvement of the Mantuan breed. His gifts of fine horses cemented his friendship with kings, while his numerous *palio* successes raised the political stock of the Gonzaga in Italy. Horses were a major economic and cultural asset for the Mantuan state and Francesco's friendship with the sultan played a vital part in its development. The giving of armor as gifts prompted Ottoman interest in another key Mantuan product. The superior Northern Italian armor, which in the words of the sancakbeyi of Shkodër "cannot be found or bought in these parts," was greatly appreciated.[86] Furthermore, Bayezid and his governors gained access to an expert in armor in the person of the Mantuan envoy.

[85] Kissling, *Sultan Bajezid's II*, 108–9.

[86] ASMn, AG, b. 795, fasc. 17, fol. 71: "perchè de tal cossa in queste parti non sono a trovare a camprare." See also Kissling, *Sultan Bajezid's II*, 61–62.

The costliness of gold and textiles were more readily recognizable and could thus transcend the cultural divide in expressing how the recipient was regarded. However, other meanings assigned by the giver to certain objects, such as the robe of honor, the portraits and the turban, might have been interpreted differently at the gift's final destination. The diverse, sometimes unusual, and even illicit gifts exchanged between the marquis and the Sultan reveal much about this relationship and are a reminder of how varied the interaction was between the Ottomans and the Italian city-states. In fact, the fractured political system of the Italian city-states offered fertile ground for smaller states to nurture such a friendship with the Ottomans that enhanced the status of the Mantuan court and was facilitated in no small part by the exchange of gifts.

2

Material Diplomacy

Venetian Luxury Gifts for the Ottoman Empire in the Late Renaissance

Luca Molà

In 1585 the Venetian Republic received a tempting proposal from King Philip II of Spain and Portugal. The monarch offered Venice the purchase of the royal monopoly of the pepper trade carried to Europe through the Cape of Good Hope, which had proven difficult to manage by the Spanish crown. A long debate ensued among the Venetian ruling class, enticed by the possibility of plugging the city's commercial structure into a global network, but also wary of binding its fate too closely to the international politics of Philip II. After years of inconclusive talks, the decision of retaining the traditional Mediterranean trading structure prevailed in the state councils, and the pepper deal was never done.[1] The provision of Asian spices through the Portuguese routes under Spanish military protection would have meant the end of Venice's diplomatic relations with the Ottoman Empire, a naval power that posed a continuous threat to the eastern possessions of the Republic but at the same time was its main trading partner.

Indeed, in the second half of the sixteenth century the Ottoman markets absorbed a great part of the flourishing Venetian production of silk and woolen cloth, the two most important products of the city and a source of employment for tens of thousands of people.[2] Large and

[1] Innocenzo Cervelli, "Intorno alla decadenza di Venezia: un episodio di storia economica, ovvero un affare mancato," *Nuova Rivista Storica* 50 (1966): 596–42; Fernand Braudel, *The Mediterranean and the Mediterranean World in the Age of Philip II* (Berkeley and Los Angeles: University of California Press, 1995), 1: 558–60.

[2] Domenico Sella, *Commerci e industrie a Venezia nel secolo XVII* (Venice and Rome: Istituto per la collaborazione culturale, 1961), 1–15; id., "L'economia," in *Storia di Venezia dalle origini alla caduta della Serenissima*, ed. Gaetano Cozzi and Paolo Prodi (Rome: Istituto

valuable shipments of Venetian silk cloth are regularly recorded in the commercial correspondence between Venice and Constantinople in this period.[3] They were sold on the open market or went to supply the insatiable appetite for luxury fabrics at the court of the Sultan.[4] The Ottoman elites frequently placed orders directly in Venice through the intermediation of local Jewish or Turkish merchants and agents. In 1589, for instance, 2,000 *braccia* (each silk *braccio* was equal to 0.63 meters) of the most valuable cloth of gold were bought for the needs of the Imperial Palace, something that was done at regular intervals.[5] In the same year, the Great Admiral of the Ottoman fleet ordered 1100 braccia of silk satins and damasks, in 22 different colors.[6] In the late sixteenth century around 100,000 braccia (63 kilometers) of precious silk fabrics made in Venice were sent each year to the Syrian market.[7] The manufacture of woolen cloth was even more tied to demand from the Ottoman Empire. According to a report from a Florentine spy compiled in 1592, around three-quarters of the 27,000 bolts (each about 50–55 braccia long) produced in Venice were exported to different parts of the Ottoman realm. Constantinople consumed 3,000 bolts of the best quality; Egypt 4,000 and Bosnia and the Balkans 5,000. Syria absorbed an even larger share of this production, with 10–12,000 bolts imported each year, partly to be sold to local customers and partly to be traded by Armenian merchants to Persia and other Asian regions.[8] The Venetian Consul based in Aleppo estimated that between 1589 and 1592 the silk and woolen cloth trade to Syria was worth one million ducats a year.[9] The same Florentine spy mentioned earlier tells

Treccani, 1994), 666–69; Ugo Tucci, "Venezia nel Cinquecento: una città industriale?," in *Crisi e rinnovamenti nell'autunno del Rinascimento a Venezia*, ed. Vittore Branca and Carlo Ossola (Florence: Olschki Editore, 1991), 61–83; Luca Molà, *The Silk Industry of Renaissance Venice* (Baltimore and London: Johns Hopkins University Press, 2000).

3 See, for example, the commercial letters in the Archivio di Stato di Venezia (hereafter ASV), Miscellanea Gregolin, buste 12 ter I and 12 ter II.

4 On the role of silk cloth at the Porte, see Nurhan Atasoy et al., *İpek: The Crescent and the Rose: Imperial Ottoman Silks and Velvets* (London: Azimuth, 2001), 21–35.

5 Maria Pia Pedani and Alessio Bombaci, eds., *I "Documenti Turchi" dell'Archivio di Stato di Venezia* (Rome: Ministero per i beni ambientali e culturali, 1994), n. 991; Atasoy, *İpek*, 185–86.

6 ASV, Senato, Deliberazioni Costantinopoli (hereafter DELC), filza 7, 9 June 1589.

7 Guglielmo Berchet, *Relazioni dei Consoli Veneti nella Siria* (Turin: Paravia, 1866), 79–80.

8 Archivio di Stato di Firenze, Miscellanea Medicea, 27 III, fol. 1070r-v, 1592; the document is briefly mentioned in Ruggiero Romano, "La storia economica. Dal secolo XIV al Settecento," in *Storia d'Italia, vol. 2: Dalla caduta dell'Impero romano al secolo XVIII* (Turin: Einaudi, 1974), 1910.

9 Berchet, *Relazioni*, 77.

us that in 1592 considerable amounts of Murano glass and mirrors were also shipped to the three main centers of the Ottoman Empire: to Constantinople (for a total value of 10,000 ducats); to Alexandria and Egypt (5,000 ducats) and to Syria and Aleppo (20,000 ducats). These areas accounted for almost one-third of the total export of glass from Venice.[10]

These three products – silk fabrics, woolen cloth and glass – were not just items of trade. They also constituted the greatest part of the gifts that the Venetian Republic sent to the Porte during the sixteenth and early seventeenth centuries. Seminal studies by Antonio Fabris, Deborah Howard, Julian Raby and Maria Pia Pedani have shown the relevance of gifts in the relations between Venice and the Ottoman Empire, describing the wide range of luxury items involved in this diplomatic exchange and highlighting some of its complexities.[11] Building on this solid ground, the analysis of new archival material and a closer study of some key episodes will allow us to obtain a more systematic view of Venetian gift-giving to the Sublime Porte, thus understanding in greater detail its evolution and its importance not only in the field of international politics but also for the economic and technical development of Venice in the late Renaissance.

BAILI AND AMBASSADORS

There were two main types of occasion for the delivery of large amounts of diplomatic presents to the Ottoman Court. The first, and most common occasion, was on the arrival of a new Venetian permanent representative in Constantinople, who since medieval times received the title of *Bailo*. The government selected one of the most experienced Venetian noblemen for this task, and his position was to be renewed every two to three years (even though at times, due to various circumstances, *Baili* remained

10 Gino Corti, "L'industria del vetro di Murano alla fine del secolo XVI in una relazione al Granduca di Toscana," *Studi Veneziani* new series 13 (1971): 649–54.

11 Antonio Fabris, "Artisanat et culture: recherces sur la production Venitienne et le marché Ottoman au XVIe siècle," *Arab Historical Review for Ottoman Studies* 3, no. 4 (1991): 51–60; Deborah Howard, "Cultural Transfer between Venice and the Ottomans in the Fifteenth and Sixteenth Centuries," in *Forging European Identities, 1400–1700*, ed. Herman Roodenburg (Cambridge: Cambridge University Press, 2007), 138–77; Julian Raby, "The Serenissima and the Sublime Porte: Art in the Art of Diplomacy, 1453–1600," in *Venice and the Islamic World, 828–1797*, ed. Stefano Carboni (New Haven and London: Yale University Press and Metropolitan Museum of Art, 2007), 90–119; Maria Pia Pedani, *Venezia porta d'Oriente* (Bologna: Il Mulino, 2010), 100–9.

in Constantinople for longer periods).[12] The second type of occasion took place when the Venetian government appointed a special envoy with the title of ambassador. This diplomat had only a limited and circumscribed mission, tied to a particular event, such as the signing of a peace treaty, the congratulations for a major Turkish military victory, the festivities for the circumcision of the Sultan's sons or the coming to power of a new ruler. Before their departure from Venice, the Senate allotted the money for commissioning or buying the gifts that had to be formally presented to various members of the Ottoman court. The amount spent on each occasion was considerable, ranging from almost 14,000 to over 20,000 ducats.[13] The financial and organizational effort involved can be easily gauged considering that the Republic sent 70 nobles as ambassadors or Baili to the Porte between 1500 and 1600.[14]

The most complete and detailed list of gifts to be found in the Venetian archives relates to the mission of Bailo Vincenzo Gradenigo in 1599. It was drawn up as usual by the Venetian state office in charge of diplomatic gifts, the *Ufficiali alle Rason Vecchie*, which punctiliously recorded the names of all suppliers and the expenditure involved, down to the cost of the paper and strings needed to wrap and tie the most fragile objects and their containers, and the drinks offered to porters. Silks abounded with almost 3.5 kilometers of various kinds of fabrics, the most precious of which was the regal cloth of gold (*soprarizo d'oro regal*) for the Ottoman Sultan that at 40 ducats per braccio cost 550 ducats alone. Woolen cloth followed suit, with 22 bolts shipped at a value on average of 200–220 ducats each. Almost 1,200 pieces of Murano glass came in a surprising variety of names, shapes, sizes, colors and decorations. There were large vases, smaller vases for flowers with several spouts (probably for holding

[12] On the Venetian Bailo, see Tommaso Bertelè, *Il palazzo degli ambasciatori di Costantinopoli a Venezia* (Bologna: Apollo, 1932); Eric R. Dursteler, "The Bailo in Constantinople: Crisis and Career in Venice's Early Modern Diplomatic Corps," *Mediterranean Historical Review* 16, no. 2 (2001): 1–30; Stefan Hanss, "Baili and Ambassadors," in *Il Palazzo di Venezia a Constantinople e i suoi antichi abitanti/İstanbul'daki Venedik Sarayı ve Eski Yaşayanları*, ed. Maria Pia Pedani (Venice: Edizioni Ca' Foscari, 2013), 35–52.

[13] The cost of the gifts sent from Venice to Constantinople with Baili and Ambassadors was: in 1573: 15,825 ducats; 1575: 18,455; 1582: 20,758; 1590: 13,904; 1591: 14,180; 1599: 16,270; and 1602: 17,587. Biblioteca del Museo Civico Correr di Venezia (hereafter BMCCV): Mss. Donà dalle Rose 148, fols. 138r–139r, 19 July 1573, 28 May 1575 and 29 March 1582; Mss. P.D. 943, fasc. 6, 9 April 1590. ASV, DELC reg. 8, fol. 81v, 27 November 1591; filza 9, 6 July 1599; filza 10, 22 April, 7 June and 31 August 1602; filza 12, 5 November 1611.

[14] Maria Pia Pedani, "Elenco degli inviati diplomatici veneziani presso i sovrani ottomani," *Electronic Journal of Oriental Studies* 5, no. 4 (2002): 1–54.

tulips), basins, home or mosque lamps (*ferali* and *cesendelli*), drinking vessels with lids (*mastrapani*), drinking glasses (*ziati*), plates (*tapsi*), bottles and cruets (*acanini* and *zame*) and the many *bembi*, *ocche*, *cattelani* and *soltanie* that still defy historians' understanding.[15] Several of them had a form that was defined as "cut" (*tagiadi*), "twisted" (*torti*), "pine-like" (*a pigne*) or "strawberry-like" (*a fragole*). Most of these pieces were gilded, catering probably to a specific Turkish taste for glitter that was testified also in the Ottoman preference for textiles interwoven with precious metals and the frequent embellishment of porcelain and jade with gold. Hundreds of spectacles made of crystal glass were also part of the list of the Bailo's gifts to the Porte, together with those of rock crystal and mirrors.[16]

Fifteen densely written pages record a myriad other luxury objects or consumables: ivory boxes, sand and mechanical clocks, chairs and musical instruments, gloves, perfumes and "perfumed compositions," animals, candles, sugar, Parmesan cheese (particularly appreciated in Constantinople), and a variety of sweet and spicy preserves as well as marzipan fruits in the shape of apples, pears, figs, cherries, apricots, peaches, plums, carobs and broad beans (Table 2.1).

Many of these luxury goods were the characteristic gifts that Venice offered to the members of the Ottoman Court on many occasions. They were the best among the Venetian products, and therefore an advertisement for the city's industrial and artisanal skills. A small army of highly specialized craftsmen was mobilized for their production and preparation every time a Bailo or an ambassador left Venice. There must have been a clear understanding among these artisans of the political importance and prestige resulting from their work, and perhaps some of them became local celebrities in connection with their supplying the Ottoman Court. Finally, the packaging and presentation of all these luxuries was of the highest importance: the list mentions hundreds of large and small golden

[15] For the identification of some of these glasses, see Astone Gasparetto, "Vetri veneziani da un naufragio in Dalmazia e da alcuni documenti dell'ultimo Cinquecento," *Studi Veneziani* 17/18 (1975–76): 411–46.

[16] The Ottoman taste was partly at odds with the contemporary choices of consumers in China. As a Florentine merchant visiting the market of Canton (Guangzhou) in 1599 reported, the Chinese appreciated Venetian "glasses, particularly those in the shape of vases and plates, with white canes inside, and also of other types, so long as they were not gilded, which they did not esteem in the least; and similarly spectacles of all kinds, and particularly those with coloured lenses." See Francesco Carletti, *Ragionamenti del mio viaggio intorno al mondo* (Milan: Mursia, 1987), 138.

TABLE 2.1 *Composition of the Bailo's Gifts Sent to Constantinople in 1599*

256 silk robes (*veste*)
22 bolts of woolen cloth
72 rock crystal spectacles
500 crystal glass spectacles
1,196 pieces of glass of various kinds
48 mirrors
64 ivory boxes
5 sand clocks of six and twelve hours
3 mechanical clocks
6 chairs
2 small dogs
1 organ (*regal*) lacquered and painted with arabesques
Silk flowers of various kinds
50 silk *pumpkins*
24 pairs of gloves embroidered with gold
18 gloves from Rome
300 perfumed balls
290 big candles of various weight
14 pieces of Parmesan cheese
100 blocks of sugar
Musk, ambergris, perfumes, perfumed waters and oils of various kinds
Preserves and confections
Quince jam
Sugared cinnamon and cloves
Candied fruit
Marzipan fruits (*fruti de pasta real*)

Source: Archivio di Stato di Venezia, Senato, Deliberazioni Costantinopoli, filza 9, 6 July 1599.

boxes, gilded chests, copper vessels and other miscellaneous containers in which food, perfumed oils and smaller items were stored. The most valuable cloths were carefully arranged into costly envelopes made of cheaper fabrics, and even the plain boxes containing the largest artifacts had a lion of St. Mark drawn on them by a painter.

Other lists of Baili's gifts have survived for 1590 and 1611, including a similar range of artifacts.[17] The presents for the ambassadors' missions followed the same pattern, but in this case the Republic – starting in 1573 – used to add a set of elaborate silver objects for the table composed

[17] BMCCV, Mss. P.D. C 943, fasc. 6, 9 April 1590; DELC, filza 12, 5 November 1611.

of cups, bowls, flasks, basins, buckets, candlesticks and saltcellars.[18] On particular occasions the ambassadorial gift was truly unique and extraordinary. In 1531, for the circumcision of the sons of Suleyman I and acceding to a direct and insistent request from Ibrahim Pasha, Pietro Zen presented the Sultan with one of the three pieces of the unicorn that were kept in the treasury of the Church of St. Mark.[19] Likewise, in 1573, when Andrea Badoer reached Constantinople to seal the peace agreements after the War of Cyprus, the Senate decided to send along twenty-five Turkish slaves all dressed in Venetian woolen cloth.[20]

THE GIFT-GIVING SYSTEM: ORDINARY AND EXTRAORDINARY PRESENTS

Cloths of gold, velvets, satins, damasks and several other types of silk fabrics constituted around two-thirds of the total value of the Baili's and ambassadors' gifts. The precious cloth was provided by a limited number of top mercers and merchant-entrepreneurs of Venice. The leading suppliers in the late sixteenth century were Bartolomeo Bontempelli dal Calice and Agostino dal Ponte, who ran the best silk shops in the city – the first one located in the Mercerie, the main shopping street in Europe, the second on the Rialto Bridge – and were renowned for their trading connections with Constantinople.[21] The two of them, for instance, gave the government 137 of the 260 robes (*veste*) handed over to Ambassador Leonardo Donà in 1595, and a large part of the 256 robes sent in 1599.[22]

Veste, however, were not real tailored garments, but a ghost luxury unit of measure, like the ducat or lira of account that were commonly

[18] BMCCV, Mss. Donà dalle Rose 23, fols. 76r–80v, 390r; BMCCV, Mss. Donà dalle Rose 249, fasc. 3; DELC, reg. 4, fol. 43r, 22 May 1573; DELC, reg. 6, fol. 71r, 16 December 1581; DELC, reg. 9, fol. 25r, 30 March 1595.

[19] Carla Coco and Flora Manzonetto, *Baili veneziani alla Sublime Porta. Storia e caratteristiche dell'ambasciata veneta a Costantinopoli* (Venice: Stamperia di Venezia, 1985), 87–88; Giovanni Curatola, "Marin Sanudo, Venezia, i doni diplomatici e le merci orientali islamiche," in *Islamic Artefacts in the Mediterranean World: Trade, Gift Exchange and Artistic Transfer*, ed. Catarina Schmidt Arcangeli and Gerhard Wolf (Venice: Marsilio, 2010), 176.

[20] DELC, reg. 4, fol. 43r, 22 May 1573; fol. 44r-v, 9 June 1573.

[21] Michela Sermidi, ed., *Le collezioni Gonzaga. Il carteggio tra Venezia e Mantova (1588–1612)* (Milan: Silvana Editoriale, 2003), nn. 394 and 828. On Bontempelli, see also Gigi Corazzol, "Varietà notarile: scorci di vita economica e sociale," in *Storia di Venezia dalle origini alla caduta della Serenissima*, 775–91.

[22] BMCCV, Mss. Donà dalle Rose 148, fol. 76r ff., and Pedani, "Elenco degli inviati diplomatici veneziani presso i sovrani ottomani."

used instead of minted coins for easing transactions and calculations. Starting in the 1540s, in fact, the Venetian Republic developed a diplomatic gift system for the Ottoman Empire that was based principally on the presentation of a fixed measure of silk, the veste, each presumably equal to the amount of fabric needed to make a single robe. During the sixteenth century this unit ranged between 13 and 14 braccia of cloth, but a law of the Senate issued in 1605 limited its length to 12¾ braccia, so as to reduce the costs of official gifts to the Porte.[23] By contrast, Venetian diplomats in Constantinople received real robes of honor (*hil'at*) when they had the first meeting with the Sultan and when they presented their successors before leaving the city, plus occasionally as a special token of respect from eminent members of the court. The Venetian Republic, too, had adopted the Asian tradition of giving ceremonial silk robes to the Ottoman envoys since the fifteenth century. Usually Turkish ambassadors were entitled to two or three valuable garments on their departure, while other robes, some of them made of wool, were granted to members of their retinue.[24]

Veste were thus at the heart of a complex and continuously evolving strategy of gift-giving to the Porte. Hundreds, and at times thousands, of veste were handed out at different occasions each year, and following a rooted Ottoman tradition of redistribution they circulated among Turkish elites in the form of presents.[25] They constituted the bulk of the so-called ordinary gifts (*presenti* or *donativi ordinari*), which followed a precise protocol guiding the actions of the Republic's diplomats. A handbook that Bailo Giovanni Moro drew up in the late 1580s for the needs of his mission, based on the records left by his predecessors over the decades and his own experience, provides detailed information on what different members of the Ottoman court expected to receive from the Venetian resident diplomats.[26] First of all, the handbook lists how the Bailo's presents were distributed on his arrival to specific individuals according to their rank. For instance, in addition to the regal cloth of gold, the Sultan was given a veste with silver thread, another of velvet with the pile

[23] DELC, filza 10, 16 February 1605.

[24] Maria Pia Pedani, *In nome del Gran Signore. Inviati Ottomani a Venezia dalla caduta di Costantinopoli alla guerra di Candia* (Venice: Deputazione Editrice, 1994), 75, and 90–91.

[25] On the Ottoman Court's tradition of gifts, see Tim Stanley, "Ottoman Gift Exchange: Royal Give and Take," in *Gifts for the Sultan: The Arts of Giving at the Islamic Courts*, ed. Linda Komaroff (New Haven and London: Yale University Press, 2011), 149–66.

[26] BMCCV, Mss. Donà dalle Rose 23, fols. 430r–442r; copy made by the ambassador Leonardo Donà for his mission in 1595.

cut at different heights (*velluto altobasso*), two of satin, and lengths of scarlet and purple woolen cloth; the Grand Vizier had a veste of crimson and gold velvet, two of plain velvet, four of satin and damask, and two of woolen cloth; the Great Admiral of the Turkish fleet received two veste of velvet, six of satin and damask, and two of woolen cloth; and so on for their lieutenants and other court members and officers who usually received only a single veste or some cash.

Bailo Giovanni Moro also recorded a number of specific occasions during a Bailo's period of office that would require additional gifts. The wedding of a Grand Vizier's daughter required five veste (of velvet, damask, satin, tabby and brocatel), a large mirror and a writing desk, both inlaid with mother-of-pearl, whereas twenty-four veste (fourteen of silk and ten of wool) were given if one of the Viziers married a daughter of the Sultan. More important, any new appointment at court taking place during the period in which the Bailo was in Constantinople required its own gift, frequently of the same nature as the one given at the beginning of his term to the equivalent official. This tradition created major problems in the last decades of the sixteenth century, when the growing instability of the Ottoman government meant a constant replacement of the Grand Viziers, reaching a record four new appointments in 1595. Frequently the men that had been removed just a few years or even months earlier came back to power after a short period of time. In such a fluid political situation, the Venetian government decided to widen its ordinary gifting policy to include also the dismissed Grand Viziers (*bassà dismessi*), so as not to alienate their favor if they got back to their former position. In the meantime, the total number of viziers grew from the usual four to six and then eight, while also several other key positions in the Empire that were included in the roll of ordinary gifts changed hands at a higher rate of speed.[27]

The Great Admiral deserved special attention, given his capacity to influence the expansionist policies of the Sultans against the dominions of Venice in the Levant. The Bailo offered him nine veste and a wheel of Parmesan cheese when he left Constantinople with the fleet in the spring, seven veste when he was back and another one every time he ordered the

[27] See the Baili's reports of the 1580s and 1590s in Eugenio Alberi, *Relazioni degli ambasciatori veneti al Senato*, series 3, vol. 2 (Florence: Tipografia all'Insegna di Clio, 1844), and vol. 3 (Florence: Società Editrice Fiorentina, 1855). For a clear statement on the quick rotation of Viziers, and the need to give them silk *veste* instead of cash, see DELC, filza 9, 30 December 1597.

construction of a new galley in Constantinople's Arsenal.[28] The Admiral, however, received gifts not just from Venice; ordinary presents were given to him on a yearly basis by the governors of Corfu and Zante (Zakhintos), two key islands of Venice's maritime state in the Ionian Sea, when the Turkish navy cruised in the Eastern Mediterranean.[29] On another front, the Venetian officials presiding over the cities of Zara (Zadar), Spalato (Split), Traù (Trogir), Sebenico (Sibenik) and Cattaro (Kotor) on the Adriatic coast maintained a similar obliging attitude toward the provincial and regional Ottoman governors (*sanjacks* and *beylerbeys*) of the areas bordering the possessions of the Republic in the Balkans.[30]

Indeed, the gifts that Venice offered to Ottoman officials outside Constantinople formed a parallel and quite complex system of diplomatic exchange in its own right, which was almost unidirectional. It too involved a large amount of veste and other items such as glass and sweets, called, respectively, "kindnesses" (*gentilezze*) and "refreshments" (*rifrescamenti*). Therefore the whole organization of timed ordinary presents for the Ottomans, both at the Porte and in the eastern territories of Venice, needed a steady supply of silks, woolens and other luxury goods that Baili and Venetian governors carefully kept at hand.[31]

Fabrics and a panoply of different luxury items were even more important for the unpredictable distribution of "extraordinary gifts" (*presenti straordinari*). These were necessary in critical moments in order to oil the wheels of the Ottoman government or appease tense situations. Obtaining commercial concessions, liberating Christian slaves, settling territorial disputes, solving military confrontations or legal cases between Venetians and Turkish subjects could frequently be eased through the use of presents. The initiative would be taken directly by the Bailo on the spot or after consulting the home government and receiving its approval, by using his stock, buying the items

[28] BMCCV, Mss. Donà dalle Rose 23, fols. 433v–434v.

[29] DELC, reg. 4, fols. 81v–82v, 20 April 1574; DELC, filza 7, 28 March 1589 (with copy of the gift of Zante in 1586); DELC, filza 9, 27 February 1598; DELC, filza 10, 3 July 1601 (with copies of the gifts of Zante in 1596, 1598 and 1600); DELC, filza 11, 26 June 1608 (with copies of the gifts of Corfu in 1592, 1601 and 1603).

[30] DELC, reg. 2, fols. 71v–72v, 24 September 1562 (Zara, Sebenico, Traù and Spalato); DELC, reg. 4, fol. 89r-v, 24 August 1574 (Cattaro); DELC, filza 4, 3 March 1578 (Zara, Sebenico, Traù and Spalato, also with list of gifts in 1573); DELC, filza 6, 13 July 1587 (Zara); DELC, filza 7, 3 November 1590 (Sebenico and Zara); DELC, reg. 8, fol. 62r, 1 June 1591 (Traù); DELC, filza 10, 7 June 1602 and 5 June 1604 (Cattaro); DELC, filza 11, 5 March 1608 (Traù); DELC, filza 12, 19 May 1612 (Traù and Sebenico).

[31] For the supply of Venetian governors, see, for instance, DELC, reg. 8, fol. 159v, 22 January 1594; DELC, filza 12, 19 May 1612; Hanss, "Baili," 48–51.

from Venetian merchants in Constantinople or waiting for the goods to be shipped from Venice. More commonly, it originated from the explicit demands of the Ottoman court and governors. Glass products, for instance, were among the most prized gifts. Single orders of hundreds of lamps and thousands of round and square windowpanes for a new mosque, for the Topkapi Palace or other public buildings in the capital were not uncommon, as were requests for crystal glasses for private consumption (Table 2.2). For the Senate it was of crucial importance that a clear distinction be made between ordinary and extraordinary gifts, so that the latter would not become a tradition (*kanun*, or *canon* in Venetian) and thus enter into the previous category as things to be expected at regular intervals.[32] Equally important was the timely delivery of presents. The Sultana was very pleased when in 1584 the Venetian government, unable to find any ships that were leaving for Turkey, hurried the consignment of thirteen silk veste to her by sending men who carried them on their shoulders all the way to Constantinople.[33] Incidentally this caused great envy on the part of the Grand Vizier, who just a month later asked for a richly adorned chair and wanted it to be delivered as soon as possible overland, saying he knew it could well be done if the Bailo wanted.[34] When important matters were at stake, the Republic's representative would postpone discussing them with the Grand Vizier until a valuable gift – that had often been asked and promised – was ready available.

The high expenditure on extraordinary gifts and the promptness and zeal required to respond to every whim of the Ottoman elites were the source of numerous complaints and sometimes a sense of frustration among the Venetian ruling class. In 1568 the Senate, annoyed at the persistent requests of glass windowpanes coming from the Porte, proposed to let the Turks know how much these goods cost, thus making them aware of the value of Venetian gifts.[35] A Bailo could caustically remark that if he had to satisfy all the people who, "like bees around honey," asked for presents, then the embassy would be busier than a shop on the Rialto Bridge.[36] By the late sixteenth century the issue of extraordinary gifts, their handling and the necessity to moderate them, or at least

[32] For some examples, see DELC, reg. 8, fol. 68r-v, 10 August 1591; fol. 72v, 2 September 1591; fols. 73v–74r, 15 September 1591; fol. 111r-v, 14 October 1592.

[33] ASV, Senato, Dispacci Costantinopoli (hereafter DISPC), filza 20, fol. 10r, 4 September 1584.

[34] DISPC, filza 20, fols. 85r–86r, 2 October 1584.

[35] DELC, reg. 3, fol. 119v, 6 May 1568.

[36] Alberi, *Relazioni*, 2: 407. For similar remarks, see also Maria Pia Pedani, "Safiye's Household and Venetian Diplomacy," *Turcica* 32 (2000): 12.

TABLE 2.2 *Glassware Ordered by the Senate as Gifts for Members of the Ottoman Court, 1557–92*

Date	Glassware	Source
September 1557	Cesendelli (small lamps)	DELC reg. 1: 58v
September 1557	Two ferali (big lamps for interiors or boats)	DELC reg. 1: 58v
January 1558	200 pieces of crystal glass	DELC reg. 1: 71r
March 1560	Window panes	DELC reg. 2: 12r
March 1560	1,500 small red panes	DELC reg. 2: 14r
May 1560	350 hourglasses of various types made of crystal glass	DELC reg. 2: 14r
April 1562	10,000 window panes	DELC reg. 2: 56v–57r
April 1562	5 ferali	DELC reg. 2: 56v–57r
September 1562	100 pieces of crystal glass	DELC reg. 2: 71v–72v
August 1563	2 cesendelli	DELC reg. 2: 97v
October 1563	300 pieces of glass	DELC reg. 2: 99r, 103r-v
December 1563	400 windowpanes	DELC reg. 2: 103r-v
September 1564	400 pieces of crystal glass	DELC reg. 2: 131r
September 1564	200 pieces of crystal glass	DELC reg. 2: 131r
December 1564	5,000 rui (small round or square window eyes)	DELC reg. 2: 142v
March 1567	400 glasses for fanò (a big lamp for a ship)	DELC reg. 3: 79v, 82r-v
April 1567	400 pieces of glass	DELC reg. 3: 82r-v
April 1567	2,000 windowpanes	DELC reg. 3: 85v–86r
December 1567	1,000 windowpanes	DELC reg. 3: 103r
December 1567	800 large square panes and 800 small round panes	DELC reg. 3: 103r
February 1568	Windowpanes and cesendelli in Frankish style	DELC reg. 3: 110v
October 1568	1,000 windowpanes	DELC reg. 3: 133r
May 1569	3,000 round windowpanes	DELC reg. 4: 16r
July 1569	900 cesendelli	DELC reg. 4: 22v
October 1569	10 large ferali	DELC reg. 4: 27v, 31v
June 1576	Pieces of crystal glass and rui	DELC reg. 5: 36r
August 1576	1,000 round windowpanes	DELC reg. 5: 43v
August 1576	100 panes of crystal glass	DELC reg. 5: 43v
December 1576	200 panes for lamps	DELC reg. 5: 48r
June 1578	2,000 rui of crystal glass	DELC reg. 5: 98r-v
June 1579	Rui and ferali	DELC reg. 5: 135v
September 1579	One crystal plate	DELC reg. 5: 146v
June 1580	400 panes for lamps	DELC reg. 6: 33r
October 1580	Rui	DELC reg. 6: 41r
April 1581	320 windowpanes	DELC reg. 6: 52v

(*continued*)

TABLE 2.2 (*continued*)

Date	Glassware	Source
September 1583	5,000 rui	DELC reg. 6: 140v
October 1584	150 cesendelli	DELC reg. 6: 175r
October 1584	2,000 rui, half square and half round	DELC reg. 6: 175r
October 1584	50 cesendelli	DELC reg. 6: 175r
February 1585	Cesendelli and crystal panes	DELC reg. 6: 203r
September 1585	Cesendelli	DELC reg. 7: 40v–41v
May 1586	150 cesendelli	DELC reg. 7: 59r
September 1590	75 vases of chalcedony glass	DELC reg. 8: 35r
November 1590	40 cesendelli and 400 square white crystal panes	DELC reg. 8: 45v–47r
June 1592	300 colored panes	DELC reg. 8: 99v–100r
June 1592	20 glass balls	DELC reg. 8: 99v–100r

place greater attention to their distribution, recurs regularly in the Baili's dispatches and becomes almost a topos in their final reports to the Senate when they returned to Venice. Bailo Lorenzo Bernardo, writing in 1592, judged these gifts degrading and thought they should be used like wine, which doctors prescribe on two occasions: in people's sanity and in their extreme infirmity; in the first case a moderate amount of wine keeps the body in good shape, in the second it could remedy a desperate situation and revive a dying patient. Likewise, small presents given with measure in normal and peaceful circumstances smoothed the relations with the Turks; if they were used in extraordinary occasions, as in the threat of war, but in large amounts, they could avert disaster. Bailo Cristoforo Valier, reporting in 1616, was of a different opinion. He understood interpersonal relationships in the Ottoman Empire, based as they were mainly on donations, a practice commonly and universally approved. Even fathers and sons, or brothers, would deal with each other through gifts, "as the true sign of honour and the true fruit of love." For Valier gift-giving was like a spiral starting at the bottom with an individual offering to his superior, and ascending through the social scale all the way to the Sultan, who then donated back to all. To show the power of presents in that society, he translated in Venetian a Turkish proverb saying that "a hand that brings [gifts] to the Porte and gives [them] is never cut" (*man che porta alla Porta e che dà, mai non vien tagià*).[37] With similar perceptiveness, other Baili

[37] Alberi, *Relazioni*, 2: 404–10; Nicolò Barozzi and Guglielmo Berchet, eds., *Le relazioni degli stati europei lette al Senato dagli ambasciatori veneziani nel secolo decimosettimo.*

considered that if Ottoman requests needed to be quickly satisfied, the timely delivery of gifts showed interest and care for the person making the request, who in due time would reciprocate the donor with favors.

TECHNICAL CHALLENGES AND THE OTTOMAN TASTE FOR NOVELTIES

The frequent demands of the Ottoman court for silk fabrics of unusual or altogether new patterns, measures or colors posed serious technical challenges to the Venetian government and craftsmen. In 1543, for instance, the Bailo sent to Venice samples of a pure silk fabric and of cloth of gold that had been requested for the Sultan's treasury, together with a detailed list of the quantities that had to be produced. After careful investigation, the Senators replied that while the silk-only fabrics could be made without delay and in ever greater numbers than required, those with gold thread were too narrow for the standards of the city's artisans and there were no looms or other implements that could be adapted to the task. The only possibility of accommodating Suleyman's requests was to weave the cloth according to the Venetian measures, even though – probably because of the need to adapt the design – it would take a long time.[38] Again, in June 1562, during a meeting at the Divan, the Great Vizier Ali Pasha ordered that a sample of cloth of gold be brought from the Sultan's treasury and gave it to the Venetian dragoman, asking the government of Venice to make over 200 braccia of fabrics of the same quality and design for the Sultan. The reason for such a request derived in part from the huge number of robes that had been recently sent to the Persian Shah as gifts. Even more important, Suleyman I had distributed many other silk fabrics for the wedding of the three daughters of Prince Selim, who had arrived in Constantinople in March in order to be married, respectively, to the Head of the Jannissaries, the Great Admiral and Ali Pasha himself. These two events had left the imperial treasury almost empty of silk robes, which could not be found even among the European merchants or in the Grand Bazaar.[39] Similarly complex was the request in 1584 by the Chief Chamberlain (*Capi Agà*) of the Sultan for 100 braccia of satin of a peach-like color (*perseghin*). He wanted them to be made in Venice and not bought elsewhere. The Venetian government had

Serie V. Turchia (Venice: Pietro Naratovich, 1866), 305–7; Coco-Manzonetto, *Baili*, 87, and 89–90; Pedani, *Venezia*, 108–9.

38 ASV, Senato Secreta, reg. 63, fol. 25r, 16 March 1543.

39 DISPC, filza 3C, fol. 194r-v, 16 June 1562. For the arrival of Selim's daughters, the order of 100,000 ducats in gems and jewelry, and the distribution of money and vests for this reason, see ibid., fols. 148r–149v, 22 March 1562.

to commission them for the purpose since the shade was uncommon in the city.[40] Indeed, in the past that color had been usually associated with fabrics coming from the East, such as the Levantine bolt of *ermisino persegin* deposited in the shop of a silk merchant at the Rialto in the 1550s.[41] After 1584, however, the peach-like color appeared frequently among the cloth sent as a present to the Ottoman Court.[42]

An important example of long and complex cross-cultural and cross-linguistic textile production is represented by two commissions that Grand Vizier Rustem Pasha placed to the Bailo Antonio Erizzo. First, in October 1555, he asked for a set of gold and silk fabrics that had to furnish a chamber on the occasion of his daughter's marriage. After the initial arrangements were discussed between the Venetian representative and an agent of Rustem Pasha, the Vizier's master tailor was dispatched to the Bailo's residence in order to explain the details of the order through the means of some drawings containing annotations and the measures of the fabrics, papers that were then forwarded to Venice. In February 1556, Erizzo excused himself with the Vizier for the delay in fulfilling his requests, explaining that such fabrics were not commonly produced in Venice and that only few artisans were able to make them. Indeed, the first master who had been entrusted with the task had totally spoiled the cloth, so that the government had been forced to find a more skilled weaver. Besides, Venetians faced serious problems regarding the interpretation of the instructions. As the Senate wrote to Erizzo in March, a recent consultation with a group of master weavers had raised a series of questions on the three drawings sent from Constantinople. The first inscribed image represented a cloth with a gold-thread design that, according to the artisans, should be reversed, while it was not clear if the color of the fabric beneath should be black or the deep green that was usually called "duck neck" (*collo d'anera*). The second one did not specify if it was intended to be a velvet or a satin, and regarding the third, which appeared smaller and narrower, there were

40 DISPC, filza 18, fol. 426r-v, 24 January 1584; DISPC, filza 19, fol. 16r, 6 March 1584; DELC, reg. 6, fol. 165v, 14 April 1584.

41 ASV, Cancelleria Inferiore, Miscellanea Notai Diversi, busta 39, n. 43, inventory of the shop of the late Pietro Verde, 18 November 1556.

42 It is included, for instance, in the Great Admiral's list of satins ordered in 1589, together with 21 other colors: "cremexin, paonazo, lagiverdi, turchino, latado, biancho, sguardo, persegin, color d'argiento, color de chaveli, arzentin fratescho, col d'anera, rosasecha, incarnado, zallo, paiescho, verde, festechin, canelado, rovan, agua de mar, naranzato" (see note 6 above). For another example, see BMCCV, Mss. Donà dalle Rose 236, Dispacci del Bailo Venier, fol. 13v, 15 October 1594.

doubts about its width. In May the Bailo, after a second consultation with the Vizier's master tailor, replied, clarifying in detail all points. It took another two years, though, to finish all the pieces, which the special ambassador Marino Cavalli carried with him to the Ottoman capital and presented to a delighted Grand Vizier only in August 1558.[43]

Rustem Pasha, however, was to take the challenge even further: a year later, in 1556, he asked for silk cloth for making cushions (*minderi*) in velvet and gold of a width of seven *quarte*. This was once again a technical challenge as the standard measure adopted by Venetian producers and regulated by the guild was of just four quarte (or a braccio). At first the Bailo and the government tried to take time, alleging a lack of expertise and the plague epidemic that afflicted the city. In the end, due to the insistence of the Grand Vizier, the Senators decided to send a more articulated explanation in February 1557. They reported to have conducted an investigation among Venetian artisans who, in a written statement, remarked on not just the difficulty but the technical impossibility of weaving such a large cloth in velvet and gold. They were ready to make the fabric with the usual width of four quarte, but in that case the design submitted – certainly through another drawing – would need to be altered so much that the patterns would be unrecognizable. What the masters proposed as a solution, then, was to weave a seven-braccia cloth in satin and gold, which preserved the harmony of the pattern and presented less of a technical challenge. In March the artisan's report reached the new Bailo, Antonio Barbarigo, in Edirne, where he had followed the Ottoman court. During a meeting with the Grand Vizier, after discussing international politics, Barbarigo presented the report, which had been translated into Turkish. Rustem insisted that he wanted the fabrics made exactly as he had instructed, stating that they could be produced in Turkey. Then, struck with a new idea elicited by what he had just read, he proposed that the Venetian government should commission for him two cloths with his desired measures, one of velvet and gold and another of satin and gold, so that he could see how they turned out.[44]

It is easy to detect an element of challenge in the words of the Grand Vizier, a willingness to push Venetian productive skills to their limit and

[43] DISPC, filza 1A, fol. 181v, 18 October 1555; fol. 222 r-v, 7 February 1556; fol. 280v, 2 May 1556; DELC, reg. 1, fol. 17v, 7 March 1556; fol. 18v, 12 March 1556; fol. 77v, 2 May 1558; fol. 98v, 29 September 1558.

[44] DISPC, filza 1A, fol. 228 r-v, 7 February 1556; fol. 358r, 30 November 1556; DELC, reg. 1, fols. 39v–40v, 6 February 1557; DISPC, filza 1A, fol. 397v, 30 March 1557.

test their capacity to satisfy his wishes. Several other members of the Ottoman court seem to have vied with each other for obtaining ever-changing types of cloth, producing frequently a cautious and at times worried reply from Venice. Such requests included, for instance, a checkered damask, "which is a new work," in 1559; covers with a new design of difficult production in 1560; crimson and purple satin of unusual measures, in 1563; saddle-cloth of velvet with gold and silver thread, never made before in Venice, in 1578; complex fabrics for cushions and cloth of gold in 1583; veste of an unseen type, requiring a careful search for suitable weavers in 1593; or challenging printed satin and velvet in 1595.[45] Some of these fabrics were meant to copy Turkish designs, based on the cloth produced either in the main textile center of Bursa or in the court workshop that Grand Vizier Rustem Pasha created in Constantinople in the 1540s and 1550s and that employed over a hundred weavers.[46] It is also possible that the development of this state manufacture involved experimentations in new patterns and weaves that could be performed through the efforts of the Venetian artisans. Moreover, the Ottoman commercial and diplomatic exchanges with other empires involved the arrival in the capital of a wide range of Asian silk textiles, samples of which might have been sent to Venice for their reproduction. For sure, by the end of the sixteenth century Venetian weavers had acquired a good competence in producing silk fabrics that imitated traditional Ottoman patterns. The veste in the Bailo's 1599 list of ordinary gifts include milky velvet with pyramids on a silver background (*veludo latado a piramide fondi d'arzento*); crimson damask with little flames and balls (*damasco cremesin a fiamole e bale*) or with leeches (*damasco cremesin a sansuge*); white and silver *canevaza* with moons and stars (*canevaza biancha e arzento a lune e stele*); or dark pink on a light blue and silver background velvet with tulips and moons (*veludo sguardo con fondi turchin e d'arzento a tulipanti e lune*). This documentary evidence complements recent findings by textile experts regarding the

45 DELC, reg. 1, fol. 121v, 8 July 1559; DELC, reg. 2, fol. 22r, 20 June 1560; fol. 103r-v, 14 December 1563; DISPC, filza 12, fols. 303v–304r, 2 November 1578; DISPC, filza 18, fols. 235r–237r, 29 November 1583; DELC, reg. 8, fols. 121v–122r, 6 February 1593; DELC, reg. 9, fol. 44v, 22 September 1595.

46 Murat Çizakça, "A Short History of the Bursa Silk Industry (1500–1900)," *Journal of the Economic and Social History of the Orient* 23 (1980): 145–52; Gülru Necipoğlu, "A Kânûn for the State, a Canon for the Arts: Conceptualizing the Classical Synthesis of Ottoman Art and Architecture," in *Soliman le Magnifique et son temps/Süleymân the Magnificent and His Time*, ed. Gilles Veinstein (Paris: La Documentacion Française, 1992), 198–201; Atasoy, *İpek*, 152–75.

FIGURE 2.1 Mosque lamp in clear colorless glass, blown, with traces of original adhesive for gilding. Probably made in Venice, c. 1550–1600. Victoria and Albert Museum 332–1900.

presence of late sixteenth-/early seventeenth-century fabrics made in Venice with Turkish designs among the kaftans of the Topkapi Palace's collections.[47]

Gifts of glassware to the Ottomans were the cause of further technical challenges for Venetian producers. Usually, orders of lamps, crystal glass and other items included drawings and descriptions with the desired shapes and measures (Figure 2.1).[48]

Sometimes the objects commissioned were so oversized that the craftsmen of Murano could make them only with great difficulty, as in the case of the 400 pieces ordered in 1563.[49] In other instances old techniques, almost forgotten, had to be revived. In 1590 the Sultana Safiye wanted

[47] Atasoy, *İpek*, 187–90; Sandra Sarjono, "Ottoman or Italian Velvets? A Technical Investigation," in *Venice and the Islamic World*, 192–99.

[48] Fabris, "Artisanat," 52; Howard, "Cultural Transfer," 157–61; Pedani, *Venezia*, 103–4; Ayşe Aldemir Kilercik, "I vetri veneziani nei territori ottomani," in *Venezia e Constantinople in epoca ottomana/Osmanli Döneminde Venedik ve İstanbul* (Milan: Electa, 2009), 182–91; Gülru Necipoğlu, *The Age of Sinan. Architectural Culture in the Ottoman Empire* (London: Reaktion Books, 2011), *ad vocem* "glass."

[49] DELC, reg. 2, fol. 103r-v, 14 December 1563.

seventy-five glass vases imitating chalcedony stone, a product invented in Venice around 1460 and of great popularity until the early decades of the sixteenth century, but totally out of fashion by the end of the century. The Senate had trouble in finding the only master in the city still able to produce chalcedony glass, someone who was not even particularly skilled at that: he managed to complete just ten vases with great effort, breaking many others in the process.[50] An even more complex request came in 1583, when the wife of Grand Vizier Mehmed Sokollu asked to receive from Venice the smallest gold chains possible and the biggest mirror ever made, with a height of two braccia and a width of one braccio (136 cm × 68 cm). At first, the lady had contacted Guglielmo Helman, a rich international merchant of Flemish origins based in Venice, who was unable to find an object of the size required.[51] Then the Republic took the matter directly in its hands, opening a public competition for the making of an even larger mirror of two by one-and-a-half braccia (136 cm × 102 cm). Since nothing of the kind had been produced before in crystal glass, an artisan came forward proposing to make the mirror in polished steel and was officially entrusted with the task; once the mirror was completed, however, he asked the exorbitant sum of 3,000 ducats, which the Senate refused to pay. At that point another craftsman, Piero Ballarin – who ran one of the most important furnaces in Murano and was the official purveyor of luxury glass for the gifts sent by the Venetian state to the Ottoman Empire – offered to "put all his energies and skills in experimenting how to make such a mirror in crystal." Asking just financial help to cover the high costs of the enterprise, in 1585 the Senate granted him a loan of 100 ducats to be deducted from the final compensation if he succeeded.[52] His attempt, however, must have failed as in 1591 two other glass-makers claimed to have been able to make such a big mirror and petitioned the state to obtain a patent for the monopoly on its production for thirty years.[53]

[50] DELC, reg. 8, fol. 35r, 23 September 1590; fol. 49r-v, 19 January 1591.

[51] ASV, Miscellanea Gregolin, busta 12 ter I, letter of Guglielmo Helman from Venice to Antonio Paruta in Constantinople, 27 August 1583. On Helman, see Maartje Van Gelder, *Trading Places: The Netherlandish Merchants in Early Modern Venice* (Leiden-Boston: Brill, 2009), *ad vocem*.

[52] ASV, Senato Mar, reg. 47, fols. 131v–132r, 19 December 1585. For Ballarin's products included in the Bailo's gift of 1590 and his request of a patent for a new color for glass in 1595, see Luigi Zecchin, *Vetro e vetrai di Murano. Studi sulla storia del vetro* (Venice: Arsenale Editrice, 1989), 1: 166–67.

[53] ASV, Collegio, Risposte di dentro, filza 9, n. 263, 13 March 1591. One of the two artisans, Bernardino Bigagia, was the supplier of glassware for the Bailo's gift of 1611.

Requests for new and unusual products increasingly came to characterize the Ottomans' gifts from Venice. This was probably due to the growing competition among individuals and factions at the Porte, which was played out also through the conspicuous display and redistribution of luxury goods. In 1584, for example, Bailo Giovan Francesco Morosini obtained the liberation of twenty-five out of thirty slaves in the Sultan's Hamam who were subjects of Venice; when he asked for the freedom of the remaining ones, the Grand Vizier replied laughing: "when a ship from Venice will arrive, send me some nice object of these new things that are made in those parts, and I promise to free the last five of them."[54] In 1592 the Venetian representative advised the Senate on the opportunity of "sending every year some new things that could be agreeable to the Sultan."[55] A similar reference to curiosity and novelty is to be found in the instructions of the Senate for the production of silk fabrics with extravagant colors (*colori stravaccanti*), or "of new and charming works" (*opera nova et vaga*, *opera nova et bella*) for various members of the Porte.[56] In 1593 the Venetian governement officially thanked the Sultana Safiye for the detailed advice she had provided the Bailo on the "veste and new things that are sent to Constantinople as a present" to both her and Sultan Murad III.[57] The taste of her son, Sultan Mehmed III, for Venetian luxuries is also well known. Bailo Girolamo Cappello recorded an entire conversation that he had in the garden of the Capi Agà of the Sultan in July 1598. When Cappello asked for tips on the matter, he was told to send small objects frequently, "because the Sultan is like a child, whatever he sees, he likes it and then he wants it. He had some rock-crystal balls the size of playing balls, and now two of them are lost and he greatly desires to have new ones; if they could be obtained from Venice he would consider them as very dear." This was a wish that the Venetian government could not ignore, shipping six crystal balls to Constantinople right away.[58]

The importation of new items into Constantinople by Venetian merchants could sometimes produce unexpected consequences. In early August 1594 the all-powerful Safiye, already defining herself as the mother of Sultan Mehmed III, penned a fiery and highly menacing letter to the Bailo:

[54] DISPC, filza 19, fols. 1r–2r, 6 March 1584.

[55] DELC, reg. 8, fol. 113r-v, 31 October 1592.

[56] DISPC, filza 19, fol. 16r, 6 March 1584; DELC, reg. 8, fol. 181r, 24 September 1594; DELC, filza 10, 9 September 1603.

[57] DELC, reg. 8, fol. 156v, 13 November 1593.

[58] DISPC, filza 47, fols. 302r–303v, 25 July 1598; DELC, reg. 9, fol. 119v, 29 August 1598.

> You should know that with the last ships coming from Venice some aigrettes (*penachi*) have been brought here, which being a new thing we bought them all, so that they will not fall into other people's hands. For this reason you will write to the Lords of Venice that they have to forbid such works that resemble aigrettes, and as a consequence they will not be brought here anymore. Otherwise, due to the displeasure I feel, our friendship will be broken, and I will not favour your negotiations anymore. But make sure that the Lords of Venice issue a prohibition that similar works of feather-like aigrettes should not be made and brought here, and if they will still be seen I declare that our friendship will be over. Write therefore to those Lords of Venice that they should not let them be manufactured, having the possibility of allowing the production of many other kinds of merchandise that could be carried here, but not these in any way. And if you want to see a sample of them I will send you one, so that once seen you will send it back, and beware that no one will see it. [Signed:] The Mother of Sultan Mehemet.

Taken aback and not knowing anything regarding these new objects, the Bailo tried to understand what was the matter of complaint. He collected information and soon realized that the *penachi* the Sultana resented so much were composed of "several thin glasses in various colours, put together in a way to resemble the feathers of herons and other birds, which look beautiful and compete successfully with the true feathers and aigrettes that are worked with great craftmanship and at high cost." He replied to the letter assuring Safiye that the government of Venice would be duly informed, in order "to calm her down, seeing how distressed she was." Then he suggested the Senate to comply immediately with the Sultan Mother's wishes, since she had been one of the major supporters of the Republic.[59]

It must have been unclear if the request to stop the importation of the glass *penachi* under the threat of dissolving Safiye's ties with Venice derived from her desire to have the exclusive privilege of wearing them. Considering the emotional response, she was probably offended by the arrival of a fanciful and original object that should have being brought as a prized gift, and not put on offer in the open market. The Venetian Senate presented its apologies, stating that the glass imitations had been exported "as a new and charming thing," not imagining that this could cause any disappointment. An order was immediately issued that no future consignment of *penachi* could be made to Constantinople under the penalty of confiscation, while the Bailo alerted the Venetian merchants in Turkey of the new prohibition. A public officer was then sent touring

[59] DISPC, filza 39, fol. 607r-v, 6 August 1594. On the power of the Queen Mothers at the Porte during the last decades of the sixteenth century, see Leslie P. Peirce, *The Imperial Harem: Women and Sovereignty in the Ottoman Empire* (New York and Oxford: Oxford University Press, 1993), 91–112 and 222–28. On Safiye in particular, see Pedani, "Safiye's Household," who also briefly mentions this episode.

the glass furnaces in Murano and a series of shops in Venice, warning artisans and mercers of the new regulation. The craftsmen and traders promised to comply with it, even though noticing that they could not possibly know or check where people would take the glass feathers after buying them. Moreover, as the Senate itself remarked, those aigrettes were produced also in the states of other Italian princes and sent directly from there to the Ottoman markets.[60] Indeed, we can recognize such a fragile object – which by its very nature had no chance of surviving over the centuries and being kept until today in collections and museums – in the drawings of the fantastic glass vessels made by the painter Jacopo Ligozzi in the early seventeenth century for the Grand Duke of Tuscany's court in Florence, where the *penachi* were also probably manufactured (Figure 2.2). At any rate, soon afterward the problem vanished as quickly as it had arisen. In November 1594 the Sultan's Mother wrote again to the Bailo, saying he should not bother to prohibit Venetian merchants from importing *penachi* anymore: "let in the future come as many as they want, because they [the aigrettes] are already in no esteem at all, and if they want to send a thousand ships of them, let them come."[61]

JEWELS AND CASKETS

Venice had a long-standing tradition of producing luxury objects in rock crystal, jewels, hard stones and gold or silver works for the courts of Asian princes. Such a specialization dated back to the times of Marco Polo and the opening of the silk roads to Western traders.[62] By the early sixteenth century Venetian jewelers, in collaboration with other artisans, took a new step in the creation of highly elaborate and imaginative pieces for Asian rulers and elites. In 1512, for instance, the merchant Martino Merlini wrote from Venice to his younger brother in Syria, asking him to send either a real Middle Eastern armor or a model in leather, wood, cloth or a drawing on paper. Martino had devised the audacious plan of creating a unique object, "of a kind that a similar one won't be found in the whole world": a full battle-set for a mounted warrior – composed of a helmet, cuirass, gauntlets and all other protections for shoulders and legs – made in crystal glass and

60 DELC, reg. 8, fol. 181r, 24 September 1594; ASV, Bailo a Costantinopoli, busta 269, Protocollo Atti e Sentenze 382, fol. 58r, 31 October 1594.

61 BMC Correr, Mss. Donà dalle Rose, 236, Dispacci del Bailo Venier, fols. 45v–46r, 25 November 1594.

62 Luca Molà, "Venezia, Genova e l'Oriente: i mercanti italiani sulle Vie della Seta tra XIII e XIV secolo," in *Sulla Via della Seta. Antichi sentieri tra Oriente e Occidente*, ed. Mark Norrell et al. (Turin: Codice Edizioni, 2012), 137–39.

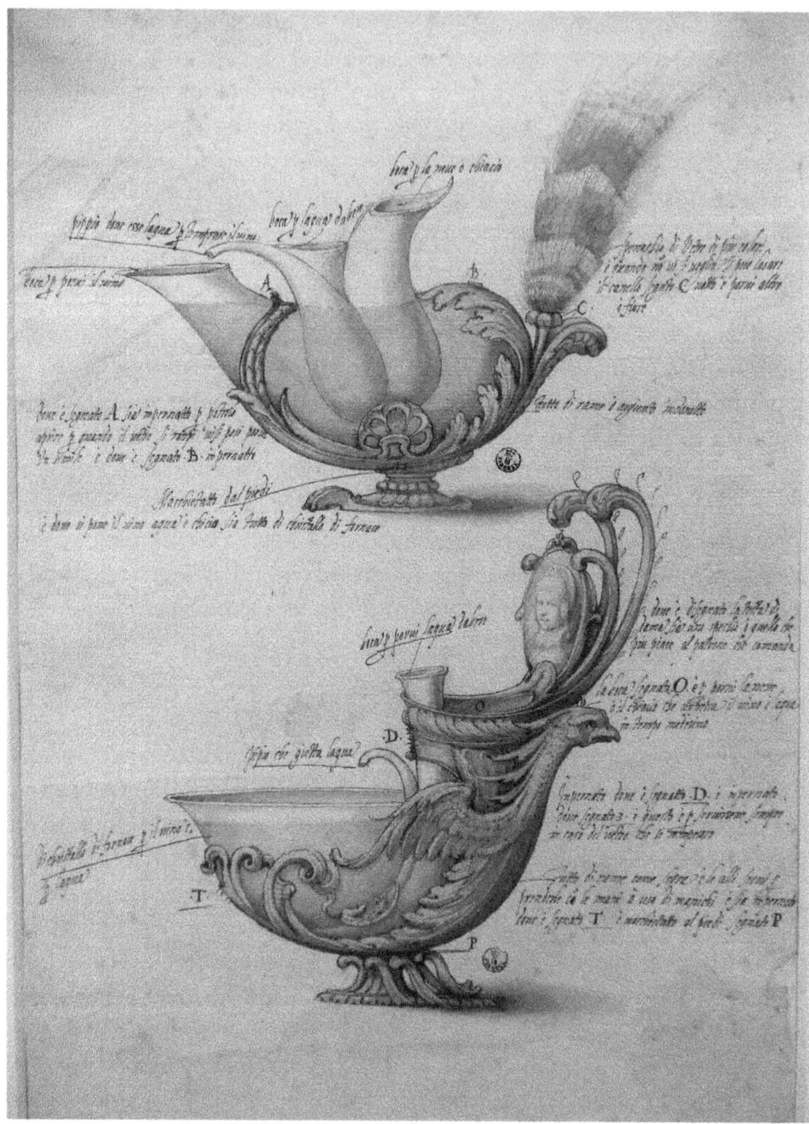

FIGURE 2.2 Jacopo Ligozzi, "Drawing of Vessel with Glass Aigrette (*Penachio*)," early seventeenth century, Gabinetto dei Disegni e delle Stampe degli Uffizi, Florence.

splendidly decorated with enameled silver, rubies, diamonds, emeralds and sapphires, so that "in the sun and in full light there won't be a man who could stare at it, because of the great brightness that will reverberate from all those jewels, glass and enamels." The Venetian merchant, of course, was not so naive as to think that the armor would be apt for fighting, but, as he said, it could be used "as adornment, to be worn by a slave who would precede the Sultan, for pomp and lustre." The craftsman who could produce such a wonder was the glass-maker Vettor dei Anzoli of Murano, who had just finished a crystal saddle and had insisted with him to have suggestions for "a new fantasy" that could be made for the Levant. The plan was to sell the armor to the Mamluk Sultan of Egypt, possibly through the intermediation of one of his top officers. In another letter, Martino proposed even to create a second identical set for the Persian Shah, emblazoned with this ruler's coat of arms.[63]

The same adaptability of a luxury object to different Asian princes emerged in 1527, when a round chessboard "wrought with gold and silver and set with chalcedony, jasper, and other jewels," and chess pieces "made of the purest crystal" was brought to the Ducal Palace and shown to the Doge and Senators. This unique artifact had been commissioned more than ten years earlier by a Venetian nobleman with the aim of selling it to the Mamluk Sultan al-Ghawri. However, after the fall of the Mamluk dynasty in 1517 the chessboard had remained in the family's possession. It was now proposed to the government – for the considerable price of 5,000 ducats – as a possible gift to be sent to Suleyman the Magnificent with the new Bailo leaving for Constantinople.[64] Over the following years partnerships of Venetian goldsmiths and merchants, several of them belonging to the nobility, invested large sums of money and employed the most skillful workers to produce a number of refined and valuable "gadgets" and ritual objects in response to the passion for jewelry prevailing at court in Constantinople under Grand Vizier Ibrahim Pasha (1523–36). This was the case, for instance, of the gold ring with a miniature watch shown by Francesco Zen around the Rialto in 1531, which was intended for sale in the Turkish capital. Even more remarkable was the output of two partnerships operating in the following years, each of which invested over 100,000 ducats in the production of objects for the Ottoman court: they created the famous four-tiered imperial crown, a jewel-studded saddle, a throne, a scepter, a horse cloth with precious stones and pearls, a – supposedly – perpetual-motion

[63] Giuseppe Dalla Santa, "Commerci, vita privata e notizie politiche dei giorni della lega di Cambrai (da lettere del mercante veneziano Martino Merlini)," *Atti del Reale Istituto Veneto di Scienze, Lettere ed Arti* 76 (1916–17): 1566–69. See also Benjamin Arbel, "The Last Decades of Venice's Trade with the Mamluks: Importation into Egypt and Syria," *Mamluk Studies Review* 8 (2004): 57–58.

[64] Marin Sanudo, *I diarii di Marino Sanuto* (Venice: Fratelli Visentini, 1895), 43, col. 599; Curatola, "Marin Sanudo," 175; Patricia H. Labalme and Laura Sanguineti White, eds., *Venice, Città Excelentissima: Selections from the Renaissance Diaries of Marin Sanudo* (Baltimore: Johns Hopkins University Press, 2008), 263–64.

clock and other valuable things. Several of these marvels were paraded in the Ducal Palace before leaving the city, demonstrating that even private commercial enterprises had a public dimension when they concerned the exchange between Venice and Constantinople.[65]

The interplay between Venetian mercantile profits and state diplomatic gifts, and between the Ottoman elite's generic demand for jewels and the official requests for luxury presents, can be further investigated through the analysis of the production, sale or donation of luxury caskets. Grand Viziers had asked the Republic to receive such items as presents already in the 1550s and 1560s,[66] but the problem of constructing box-like jewels of large dimensions became crucial for Venice in the 1580s, when a commission came from Great Admiral Uluc Ali (in Venice called "Occhiali," Spectacles), a Calabrian convert who since his appointment in 1571 had kept a threatening stance toward the Venetian dominions in the Levant. In November 1583 his moves were carefully monitored by the Venetians. After his return to Constantinople with the fleet, rumor spread that he was openly speaking about attacking Crete.[67] According to Bailo Giovan Francesco Morosini's informers, the Great Admiral had even drafted a written proposal to that effect for the Sultan, and it was only thanks to the strong opposition of the Queen Mother Nur Banu that he decided to put aside his military project.[68] Nur Banu, who claimed to be a Venetian noblewoman abducted by the Turks at a young age, was one of the main supporters of Venice at the Porte. This was in connection with a particular fondness for new and extravagant Venetian silk fabrics, which she continually requested of the Bailo.[69] Averting the Ottoman conquest of Crete,

[65] Curatola, "Marin Sanudo," 178; Otto Kurz, "A Gold Helmet Made in Venice for Sultan Sulayman the Magnificent," *Gazette des Beaux-Arts* 74 (1969): 249–58; Gülru Necipoğlu, "Süleyman the Magnificent and the Representation of Power in the Context of Ottoman-Habsburg-Papal Rivalry," *The Art Bulletin* 71 (1989): 401–27; Ennio Concina, *Il Doge e il Sultano. Mercatura, arte e relazioni nel primo '500/Doç ve Sultan. 16 yüzyul başlarında ticaret, sanat ve ilişkiler* (Rome: Logart Press, 1994), 136–45.

[66] DELC, reg. 1, fol. 104r, 31 December 1558; fols. 105v–106r, 20 February 1559; fol. 112v, 27 April 1559; fol. 132r, 14 October 1559; fol. 140r, 7 November 1559; DELC, reg. 2, fol. 12r, 15 March 1560; fol. 14r, 2 May 1560; fol. 17v, 4 May 1560; fol. 23r, 5 September 1560; fols. 56v–57r, 11 April 1562; fol. 75v, 28 November 1562; fol. 77r, 16 January 1563; fol. 82r, 17 April 1563; fol. 85r, 12 June 1563; DISPC, filza 3C, fol. 220r, 1 September 1562; fol. 248r, 7 November 1562.

[67] DISPC, filza 18, fols. 202r–204r, 29 November 1583.

[68] DISPC, reg. 18, fol. 242r, 13 December 1583; Emilio Spagni, "Una sultana veneziana," *Nuovo Archivio Veneto* 29 (1900): 241–348.

[69] On Nur Banu's orders of silk cloth, see Raby, "The Serenissima," 111–12; Susan A. Skilliter, "The Letters of the Venetian 'Sultana' Nūr Bānū and Her Kira to Venice," in

however, was the last act that the Sultan's Mother could perform in favor of the Republic. She had been ill for some time with strong abdominal pain – maybe cancer, perhaps because of poisoning – until she finally died on 7 December 1583, only days after ordering new cloths of gold from Venice and without knowing that three bolts of satin she was waiting to receive had been lost in a shipwreck off the coast of Dalmatia.[70] After the death of its main ally, the Republic and its Bailo were understandably concerned when in January the following year a request arrived for an expensive casket of rock crystal and silver from Uluc Ali. On the occasion of the prince's circumcision he had bought a similar casket worth 5,000 ducats for the Sultan from the merchant Antonio Helman, the brother and partner of Guglielmo who was based in Constantinople. The casket, made in Venice by the jeweler Ancileo Diana, had pleased Murad III so much that now he wanted an exact copy of it as quickly as possible, forcing the Great Admiral to seek the help of the Bailo.[71]

Morosini forwarded the measurements to Venice, knowing that the matter would not be easily solved. Between late March and early April 1584, the Senate dedicated long debates to the casket. The difference of opinions shows the crucial importance of making the right choice in delicate circumstances. The search for a ready-made object of the shape and size needed was unsuccessful, so the government decided to order a new one from Venetian artisans.[72] But the men who accepted the commission went back to the council a few days later stating that it was impossible to produce it in less than a year, even if they put ten masters to work on it. The jeweler Diana, asked for his opinion, confirmed the difficulty of creating such a beautiful thing rapidly; he himself had spent two and a half years completing the original casket. In the meantime,

Studia turcologica memoriae Alexii Bombaci dicata (Naples: Istituto Universitario Orientale, 1982), 527 and 536. On her pretended origins, see Benjamin Arbel, "Nūr Bānū: A Venetian Sultana?," *Turcica* 24/25 (1992–93): 241–59.

70 DISPC, reg. 18, fol. 190r, 15 November 1583. For the satins and the shipwreck, see DELC, reg. 6, fol. 151v, 9 November 1583; *Gnalić – Blago Potonulog Broda iz 16. Stoljeća* (Zagreb: Hrvatski Povijesni Muzej, 2013).

71 DISPC, filza 18, fols. 377r–379v, 21 January 1584; fols. 448v–449r, 14 February 1584; DISPC, filza 19, fol. 111v, 3 April 1584. On the government's commission to Diana of three lamps in gilded silver for the Sultan in 1599, of which a drawing has remained, see Ennio Concina, ed., *Venezia e Constantinople. Incontri, confronti e scambi* (Udine: Forum, 2006), 148–49; Maria Pia Pedani, ed., *Inventory of the Lettere e Scritture Turchesche in the Venetian State Archives* (Leiden and Boston: Brill, 2010), nos. 588–89; Pedani, *Venezia*, 104.

72 DELC, reg. 6, fol. 163r, 24 March 1584.

another container had been found, which was slightly smaller but of high quality and could be purchased at the reasonable price of 1,900 ducats. Even more important, it could be sent after only some final touches were made. Two groups opposed each other in the Senate: the first group wanted to send the measurements and description of the smaller casket to Uluc Ali and wait to see if he liked it, otherwise a new one was to be ordered; the second party, considering the urgency of the situation and the universally known fact that artisans could not be trusted for meeting a deadline, suggested shipping what was at hand without delay. After several inconclusive votes, the second option reached the required majority and the casket was loaded onto a vessel due to leave in a few days, "being sure that this rapidity will give the highest satisfaction" to the Great Admiral.[73] It is likely that the owner of this casket was Guglielmo Helman. In a letter sent to his agent in Constantinople in September 1583 he had asked to get a note from Nur Banu in order to avoid problems at the customs when collecting "a very beautiful and rich jewelled crystal casket, and also a similar and very rare jewelled crystal cabinet, both with a structure in gilded silver," which he planned to send the following spring.[74]

When in late May the Bailo received the letters of the Senate reporting its decision, he strongly approved it. The only worry he still had concerned the timing of the casket's arrival, which he hoped would be in his hands before the return of Uluc Ali and his fleet from the Black Sea.[75] Fortunately, things went according to plan. In his visit to the Great Admiral in July 1584, Morosini first explained the decision taken by his government and then proudly had the casket brought in and opened, saying it was a gift from the Republic of Venice. At this, Uluc Ali expressed his thanks many times to the Signoria, with "extraordinary signs of happiness and pleasure" and "with such an abundance of words that more could not have been desired." A box full of gold *zecchini* would not have pleased him better, he said, and he promised to keep perpetual memory of these "acts of love," intending to reciprocate them at the right time. As a final gesture of gratefulness, he freed a Venetian caulker who was a slave in the admiral galley.[76] Uluc Ali's high spirits, however, must

[73] DELC, reg. 6, fol. 164r-v, 5 and 10 April 1584.

[74] ASV, Miscellanea Gregolin, busta 12 ter I, letter of Guglielmo Helman from Venice to Antonio Paruta in Constantinople, 26 September 1583.

[75] DISPC, filza 19, fol. 229r, 22 May 1584.

[76] DISPC, filza 19, fols. 354v–355r, 4 July 1584.

have lasted for just a short time. Less than a week later he informed the Bailo about the Sultan's reception of the present. Murad III had simply reiterated his wish of having a casket of the measurements he had sent, of the greatest possible beauty, even if it took two and a half years to complete it. This time Morosini was not totally disappointed. As he wrote to the government informing it of the new request, keeping the Great Admiral waiting for the casket such a long time might keep him from harming the interests of Venice during the whole period. In the meantime, "God knows what could happen, maybe he will die, or will be removed from his office, or other occurrences will save us from this expense."[77]

On 29 August 1584 a resigned Senate accepted Morosini's advice and deliberated the manufacturing of the casket, but without hurry.[78] A sudden change of pace took place in early November, though, when news reached Venice of a savage attack perpetrated by Venetian ships near Cefalonia against a galley taking the Bey of Gerba, his mother (widow of the Governor of Tripoli) and several women and dignitaries of their court from the Barbary Coast to Constantinople. Most of the people on board had been massacred, others had been sold as slaves. The fabulously rich cargo of the galley had disappeared: sacks of coins, gold ingots, jewels, forty boxes of silk fabrics and even a unicorn's horn. These were items that in large part the Bey was carrying as gifts to the Porte, for the Sultanas and especially for his close ally Uluc Ali. To appease the fury of the Great Admiral and the Sultan, on 10 November the same year the Senate gave Morosini the power of spending up to 10,000 *zecchini* in presents for several members of the Ottoman Court.[79] The council then went back to the casket with renewed energy.[80] In January 1585 the Senators approved a contract agreement with the goldsmith Giovan Battista Rizzoletti – whom the Republic had already employed for making the caskets sent as gifts to the Habsburg Empress and the Duke of Mantua – and the "illuminator" (*miniador*) Francesco Moro.[81] The two

[77] DISPC, filza 19, fols. 363r–364v, 13 July 1584.

[78] DELC, reg. 6, fol. 173r, 29 August 1584.

[79] For a detailed reconstruction of the incident, see Antonio Fabris, "Un caso di pirateria veneziana: la cattura della galea del Bey di Gerba (21 ottobre 1584)," *Quaderni di Studi Arabi* 8 (1990): 91–112. The instructions to the Bailo are in DELC, reg. 6, fols. 176r–177r, 10 November 1584.

[80] DELC, reg. 6, fol. 181r-v, 29 December 1584.

[81] See the declarations of Rizzoletti in DELC, filza 7, 10 November 1589; Raffaella Morselli, ed., *Gonzaga. La Celeste Galeria. Le raccolte* (Milan: Skira, 2002), 281–82, 306–7, for the casket given to the Duke of Mantua in 1582.

craftsmen promised that their workshops would operate in synergy and complete the object in eighteen months, at a cost of 7,125 ducats. They also prepared a drawing of the casket on parchment, illuminated with gold, which the new Bailo, Lorenzo Bernardo, took with him to Constantinople in the spring as proof that the actual box was being made.[82]

Meanwhile, rumors spread among foreign diplomats in Venice regarding the Porte's rage for the galley's incident and the Republic's strenuous attempts at defusing it. The making of the casket became common knowledge in the city, and in the public imagination its value reached the astronomical sum of 12,000 *zecchini*, growing over time to 25–30,000 *scudi*.[83] In the following two years the Senate constantly informed Uluc Ali about the progress of the work, slowed down unfortunately by the untimely death of Francesco Moro. In June 1587, finally, the ship *Fontana* set sail for Constantinople with the casket, while a cargo note had been sent to the Bailo in advance so as to confirm its next arrival to the Great Admiral.[84] A contemporary Venetian chronicle contains a drawing and a detailed description of the famous casket. It was composed of 4,000 pieces, screws included, that could be assembled and disassembled very easily; the body was of massive gilded silver with arabesqued decorations both outside and inside; and it was surrounded by twenty-four twisted columns, five large convex pieces – on the four sides and on top – and several smaller ones made of rock crystal. Uluc Ali would have been very happy to see it, had he still been alive when the *Fontana* dropped its anchor in Constantinople. Bailo Morosini was a good prophet in foreseeing the Admiral's death before its delivery, though not as much on the possible savings for the Republic. The casket's final cost reached 9,640 ducats, plus the cost of the black leather box lined with crimson velvet and adorned outside with gold fringes in which it was packaged. It pleased the Sultan, as shown by the four robes of gold and silver brocatel with flowers made in Bursa that he handed

[82] DELC, filza 6, contract signed on 22 January 1585; DELC, reg. 6, fol. 186v, 23 January 1585; DELC, reg. 7, fol. 36r, 6 June 1585.

[83] Archivio di Stato di Mantova, Archivio Gonzaga, busta 1515, f. I, fols. 25–26, 26 January 1585; busta 1518, f. I, fols. 142–143, 30 May 1587; documents consulted from the database of the website *Collezionismo Gonzaghesco 1563–1630*, Centro Internazionale di Cultura e d'Arte di Palazzo Te e Archivio di Stato di Mantova, http://banchedatigonzaga.centropalazzote.it/collezionismo/index.php?page=Home (last accessed on 18 September 2015).

[84] DELC, reg. 6, fol. 203r, 7 February 1585; DELC, reg. 7, fols. 40v–41r, 7 September 1585; fol. 69r-v, 2 August 1586; fol. 72v, 8 November 1586; fol. 84r, 23 May 1587.

out to Lorenzo Bernardo's secretary and the three Venetian dragomans who brought him the splendid gift.[85]

After this famous incident, rock crystal and silver caskets became even more popular in diplomatic exchanges and as elite luxuries. Already in 1588 the Ottoman Governor of Rumelia (Beylerbey of Greece in the sources), one of the most powerful individuals in the Empire, asked the Venetian government for a smaller casket. And the Senate once again chose Giovan Battista Rizzoletti for the task, with another contract for a lower sum and a shorter period of time.[86] But when in 1589 another complex commission arrived from the Sultan himself, Rizzoletti was put in competition with the jeweler (and art collector) Domenico dalle Due Regine.[87] In 1590 both men presented a project with a cost estimate and drawings: dalle Due Regine offered to produce the object in thirty months for 10,000 ducats, materials included; Rizzoletti proposed a slightly lower sum of 9,800 ducats and the same time for completing the work. He also suggested the opportunity of moving the enterprise inside the state mint in St. Mark's Square, for two reasons: first, because there the work would not be seen by too many people, avoiding the possibility of having his design copied; second, because the precious metals and stones would remain in a safer place. Clearly the wide fame obtained in the city thanks to the previous caskets had made him more cautious about plagiarism and thefts. In the end Rizzoletti won the competition, and again the Porte kept constantly pressing the Bailo for the casket until its completion and shipment in September 1593.[88] In the following decade there is further

85 Lionello Venturi, "Cassetta d'argento decorato e cristallo di rocca eseguita in Venezia prima del 1587," *Arte italiana decorativa e industriale* 15 (1906): 99–100; Amato Bacchini, "Un prezioso dono artistico della Rep. di Venezia alle Sultane di Costantinopoli," *Arte e Storia* 6th series, 34, no. 1 (1915): 6–13.

86 DELC, reg. 7, fols. 112v–113r, 19 March 1588; DELC, filza 7, 13 December 1589 and 10 November 1589 for the contract.

87 On his life, see the biographical entry by Michel Hockmann, "Domenico dalle Due Regine (Domenico Franceschi detto dalle due Regine)," in *Il collezionismo d'arte a Venezia. Dalle origini al Cinquecento*, ed. Michel Hockmann, Rosella Lauber and Stefania Mason (Venice: Marsilio, 2008), 268.

88 DELC, reg. 7, fol. 176r-v, 15 April 1589; DELC, reg. 8, fol. 35r, 23 September 1590; fols. 42v–43r, 24 November 1590; fols. 45v–47r, 7 December 1590; fol. 48v, 22 December 1590; fol. 51v–53r, 9 February 1591; fol. 68r-v, 10 August 1591; fol. 80r, 28 October 1591; fols. 99v–100r, 5 June 1592; fols. 100v–101r, 25 July 1592; fol. 109v, 24 September 1592; fol. 115v, 14 November 1592; fol. 120r, 6 February 1593; fols. 131v–132r, 22 April 1593; fol. 137v, 21 June 1593; fol. 143r-v, 10 August 1593; fol. 146v, 27 August 1594; fols. 154v–155r, 28 October 1593; DELC, filza 7, 24 May 1590 (in the file of the decree of 29 June 1590) for the competition between Rizzoletti and dalle Due Regine.

information on luxury containers of a similar type offered for sale in the Venetian market by private dealers or given as diplomatic gifts. In 1594 and again in 1600, the ambassador of the Duke of Mantua proposed that his lord buy a casket made of rock crystal and silver, in the second case sending a drawing with exactly the same measurements as those of Uluc Ali;[89] in 1603 the Persian envoy to the Doge left the city with one of those caskets;[90] and in the early seventeenth century Venetian merchants presented a particularly showy casket to the Sultan of Hormuz, an object that is now in the Museu de Arte Antiga in Lisbon (other public and private collections around the world still preserve several of these precious jewels made in Venice).[91]

CONCLUSION

In 1591 the Venetian silk-cloth producers and merchants discussed the miserable situation of their ancient guildhall, located in the crowded district of Cannaregio since the early fourteenth century. They decided it was time to find a more dignified and reputable seat at Rialto. After a long search and a rebuilding campaign, in 1602 Bartolomeo Bontempelli and the other members of the committee in charge of the operation could proudly look at what no other Venetian guild could boast: a three-story guildhall standing along the Grand Canal, just a few steps from the Rialto Bridge.[92] The Ottoman Court's ceaseless request for gifts of luxury fabrics had certainly enhanced the prestige of silk entrepreneurs in Venice, and together with the flourishing trade in the Levant it helped increase their wealth. The technical difficulties faced in order to satisfy the Porte certainly contributed to a continuous refinement of the city's textile technology, with a specialization in products for the Asian markets that remained a hallmark of Venice in the following centuries. The government of the Republic supported this evolution through its diplomatic and political structures, providing the logistics

A brief mention of Rizzoletti's caskets for the Ottoman court is also in Fabris, "Artisanat," 53.

89 Sermidi, *Le collezioni*, nn. 262, 264, 458.

90 DELC, filza 10, 16 February 1605.

91 Hans Huth, "A Venetian Renaissance Casket," in *Museum Monographs I. Papers on Objects in the Collection of City Art Museum of St. Louis* (St. Louis: St. Louis Museum of Art, 1968), 42–50.

92 The guild of the silk merchants remained in this building until the fall of the Republic in 1797, even though the fact is unknown to the Venetian historiography. A forthcoming publication on the history of this guildhall will provide full information and references soon.

for the exchange of information across space, time and languages that made possible an intercontinental production of fabrics.

The need for diplomatic gifts for the Ottomans, moreover, acted as a lever for technological growth also in other artisanal sectors. By calling for public competitions among craftsmen and employing scores of them for the production of extremely refined objects almost every year, the Senate favored the professional improvement of glass-makers, jewelers, producers of furniture and other specialized artisans. And the need to promote ever new designs and better quality objects and fabrics necessarily sparked an innovative dynamic in the industrial world of Venice. Of course, this combined effort of Venetian nobles, merchants and craftsmen in making and delivering the right gifts on time to the Porte had a purely political dimension. It was crucial for smoothing relations with the Ottomans during more than half a century after Lepanto, and probably contributed to saving Venice from military attacks on its maritime dominions in the same period. Against all these benefits, one should consider the financial cost of sustaining this material diplomacy, a cost that is difficult to assess. The Baili could mention with disdain the Ragusans, who had to pay 12,500 ducats every year to the Ottomans to preserve their freedom, but they probably knew that Venice itself was willingly accepting to pay a covered tribute that was even bigger.[93]

This chapter has considered the production and offer of gifts to the Ottoman empire from the Venetian perspective. However, like the Ragusans, other European and Asian states followed a parallel and partially different gift policy in their relations with the Porte. Between the late sixteenth and the early seventeenth century more and more diplomats appeared in Constantinople with luxury presents, coming from France, the Habsburg empire, Spain, England, the Dutch Republic, Genoa, Florence, Russia or Persia. While there are studies discussing single cases, there is still no systematic investigation on the interplay or clash among the gift strategies of different countries. Future research on the competition among states in this field, the circulation of information among ambassadors and politicians and the reactions of the Ottoman Court to their choices would certainly constitute a stimulating and novel contribution to the history of diplomatic gift-giving.

93 Alberi, *Relazioni*, 2: 403. On Ragusa's tribute and gifts, see James D. Tracy, "The Grand Vezir and the Small Republic: Dubrovnik and Rüstem Paşa, 1544–1561," *Turkish Historical Review* 1 (2010): 196–214.

3

Diplomatic Ivories

Sri Lankan Caskets and the Portuguese-Asian Exchange in the Sixteenth Century

Zoltán Biedermann

Ivories played a pivotal role in the making of Sri Lankan diplomatic exchanges with Portugal, an early high point in European-Asian diplomacy.[1] In 1541, the Sinhalese monarch Bhuvanekabāhu VII (1521–51) sent an ivory casket of exceptional quality to King John III (1521–57) in Lisbon. This outstanding work of art, now in Munich and known as the "coronation casket," inaugurates an important corpus of materials dispatched from various Sri Lankan courts to the Portuguese monarch John III, his wife Catherine of Habsburg (regent 1557–62), and their successor Sebastian (1562/68–78) (Figure 3.1).[2] Like many ivories from Asia and Africa, these objects integrate motifs taken from Renaissance art into an iconography anchored in other regional traditions and executed, in this case, by South Asian artists. But what was it that drove the invention of such combinations in the local political context, what made it possible for images to travel between Sri Lanka, Goa, Lisbon and other places in Europe, and how did composite ivory

[1] I wish to thank Sujatha Arundhati Meegama for sharing her thoughts on the ivory caskets at a time when much of her work was yet unpublished. This piece is best read alongside with Meegama, "The Local and the Global: The Multiple Visual Worlds of Sixteenth-Century Sri Lanka," in *Sri Lanka at the Crossroads of History*, ed. Alan Strathern and Zoltán Biedermann (London: UCL Press, 2017), 113–40. I also thank Annemarie Jordan Gschwend for her kind support, including an invitation to the opening of the exhibition on Sri Lankan ivories at the Museum Rietberg in Zurich in 2010. The catalogue to the exhibition now offers the finest overview of the subject. Annemarie Jordan Gschwend and Johannes Beltz, *Elfenbeine aus Ceylon: Luxusgüter für Katharina von Habsburg (1507–1578)* (Zurich: Museum Rietberg, 2010).

[2] Nothing is known about such gifts during the regency of Cardinal Henry, 1562–68.

FIGURE 3.1 "Coronation casket," Kōṭṭe, Sri Lanka, c. 1541. Munich, Bayerische Verwaltung der staatlichen Schlösser, Gärten und Seen, Residenz München, Schatzkammer, Inv.-Nr. 1241.

objects achieve their diplomatic goals at distant courts? Exploring such matters allows us to address the wider issue of how value(s) – political, commercial and aesthetic – could be understood across cultural boundaries and how the imperfections of cross-cultural readings in the sixteenth century were linked to the making of unequal power relations on the global stage.[3]

A SRI LANKAN EMBASSY TO LISBON, 1541–43

Carrying the "coronation casket" was a Tamil ambassador whose principal duty was to conduct talks about his Sinhalese patron's vassalage to the Portuguese crown.[4] In Sri Lanka, Bhuvanekabāhu VII ruled over a relatively small kingdom extending across the fertile hinterland of Colombo, organized around the capital city of Kōṭṭe. He also claimed overlordship over a number of other rulers in the island and, occasionally, laid claim to the much-coveted imperial title of *cakravarti* ("Turner of the Wheel"). In sixteenth-century Sri Lanka, this title designated not so much the ability to conquer the world as the ability to impose tribute over other rulers across the island. The overlordship of Kōṭṭe over other parts of Sri Lanka was an inherently diplomatic affair as relations of authority were almost permanently under renegotiation.[5]

It was one of the peculiarities of the Lankan political arrangement that imperial ambitions within the island could be combined with the payment of tribute outside. In the heyday of Chinese maritime expansion, the *cakravarti* of Kōṭṭe Parākramabāhu VI (c. 1411–67), while receiving tribute from rulers across Sri Lanka, also sent a series of tributary embassies to the Ming court in China. Although nothing is known about the material culture of those missions, the practice must have left an

[3] On the wider context of Portuguese diplomacy in Asia, see Zoltán Biedermann, *The Portuguese in Sri Lanka and South India: Studies in the History of Empire, Diplomacy and Trade* (Wiesbaden: Harrassowitz, 2014), 33–72, and António Vasconcelos de Saldanha, *Iustum Imperium. Dos tratados como fundamento do império dos portugueses no Oriente. Estudo de história do direito internacional e do direito português* (Lisbon and Macao: Fundação Oriente and Instituto Português do Oriente, 1997).

[4] On the vassalage and its political and symbolic implications, see Zoltán Biedermann, "The *Matrioshka* Principle and How It Was Overcome: Portuguese and Habsburg Attitudes toward Imperial Authority in Sri Lanka and the Responses of the Rulers of Kotte (1506–1656)," *Journal of Early Modern History* 13, no. 4 (2009): 265–310.

[5] Michael Roberts, *Sinhala Consciousness in the Kandyan Period 1590s to 1815* (Colombo: Vijitha Yapa Publications, 2003); Alan Strathern, *Kingship and Conversion in Sixteenth-Century Sri Lanka: Portuguese Imperialism in a Buddhist Land* (Cambridge: Cambridge University Press, 2007).

imprint on the way gifts were put together in Sri Lanka to please distant courtly audiences.[6] During the early sixteenth century, attention shifted to the emerging Indian Ocean empire of the Portuguese, the *Estado da Índia*. Bhuvanekabāhu VII saw himself as a key vassal of the Portuguese crown especially from the late 1520s onward, and while he had many things to complain about – for example, the Portuguese purchased Lankan cinnamon below market value – the agreement also carried advantages for him. By maintaining his status as the sole vassal of John III in Sri Lanka, the king of Kōṭṭe could hope to keep his Lankan rivals at bay. Tributary payments, generally in the form of cinnamon, elephants and precious stones, served to strengthen a military alliance that others in the island also longed for, but struggled to obtain.[7] In this sense, certain commodities offered by Lankan rulers to the Portuguese served a function close to that of diplomatic gifts.

The embassy dispatched to Lisbon in 1541, however, responded to a specific moment in the political life of the kingdom of Kōṭṭe, for which a special kind of gift was required. In 1539, Bhuvanekabāhu VII had welcomed the birth of a grandson and declared his desire to see this child become the next king. The project went against the ambitions of Māyādunnē, Bhuvanekabāhu's younger brother ruling in nearby Sītāvaka (1521–78), himself intent on taking over Kōṭṭe and becoming the supreme overlord of Sri Lanka. As one would expect, the decision of promoting a younger candidate left many unhappy, and, confronted with the uproar, the monarch turned to his Portuguese allies to consolidate his position. He had some leverage on this front, since it was widely known that the royal treasury of John III owed him a sizeable sum of money, much needed to run Portuguese operations in Asia. The unofficial mid-sixteenth-century chronicler Gaspar Correia went so far as to suggest that the Portuguese monarch accepted to receive the Lankan embassy in the hope of seeing his debts pardoned.[8] Much of what ensued was, then, of an ambiguous hierarchical order and traversed, from the Lankan point of view at least, by a strong sense of mutuality. The monarch of Kōṭṭe offered his personal vassalage, which in practice amounted to monetary

[6] Embassies have been documented for 1416, 1432, 1433, 1435, 1436, 1445 and 1459. See K. M. M. Werake, "A Re-Examination of Chinese Relations with Sri Lanka during the 15th Century A.D.," *Modern Sri Lanka Studies* 2, nos. 1–2 (1987): 89–102.

[7] Jorge Manuel Flores, *Os Portugueses e o Mar de Ceilão, 1498–1543: Trato, Diplomacia e Guerra* (Lisbon: Cosmos, 1998); Biedermann, "The *Matrioshka* Principle."

[8] Gaspar Correia, *Lendas da Índia*, ed. M. Lopes de Almeida, 4 vols. (Porto: Lello & Irmão Editores, 1975), 4: 307.

and commercial support for the *Estado*, in exchange for further military assistance.[9]

The "coronation casket" was reportedly used as a container for a gold statuette representing the chosen successor to the Lankan throne, Dharmapāla.[10] Its diplomatic function, however, was to convey a political message through its complex iconographic program. The same story regarding the coronation of Dharmapāla and the ambitioned imperial authority of Bhuvanekabāhu VII in Sri Lanka needed to be told to two different audiences. First, it had to be exposed to the members of the court of Kōṭṭe, especially those who may have expressed doubts about the project. The fact that the mission was led by a man serving in Kōṭṭe as *purōhita*, an alter ego of the ruler and a figure guaranteeing that courtly acts were ritually appropriate, was key in this regard. Second, the notion of a coronation in Lisbon and how it related to Kōṭṭe's supremacy in Lanka had to be expounded to the Portuguese court – especially since traditionally Portuguese kings were not crowned but anointed and acclaimed. It was important to achieve the perpetuation of Kōṭṭe's alliance with Lisbon and to do so following certain formal precepts of Lankan political lore. It was also crucial that the Portuguese elite understood all that was expected.

The front panel of the casket gives a vivid account of the key moment of the embassy.[11] Prince Dharmapāla is presented in effigy to John III by Śrī Rāmarakṣa or possibly Bhuvanekabāhu himself, the child's hand placed into that of the overlord. In another vignette, the Portuguese monarch places a crown on the head of the Lankan prince, anticipating his future coronation in Kōṭṭe. Dharmapāla would, so the agreement, continue the vassalage practiced by Bhuvanekabāhu VII, providing a stable ally in a troubled region. John III, in his turn, would support the house of Kōṭṭe, shielding it from common enemies such as the kings of

[9] Fernão de Queiroz, *Conquista Temporal e Espiritual de Ceilão* (Colombo: The Government Press, 1916), 185.

[10] There remains some uncertainty about whether this exact casket is indeed identical with the mentioned container, or whether it may have been produced after the events to commemorate them. The former hypothesis is favored by Annemarie Jordan Gschwend and myself, the latter by Amin Jaffer and Melanie Anne Schwabe, "A Group of Sixteenth-Century Ivory Caskets from Ceylon," *Apollo* 445 (1999): 3–14.

[11] Despite much subsequent scholarship, the initial analysis given by Vilhelm Slomann in 1937–38 remains largely valid, and the reproductions then published are among the best available: "Elfenbeinreliefs auf zwei singhalesischen Schreinen des 16. Jahrhunderts," *Pantheon* 20 (1937): 357–53 and 21 (1938): 12–19. Also see the detailed reconstruction of the 1542 events in Gschwend and Beltz, *Elfenbeine aus Ceylon*, 35–40.

Sītāvaka, who maintained their own diplomatic and military network in South India, cooperating with the Hindu Nayaks of Tanjore and the Muslim Mappilas of the Malabar Coast.[12]

The "coronation casket" is a rather extraordinary piece of political artwork. It is a gift representing the very diplomatic act during which it was transacted. In this sense, it is the diplomatic gift par excellence. On the surface of it, the scenes mentioned may be read as either an unambiguous sign of Portuguese imperial superiority (John III as a "king of kings" capable of projecting his power into a distant, defenseless realm) or as an affirmation of a proud Lankan understanding of the deal of vassalage (Bhuvanekabāhu VII as a cakravarti reaching out to his very special foreign overlord on the global stage – a representation of the Buddhist monarch with a whole range of imperial attributes appears on the side panel in Figure 3.2).[13] What makes the casket most interesting, however, is the dynamism of these two narratives taken together in a context going from local production (with borrowings from Western images for the representation of John III and two soldier figures), transcontinental displacement, display, and courtly reception and appropriation in Lisbon.

In contrast with the written grievances and requests presented to John III by the Lankan monarch, which may not have been made widely accessible, the casket is likely to have been on display for key members of the court, making an amply readable statement about the Luso-Lankan alliance. It probably moved on from Lisbon to the royal palace at Almeirim, where Śrī Rāmarakṣa spent time with the Portuguese royal family before returning to Asia in the spring of 1543. The *purōhita* did, by all means, an outstanding diplomatic job if we take into account the results of the embassy. He – and perhaps the casket itself – created lasting bonds with John III, Catherine of Habsburg (a figure much interested in ivories) and several other high-ranking personalities, to which he himself and Bhuvanekabāhu VII would come back time and again in their diplomatic correspondence over the following years.[14] As Kōṭṭe entered a decade of troubles, the memory of the events in Lisbon kept the alliance alive. In Colombo, the Franciscans complained about Bhuvanekabāhu's

[12] Flores, *Os Portugueses e o Mar de Ceilão*.

[13] More on the parallels between the two imperial ideologies in Biedermann, "The *Matrioshka* Principle."

[14] On Catherine as a "collecting queen," see Annemarie Jordan Gschwend, *A rainha colecionadora: Catarina de Áustria* (Lisbon: Círculo de Leitores, 2012).

FIGURE 3.2 "Coronation casket" (lateral panel), Kōṭṭe, Sri Lanka, c. 1541. Munich, Bayerische Verwaltung der staatlichen Schlösser, Gärten und Seen, Residenz München, Schatzkammer, Inv.-Nr. 1241.

reluctance to convert. The king's brother Māyādunnē did all he could to invert the political hacking order in the island and become a vassal of John III himself. And other disgruntled princes and pretenders to Lankan thrones approached the Portuguese authorities with promises of conversion directed against Bhuvanekabāhu's symbolic paramountcy. Yet while the pressure mounted on John III to change the status quo, the ties consolidated in 1542 remained remarkably resilient.[15]

[15] All this is abundantly documented in Georg Schurhammer and E. A. Voretzsch, *Ceylon zur Zeit des Königs Bhuvaneka Bahu und Franz Xavers 1539–1552. Quellen zur*

All this being said, it is important not to overidealize things on grounds of an isolated exegesis of the casket in its Sri Lankan context. As the casket was, during the main audience in 1542, carried through the great hall of the royal palace on the Lisbon waterfront, the Paço da Ribeira, it became surrounded by a visual apparatus set up by John III. The audience hall is likely to have been decorated at the time with a series of very large tapestries originally commissioned in Flanders by Manuel I (r. 1495–1521), representing scenes from the early years of Asian expansion.[16] The "discoveries" depicted were an extremely ambiguous matter when it came to questions of hierarchy. In principle it is quite right to emphasize, in opposition to the older narratives of Eurocentric imperial history, that Portuguese diplomacy in Asia (and indeed in Africa) rested on a notionally level playing field.[17] At the basis of all diplomatic interactions was an understanding that, on the other side of the divide, there were rulers sharing with the Portuguese monarchs the universal qualities of kingship. In other words, a king was a king, and an ambassador an ambassador. In fact, the Portuguese were often humbled during diplomatic encounters especially in the larger empires of mainland Asia. But to the participants in the 1542 reception, the overlord on whom things converged in that particular moment was the man sitting in the hall – notwithstanding his debts – rather than the one coming toward him. It was the former, after all, who had the power to dispatch troops to the realm of the latter, and not vice versa.

Naturally, the casket had been produced in Kōṭṭe without knowledge of the precise context in which it would be used in Lisbon. It expressed a Lankan point of view, where mutuality was the key quality of the alliance with the Portuguese. In Lisbon, the royal palace reframed the visual narrative, putting it into perspective and in line with the Portuguese imperial imagination. Here the story became one of imperial expansion and the establishment of hierarchical diplomatic relations across the globe. The notion of Portuguese superiority found expression in a gesture

Geschichte der Portugiesen, sowie der Franziskaner- und Jesuitenmission auf Ceylon, im Urtext herausgegeben und erklärt, 2 vols. (Leipzig: Verlag der Asia Major, 1928).

16 Gschwend and Beltz, *Elfenbeine aus Ceylon*, 36. On the imperial message of such tapestries and their complex iconographic programs, see Pedro Dias, *À Maneira de Portugal. Uma tapeçaria inédita*, Porto, VOC Antiguidades, 2007 (available online at www.pab.pt/_usr/downloads/À Maneira de Portugal e da Índia.pdf, accessed 29 July 2016).

17 Elbl, Ivana, "Cross-Cultural Trade and Diplomacy: Portuguese Relations with West Africa, 1441–1521," *Journal of World History* 3, no. 2 (1992): 165–204.

that modern historians, as their early modern precursors, have chosen to ignore. It is, to be more precise, an absence that strikes us as we go through the written record. After the casket was presented, John III does not seem to have offered anything of substantial material value in return. There is a possibility that the Portuguese monarch may have reciprocated a *cabaia* from Bhuvanekabāhu (a robe of the sort worn by him as shown on the casket) by offering a similar piece.[18] But there are no further textual clues on this. The silence is in itself noteworthy.

The logic of receiving without giving reverberated through the following decades. It manifested itself in the sustained hesitation of the Portuguese authorities to send more troops to Bhuvanekabāhu VII, even when the latter kept producing material incentives including precious ivory objects to obtain such support. The politics of this increasingly asymmetrical exchange call to be spelled out. For Annemarie Jordan Gschwend, Catherine of Habsburg's biographer, the queen not only received diplomatic gifts, she was also on a veritable shopping spree in the 1540s to obtain Lankan ivories that she then redistributed across her vast family. Recipients of Lankan ivory objects – for example, combs and large fans – included Maria of Parma, wife of Alessandro Farnese; Catherine's niece and daughter-in-law Joanna of Austria; her daughter Dona Maria, wife of Philip II of Spain; Emperor Rudolf II; Ferdinand II of Tyrol; and Albrecht V of Bavaria.[19] But what exactly was the nature of this trading, collecting and distributing? Can we ignore the ways in which the production of ivories in Sri Lanka was tied up with the new imperial order overseen by Portugal's elite? It was on imperial power that the fulfillment of Catherine's orders in Sri Lanka rested. The supply of ivories was discussed between Lisbon and Kōṭṭe at the highest political level.[20]

[18] Gschwend and Beltz, *Elfenbeine aus Ceylon*, 39. Gschwend has also suggested that the king may have sent some valuable weaponry in return, as he did to the Sultan of Cambay in 1537. Ibid., 43.

[19] Gschwend, "Ivory Caskets, Combs and Fans from Ceylon," in *The Heritage of Raulu-chantim* (Lisbon: 1996), 108; Jaffer and Schwabe, "A Group of Sixteenth-Century Ivory Caskets," 4.

[20] In 1551 the Portuguese viceroy mentioned, in a letter arguing for the launch of a military campaign in the island, that the royal couple should not worry about the supply of ivories so dear to the queen – a sign of how Bhuvanekabāhu VII had managed to tie the maintenance of the political status quo to the prospect of further ivory shipments. Catherine's agent Diogo Vaz obtained, according to the same letter, over a thousand rubies, five hundred emeralds, a large rock crystal, and numerous objects made of gold. Sebastião Ferreira to Catherine, Cochin, January 24, 1551, published in Schurhammer and Voretzsch, *Ceylon*, 558.

It is important to distinguish here between at least two categories of objects handed over to Portuguese agents in the island. They may all have been part of the complex political and diplomatic operations of Bhuvanekabāhu VII, but objects such as ivory fans, combs, small jewelry boxes and rock crystal figures do not seem to have carried the same political weight as caskets with their more elaborate iconographic programs.[21] The potential for depoliticization and commodification was significantly lower with the latter than the former. While historians long believed the ivory caskets now in Munich to have been purchased in Lisbon by an agent of Markus Fugger on behalf of Duke Albert V, in 1566 – in other words, sold for money[22] – recent research has shown that they were in fact sent to Bavaria by Catherine in 1573 as gifts, to help pave the way for a marriage between Princess Maximiliana, daughter of Albrecht V, and Sebastian of Portugal.[23] In other words, they remained firmly within the remit of high diplomacy.

What is striking though is how a casket intended by Bhuvanekabāhu VII to stand in Lisbon as a reminder of his and his successor's vassalage was given away at a time when Dharmapāla (1551–97), the king crowned on the front panel, was still on the throne and more reliant than ever on Portuguese support.[24] What remained in Lisbon after 1573 were the papers containing Bhuvanekabāhu's demands from 1541 along with a series of royal decrees responding to them, issued in 1543. An important shift was under way. The papers, which had not received an exposure comparable to the casket during the actual diplomatic events, now became the principal testimony of the arrangement. They were retained in the state archive – where they remain today – while the casket was allowed to leave and perform new diplomatic functions. This bifurcation may be indicative of the progressive bureaucratization of the imperial

[21] A remarkable corpus of such objects has been gathered in Gschwend and Beltz, *Elfenbeine aus Ceylon*.

[22] Lorenz Seelig, "Exotica in der Münchner Kunstkammer des Bayerischen Wittelsbacher," *Jahrbuch des Kunsthistorischen Museums Wien* 3 (2003): 148.

[23] Annemarie Jordan Gschwend, "Exotica for the Munich Kunstkammer. Anthonio Meyting: Fugger Agent, Art Dealer and Ducal Ambassador in Spain," in *Exotica: Kunstkammer Georg Laue* (Munich: Georg Laue, 2012), 21–22.

[24] It has been suggested that the queen lost interest in Lankan art after the middle of the century, when she began to look for objects from China and Japan instead. Annemarie Jordan Gschwend, "O fascínio de Cipango: Artes decorativas e lacas da Ásia Oriental em Portugal, Espanha e Áustria (1511–1598)," in *Os Construtores do Oriente Português* (Lisbon: CNCDP, 1998), 195–227. This shift alone, however, may not suffice to explain the dispatching of the casket in 1573.

administration, and a relative loss of power of objects such as the "coronation casket." The symbolic ascent of paperwork, now the key signifier of imperial reach, may have made other material remainders of diplomacy more dispensable at the Portuguese court than before.

KINGSHIP, CASKETS AND CONVERSIONS: SOME OTHER DIPLOMATIC IVORIES

As is often the case with objects falling under the category of "decorative arts" in museums today, even high-profile diplomatic gifts are difficult to track down in historical inventories since their descriptions tend to be generic. The "coronation casket" is the only one that can be unambiguously linked to a specific diplomatic event. A number of other caskets made their way from Sri Lanka to Europe during the sixteenth century, but their history remains shrouded in uncertainty. Different narratives have evolved as historians of art have attempted to make sense of them.

The best-known summary of the caskets was produced nearly two decades ago by Melanie Schwabe in an article coauthored with Amin Jaffer.[25] For Schwabe and Jaffer, there is a clear succession of caskets linked to the story of Luso-Lankan diplomacy. The first of these caskets, today in the Victoria and Albert Museum and known as the "Robinson casket," was possibly the earliest to display Christian motifs (Figure 3.3). It only seems right to read it in connection with the conversion, in 1557, of King Dharmapāla (r. 1551–97) to Catholicism.[26] While this event did not prompt a diplomatic episode comparable to that of 1542, it was closely connected with the earlier deal. On being baptized, Dharmapāla took the name of Dom João in honor of John III and pursued fundamentally the same objective as Bhuvanekabāhu VII had before: to offer tributary submission in exchange for Portuguese military support. By converting, Dharmapāla took things one significant step further, and that is precisely what the casket did, too. This time around, the carvers represented not just themes of kingship and overlordship, but also their religious conditions in the new Catholic imperial order. From the 1540s onward, Christianization had become a central and explicitly pursued objective of the Portuguese authorities. As an increasing number of Asian subjects opted for baptism,

[25] Jaffer and Schwabe, "A Group of Sixteenth-Century Ivory Caskets."

[26] Jaffer and Schwabe, "A Group of Sixteenth-Century Caskets," 8–10. Photographs of this casket are on the Victoria and Albert Museum's website at http://collections.vam.ac.uk/item/O18316/the-robinson-casket-casket-unknown/ (accessed 17 September 2016).

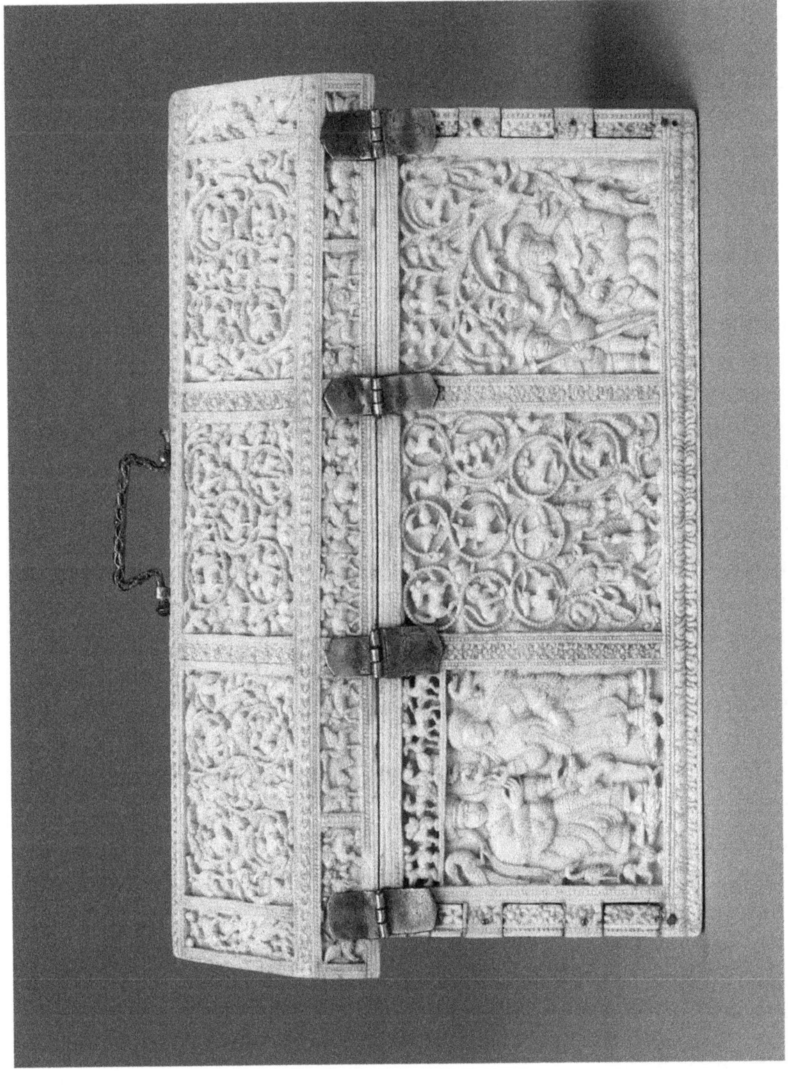

FIGURE 3.3. “Robinson casket” (rear panel), Kōṭṭe, Sri Lanka, c. 1557. London, Victoria and Albert Museum, Inv.-Nr. IS.41–1980.

questions were asked about the comparable value of being a Christian by birth (*generatio*) or by conversion (*regeneratio*).[27]

Birth and rebirth are indeed the central themes addressed by the "Robinson casket" with the help of Western and South Asian motifs.[28] Among the biblical references on the various panels of the caskets, the Betrothal of the Virgin, the Rest on the Flight to Egypt and a magnificent Tree of Jesse on one of the lateral panels stand out (see Figure 3.6; more on this below). A female head with a royal sunflower appears depicted on the lid, once in Sinhalese and once in European dress, suggesting the transformation of a Lankan queen – possibly Dharmapāla's first wife – into a Catholic figure. All this is accompanied by Lankan motifs revolving around the same topics, namely, a pair of *kinnaras*, half-human mythical being, the tails of which become beaded ropes known as "cords of life" encircling every creature in the world. On the lid, an unusual combination of regal lion bodies with symbolic *makara* heads further explores the link between kingship and creation/re-creation.[29] Such themes are best seen in connection with the conversion of a Lankan monarch and his need to affirm himself as a Catholic by *regeneratio* in the new imperial order.

Another casket, today in Berlin, has been dated by Schwabe to 1578–80. The first date refers to the disappearance and likely death of King Sebastian in Morocco, the second to the signing of the donation of Kōṭṭe by Dom João Dharmapāla, naming the Portuguese monarch as his successor to the Lankan throne. Here the majority of the iconographic program is Christian.[30] There are references to the Life of Christ and the Martyrdom of Sebastian as well as the attempted martyrdom of John the Evangelist – a barely veiled allusion to the continued attacks that Dom João Dharmapāla suffered throughout his reign, namely, from his Sītāvakan rival Rājasiṃha I (1578–93), the successor of Māyādunnē. A full reading of the twenty-two scenes on this casket has yet to be produced, but there is, again, a very plausible association between the

[27] Ângela Barreto Xavier, "Dissolver a Diferença – Conversão e Mestiçagem no Império Português," in *Itinerários: A Investigação nos 25 Anos do ICS*, ed. Manuel Villaverde, Karin Wall, Sofia Aboim and Filipe Carreira da Silva (Lisbon: Imprensa de Ciências Sociais, 2008), 709–27.

[28] Jaffer and Schwabe, "A Group of Sixteenth-Century Caskets," 9.

[29] Ibid., 9–10. Also see Meegama, "The Local and the Global."

[30] See Jaffer and Schwabe, "A Group of Sixteenth-Century Caskets." A picture of this casket can be found in the online collections database of the Museum für Asiatische Kunst at www.smb.museum/en/museums-institutions/museum-fuer-asiatische-kunst/home.html (accessed 17 September 2016).

object and a key event – the signing of the testamentary donation of Kōṭṭe in 1580 and the expressed hope that the vanished Sebastian may reappear. The casket could well have accompanied a copy of the testament as it was dispatched to Lisbon. It was on grounds of this donation that, after Dharmapāla's death in 1597, Phillip II of Spain became, as king of Portugal, the new king of Kōṭṭe.[31]

Both the 1557 and the 1580 caskets seem to have been ordered by Dom João Dharmapāla to express his commitment to Portuguese overlords and, thus, pursue his own agenda to obtain increased military support. At a time when sending full-blown embassies to Lisbon posed practical problems – such missions were costly for all parties involved, and indeed not encouraged by the Portuguese crown – the caskets themselves served as visual reminders, certainly accompanied by explanatory letters, of the importance of maintaining the old alliance between Lisbon and Kōṭṭe. There is scope to consider them not only as diplomatic gifts, but also as objects that travelled with a certain autonomy on diplomatic missions.

A sharp critique of the narrative proposed by Schwabe and Jaffer has been formulated recently by Annemarie Jordan Gschwend.[32] To Gschwend, the considerations summarized above call to be reexamined in the light of a closer reading of European royal inventories. In Gschwend's view, at least four or five of the high-quality caskets now extant in Europe must have been collected by Catherine of Habsburg during the 1540s. The merit of Gschwend's proposal is, as we shall see, that it reopens the debate for new considerations of chronology. The main problem is that a rich iconographic reading of the caskets themselves is challenged by means of references to usually very plain textual evidence extant in inventories, where no details other than the type of object ("a casket") and their materials are given. This is then an unresolved methodological issue, and, for the time being, the assumption that some of the high-end ivory caskets from Sri Lanka make most sense in conjunction with diplomatic developments over several decades remains as valid as the more recent thesis about the concentrated protagonism of Queen Catherine as a collector. Gschwend's suggestions are most valuable in that they encourage us to revisit the corpus and ask new questions of it.

31 On this transition, see Biedermann, *The Portuguese in Sri Lanka and South India*, 87–102.

32 Repeatedly in *Elfenbeine aus Ceylon*.

GIFTED COMMODITIES: CASKETS AND DIPLOMATIC COMPETITION

That nothing is set in stone is best illustrated by a rereading of two ivory caskets not mentioned so far, one preserved in Munich and the other in Vienna. The so-called second Munich casket has been placed by Schwabe, who here argues on grounds of the earlier work of the Portuguese scholars Luís Keil and Xavier Coutinho, in the context of a diplomatic mission launched by Māyādunnē, king of Sītāvaka, to lobby the Portuguese viceroy Dom João de Castro in the late 1540s (Figure 3.4). Only the association with Castro is tenable, however, and even this has been drawn into question by Gschwend.[33] Some motifs have been linked to a later cycle of tapestries commissioned by Castro to commemorate his victory over the Turks at Diu in 1548, today at the Kunsthistorisches Museum in Vienna, though the similarities are weak.[34] The bearded man sitting at a table may represent the viceroy himself, and the lady his wife Dona Leonor Coutinho – though other readings are possible identifying the latter figure as Bhuvanekabāhu VII, Māyādunnē, Śrī Rāmarakṣa or Proytila Rala, another diplomat from Kōṭṭe. In principle, the two figures could also be the Portuguese royal couple, John III and Catherine.

The casket displays numerous references to warfare, chivalry and kingship, but not a single Christian motif. If it was produced in Kōṭṭe, then it makes sense to assume that it must have been made before the death of the unbaptized Bhuvanekabāhu VII in 1551, or at the very latest during the early years of the reign of Dharmapāla, before he converted in 1557. The thesis of a royal patronage with a Buddhist background is reinforced by magnificent representations of Lankan kingship (the monarch sitting on a war elephant and on the imperial throne) on the two lateral panels of the casket.[35] Both are remarkably similar to those of the "coronation casket" and may well have been produced by the same workshop. The main argument in favor of a provenance from Kōṭṭe rather than Sītāvaka emerges once we place the "second Munich casket" in connection with another casket, held today

[33] On the front panel, a footman seems to carry a shield with the six *arruelas*, the symbol of the Castro family; cf. Luís Keil, "Influência artística portuguesa no Oriente. Três cofres de marfim indianos do século XVI," *Boletim da Academia Nacional de Belas-Artes* 2 (1938): 39–43.

[34] See *Tapeçarias de D. João de Castro* (Lisbon: CNCDP, 1995), esp. 44–45 for an overview of the tapestries.

[35] The elephant scene is similar – albeit with some differences – to the one that can be seen from an angle in Figure 3.1.

FIGURE 3.4 Second Munich casket (frontal view), probably Kōṭṭe, Sri Lanka, late 1540s. Munich, Bayerische Verwaltung der staatlichen Schlösser, Gärten und Seen, Residenz München, Schatzkammer, Inv.-Nr. 1242.

in Vienna (Figure 3.5). The latter, known as the "Rāmāyaṇa casket," has been recently redated by Annemarie Jordan Gschwend, who believes that it may be precisely a gift produced by Māyādunnē in the late 1540s. It could have been forwarded from Goa to Catherine, as other *exotica* were, and be identical with a casket appearing in the queen's 1550–55 inventory for the first time.[36]

We are here best advised, it seems, to read the objects in the context of a wider struggle involving competing diplomatic gifts. Dom João de Castro's term as viceroy between 1545 and 1548 fell into a period of intense diplomatic rivalry between Bhuvanekabāhu VII and Māyādunnē. While the former remained the sole formally recognized vassal of John III in Sri Lanka, his younger brother relentlessly pursued the objective of becoming a Portuguese vassal himself and then launching a reinvigorated attack on Kōṭṭe. An ambassador of Māyādunnē made it to Goa in November 1547,[37] and Bhuvanekabāhu was forced to send his own ambassador, a nephew of his, about a month or two later in order to counter the potentially damaging effects.[38] The "second Munich casket" makes most sense in this context as an object combining references to Bhuvanekabāhu VII as the supreme Lankan overlord, to Castro (or indeed John III) as the head of the Portuguese Empire in Asia and to motifs of chivalry, but also what seem to be more leisurely hunting scenes on the back of the casket. These vignettes, all of impeccable artistic quality, exude a firm command of the most distinguished iconographic traditions pertaining to kingship and nobility in Lanka *and* in Portugal. The hunting scenes in particular suggest familiarity and the possibility of mutual understandings grounded in common values and in a protracted relationship between the two dynasties.[39]

The "Rāmāyaṇa casket," in contrast, makes no references at all to the European visual idiom. If this is indeed a gift from Sītāvaka, then there is in this absence a striking honesty. Between Māyādunnē and the Portuguese, the

36 Gschwend and Beltz, *Elfenbeine aus Ceylon*, 70–71.

37 Cf. Register of the gifts sent by Māyādunnē to Dom João de Castro, Goa, November 27, 1547, published in Schurhammer and Voretzsch, *Ceylon*, 498.

38 Schurhammer and Voretzsch, *Ceylon*, 500. Which is not to say, evidently, that the casket was produced spontaneously at short notice – it must have been under preparation for a considerable amount of time, and indeed Māyādunnē may well have known about it.

39 Another line of inquiry would concern the numerous dancing scenes in this and other caskets (see for example the lid in Figure 3.1). On the perceived universality of dancing and the gesturing it involved during the medieval period, see Paul Zumthor, *La mesure du monde. Représentation de l'espace au Moyen Âge* (Paris: Seuil, 1993), 38–39.

FIGURE 3.5 "Rāmāyaṇa casket" (lateral panel), probably Sītāvaka, Sri Lanka, c. 1547. Vienna, Kunsthistorisches Museum, Kunskammer, Inv.-Nr. KK 4743.

relationship had been strained for decades. Sītāvaka maintained its abovementioned alliances with Hindu and Muslim enemies of the *Estado in India.* If a new alliance was to be built, there would have to be a fresh start. Much of the iconography on this casket is grounded in the Rāmāyaṇa and would have required verbal explanations by the king's ambassador when the gift was delivered in Goa. The tone is confidently bellicose with a slightly strident emphasis on legitimacy and unrightful dispossession. Māyādunnē was, after all, in principle the heir of Bhuvanekabāhu VII until the latter chose Dharmapāla to succeed him and John III decided to crown the child's effigy in 1542. The most remarkable aspect is perhaps how Māyādunnē, while having himself represented on a war elephant as Bhuvanekabāhu was on one lateral panel of the casket, did not include an image of himself on the imperial throne on the other. Perhaps an act of visual usurpation involving the throne would have been deemed excessive and counterproductive in the context of Lankan notions of kingship and ritual purity.[40]

On the lateral panel where the Munich caskets show Bhuvanekabāhu in full imperial glory, Māyādunnē opted for a very different motif. What we see here is not a monarch sitting on the lion throne, but Sīta, the principal female figure of the Rāmāyaṇa – after whom the city of Sītāvaka was named. This feminine reference may seem disconcerting, but the values associated with the spouse of Rāma may well have been what Māyādunnē wished to emphasize: dedication, self-sacrifice, purity, legitimacy and courage. Sīta accompanies Rāma into exile and undergoes, in the great epic, terrible trials before being made a queen – only to be sent away again in the end, unjustly accused of having been unfaithful. She is, in other words, a legitimate royal figure who has her moments of glory but is also forced into limbo by circumstances for which she bears no responsibility.[41]

The figure of Sīta calls for a complex reading. On the one hand, the Rāmāyaṇa's key female protagonist carries necessarily the message of her undeserved fall from grace. Through Sīta, Māyādunnē could allude to things as they were rather than as he wished them to be, skillfully striking a realistic tone at a time when the *Estado* discussed more pragmatically than before the possibilities of switching vassals in Ceylon. Presenting himself as the chief victim of decades of misunderstandings grounded in the perfidious diplomacy of Bhuvanekabāhu VII, Māyādunnē could attempt to make himself heard as the pure-at-heart, reliable ally that the Portuguese were looking for. He was the very man who, in the Lisbon agreement of 1542, had been unduly barred from succeeding on the Lankan imperial throne. It may well have been hoped in Sītāvaka that the dramatic tone of all this would relativize the fact that Māyādunnē, like Bhuvanekabāhu, still refused to convert.[42] Complementing such a reading, on the other hand, is the fact that the iconography of the casket,

[40] A detailed identification of the various Rāmāyaṇa scenes can be found in Gschwend and Beltz, *Elfenbeine aus Ceylon*, 70–71.

[41] See Jorrit Britschgi and Eberhard Fischer, *Rama und Sita: Das Ramayana in der Malerei Indiens* (Zurich: Museum Rietberg, 2008).

[42] This is in contrast with some disgruntled princes and the more peripheral king of Kandy, who began to promise baptism in exchange for support during the early 1540s. On ivory production in Kandy, see Martha Chaiklin, "Ivory in Early Modern Ceylon: A Case Study in What Documents Don't Reveal," *International Journal of Asian Studies* 6, no. 1 (2009): 37–63.

namely, the posture given to Sīta on the lateral panel, points to her triumph rather than her trials. Sīta did, after all, become the spouse of Rāma. In this vein, one could add to the previous considerations that Māyādunnē was striking an increasingly defiant, self-aggrandizing and forward-projecting tone. This was very much in line with his proactive diplomatic stance at a time when the Goan authorities manifested openness to a change in their regime of alliances. It also reflected the real accrual of Sītāvakan military power during this period.

The "Rāmāyaṇa casket" would have required explanations in a diplomatic context where the Goan elite had a limited grasp only of the stories of the great epic. It is not clear to what extent even Dom João de Castro, otherwise known for his appreciation of the South Asian art, would have fully understood the references on the casket without an interpreter. Observers in Goa less versed in Hindu mythology might simply have read the female figure as, say, an exotic personification of *Iustitia*[43] or an opaque piece of Asian luxuriousness *tout court*. What seems certain, however, is that studying these objects as Habsburg collectibles at one end of the exchange does not entitle us to neglect the complex political contexts that generated them at the other.

DID DÜRER MEET THE RĀMĀYAṆA? THE PROBLEM OF VALUE AND VALUES

As a picture emerges of how the study of diplomacy may add something to our understanding of early modern material culture and art, we must also ask ourselves how, inversely, insights from the history of material culture and art may enrich the way we study European-Asian diplomacy. Ivory caskets void of European imagery, Jaffer and Schwabe argued, could be assumed to be the oldest because, naturally, they originated before the European artistic influence reached them.[44] Yet the underlying notion of linear historical change is as problematic from

[43] I thank Barbara Karl for this suggestion.

[44] Jaffer and Schwabe, "A Group of Sixteenth-Century Caskets." A similar proposal is in Keil, "Influência artística portuguesa," 42. To be fair, the authors themselves admitted that this notion was a weak point in their theory. It can also be added that ultimately the political reading of the "coronation casket" itself does not change radically even if we assume, with Jaffer and Schwabe, that it may have been made after the embassy rather than before it.

an art historical point of view as from that of diplomatic history. It may seem straightforward to imagine how, at an early moment of the exchange, a Lankan king decided to present a "purely" South Asian casket to the Portuguese (for example, with scenes from the Rāmāyaṇa), and how then, over the years, new iconographic elements were introduced on other caskets (for example, a bagpiper taken from a Dürer print on the front panel of the "Robinson casket"). This is, after all, a story that seems to resonate with processes of exposure, adaptation and "hybridization" – a problematic but far from useless concept – in the arts and politics of Africa, America and Asia.[45] In West Africa, spectacular "hybrid" ivories were produced in the fifteenth and sixteenth centuries combining regional craftsmanship and materials with imagery of European origins. At the same time, African rulers and princes interacted diplomatically with the Portuguese.[46] But while it is logical to assume that no innovations of this kind could have existed before the arrival of Western travelers and motifs, the reverse argument is not tenable. Even after having produced an object including some Western elements, or after having exchanged ambassadors with a Western monarch, a workshop could perfectly go back to producing other objects without them, and a ruler could return to his old alliances. These were matters of choice.

Agency is a contentious topic across early colonial history. The agency of African and Asian craftspeople (and by extension their diplomatically engaged patrons) has been persistently minimized by art historians who have here, perhaps more than in any other subfield, clung to an outdated vocabulary built around a hierarchical notion of "influence."[47] For the Portuguese art historian Nuno Vassallo e Silva, for example, there can be

45 On the problems raised by the term "hybridity," see Carolyn Dean and Dana Leibsohn, "Hybridity and Its Discontents: Considering Visual Culture in Colonial Spanish America," *Colonial Latin American Review* 12, no. 1 (2003): 5–35.

46 For an introduction, see Peter Mark, "Portugal in West Africa: The Afro-Portuguese Ivories," in *Encompassing the Globe: Portugal and the World in the 16th and 17th Centuries*, 3 vols., ed. Jay Levenson (Washington, DC: Freer & Sackler Gallery, 2007), 2: 77–85. A more recent overview is in Kate Lowe, "Made in Africa: West African Luxury Goods for Lisbon's Markets," in *The Global City: On the Streets of Renaissance Lisbon*, ed. Annemarie Jordan Gschwend and K. J. P. Lowe (London: Paul Holberton, 2015), 163–77.

47 Peter Mark has recently suggested the term "Luso-African" to replace "Afro-Portuguese" because it reflects more accurately the origins of these objects. "Towards a Reassessment of the Dating and the Geographical Origins of the Luso-African Ivories," *History in Africa* 34 (2007): 189–90. Similarly, "Luso-Lankan" might here be more appropriate than "Indo-Portuguese" or "Sri Lankan Portuguese."

no doubt that the same commissioners sitting in Lisbon determined the making of ivories in West Africa and in Sri Lanka, and that this is, in essence, the story to be told.[48] Once this sort of chronologically anterior, hierarchically superior Portuguese agency is established in our imagination, the complex reception and adaptation of Western imagery by Asian carvers is easily reduced to a unidirectional process by which Asian artists and patrons were made to churn out passive and uncritical imitations of European inventions. In fact, it is only a small step from here to affirming that Asians did not understand what they were doing, combining European motifs "in an apparently random manner, without a coherent repertoire."[49]

Only very recently has this argumentation been challenged for the Sri Lankan case by the art historian Sujatha Meegama. To avoid perpetuating traditional interpretative schemes, Meegama argues, we should start by replacing the word "influence" by "appropriation."[50] Rather than stating that Lankan artists "followed faithfully" a model from a European "source" or proceeded to a "direct reproduction,"[51] we need to acknowledge that the inspiration derived from a foreign model stood in a wider context of artistic and political selection and (re)creation. Of course, motifs were copied, as they were throughout history in many parts of the world including Europe, but by whom, how, why and what for? If insisting on the push factors subjacent to diffusionist theories of empire and of art is problematic, should we not explore more vigorously the pull factors that made the appropriation of certain motifs by people in Africa, Asia and the Americas possible? What exactly would the perceived difference be, in Sri Lanka (and also in Portugal), between a "purely" South Asian object and one that made use of some European imagery?

48 Nuno Vassallo e Silva, "'Ingenuity and Excellence': Ivory Art in Ceylon," in *Ivories in the Portuguese Empire*, ed. Gauvin Alexander Bailey, Jean Michel Massing and Nuno Vassallo e Silva (Lisbon: Scribe, 2013), 89–141, in particular p. 99.

49 Silva on the "Robinson casket" in "Ingenuity and Excellence," 93.

50 Meegama, "The Local and the Global," here refers to three key texts: Robert S. Nelson, "Appropriation," in *Critical Terms for Art History*, 2nd ed. (Chicago and London: University of Chicago Press, 2003); Michael Baxandall, *Patterns of Intention on the Historical Explanation of Pictures* (New Haven and London: Yale University Press, 1985), 59; and Senake Bandaranayake, "Sri Lanka and Monsoon Asia: Patterns of Local and Regional Architectural Development and the Problem of the Traditional Sri Lankan Roof," in *Senerat Paranavitana Commemorative Volume*, ed. Leelananda Prematilleke et al., Studies in South Asian Culture, vol. 7 (Leiden: Brill, 1978), 22–44.

51 Silva, "Ingenuity and Excellence," 93.

How long after being included in a Lankan object would an imported motif cease to be European and become Asian? What can these caskets tell us about the translatability of values and the connectability – or even the universality – of visual idioms, the key conditions for the successful conduction of diplomacy?

To tackle such questions, a seemingly minor, but in fact key art historical concept requires to be discussed as well. Along with the placement of European above Asian agency, art historians have operated with a simplistic notion of ornamentality. Western motifs thus appear to have been "curiously adapted within the Singhalese style of ivory, with the rich texture of clothes, and the filling of backgrounds with other human figures, as well as animals."[52] The contrast is not just between the "figurative" and the "ornamental," but between an art that carries meaning opposed to one that, even in depicting the human body, is incapable of autonomous thought. The suggestion is that there were elements of a higher tradition (for example, an image originally created by Dürer) rendered in an idiom of a lower tradition that excelled, essentially, at the technical level, and could handle Western inputs only through dexterous, but ultimately passive imitation.[53]

Apart from recognizing the evident shortcomings of such notions, the truly disquieting challenge is to further explore the matter of "ornament," not on grounds of an ill-informed, anachronistic aesthetics of the Lankan ivories, but by engaging with the artistic and diplomatic discourses that surrounded them in the sixteenth century.[54] On the Lankan side, visual elements that have been misunderstood by Western art historians as mere decoration can tell stories of great subtlety and complexity. As Sujatha Meegama has argued, the Tree of Jesse on the "Robinson casket" (itself an interesting adaptation of a famous print first produced in Paris in 1499, not a copy) is best read in connection with the equally impressive, but generally ignored panel on the opposite end of the casket (Figures 3.6 and 3.7). The latter, structurally similar

[52] Silva, "Ingenuity and Excellence," 93.

[53] See for example Silva, "Ingenuity and Excellence," 98. Note that a more complex view was given already in 1938 by Luís Keil, who described the Munich caskets as the product of carvers who "insisted on a symbolist Hindu decoration, with exuberance and meticulousness" and used "European themes" as "details" signaling certain historical events ("Influência artística portuguesa," 42).

[54] On the problems caused by the assumption that aesthetics are a prerogative of Western art, see Valerie Gonzalez, *Beauty and Islam: Aesthetics in Islamic Art and Architecture* (London: I. B. Tauris, 2001).

FIGURE 3.6 “Robinson casket” (lateral panel), Kōṭṭe, Sri Lanka, c. 1557. London, Victoria and Albert Museum, Inv.-Nr. IS.41–1980.

and conceptually equivalent to the Tree of Jesse motif, has a pair of vines coming out of the mouths of two makara-headed lions at the bottom of the scene. This, Meegama shows, is as powerful a reference to the founder of the Lankan royal lineage, Vijaya (born from the union of a woman and a lion) as the Tree of Jesse is to the founder of the royal lineage leading through David to Jesus. The animals, placed on the vines as kings are in the Tree of Jesse, all carry specific auspicious associations. What we are looking at is then a very sophisticated piece of diplomatic artwork creating a profoundly meaningful dialogue with its Judeo-Christian counterpart at the very moment of Dom João Dharmapala’s conversion to Catholicism. Overall, its message is one of symmetry and

FIGURE 3.7 "Robinson casket" (lateral panel), Kōṭṭe, Sri Lanka, c. 1557. London, Victoria and Albert Museum, Inv.-Nr. IS.41–1980.

mutual intertwinement rather than rupture or the imposition of a new hierarchical order.[55] We are, again, in the presence of a diplomatic dialogue carved in ivory.

One cannot, of course, be certain that Portuguese observers in the sixteenth century did not regard the Lankan vines and animals with similar disinterest as twentieth-century art historians have done. But we need to consider at least the possibility that this was not the case. Renaissance observers were inclined to acknowledge that they stood face to face

[55] Meegama, "The Local and the Global."

in South Asia with an artistic tradition of the highest possible sophistication. A number of Portuguese travelers and decision-makers regarded Indian sculpture in particular with great admiration. To be sure, their descriptions could easily be misread as reflecting an appreciation of craftsmanship in the reductive sense observed above. Take for example one of the most remarkable descriptions of South Indian art in the account written by the traveler Domingos Pais after a visit to Vijayanagara, around 1520–22. Pais was in awe as he walked into "a room ... all of ivory, as well the chamber as the walls, from top to bottom, and the pillars of the cross-timbers at the top had roses and flowers of lotuses all of ivory, and all well executed, so that there could not be better, – it is so rich and beautiful that you would hardly find anywhere another such."[56] But this appreciation needs to be placed in conjunction, from the 1530s, with another development that carried wider cultural implications.

During the reign of John III, a strong classicist current shaped the visual culture of the Portuguese courtly elite and their perception of Asian arts. It has been pointed out that the viceroy Dom João de Castro observed Indian architecture through the lens of Vitruvius,[57] and that with him others may have sensed strong commonalities between classical ideals and the round-bossed forms of Indian sculpture.[58] Castro's description of the caves at Elephanta Island are a spectacular example of early cross-cultural admiration.[59] While no similar comments survive in the written record regarding Sri Lanka, it is very likely that the caskets brought to Goa and Lisbon in the 1540s elicited a strong appreciation precisely on these two grounds: the exceptionally high technical standard of their execution, along with an ability to represent the human body in proximity to Renaissance ideals – and hence with commensurate artistic

[56] Translation from Robert Sewell, *A Forgotten Empire (Vijayanagar): A Contribution to the History of India* (1900, reprint, New Delhi and Madras: Asian Educational Service, 2001), 285–86.

[57] Rafael Moreira, "Dom João de Castro e Vitrúvio," in *Tapeçarias de D. João de Castro* (Lisbon: MNAA, 1995), 51–56.

[58] Paulo Varela Gomes, "Perspectives of World Art Research: Form, Recognition and Empathy," paper presented at the 2012 Opler Conference, Worcester College, Oxford. I wish to thank the author, now deceased, for sharing this material. Also see Zoltán Biedermann, "Imagining Asia from the Margins: Early Portuguese Mappings of the Continent's Architecture and Space," in *Architecturalized Asia: Mapping the Continent through Architecture and Geography*, ed. V. Rujivacharakul, H. H. Hahn, K. T. Oshima and P. Christensen (Hong Kong: Hong Kong University Press, 2013), 35–51.

[59] A. Fontoura da Costa, ed., *Roteiros de D. João de Castro*, 3 vols. (Lisbon: Agência Geral das Colónias, 1940), 2: 52–53.

standards as sculpture in the West. The volume and depth of the figures, the highly accomplished play with light and shadow, the combination of fair proportions and energetic yet controlled movement, along with a sustained (and indeed unrivalled) attention to detail, all combined into an art that could not but gain appreciation.

These considerations bear relevance for our understanding of the value of the Lankan ivory caskets. The overall value of a diplomatic gift such as the "coronation casket" or the "second Munich casket" resulted from a combination of a multiplicity of factors ranging from the quantifiable to the unmeasurable. At the most fundamental level, it seems very reasonable to assume that labor and matter constituted parts of the value of any object. It does not take a Marxist conviction to see that, especially at a time when patronage involved a tight control of labor but, concurrently, highly skilled labor was hard to come by, an object made in a royal workshop over thousands of hours was in itself almost inevitably very valuable. The fact that this work was done in ivory, a material of a recognized inherent value across cultures in Europe, Africa and Asia, only consolidated the value created by labor.[60] To this, one has to add mutual aesthetic appreciation, in connection with the wider commonalities of European and Asian court societies. It was, as Sanjay Subrahmanyam has pointed out, an encounter not between "peoples" of the two continents in which such objects changed hands, but between courtly elites sharing a number of social and cultural values.[61] However exotic the pose of Bhuvanekabāhu VII on the lion throne may have been to Portuguese eyes, the royal status of the ruler depicted was evident, the quality of the artwork impeccable and the links between this figure and the coronation scenes on the front panel forceful. However exotic the animals populating the friezes above and below the hunting scene in the "second Munich casket" may have seemed, the act of hunting as such was a shared interest of European and Asian nobilities and closely connected with the military ethos.[62]

[60] The provenance of the ivory used for the caskets is unclear, though there is a strong possibility that for several of them African material was used. The whiter color of the Vienna casket may indicate a Lankan workshop with limited access to foreign ivory (Gschwend and Beltz, *Elfenbeine aus Ceylon*, 71).

[61] *Courtly Encounters: Translating Courtliness and Violence in Early Modern Eurasia* (Cambridge, MA: Harvard University Press, 2012).

[62] See Thomas T. Allsen, *The Royal Hunt in Eurasian History* (Philadelphia: University of Pennsylvania Press, 2006).

If elements taken from the Western tradition were used to depict the chivalrous confrontation of two horsemen (as in Figure 3.4), then this would be necessarily appreciated by Portuguese observers not as a random imitative ornament, but as a conscious and suitable nod, a bridge between two societies facing each other in diplomacy, war, trade and other forms of exchange. Shared social values contributed to the creation and recognition of sharable notions of artistic and diplomatic value. In close connection with the latter, though at a slightly more abstract level, the value of specific gifts also depended on their handling in politically charged contexts, mainly in moments of high diplomacy involving rulers with commensurable imperial ambitions. In those moments, the said and the unsaid were necessarily intertwined. Political ideas are likely to have been uttered in the guise of explanations regarding the iconography, while majesty as such – like the high material and artistic value of these caskets – required no comments.

Crucially in these objects, all indicators of value seem to have been relevant both at the point of origin and at the port of destination. It becomes inevitable to ask whether the notion of distinct "regimes of value" is not of limited bearing in comparison to that of "mechanisms of commensuration" mediating between them.[63] While one might think that the aura of a regime of high diplomacy was easily effaced again once the object was de- and recontextualized as, for example, a simple curiosity in a Renaissance *Wunderkammer*, the history of the "coronation casket" suggests otherwise. It rather looks as if the value of this particular object never increased nor decreased very steeply as it was transported from Kōṭṭe to Goa, Lisbon and finally Munich. The combined impact of a high-end artistic production closely linked with royalty, a series of images pertaining to matters of state, along with a highly dramatized reception at a royal court made sure that the original aura (and not just the aura of the original) never quite vanished.[64] Perhaps it was precisely the fact that

[63] See Jean Comaroff and John Comaroff, "Beasts, Banknotes and the Colour of Money," *Archaeological Dialogues* 12 (2005): 107–32.

[64] Note that one instance at least of monetary valuation is documented in an inventory of the collections of Phillip II, the price of an ivory casket from South Asia here being given as 150 ducats. In the same inventory, a painting by Hieronymus Bosch was valued at 6 ducats, but a portrait of the monarch and his son Charles, painted by Titian, at 200 ducats (Silva, "Ingenuity and Excellence," p. 101). It is far from clear what we can conclude from these figures, but at present they seem to confirm the very high value of caskets and Annemarie Jordan Gschwend's intuition that royal courts remained the natural habitat of such artifacts throughout the sixteenth century.

value was here consolidated through a very specific, politically loaded exchange, a zone of highly charged communication, that mattered. This would then be a case of an overarching, transcultural regime of value itself being "built *through* the intercultural and international exchange."[65]

Before we conclude, a caveat is due though regarding the limits of early modern connectivity. Even within such a reduced corpus of highly "political" caskets as those preserved in Munich and in Vienna, there may be a gradation with complex implications. It could be that the continuum of value as we observe it in the two Munich caskets depended precisely on the controlled inclusion of some pictorial elements that would be immediately readable for sixteenth-century Europeans as not just commensurate to Western traditions, but taken directly from the Western visual repertoire. It may well have been these specific elements that drove the reception of certain caskets, easing the way for European eyes into a world of less familiar stories. Without such anchors, the observers might not only have felt lost, they could also have refrained from engaging with the iconography altogether. However stunning its imagery may be, the "Rāmāyaṇa casket" now attributed to the royal workshop at Sītāvaka has not come near, to this day, to achieving the symbolic status of its "hybrid" or "composite" counterparts in Munich. Whether this is down to it having come from a king not recognized as a vassal in Lisbon, or to being entirely void of graspable Western visual elements, we cannot know for sure. Nor is it clear when exactly it became just another piece of South Asian craft in a European *Kunstkammer* and the later Kunsthistorisches Museum, since the history of the perceptions of such objects in sixteenth- to nineteenth-century Europe is barely known. The only certainty is that, as an original diplomatic gift, the casket calls to be reconnected now curatorially with its distant, politically loaded past.

CONCLUSION

The inclusion of motifs that still tend to be seen as "European" on objects made in Asia for the global diplomatic marketplace can be understood in two different ways. At one level, such innovations can be read as a sign

[65] Laurier Turgeon, "Crossing Boundaries: Regimes of Value in Intercultural Colonial Contexts. Reflections on Jean and John Comaroff's 'Beasts, Banknotes and the Colour of Money,'" *Archaeological Dialogues* 12 (2005): 136 (my emphasis).

not of the fragility of their commissioners and makers, but of high diplomatic capabilities, of deliberate choices and of a remarkable sense of empathy and strategy as objects were dispatched to perform diplomatic missions on the other side of the globe. It may have been precisely through the controlled incorporation of the foreign that Lankan (and particularly Kōṭṭe-based) diplomatic and artistic agency came into full bloom. In fact, one is compelled to note that it was the European elite that often stood by passively, watching casket after casket reaching its courts without being able to control their making or even fully read the stories they told. On the other hand, we are again well advised not to overstretch this argument. The appearance of pictorial elements and themes taken from Western art does signal quite clearly the beginnings of a global power imbalance, at least in this specific case. It was the rulers of Sri Lanka who courted the Portuguese monarchs with exquisite diplomatic gifts after all, and not the other way around.[66]

Sadly enough, Dürer did not quite meet the Rāmāyaṇa in the end. The famous bagpiper appears on the "Robinson casket," which makes no reference to the epic, and also on another casket predominantly displaying motifs taken from Western models, now in a private collection in Paris.[67] This being said, we are still awaiting a systematic survey of Lankan ivory caskets. A thorough comparison of these objects with other manifestations of sixteenth-century Lankan and South Indian sculptural practice is still outstanding. Stories of great significance may be hiding in the numerous vignettes covering the caskets – and indeed, perhaps, on other objects such as fans and combs – most of which await a full and thorough investigation.[68] New connections will inevitably surface. For the time being, this incursion into the history of a handful of caskets may suffice to whet our appetites. It exemplifies how examining art objects as diplomatic gifts may help us understand their iconographies, and vice versa. The new readings are worthwhile if through

[66] This said, we know nothing about the ways in which for example churches in sixteenth-century Sri Lanka may have gone through similar processes of visual blending and adaptation.

[67] The Paris casket is analyzed in Gschwend and Beltz, *Elfenbeine aus Ceylon*, 60–69.

[68] A single, spectacular ivory casket with scenes from the Rāmāyaṇa survives in the collection of the University of Peradeniya and has only recently been pictured in Meegama, "The Local and the Global." New finds are also described in Alan Chong, "Sri Lankan Ivories for the Dutch and Portuguese," *Journal of Historians of Netherlandish Art* 5, no. 2 (2013), DOI:10.5092/jhna.2013.5.2.16. Online at www.jhna.org/index.php/past-issues/volume-5-issue-2–2013/208-sri-lankan-ivories-for-the-dutch-and-portuguese (accessed 6 October 2016).

them we gain access to a hitherto overlooked universe of cross-cultural encounters and exchanges that all contributed – by connecting the courts of Europe and Asia as, in the words of Norbert Elias, the "communicating organs" of a larger body – to the making of the early modern world.[69]

[69] Norbert Elias, *Über den Prozeß der Zivilisation: Soziogenetische und psychogenetische Untersuchungen*, 2nd ed., 2 vols. (Frankfurt: Suhrkamp Verlag, 1969), 2: 5.

4

Objects of Prestige and Spoils of War

Ottoman Objects in the Habsburg Networks of Gift-Giving in the Sixteenth Century

Barbara Karl

After the Hungarian defeat at Mohács in 1526, the Habsburg and Ottoman Empires became direct neighbors. For the Austrian Habsburgs the ensuing confrontation was a matter of survival, as their very existence was challenged. The year 1529 saw Sultan Süleyman (1494–1566) at the gates of Vienna. For the Ottomans it was a conflict on the fringes of their territory, complemented by expansionist moves in the Middle East and the Mediterranean.[1] From the battle of Mohács to 1547 the dealings between the two empires revolved mostly around the question of Hungary, a fragmented polity that both claimed. The peace treaty of 1547/48 stabilized the situation to some extent. From that time, the Habsburgs kept a permanent resident in Constantinople and agreed to send, albeit reluctantly, yearly honorific gifts/tribute to the Ottoman court.[2] The following decades saw new rulers on the thrones of both empires,

The author wishes to thank the FWF-The Austrian Science Fund, Zoltán Biedermann, Bert Fragner, Anne Gerritsen, Giorgio Riello and Karlo Ruzicic-Kessler.

[1] Still valid in many aspects on the history of the contact between the two empires: Joseph von Hammer-Purgstall, *Geschichte des osmanischen Reiches* (1829; reprint, Graz: Akademische Druck- und Verlagsanstalt, 1963), vol. 3. More general: Halil Inalcik, *The Ottoman Empire: The Classical Age 1300–1600* (New York and Washington: Weidenfeld and Nicolson, 1973); Klaus Kreiser, *Der osmanische Staat 1300–1922* (München: Oldenbourg Wissenschaftsverlag, 2001); Suraiya Faroqui, *The Ottoman Empire and the World around It* (London and New York: I. B. Tauris, 2004).

[2] Described at length by Hammer-Purgstall, *Geschichte*, vol. 3. See also Anton Schaendlinger, "Der diplomatische Verkehr zwischen Österreich und der Hohen Pforte im Zeitalter Süleymans des Prächtigen, in *Kultur des Islam*, ed. Otto Mazal (Vienna: Österreichische Nationalbibliothek, 1981), 91–104.

regular renegotiations of the fragile peace and overall the preservation of the status quo.[3] The balance of power between the two empires remained asymmetric, though, at least until the Long War of 1593–1606 and the ensuing peace of Zsitvatorok in 1606. It was the latter that established the two parties as equal players and inaugurated a new era of interimperial diplomacy. This study is concerned with the period from the battle of Mohács to the agreements of Zsitvatorok, as this allows us to engage with diplomatic gifts and other moving objects in a politically ambiguous context dominated by the Ottomans.[4]

The question of tribute is key in this regard. For about eight decades, the Habsburg emperors were obliged to send 30,000 ducats and numerous other gifts to Constantinople every year. While the sultan and his retinue viewed these as tribute and confirmation of their status as the higher imperial authority, the Habsburgs attempted to frame them as honorific gifts. Considering the Habsburg as well as the Ottoman side Ernst Petritsch has drawn attention to the terminology surrounding what we now see as gifts and/or tribute in the Habsburg-Ottoman context, but little is known about the way these ambiguities played out with regard to the actual objects that were gifted.[5] This is, then, one of the gaps the present study seeks to address.

The asymmetry of power during the period in question translates into archival asymmetries, though these run along rather complex fault lines. Overall, the reports of imperial emissaries tell more about their experiences at the Ottoman court than what we know about the receptions of

[3] Ralf C. Müller, "Der umworbene 'Erbfeind': Habsburgische Diplomatie an der Hohen Pforte von Maximilian I. bis zum langen Türkenkrieg," in *Das osmanische Reich und die Habsburgermonarchie*, ed. Marlene Kurz, Martin Scheuz, Karl Vocelka et al. (Vienna and Munich: Oldenbourg, 2005), 251–80; Jan Paul Niederkorn, *Die europäischen Mächte und der lange Türkenkrieg'Kaiser Rudolfs II. 1593–1606* (Vienna: Verlag der Akademie der Wissenschaften, 1993); see also Günes Isiksel, "Ottoman-Habsburg Relations in the Second Half of the 16th Century: The Ottoman Standpoint," in *Frieden und Konfliktmanagement in interkulturellen Räumen: Das Osmanische Reich und die Habsburgermonarchie in der Frühen Neuzeit*, ed. Arno Strohmeyer and Norbert Spannenberger (Stuttgart: Franz Steiner Verlag, 2013), 51–62; Jan Paul Niederkorn, "'Friedenspolitik' in Constantinople im Vorfeld des langen Türkenkriegs," in *Frieden und Konfliktmanagement*, ed. Strohmeyer and Spannberger, 95–108.

[4] See, for example, Gustav Beyerle, "The Compromise at Zsitvatorok," *Archivium Ottomanicum* 6 (1980): 5–53; Markus Köhbach, "Caesar oder Imperator? Zur Titulatur der römischen Kaiser durch die Osmanen nach dem Vertrag von Zsitvatorok," *Viennaer Zeitschrift für die Kunde des Morgenlandes* 82 (1992): 223–34.

[5] Ernst Petritsch, "Tribut oder Ehrengeschenk," in *Archiv und Forschung Viennaer Beiträge zur Geschichte der Neuzeit*, 20, ed. Elisabeth Springer and Leopold Kammerhofer (Vienna: Verl. f. Geschichte und Politik, 1993), 49–85.

Ottoman emissaries at the Habsburg court. While the Habsburg embassies to Constantinople in the sixteenth century are partly documented in Habsburg sources, Ottoman accounts are rather silent when it comes to imperial ambassadors in Constantinople during the period under consideration, suggesting that the sultans were not particularly interested in the Habsburgs in this regard.[6] Indeed, Hedda Reindl-Kiel points out that Ottoman sources were remarkably silent in general about European diplomatic gifts, arguably because these were not deemed valuable enough to be seen as enhancing the status of the sultans.[7] This being said, we do know what kinds of gifts Habsburg envoys took to Constantinople as a complement to the annual payments. Imperial officials had rather clear ideas about what would be well received in Constantinople's court circles. Apart from money the Habsburgs gifted, somewhat repetitively, silver articles, clocks and automata, mirrors, falcons and dogs. They presented these not only to the sultan but also to his entourage and knew about personal inclinations or even specific requests from the Porte.[8] This is in tune with what Luca Molà argues in the present volume regarding Venice, though we have so far no comparable evidence for Central European technological innovation driven by Ottoman requests.

Much less is known about what came the other way, even though it is quite certain that most Ottoman messengers sent to Vienna did not come empty handed.[9] Reports by Ottoman emissaries to the Habsburg

[6] Faroqhi, *Ottoman Empire*, 6; Harriett Rudolph, "Türkische Gesandtschaften ins Reich am Beginn der Neuzeit: Herrschaftsinszenierung, Fremdheitserfahrung und Erinnerungskultur: Die Gesandtschaft des Ibrahim Bey von 1562," in *Das osmanische Reich*, ed. Kurz, Scheuz and Vocelka, 296.

[7] Hedda Reindl-Kiel, "Der Duft der Macht: Osmanen, islamische Tradition, muslimische Mächte und der Westen im Spiegel diplomatischer Geschenke," *Viennaer Zeitschrift für die Kunde des Morgenlandes* 95 (2005): 225.

[8] Hammer-Purgstall, *Geschichte*, vol. 3, 223, 236, 271, 274, 275, 274, 331; Tim Stanley, "Ottoman Gift Exchange-Royal Give and Take," in *Gifts of the Sultan. The Arts of Giving at the Islamic Courts*, ed. Linda Komaroff (New Haven: Yale University Press, 2011), 149–66; Rudolf Neck, ed., *Österreich und die Osmanen: gemeinsame Ausstellung der Österreichischen Nationalbibliothek und des Österreichischen Staatsarchivs* (Vienna: Österr. Staatsdruckerei, 1983); 65–66, 68–69, and 71–72; Peter Burschel, "Der Sultan und das Hündchen: Zur politischen Ökonomie des Schenkens in interkultureller Perspektive," *Historische Anthropologie* 15 (2007): 408–21; Reindl-Kiel, "Duft der Macht," 216–17.

[9] Hammer-Purgstall, *Geschichte*, vols. 3 and 4; Neck, *Österreich und die Osmanen*; Hedda Reindl-Kiel, "East Is East and West Is West, and Sometimes the Twain Did Meet: Diplomatic Gift Exchange in the Ottoman Empire," in *Frontiers of Ottoman Studies: State, Province and the West*, ed. Colin Imber, Keiko Kiyotaki and Rhoads Murphey (London and New York: I. B. Tauris, 2005), 113–24; Peter Burschel, "Der Sultan und das

dominions survive only from the eighteenth century onward. As for the *Zeremonialprotokolle* (documents on ceremonial protocol) preserved in the Haus- Hof- und Staatsarchiv, where one would expect diplomatic receptions at Vienna to be described, they cover the period only from 1652 onward.[10] For earlier times, Habsburg narrative sources offer little elaboration when it comes to detailing gifts from the sultans, maybe because, as we shall see, they had the potential of throwing a rather humiliating light on the situation of the emperors. Italian archives, in their turn (Venice and the Vatican both had residents in Vienna who could have reported on diplomatic receptions), remain largely untapped as a source for Habsburg-Ottoman history.[11]

What does survive beyond the scattered written evidence on gifts made by the Ottomans during the sixteenth century[12] is a rich corpus of objects. It is in this regard that the surviving inventories of the households of various Habsburg family members prove very valuable. Numerous Ottoman objects dated to the sixteenth century survive in the imperial collections and are today in the museums of Vienna and Ambras Castle near Innsbruck. They are material witnesses to an intensifying, multilayered exchange between two empires, and can now be used to shed light on the different layers of gift-giving between the Habsburg and Ottoman courts during the second half of the sixteenth century.

A word is in place here regarding the agents who carried the objects. The asymmetry of power was reflected in the choice of personnel.

Hündchen," 412–13; Elisabeth Schmuttermeier, "Zum Schenken verpflichtet," in *Global: Lab Kunst als Botschaft, Asien und Europa 1500–1700*, ed. Peter Noever (Ostfildern: Hatje Cantz, 2009), 202–4.

10 On related documents in the Haus-, Hof- und Staatsarchiv, Vienna: Neck, *Österreich und die Osmanen*; Leopold Auer, "Diplomatisches Zeremoniell am Kaiserhof der Frühen Neuzeit," in *Diplomatisches Zeremoniell in Europa und im Mittleren Osten in der frühen Neuzeit*, ed. Ralf Kauz, Giorgio Rota and Jan Paul Niederkorn (Vienna: Verl. d. Österr. Akademie d. Wissenschaften, 2009), 38.

11 See, for example, Elisabeth Garms-Cornides, "'Per sostenere il decoro': Beobachtungen zum Zeremoniell des päpstlichen Nuntius in Vienna im Spannungsfeld von Diplomatie und Liturgie," in *Diplomatisches Zeremoniell*, ed. Kauz, Rota and Niederkorn, 97 and 98.

12 There is more information on the gifts given by the Ottomans during the seventeenth century: Burschel, "Der Sultan und das Hündchen," 408–21; Hedda Reindl-Kiel, "Pracht und Ehre: Zum Geschenkwesen im Osmanischen Reich," in *Das osmanische Reich in seinen Archivalien und Chroniken*, ed. Klaus Kreiser and Christoph K. Neumann (Stuttgart: Franz Steiner Verl., 1997), 161–89. See also Hedda Reindl-Kiel, "Symbolik, Selbstbild und Beschwichtigungsstrategien: Diplomatische Geschenke der Osmanen für den Viennaer Hof (17.-18. Jahrhundert)," in *Frieden und Konfliktmanagement*, ed. Strohmeyer and Spannberger, 265–82.

Contrary to the emperor, who sent relatively high-ranking officials to Constantinople, the sultan sent but simple emissaries (*tschausch* or *çavuş*) and occasionally a court translator, all with narrowly defined duties, as bearers of letters and different drafts of treatises. The peace negotiations generally took place at the court of the sultan, clearly indicating again the inferior status of the Austrian Habsburgs in the official view of the sultan.[13] This must have been particularly problematic for the Habsburgs since, with the exception of Ferdinand I (1503–64) before the abdication of his brother Charles V (1500–1558), they were all Holy Roman Emperors in name and adhered to an aggressively universalist concept of religiously sanctioned universal rule comparable, in theory, to that of the Ottoman sultans.[14] To them, the dealings up to 1606 were essentially humiliating. Ambassadors and envoys on both sides tended to be experienced men with a highly cosmopolitan background. Many of the sultan's messengers were recent converts, and often made splendid international careers in the service of the Porte. One has to bear in mind here how closely connected Vienna, Venice, Ragusa and Constantinople were through a tightly knit network of information channels, and what a heterogeneous group of people the different emissaries were. The emperors sent Italians, Dalmatians, Croatians, Flemish, Catholic as well as Protestant subjects. In the sultan's service were mostly converted Bavarians, Styrians, Poles, Hungarians, Italians, Albanians, Bosnians and the like. Habsburg and Ottoman emissaries often negotiated in their native languages.[15] While nothing is known about the way they talked about gifts, it certainly does bear relevance for the present study that these individuals would have an ample knowledge regarding the material cultures of both the Habsburg and the Ottoman spheres.

[13] Karl Teply, "Türkische Gesandtschaften nach Vienna (1488–1792)," *Österreich in Geschichte und Literatur* 20, no. 1 (1976): 17 and 18. For example: Hammer-Purgstall, *Geschichte*, vol. 3, 108.

[14] Franz Bosbach, *Monarchia universalis: ein politischer Leitbegriff der frühen Neuzeit* (Göttingen: Vandehoeck & Ruprecht, 1988); Sanjay Subrahmanyam, "Tale of Three Empires: Mughals, Ottomans, and Habsburgs in a Comparative Context," *Common Knowledge* 12, no. 1 (2006): 66–92.

[15] Josef Mautz, "Die Pfortendolmetscher zur Zeit Suleymans des Prächtigen," *Südost-Forschungen* 34 (1975): 26–60; Hammer-Purgstall, *Geschichte*, vol. 4, 25 and 26. For insights on the network of Habsburg agents, see also Neck, *Österreich und die Osmanen*, 33–34; Alexander H. de Groot, "Dolmetscher und Dragomane 1700–1869: Zum Verlust ihrer interkulturellen Funktion," in *Das osmanische Reich und die Habsburgermonarchie*, ed. Kurz, Scheuz and Vocelka, 473–90.

TRIBUTE AND DIPLOMATIC GIFTS

In terms of gifting, there could be no exchange on equal terms between the Ottoman sultans and the Habsburg emperors during the period under consideration. International diplomacy was in its developing phase and particularly fraught by ambiguity when it came to Ottoman-Habsburg relations. These followed parameters different from the relations between the European Christian powers, where the emperor's position was more clearly defined, though far from uncontested.[16] A gift can mirror hierarchy, indicate the rank and status of those involved and make statements about the quality of the relationship.[17] However, any gift can also be read in very different ways by different participants in the exchange. When sending objects and money to the Ottoman court, the Habsburgs did everything they could to frame these as *Ehrengeschenke* (honorific gifts). The Ottomans, in contrast, saw them as tribute. In Constantinople, the gifts from Central Europe appeared to express the superior status of the sultan, and did not call for a material reciprocation.[18] Incidentally, some vassals of the Porte in the Balkans paid more than the Habsburgs, though it is not clear how these gradations were conceptualized. The principality of Wallachia, a direct vassal of the Ottomans, for instance, sent a nonnegotiable yearly tribute of 40,000 ducats to Constantinople, and usually had to be more generous when it came to other gifts as well.[19]

Even when gifts were reciprocated, this was done under the presumption of Ottoman superiority. When a new vassal ascended a throne, the sultan would send him kaftans, flags and horse-tail standards that stressed their alliance to him. Occasionally other gifts followed. On her visit to Sultan Süleyman's camp in 1541, Queen Isabella of Hungary (1519–59),

[16] Matthew S. Andersen, *The Rise of Modern Diplomacy, 1450–1919* (London and New York: Longman, 1993), 1–40.

[17] On gift exchange: Mark Häberlein and Christof Jeggle, "Einleitung," in *Materielle Grundlagen der Diplomatie. Schenken, sammeln und verhandeln in Spätmittelalter und früher Neuzeit*, ed. Mark Häberlein and Christof Jeggle (München: UVK Verlagsgesellschaft mbH, 2013), 13–15; André Krischer, "Souveränität als sozialer Status. Zur Funktion des diplomatischen Zeremoniells in der Frühen Neuzeit," in *Diplomatisches Zeremoniell*, ed. Kauz, Rota and Niederkorn, 1–32; Reindl-Kiel, "Duft der Macht," 195–200; Marcel Mauss, "Essai sur le don: Forme et raison de l'échange dans les sociétés archaiques," *L'Année Sociologique* 1 (1925): 30–186.

[18] More detailed: Petritsch, "Tribut oder Ehrengeschenk," 49–58.

[19] Hammer-Purgstall, *Geschichte*, vol. 3, 524.

the widow of King John Zápolya (c. 1490–1540), his former vassal, received four gold chains, three caparisoned horses and various bracelets.[20] All these gifts were made "from above," to reinforce the notion of vassalage. That the Habsburgs were very much part of the Balkanic picture is also mirrored in the treatment of the Habsburg diplomats by the Ottoman court. They were dealt with similarly to the envoys of the sultan's vassals on the Balkan. Unlike their Venetian and French counterparts in Constantinople, the Habsburg ambassadors were confined to a special storehouse – the *han* of the ambassadors.[21] Acknowledgment came very slowly, and at first on a personal basis only, for instance when capable Habsburg envoys came to be asked to change sides and work for the sultan.[22]

In the way the annual reception of the 30,000 ducats and accompanying objects served to emphasize the superiority of the receiver and not the equality of both parties, this relationship was very different from that of the Ottomans with the Safavids. The latter – even though also considered by the Ottomans to be lower in rank, as tributaries and Shiite heretics – held sumptuous entries into Constantinople, and brought and received incomparably more precious gifts than any European power. The presents given by the Shah of Iran to the sultan and vice versa in 1555, and especially in 1566 and 1576, were described as being the most sumptuous gift exchanges ever witnessed. The valuable fabrics alone, which were but a fraction of the gifts, were worth more than five times the Habsburgs' yearly tribute.[23] Comparing the value of the presents brought by the Safavids to Constantinople with those of the Habsburgs, it is not difficult to understand why Habsburg emissaries were often poorly treated. The higher the value of gifts, the more the sultans could feel confirmed in their honors – and the more could also be achieved diplomatically.[24] While the Safavids knew this and played accordingly, the Habsburgs apparently did not.

[20] Ibid., vol. 3, 231.

[21] Ernst Petritsch, "Zeremoniell bei Empfängen habsburgischer Gesandter in Konstantinopel," in *Diplomatisches Zeremoniell*, ed. Kauz, Rota and Niederkorn, 303.

[22] Hammer-Purgstall, *Geschichte*, vol. 3, 226.

[23] Ibid., vol. 3, 517–22; vol. 4, 52–55. See also Lale Uluc, "Gifted Manuscripts from the Safavids to the Ottomans," in Komaroff, *Gifts of the Sultan*, 144; Stanley, "Ottoman Gift Exchange."

[24] On the concept of honor and Ottoman gift exchange, see especially Reindl-Kiel, "Duft der Macht," 196–99.

One could argue, perhaps, that this was in itself a sign of independence. But in reality the Austrian Habsburgs seem to have experienced their position in the wider diplomatic field as rather frustrating. While imperial diplomats were received with precedence all across Christian Europe, in the Ottoman context they were treated as emissaries of a tributary power and treated worse than Venetian, French or English diplomats – all of whom would be considered inferior elsewhere. It is also precisely with this in mind that the Habsburg emperors were not entitled to gifts of similar value as those offered to other Christian monarchs. Naturally, Ottoman emissaries did not come empty handed to the emperor, but their gifts were of a low value – indeed, a lesser value than the gift/tribute paid to the sultan.[25] In fact, the problem of appropriate mutual gifting was perceived to be grave enough to become a point of clarification in the treaty of Zsitvatorok in 1606. During the negotiations, as the Habsburg victories of the Long War were made into political currency, it was asked that the sultan send gifts worthy of an emperor at last, and that ambassadors of according rank should bring them to Vienna.[26]

Let us now address what exactly *was* sent to the Habsburg monarchs before this moment of redress. Ottoman gift diplomacy in general seems to have followed a set of remarkably stable patterns in the history of the Islamic Middle East. This continuity becomes evident from the objects displayed at recent exhibitions dedicated to the subject, namely, "Gifts of the Sultan," held in 2011 at the LACMA in Los Angeles, and also from the long life of a text such as the *kitab al-hadaya wa al-tuhaf*, or *Book of Gifts and Rarities*, which circulated from the ninth to the fifteenth century. Among the most popular gifts were horses and slaves (both often sumptuously dressed up), weapons, coins, jewels, textiles and other valuable objects of decorative art. From the sixteenth century onward, European clocks entered the circuit as coveted items.[27] Nor should it strike us too much that notions of value and especially nobility were

[25] Burschel, "Der Sultan und das Hündchen," 408. He refers to a quote from the diary of the Habsburg ambassador Hans Ludwig von Kuefstein, who traveled to Constantinople in 1628.

[26] Ernst Petritsch, "Zeremoniell bei Empfängen habsburgischer Gesandter in Konstantinopel," 303 and 304; Ludwig Fekete, *Türkische Schreiben aus dem Archive des Palatins Nikolaus Esterházy* (Budapest: Auftrag des Fürsten Paul Esterházy, 1932), 211; Teply, "Türkische Gesandtschaften," 18.

[27] Komaroff, *Gifts of the Sultan; Book of Gifts and Rarities (Kitab al-hadaya wa al-tuhaf)*, ed. and trans. Ghada Hijjawi Qaddumi (Cambridge: Harvard University Press, 1996); Reindl-Kiel, "Duft der Macht," 195–258.

expressed similarly, or at least commensurably, over long periods of time and across religious and cultural divides. In this sense, then, the objects surviving from the Ottoman-Habsburg exchange come as no surprise. Over the following three sections, I shall present three different categories of objects, namely, textiles, weaponry and stone items.

TEXTILES

The most fundamental and repetitive act of Ottoman-Habsburg gift exchange, frequently reported by emissaries, was the distribution along with money of valuable kaftans to the ambassadors and their retinue on the reception ceremony at the court of the sultan.[28] The money could be used for the voyage back home, and the kaftans, a sign of vassalage to the sultan (*hil'at*), could be sold as well. But they were often kept by the emissaries, and their proud owners even had their portrait painted in full *hil'at* attire. This was the case with Sigmund von Herberstein (1486–1566), a successful imperial diplomat, who traveled to meet Sultan Süleyman the Magnificent in Buda in 1541.[29] Quite possibly, the wearer was not entirely aware of the original meaning of the gift. He viewed it as a distinction rather than a sign of his submission to the sultan, though ultimately the two meanings may not have been entirely incompatible.[30] Hedda Reindl-Kiel has shown that kaftans continued to be gifted to the Habsburg emperors throughout the seventeenth century, implying the superiority of the sultan even after the Treaty of 1606 – a notion that was apparently lost on the imperial administrators in Vienna.

For example, a close look at a portrait showing Rudolph II's (1552–1612) brother, Emperor Mathias (1557–1619), in his Bohemian coronation vestments, reveals that the monarch is wearing a sixteenth-century Ottoman silk kaftan with peacock feather design under his cape. The garment was reportedly presented to him by the pasha of Buda in

[28] One such event is told for instance in Hammer-Purgstall, *Geschichte*, vol. 3, 236 and 237. For *hil'at* and gift exchange: Reindl-Kiel, "Duft der Macht," 210; Reindl-Kiel, "East Is East," 118–19; Monica Springberg-Hansen, *Die Hil'a: Studien zur Geschichte des geschenkten Gewandes im islamischen Kulturkreis* (Würzburg: Ergon, 2000); Stewart Gordon, ed., *Robes and Honour: The Medieval World of Investiture* (New York: Palgrave Macmillan, 2001) esp. chs. 6, 8, 9, 14 and 17.

[29] Reference in Neck, *Österreich und die Osmanen*, 39 and 40; for an image, see Komaroff, *Gifts of the Sultan*, 21.

[30] Amanda Phillips, "Ottoman Hil'at: Between Commodity and Charisma," in *Frontiers of Ottoman Imagination: Studies in the Honour of Rhoads Murphey*, ed. Marios Hadjianastasis (Leiden: Brill, 2015), 111–38.

1609, thus after Zsitvatorok.[31] This is notable for two reasons. First, it reminds us of the conceptual continuity in Christian Europe regarding the value of silk textiles from the East. Splendid textiles from the East often had long and complex histories, such as the sumptuously embroidered Sicilian mantle of King Roger II dating to 1133/34 that later turned into the coronation mantle of the Holy Roman Emperors. It is today preserved in the *Schatzkammer* of the Kunsthistorisches Museum in Vienna.[32] Second, gifted kaftans highlight the recurrence of cultural misunderstandings: the kaftan was considered *hil'at* by the sultan and presumably by the pasha, its acceptance expressing the wearer's acceptance of vassalage to the Ottoman sultan. What the Habsburgs may have interpreted as continuing old traditions stressing imperial splendor had another meaning for the Ottomans who through *hil'at* distributed robes to their most distinguished subordinates thus showing their superiority.[33] It is in this sense that the sultan would have most appreciated the portrait. Incidentally, Matthias's habit was later captured by the Swedish army and survives today – probably resulting from a pious gift by one of the capturers – in a church in Sweden, where it was tailored into an *antependium* of the altar.[34]

Ottoman silk kaftans and other garments could also be presented in a context very different from the one described, actually enhancing the position of the emperor vis-à-vis the sultan. For this to happen, the object needed to be taken out of its original context of circulation and injected into a new, different circuit. In 1602, Emperor Rudolf II sent an embassy with gifts to the Elector of Saxony, Christian II (1583–1611), who had just assumed his governmental duties and was an important ally in the emperor's fights against the Ottomans during the ongoing Long War. Presenting himself as a victor of the Ottomans, the emperor sent a gift consisting of five sumptuously dressed and armed Ottoman captives (one of them a *çavuş* or *tschauch*, the others a "Moor," a "Turk," a Tartar and a Janissary), three of whom were wearing kaftans, along with three horses

[31] Otto Kurz, *The Decorative Arts of Europe and the Islamic East: The Arts of Europe and Islam* (London: Dorian Press, 1977), 8.

[32] Rotraud Bauer, "Der Mantel Rogers II. und die siculo-normannischen Gewänder aus den königlichen Hofwerkstätten in Palermo," in *Nobiles Officinae: Die königlsichen Hofwerkstätten zu Palermo zur Zeit der Normannen und Staufer im 12. und 13. Jahrhundert* ed. Wilfried Seipel (Milan: Skira, 2004), 115–23.

[33] This was also remarked by Reindl-Kiel, "East Is East," 113–24; Burschel, "Der Sultan und das Hündchen," 408–20.

[34] Kurz, *Decorative Arts of Europe*, 8. For the full-length portrait of Emperor Matthias as King of Bohemia, see the work by Hans von Aachen, Prague (1612) in the Collections of the city of Prague.

heavily caparisoned in Ottoman fashion. The textiles that were part of this gift did not survive, but several of the weapons carried by the captives are still in the Türckische Cammer in Dresden, a space celebrating the triumphs of Saxony's electors and a repository for equipment used in courtly tournaments. The very detailed contemporary documentation and description of this imperial present in Saxony, recently published by Holger Schuckelt, stresses its importance.[35]

Two more fine Ottoman silk kaftans, that given their storage location were probably spoils of war, survived in Vienna until 1883 at least, when they appeared listed as numbers 651 and 669 of the catalogue of the exhibition celebrating the bicentenary of the liberation of Vienna from the Ottoman siege (1683) led by Kara Mustafa Pasha (c. 1634–1683). Originally kept in the imperial armory – a space celebrating the military triumphs of the Habsburgs – they did not survive the world wars.[36] Their inclusion in this prestigious collection points to the high symbolic value attributed to them in the Habsburg context.

Ottoman textiles were also used to cover and embellish diplomatic items other than people or animals. Also in this case they retained a strong hierarchical element. Regularly the sultans sent their messengers and official translators to the imperial court. Their most important duty was to deliver paperwork, be that draft versions of treaties and their often conflicting translations in the different languages, announcements of enthronements or important victories, laments concerning the frontier disputes on the border or invitations to the circumcision festivities of princes.[37] The sultan's letters were commonly covered with valuable textiles that subtly expressed the rank of their addressees – the more valuable the textile, the higher the rank of whoever received it. On the visit in 1541 by Sigmund von Herberstein to the camp of Sultan Süleyman near Buda, the emissary received not only a kaftan but also a letter for the emperor covered with a golden fabric. On this occasion at least, a

35 Holger Schuckelt, *Die Türckische Cammer: Sammlung orientalischer Kunst in der kurfürstlich-sächsischen Rüstkammer Dresden* (Dresden: Sandstein Verlag, 2010), 93–95.

36 Carl Weiss, ed., *Katalog der historischen Ausstellung der Stadt Vienna 1883: Aus Anlass der zweiten Säcularfeier der Befreiung Viennas von den Turken vom Gemeinderathe der Reichshaupt- und Residenzstadt Vienna veranstaltet* (Vienna: Wallishausser, 1883), nos. 651 and 669. It is unknown when these two pieces came to Vienna, and whether they were originally gifts or booty.

37 Teply, "Türkische Gesandtschaften," 17; Ernst Petritsch, "Dissimulieren in den habsburgisch-osmanischen Friedens- und Waffenstillstandsverträgen (16.-17. Jahrhundert): Differenzen und Divergenzen," in *Frieden und Konfliktmanagement*, ed. Strohmeyer and Spannberger, 145–62.

FIGURE 4.1 Ottoman flask of Emperor Rudolf II, c. 1580; leather, felt, ivory, horn, cord; 29.8 cm.
© Kunsthistorisches Museum – Museumsverband HJRK C 28.

material was chosen that would have matched the self-perception of the Habsburg emperors.[38] Two such covers survive in the Haus- Hof- und Staatsarchiv in Vienna, although they are both of a later date.

Messages and letters would also often come accompanied by objects. An elaborate flask was thus sent by Sultan Murad III (1546–95) to Emperor Rudolf II along with an invitation to attend the circumcision ceremony of his son. We know this from a letter of the Venetian ambassador in Prague, written in 1581, at a time when the formal armistice was still in place, with the emperor paying tribute to the Ottoman sultan. A flask kept today in the Hofjagd- und Rüstkammer, attributed to the court workshops in Constantinople on grounds of its exquisite appliqué embroidery, has been identified as the object described in that letter (Figure 4.1).[39] Official invitations to a spectacular event such as the circumcision of the sultan's sons were not unusual. As early as 1530, Sultan Süleyman had invited the Doge of Venice to one.[40] Sovereigns

[38] Hammer-Purgstall, *Geschichte*, vol. 3, 238. More on letter sacks: Agnes Geijer, *Oriental Textiles in Sweden* (Copenhagen: Rosenkilde und Bagger, 1951), 31 and 54–59.

[39] August Grosz and Bruno Thomas, *Katalog der Waffensammlung in der Neuen Burg* (Vienna: Kunsthistorisches Museum, 1936), 92; Esin Atil, *The Age of Sultan Suleyman the Magnificent* (Washington, DC: National Gallery of Art, 1987), 165.

[40] Hammer-Purgstall, *Geschichte*, vol. 3, 95 and 96.

from East and West were invited to the circumcision festivities of 1581, which were celebrated with the greatest possible pomp.[41] The emperor himself did not attend, but his official emissary in Constantinople and those of many other European countries did.

While in general these and other objects come to us with little or no documented ceremonial context attached to them, one Ottoman diplomatic mission in particular stands out to offer us a sense of what was going on in the courtly environments under consideration. Having negotiated the armistice agreement of 1562, the imperial resident in Constantinople, Oghier Ghislain de Busbecq, was accompanied on his way back to Central Europe by the court translator Ibrahim Bey, a Polish renegade in Ottoman service. These two high-ranking officials went on to attend the coronation of Maximilian II in Frankfurt, where Ibrahim Bey was received both by Emperor Ferdinand I and by his son Maximilian.[42] Ibrahim Bey was reportedly led through a series of rooms before encountering the emperor in the audience hall with the electors and dignitaries of the empire. At first he delivered but two letters; only in a second audience did he present the gifts. With this, according to Harriet Rudolph, he showed that the gifts were not born out of any obligation – as were those of the emperor to the sultan – but a voluntary gesture. The gifts thus still stressed the hierarchy established by the sultan, but it can also be added that they were carefully selected to please, not only impress. As Busbecq stated, the sultan "presented such gifts as are held most honourable by the Turks."[43]

Indeed, the set presented by Ibrahim Bey included a horse with gilded bridles and a woven saddle cover, two sets of crystal or alabaster tableware and four camels with valuable trappings for the emperor. In addition, four Venetian jugs, two cups decorated with precious stones, two Ottoman carpets and cushions are also mentioned.[44] There were also presents for the newly crowned Maximilian II: a horse, two camels, a dog, a set of bow and arrows including quivers and four painted pikes – quite a traditional selection, and in fact one that mirrors the sort of items often sent in the

[41] Hammer-Purgstall, *Geschichte*, vol. 4, 108–42.

[42] Teply, "Türkische Gesandtschaften," 18; Rudolph, "Türkische Gesandtschaften," 295–314; Carina L. Johnson, *Cultural Hierarchy in Sixteenth-Century Europe: The Ottomans and Mexicans* (Cambridge: Cambridge University Press, 2011), 197–229.

[43] Edward S. Forster and Karl A. Roider, ed. and trans., *The Turkish Letters of Ogier Ghiselin de Busbecq* (1927; reprint, Baton Rouge: Louisiana State University Press, 2005), 237.

[44] Rudolph, "Türkische Gesandtschaften," 301 and 302. Rudolph quotes two sources mentioning slightly different gifts.

opposite direction. It may be worth highlighting how the Ottomans, like their European diplomatic counterparts, did not restrict themselves to sending objects from their own workshops, rather sourcing a variety of items reflecting their diplomatic reach – hence the Venetian jugs. In this case, we also know that Ibrahim Bey received a personal award including money and some textiles for his service.[45]

Exotic animals were favored gifts with emperor and sultan, since both entertained menageries to impress visitors. In fact, one case shows that it was not only the Ottomans making demands, but also the Habsburg diplomats expressing their needs and ambitions. During the winter of 1567–68, the Habsburg emissary in Constantinople asked for a giraffe to be sought as a present for Maximilian II from the Grand Vizier. This was denied on the grounds that there was but one such animal in Constantinople at that moment, and that it was needed elsewhere.[46] The response may have come as a humiliation, but also as a reality check after a request quite clearly beyond the usual remit of Ottoman gifting to Vienna.

While the fate of such gifted animals is often obscure, some objects that came along with them have survived. Several sets of Ottoman horse-trappings including bridles, saddles and saddle covers survive in the Hofjagd- und Rüstkammer and the famous *Rüstkammer* or armory of Archduke Ferdinand II of Tyrol (1529–95).[47] Many of these pieces, now extremely rare, are high quality products most likely manufactured in the Ottoman court workshops with high-ranking receptors in mind. Their high quality and storage locations in the Habsburg realm indicate that they were diplomatic gifts. The famous 1596 inventory of the Ambras collections of Archduke Ferdinand II of Tyrol lists several Ottoman horse-trappings, including saddle covers woven in gold. Three of these late sixteenth-century saddle covers from Ambras today survive in the Museum für angewandte Kunst in Vienna, and while they cannot be traced to the Frankfurt reception described above, they are likely to have been transacted on an occasion of great importance (Figure 4.2).[48] Much

[45] Ibid., 303.

[46] Hammer-Purgstall, *Geschichte*, vol. 3, 516; Reindl-Kiel, "Duft der Macht," 232–35.

[47] Eduard von Sacken, *Die vorzüglichsten Rüstungen und Waffen der k.k. Ambraser Sammlung* (Vienna: Braumuller, 1859–62), vol. 1, 58, pl. 51; Laurin Luchner, *Denkmal eines Renaissancefürsten: Versuch einer Rekonstruktion des Ambraser Museums von 1583* (Vienna: Schroll, 1958), 103; Ortwin Gamber and Christian Beaufort, *Katalog der Leibrüstkammer: Zeitraum 1530–1560* (Busto Arsizio: Bramante, 1990), 212–14.

[48] Wendelin Boeheim, ed., "Urkunden und Regesten aus der k.k. Hofbibliothek: Regeste 5556, Inventari über das fürstlich gsclosz Ombras sambt den rüst- und kunstcämern,"

FIGURE 4.2 Ottoman saddle cover from Ambras Collection, second half of the sixteenth century; silk, metal threads, cotton, linen; 126 cm × 135 cm.
© MAK – Museum für angewandte Kunst/Gegenwartskunst, Vienna. T 9128.

effort was also put into displaying such pieces at Ambras Castle where large horse statues were caparisoned and shown in Ferdinand's *Rüstkammer* (armory) and *Türkenkammerl* (Turkish chamber) mounted by life-sized mannequins dressed as Ottoman soldiers. The objects, gifts as well as booty pieces, were integrated into a complex, multilayered display

Jahrbuch der kunsthistorischen Sammlungen des allerhöchsten Kaiserhauses 7, no. 2 (1888): cclxviii–cclxxix (armory). Barbara Karl, "Diplomatic Gifts and Collecting: Three Ottoman *çapraks* in the MAK – Museum für angewandte Kunst/Gegenwartskunst Vienna," in *Conference Proceedings ICDAD Cracow*, 2015 (2016), 199–210. This article is an adapted and improved version including the necessary footnotes and corrections of "When Horses Wore Silk and Gold," *HALI* 175 (2013): 25–29, which was published before the author could carry out corrections and – against the knowledge and wish of the author – without footnotes, therefore containing errors in the technical analysis of the pieces.

occupying several rooms of the castle, contributing to the celebration of the archduke and his dynasty. Many objects of sixteenth-century Ottoman manufacture survive in Ambras today, including turbans, a striped North African cloak, an embroidered undergarment, a janissary cap, leather inlaid discs, boots or an intriguing vambrace attributed to Sultan Süleyman.[49] Ambras Castle under Ferdinand II was known not only for its treasures, but also for sumptuous courtly festivals during which show fights between Ottomans and Habsburgs were staged. Some of the objects kept in the armory may well have been used on such occasions.[50] In this context, then, Ottoman objects produced in Constantinople to express the might of the sultans helped legitimize Habsburg rule by celebrating the Austrian dynasty as defenders of the Holy Roman Empire against one of its hereditary enemies.

Among the other textile objects mentioned for the Frankfurt gift exchange, there were two unspecified carpets and some cushions. It is unknown what happened to the latter. The reception of carpets, however, has been studied. They were not only fitting diplomatic gifts, but also widely traded items transporting Eastern imagery into European courtly settings. By the second half of the sixteenth century carpets were a common feature of Central European palace decoration, as both Alois Riegl and Angela Völker have shown. Ample evidence has been found for Ottoman carpets in Habsburg inventories.[51] An inventory of Emperor Maximilian II from 1568 lists among many other objects seven carpets, three of which are designated as gifts made by courtiers who had traveled abroad. One came from Venice, and the other two were from Oghier Ghislain de Busbecq.[52] By the end of the century, the numbers were

[49] Barbara Karl, *Treasury-Kunstkammer-Museum: Objects from the Islamic World in the Museum Collections of Vienna* (Vienna: Verl. d. Österr. Akademie d. Wissenschaften, 2011), 21, 22 and 59. All can be traced to the 1596 inventory, but not explicitly to a particular gift exchange.

[50] Alfred Auer, *Wir sind Helden: Habsburgische Feste in der Renaissance* (Vienna: Kunsthistorisches Museum, 2005); Veronika Sandbichler, *Türkische Kostbarkeiten aus dem kunsthistorischen Museum* (Vienna: Kunsthistorisches Museum, 1997).

[51] Alois Riegl, "Ältere orientalische Teppiche aus dem Besitze des Kaiserhauses," *Jahrbuch der kunsthistorischen Sammlungen des allerhöchsten Kaiserhauses* 13, no. 1 (1892): 267–331; Angela Völker, *Die orientalischen Knüpfteppiche des MAK* (Vienna: Böhlau, 2001).

[52] The inventory was published in the article by Karl Rudolf, "Die Kunstbestrebungen Kaiser Maximilians II. im Spannungsfeld zwischen Madrid und Vienna: Untersuchungen zu den Sammlungen der österreichischen und spanischen Habsburger im 16. Jahrhundert," *Jahrbuch der kunsthistorischen Sammlungen* 91 (1995): 242, nos. 331–33.

significantly higher. The 1596 inventory of Ambras castle alone lists about twenty carpets.[53]

Unlike many other objects of Ottoman manufacture such as weapons, however, carpets were not the object of a systematic Habsburg collecting effort, nor were they used for propaganda purposes. They may not have been deemed novel or rare or exquisite enough to compete with other categories of objects valued at the time. They were mostly used for ceremonial but essentially practical purposes in the palatial households, mainly to cover tables and benches.[54] Three days after the gift exchange between Ibrahim Bey and the emperor, for example, during the coronation of Maximilian, the future emperor knelt on an Ottoman carpet. Rudolph interpreted this politically as a metaphorical humiliation of the enemy.[55] Generally, given the increasingly ample use of carpets in palatial interiors, it is probable that the perception of the carpet was more prosaic. The Frankfurt carpet certainly enhanced the solemnity of the ceremony (not to mention that they kept the king's knees warm), but it does not seem to have attracted the attention that other objects commanded. It was only much later that carpets came to be valued as objects to be collected and studied at the highest level. Today, the carpets that went through the Habsburg imperial household constitute one of the world's most magnificent collections, housed in the Museum für angewandte Kunst in Vienna. Given the generic description of carpets in the inventories, it is not possible to link them directly to the documents of the sixteenth century – but in all likeliness, at least some of them may have arrived in Austria as diplomatic gifts.

Other kinds of Ottoman textiles are likely to be of a similar diplomatic provenance. Elaborately worked quivers containing bows and arrows were part of the gift to Archduke Maximilian in Frankfurt. Exquisite sixteenth-century quivers survive in the *Rüstkammer*/armory of the Kunsthistorisches Museum, though given the lack of detail in the original document, none of them can be positively identified with that particular set of gifts. The sumptuous surviving quivers were made of leather. They were decorated with gold or appliqué embroidery, covered with valuable textiles like silk velvet and some can be associated with Ottoman courtly

53 Wendelin Boeheim, ed., "Urkunden und Regesten, Regeste 5556," cclviii–cclxviii (inventory of the castle).

54 Riegl, "Ältere orientalische Teppiche," 330–31; Völker, *Die orientalischen Knüpfteppiche des MAK*, 7–30.

55 Rudolph, "Türkische Gesandtschaften ins Reich am Beginn der Neuzeit," 304.

production.[56] As we will see further below, these were not the only quivers transacted as part of an Ottoman diplomatic gift to the emperor. Finally, the above quoted 1568 inventory of Emperor Maximilian II also included three *unngrisch* (Hungarian) jackets brought by a courtier from *thürckey* (Turkey) – one white, woven with gold, another of red velvet and a third of green velvet, the latter two brocaded with gold. Another polychrome *gewürkht* (woven) cloth came from a courtier in Venice.[57] This and other commissions made by courtiers illustrate that Ottoman items were not only gifted and captured but also bought. Together with the presence of so many carpets in Ambras, this stresses the high appreciation courtly circles had for luxurious Ottoman material culture. The fashion lasted roughly until the beginning of the Thirty Years' War and found expression not only in interior decoration but also in courtly festivities, one of which saw the Elector of Saxony dressed as sultan in Dresden in 1607.[58]

Importantly, textiles of such high standards soon began to circulate in various directions across the complex gift-giving networks of the Habsburg family in Europe.[59] In the 1619 inventory of the estate of Emperor Mathias – a very valuable document as the object descriptions occasionally include the name of the giver and the date of giving – a gift of Queen Anna of Poland (1573–98) to either Rudolf or Mathias appears (Anna having died in 1598, the gift must have been made before that date). This included several textiles of Ottoman and Safavid manufacture, which were incidentally becoming more and more popular with the Polish nobility.[60] Most of them were probably part of women's or men's courtly toilette as they were designated as veils and handkerchiefs. Some may have been made of cotton, though one item is described as *tuech*,

[56] On bows and quivers: Gamber and Beaufort, *Katalog der Leibrüstkammer*, 230, 223 and 230–32; Atil, *Age of Sultan Suleyman*, 164; Luchner, *Denkmal eines Renaissancefürsten*, 105; Karl, *Treasury-Kunstkammer-Museum*, 56–70.

[57] Rudolf, "Kunstbestrebungen Kaiser Maximilians II," 240, nos. 247, 244 and 414.

[58] Compare Schuckelt, *Türkische Cammer*, 90–111, esp. 100.

[59] On Habsburg family gift-giving: Annemarie Jordan Gschwend, and Almudena Perez de Tudela, "Luxury Goods for Royal Collectors: Exotica, Princely Gifts and Rare Animals Exchanged between the Iberian Courts and Central Europe in the Renaissance (1560–1612)," in *Exotica: Portugals Entdeckungen im Spiegel furstlicher Kunst- und Wunderkammern der Renaissance*, ed. Helmut Trnek and Sabine Haag (Mainz: Zabern, 2001), vol. 3, 1–127.

[60] Inventar Kaiser Mathias, 1619: Hans von Voltelini, ed., "Urkunden und Regesten aus dem k. Und k. Haus-Hof- und Staatsarchiv, Regeste: 17408," *Jahrbuch der kunsthistorischen Sammlungen des allerhöchsten Kaiserhauses* 20, no. 2 (1899): lxxxv, entry 1980.

suggesting a woolen fabric. In addition, a pouch with gold and silver decoration (probably embroidered) is also mentioned. The position of these objects in the inventory, among the more valuable goods, stresses their importance in the Habsburg courtly context. They would have been kept for their rarity, their quality as curiosities, and to commemorate the late queen.

WEAPONRY

Weapons take us into a complex field in the context of this study since their provenance was likely to be of either a diplomatic or bellicose kind. While diplomats negotiated and exchanged gifts in courtly setting, frontier skirmishes on the Balkans continued and brought abundant booty.[61] This made arms particularly susceptible of being used as tools of propaganda, thus adding to the ambiguities already discussed. Given by the Ottomans to the emperor, weapons were gifts that could express hierarchy like many others, illustrating the superior position of the sultan. Coming to Vienna as the spoils of war, in contrast, they would manifest the growing power of the emperor. The latter appeared here as the defender not only of his dominions, but also of the whole of Christendom, a lord to whom the spoils of triumph were regularly dedicated by his generals. Weapons are today the largest group of Ottoman items to survive in the Habsburg context from the late sixteenth century. They were much appreciated for their material as well as for their propagandistic value.[62]

Weapons of the highest value were kept in the various *Kunstkammern* and *Rüstkammern* of the Habsburgs. The collections of Ferdinand II of Tyrol and his three nephews, Emperor Rudolf II, Emperor Mathias and Maximilian III (1558–1618), the Grand Master of the Teutonic Order, included numerous Ottoman but also Safavid weapons from the period in question. Together with mail shirts and helmets, wicker shields, sabers, daggers, bows and arrows they constitute a unique nucleus of sixteenth-century Ottoman weaponry. It would be plausible to assume that the most outstandingly valuable items may have been part of diplomatic exchanges, while others of lesser value, including many pieces today stored in Ambras Castle, represent booty (Figure 4.3).

[61] Hedda Reindl-Kiel, "Der Duft der Macht," 218–19.

[62] Karl, *Treasury-Kunstkammer-Museum*, 56–70, 76–79 and 82–84.

FIGURE 4.3 Ottoman wicker shields from Ambras Collection, sixteenth century; iron, silk, wicker; diam. 63.5 cm and 52 cm.

Valuable weapons and accoutrements of war, among them many textiles, were the ideal princely gift. It must be added though that they originated not only from the Porte, but also from other, intermediary nodes in the diplomatic network, such as Buda in what had been the heart of Hungary. This slightly complicates the geography of diplomatic gifting and adds complexity to the notion of imperial centers of power. Diplomatic exchanges between the Habsburgs and their neighboring pashas were more frequent than those on the highest level. The pashas of Buda represented an important position in the relations between Constantinople and Vienna, as all embassies went through their territory and they themselves were in constant exchange with both the Habsburg and the Ottoman court. The importance of this post is stressed by the fact that some men holding it were related to the sultan through marriage.[63] Given

[63] Teply, "Türkiche Gesandtschaften," 16; Gisela Prohazka-Eisl and Claudia Römer, "Raub, Mord und Übergriffe an der habsburgisch-osmanischen Grenze," in *Diplomatisches Zeremoniell in Europa und im Mittleren Osten*, ed. Kauz, Rota and Niederkorn, 254.

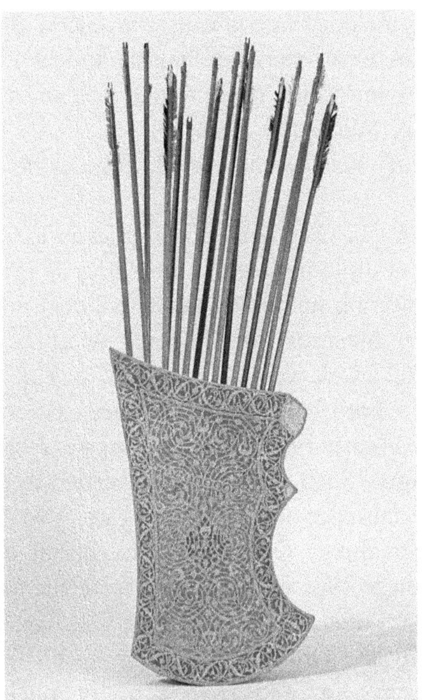

FIGURE 4.4 Ottoman quiver for arrows, c. 1550; leather, silk, linen; 42 cm × 26 cm. © Kunsthistorisches Museum – Museumsverband HJRK C 5a.

these pashas' important rank and connections to the court in Constantinople, they had access to top quality products such as jewel-encrusted sabers, daggers and quivers (Figure 4.4). According to a report to the Grand Duke of Tuscany, Francesco de' Medici (a brother-in-law of Emperor Maximilian II), "six beautiful horses [probably sumptuously caparisoned], some sabres, bows and arrows and an offer of friendship" were presented by the pasha of Buda to Emperor Maximilian II in 1567.[64]

The 1568 inventory of Maximilian also lists twelve items as "*Etliche türckhische Sachen so der Pascha von Ofen verert*" (various Turkish things given by the pasha of Buda). It is not clear on which occasion these

[64] Archivio di Stato di Firenze, Mediceo del Principato 21659, fol. 128. Quotation: Documentary sources for the Arts and Humanities (The Medici Archive Database, Inc.). On the concept of friendship in this context: Arno Strohmeyer, "Die habsburgisch-osmanische Freundschaft (16.–18. Jahrhundert)," in *Frieden und Konfliktmanagement*, ed. Strohmeyer and Spannberger, 223–38.

gifts arrived. They included falcon caps and falcon gloves for hunting, a dagger with a black jewel-encrusted handle and two bows. In addition, there were probably matching items wrought in silver, such as a flask, a cup and small jug, and small pieces of jewelry.[65] The quality of the pasha's gifts was, it must be underlined, impeccable and of the highest standards.

Valuable weapons of Ottoman and, to a lesser extent, Safavid origins circulated widely as diplomatic gifts, affording us insights into a diplomatic culture connecting numerous lower political powers and communities.[66] The 1619 inventory of Emperor Mathias reveals that such precious swords and jewels were presented by the embassies of Wallachia and Transylvania – both having formerly been Ottoman vassals before they sided with the Habsburgs during the Long War – and even the Jewish community of Prague. Such cases certainly added to the growing Habsburg sense of imperial superiority. Both instances also illustrate, again, the increasing taste for things Ottoman in European courtly circles and beyond. In addition to this, we also learn from the inventory that some objects, namely, a set of saddle covers, were sent from Constantinople to the emperor not by the Ottoman elite, but by his own emissaries and courtiers.[67] Between 1600 and 1610 a polity much further east and sharing some strategic interests with various European powers, Safavid Persia, sent several embassies including gifts to Europe, bypassing the Porte at a delicate moment in time. According to an inventory of the collection of Rudolf II, the Persian gifts included various jewel-encrusted knives brought to Rudolf in 1610.[68]

As mentioned already, weapons and other martial accessories often represented spoils of war.[69] While during the period in question the Habsburg army entered in very few open field battles against the

[65] Rudolf, "Kunstbestrebungen Kaiser Maximilians II," 247, nos. 508–16.

[66] Schuckelt, *Türkische Cammer*, 20–111.

[67] Voltelini, "Urkunden und Regesten," lxxxiii–xc.

[68] Inventory of Emperor Rudolf II, 1607/11: Rotraud Bauer and Herbert Haupt, eds., *Das Kunstkammerinventar Kaiser Rudolfs II., 1607–1611* (Jahrbuch der kunsthistorischen Sammlungen in Vienna, vol. 72, 1976), 19, 30 and 72. Barbara Karl, "On the Crossroads: Habsburg Collecting of Objects from the Islamic World, 16th and 17th Centuries," *Ars Orientalis* 42 (2012): 114–26.

[69] For flags, see Barbara Karl, "Silk and Propaganda: Two Ottoman Silk Flags and the Relief of Vienna, 1683," *Textile History* 45, no. 2 (2014): 192–215; id., "Zwei osmanische Fahnen in der kaiserlichen Sammlung," in *Orient & Okzident: Begegnungen und Wahrnehmungen and fünf Jahrhunderten*, ed. Barbara Haider-Wilson and Maximilian Graf (Wien: Neue Welt Verl, 2016), 245–69.

Ottoman army (the most famous being their devastating defeat at Mezőkeresztes in 1596), frontier skirmishes and the occupation of frontier castles or cities occurred far more often. Unless the tent of a high-ranking official was looted, the booty emerging from such occasions could generally not compete in quality and status with gifted weapons from diplomatic contexts. Yet booty could be instrumentalized very effectively for propaganda purposes to stress Habsburg superiority, especially when dedicated to members of the imperial family. As early as 1584 five captured flags, several Ottoman officials of high rank and the decapitated heads of Ottoman soldiers were dedicated to Archduke Ernst (1553–95), a brother of Rudolf II.[70] Naturally, the Ottomans celebrated their triumphs similarly. In 1587, for instance, a triumphal entry into Constantinople was organized including 18 captured imperial flags and 120 captives carrying the heads of decapitated soldiers, all being accompanied by music.[71] It is notable that both events took place before the Long War, in more peaceful times.

An important nucleus of documented booty taken from the Ottomans survives in the Ambras collection. The spoils resulted from the defeat of a lesser division of the Ottoman army in 1566, under a campaign headed by the imperial General Lazarus von Schwendi (1522–83). The general, who fought in Hungary since 1564, dedicated the captured pieces to Archduke Ferdinand II, who had himself fought against the Ottomans and at that time resided in Prague. Schwendi's booty supplemented the spoils he had already taken himself on a previous occasion.[72] When the materials moved to Ambras Castle, most Ottoman spoils were exhibited in the *Türkenkammerl* (Turkish chamber), the smallest room of his famous armory, to celebrate the archduke's successes against the Ottomans.[73] The centerpieces were three horses with their riders in full attire. Two were designated as *türggisch* (Turkish), and one as *hungerisch* (Hungarian). The presence of *mumereiclaider* (disguise costumes) in the same room suggests that at least a few of the objects may have been used in show tournaments, just as had been the case in Dresden.[74] Attached to the

[70] Hammer-Purgstall, *Geschichte*, vol. 4, 145. [71] Ibid., vol. 4, 148 and 149.

[72] For a list of inventories on the Ambras castle: Luchner, *Denkmal eines Renaissancefürsten*, 137.

[73] See, especially, Luchner, *Denkmal eines Renaissancefürsten*, 103, 104 and 129; Gamber, and Beaufort, *Katalog der Leibrüstkammer*, 218–20, 224 and 227; Sandbichler, *Türkische Kostbarkeiten*, 11–12.

[74] Inventory Archduke Ferdinand II of Tyrol, 1596: Boeheim, "Urkunden und Regesten, Regeste 5556," cccxxvi–cccxiii. Inventory of the armory of Archduke Ferdinand II of

Türkenkammerl was Ambras's famous *Kunstkammer*, which also included Ottoman objects, though none of these items of higher value can be associated with documented acts of gifting or looting.[75]

Ferdinand's nephew Emperor Rudolf II owned the most famous *Kunstkammer* of his time. Several sections of its 1607/11 inventory are dedicated to Ottoman objects, among them about seventy daggers and swords. Only a few of the entries have additions that show they were looted and then dedicated to the emperor, serving as proof of victory. Among these, the list contains a strong iron padlock with its key, which reportedly hung at the city gates of Visegrád when the Habsburgs took it in 1595.[76] The year of 1595 proved particularly successful for the imperials along the Danube, as they also took the fortresses of Győr and Esztergom. The latter brought large booty since an entire Ottoman camp was plundered, including flags, tents and weaponry.[77] In 1598 Emperor Rudolf II was presented with the armor of a pasha who had been killed at Győr.[78] Another entry in Rudolf's inventory describes a saber captured at the siege of Székesfehérvár and given to the emperor in 1602, still during the Long War.

The 1619 inventory of the most important parts of the estate of Emperor Mathias, Rudolf's brother, compiled after the peace of Zitvatorok but referring to many objects received before it, is the most interesting document for this study. It lists not only many sumptuous gifts that came with Ottoman embassies after 1606, but also Ottoman objects that, thanks to specifications, can be attributed to the time before the treaty. The majority of the relevant gifted Ottoman objects are listed, along with other objects mainly from the closer Islamic world, on eight(!) pages of the transcribed inventory. Occasionally, the provenance, the date of gifting and the presenter are included in the description of an object.[79]

Tyrol, 1583: Wendelin Boeheim, "Urkunden und Regesten aus der k.k. Hofbibliothek, Regeste: 5440," *Jahrbuch der kunsthistorischen Sammlungen des allerhöchsten Kaiserhauses* 7, no. 2 (1888): ccxiv–ccxviii (*Türkenkammerl*) and: Boeheim, "Urkunden und Regesten, Regeste 5556," cclxxiv–cclxxix (*Türkenkammerl*).

75 In cupboard 16 of his *Kunstkammer* there were three pieces of Ottoman weapons, and in cupboard 17, several decorative Ottoman items such as pouches, flasks, a bowl and writing utensils: Boeheim, "Urkunden und Regesten, Regeste 5556," cclxviii–cclxxix (*Rüstkammer*), cclxxix–cccxiii (*Kunstkammer*), ccciii–cccx (cupboards 16 and 17).

76 Bauer, and Haupt, *Das Kunstkammerinventar Kaiser Rudolfs II.*, 46, entry 841.

77 Hammer-Purgstall, *Geschichte*, vol. 4, 251 and 252.

78 Alphons Lhotsky, *Festschrift des Kunsthistorischen Museums in Vienna. Die Geschichte der Sammlungen*, 2nd part, 1st half (Vienna: Verlag Ferdinand Berger, 1941–45), 280.

79 Inventory of Emperor Mathias 1619: Voltelini, "Urkunden und Regesten," xlix–cxxii; here especially lxxxiii–lxxxix.

Numerous Ottoman pieces in the inventory feature details of provenance identifying them as booty, dedicated to either Rudolf or Mathias before 1606 (it is possible that some pieces in Mathias's inventory are identical with those in Rudolf's). The inventory lists weapons taken at Győr, Székesfehérvár and Buda, the last entry providing the date 1603.[80] The document also lists weapons given by imperial military officials and generals – again most likely originating from spoils of war made before 1606. Among these military commanders was Giorgio Basta (1550–1607), an Italian in the service of Rudolf II, who was active during the Long War. Basta dedicated a sumptuous Ottoman horse harness, a gilded stabbing weapon and a mace – the latter in 1604 – to either Rudolf or Mathias.[81] Shortly before his death in 1607, he also sent a mace and a dagger to the Elector of Saxony, Rudolf's key ally.[82] Apart from weapons, two valuable Ottoman silk flags were listed in the 1619 inventory alongside diplomatic gifts. They were quite certainly captured in battle too and thus most likely gifted by an imperial general before 1606. It is difficult to imagine them being a diplomatic gift made by the sultan.[83]

The inventory again shows that Ottoman weaponry circulated at different levels of gift-giving, and that objects and gift-givers crossed paths in manifold ways. Not all derive from booty contexts; nonetheless, they emphasized the superiority of the emperor. In February to March 1601, Michael the Brave, the prince of Wallachia (1558–1601), Transylvania and Moldova (enthroned by Sultan Murad III in 1593 but soon attracted to the imperial side), visited Rudolf II in Prague to foster his good relationship with the Habsburgs, secure his position against the challenge of the Hungarian nobility led by Sigismund Báthory (himself a vassal of the Porte) and obtain funds for further campaigns against the Ottomans. He offered a sword and a saddle with a sumptuous cover. In the end, however, his mission did not yield the expected results. Only a few months later, Michael was killed by the general Giorgio Basta, following imperial orders.[84]

[80] Voltelini, "Urkunden und Regesten," lxxxiii–lxxxix, entries 1994, 2049, 2054, 2057, 2082, 2087 and 2089.

[81] Ibid., lxxxvi, entry 2014, and lxxxviii, entries 2083 and 2032.

[82] Schuckelt, *Türkische Cammer*, 99.

[83] Voltelini, "Urkunden und Regesten," C, entries 2680 and 2681.

[84] Ibid., lxxxviii, entry 2079. The objects are not explicitly described as Turkish but are listed with similar Ottoman objects.

Another entry in the 1619 inventory shows that Ottoman dignitaries presented not only objects of Ottoman manufacture, but also others, quite possibly recycled, leaving us in need of finding out more about the Middle Eastern channels feeding into the Central European networks. Here we find "a Persian [Safavid] coverlet of gold, silver and silk [most likely for a horse]," which was "received from an [Ottoman] *bassa* near Novigrad in 1594."[85] One has to be careful with the attributions in the inventories, but it is not unlikely that an Ottoman dignitary should have gifted Safavid art objects, as they were highly appreciated and circulated widely in the Ottoman Empire. In fact, Ottoman art of the time drew rich inspiration from Timurid and Safavid works of art.[86]

As the inventories illustrated, the intensification of the conflict at the end of the sixteenth century was accompanied by a growing accumulation of Ottoman trophies in Habsburg hands, and vice versa. Pieces of booty continued to be dedicated to the emperor and or used for propaganda purposes, stressing his superiority. In 1594 the imperial troops celebrated a triumphal procession with captured Ottoman weapons and standards, flags and banners among them. Other such processions with captured booty followed in 1595 and 1601.[87] A special function was imparted to the Ottoman trophies presented in 1604/5 on the visit of two Persian envoys. They were in Prague in order to sound out the possibility of an alliance between the emperor and the Safavid ruler against the Ottomans. The exhibited Ottoman trophies documented Habsburg activities of this sort to the Iranians and underlined the hope for closer collaboration.[88] The example illustrates the political profit that could be gained by the display of booty to the wider population and to a targeted group of diplomats.

As we have also seen, Ottoman textiles, pieces of arms and armor, horses and captives also circulated as gifts between the highest European courtly circles. As pointed out by Schuckelt, the importance of the role of the Electors of Saxony for the Habsburgs, for the imperial elections and for the fight against the Ottomans is stressed by further imperial visits and gifts. In 1617 Emperor Mathias and his chosen – but not yet elected – successor

[85] Ibid., lxxxiii, entry 1897.

[86] See, for example, Suraiya Faroquhi, *A Cultural History of the Ottomans* (London: I. B. Tauris, 2016), 34–59.

[87] Karl Vocelka, *Die politische Propaganda Kaiser Rudolfs II, 1572–1612*, Veröffentlichungen der Kommission für die Geschichte Österreichs 9 (Vienna: Verl. d. österr. Akademie d. Wissenschaften, 1981), 275–78.

[88] Niederkorn, *Die europäischen Mächte*, 322.

Archduke Ferdinand personally visited Johann Georg I of Saxony (1585–1656). As a reminder of Habsburg successes, the emperor brought a horse sumptuously decorated with Ottoman bridles and accoutrements and weapons, most of which are still in Dresden's *Türckische Cammer* today. After his successful election, Emperor Ferdinand II sent another caparisoned Ottoman horse and Ottoman weapons to the Elector in 1620. As the Thirty Years' War unfolded, the relationship between the two sovereigns became strained. The elector was a Protestant, and Ferdinand II (1587–1637) an ardent Catholic. Ironically, however, it has been suggested that in sending a further selection of Ottoman weapons to Saxony, the Emperor may have been emulating precisely the Porte's practice of sending maces and swords to its vassals.[89]

PRECIOUS STONE OBJECTS AND OTHER ITEMS

The following section largely leaves the war and booty context and focuses on yet another nucleus of Habsburg collecting, the *Kunstkammern* – mirroring the world according to the ideas of the ideal prince. A group of items that were far less politically charged but very appreciated at early modern courts were objects made of or decorated with stones. The lines between the different categories are blurry, given that stone-encrusted sabers or daggers, already dealt with above, technically also fall into this group. Stone carving was considered a craft worthy of princes and it could be turned into a flourishing trade. The Florentine *pietra dura* production, for instance, was a profitable luxury export branch. In Prague, famous stonecutters worked for Rudolf II, whose passion for precious stones is reflected in their abundant presence in his *Kunstkammer*. Some of the finest stone objects of that period came from the Islamic world. Several carved Timurid jade cups survive in the *Kunstkammer* collections of the Kunsthistorisches Museum and the collection of Maximilian III in the Teutonic Order, their high value and rarity suggesting that they may have been diplomatic gifts.[90] Their placement in one of the most exclusive nuclei of Habsburg collecting underlines how

89 Schuckelt, *Türkische Cammer*, 104–6.

90 Two of them were identified in the *Rudolfsinventar* of 1607/8: Seipel, ed., *Exotica*, 143–46, nos. 54, 56, 180–82 and 93; David Roxburgh, ed., *Turks: A Journey of a Thousand Years 600–1600* (London: Royal Academy of Arts, 2005), 423, 424, nos. 184 and 191; Karin Rührdanz, "Ein kändlein von schwartzgriener Igiada: Persianate Nephrite Vessels," in *Mediaeval and Modern Iranian Studies*, ed. Maria Szuppe, Anna Krasnowolska and Claus V. Pedersen (Proceedings of the 6th European Conference of

much they were appreciated. Objects like those could be used as models by stonecutters working at court, who were indeed allowed to visit Rudolf's collection. They also stress the taste for the rare and novel of the Habsburg collectors, two vital factors determining whether or not an object was included in the *Kunstkammer* and fitted into the cosmic program of these spaces.

The aforementioned Frankfurt gift exchange of 1562 also included a set of stone carved tableware. Among other things, two sets of crystal or alabaster tableware and two Iranian cups decorated with precious stones were given to Emperor Ferdinand I.[91] It is notable that they were antique at the time of giving, possibly being recycled gifts from one of the sumptuous Safavid embassies to Constantinople.[92] The 1606/11 *Kunstkammer* inventory of Rudolf II mentions a gilded walking stick decorated with precious stones in the section of *Türckische Sachen* (Turkish things), and explains that it came as gift of the Elector of Saxony to Rudolf II in 1610 – thus showing yet another channel of object circulation involving vast detours.[93] Some less expensive yet still novel items were sent to the emperor by an emissary directly from Constantinople in 1593: in the section *Türckische Bücher und Papir* (Turkish books and paper) – the attributions in the inventory have to be interpreted carefully – we find 206 folios of Safavid/Persian paper decorated with flowers.[94] Yet another entry of the inventory mentions an Ottoman *terra sigillata* jug, a medicinal tool gifted to the emperor by a courtier in 1606.[95] Ottoman *terra*

Iranian Studies held in Vienna on 18–22 September 2007 by the Societas Iranologica Europaea (*Cahiers de Studia Iranica* 45 (2011)), 179–92.

[91] Riegl, "Ältere orientalische Teppiche," 330. Unfortunately, Riegl does not specify his source; Busbecq briefly describes the reception but he provides no details of gifts: Forster and Roider, *Turkish Letters*, 237; Rudolph, "Türkische Gesandtschaften ins Reich am Beginn der Neuzeit," 301 and 302. Rudolph quotes two sources mentioning slightly different gifts.

[92] Reindl-Kiel, "Duft der Macht," 235–36.

[93] Bauer and Haupt, *Das Kunstkammerinventar Kaiser Rudolfs II.*, 45, entry 820.

[94] Ibid., 46, entry 829. The quality of an inventory always depends on the knowledge of the compiler; misinterpretations are frequent. In this case it was most likely David Fröschl. The sheets of paper are described as Persian/Safavid in a section clearly dedicated to Ottoman objects. Safavid art was available in Constantinople, the inventory also includes a section with Persian items, and it is possible that the papers were indeed of Persian origin. However, since they did not survive, the inventorist's attribution could also be wrong.

[95] Bauer and Haupt, *Das Kunstkammerinventar Kaiser Rudolfs II.*, 56, entry 1062. Julian Raby, "Terra Lemnia and the Potteries of the Golden Horn: An Antique Revival under Ottoman Auspices," *Byzantinische Forschungen (Essays in Honour of Cyril Mango)* 21 (1995): 305–42; Gisela Helmecke and Karin Rührdanz, "Turkish Terra Sigillata Vessels

sigillata vessels and other clay tableware are also listed in the estate inventory of Emperor Ferdinand I from 1568, the former having been brought by a priest from Jerusalem and given to Ferdinand, and the latter sent by Busbecq from Constantinople between 1554 and 1562.

Among the stone objects, cut and uncut precious stones and jewelry were common gifts too. At the beginning of this study, the seemingly gender-conscious gifting of golden necklaces and bracelets to Queen Isabella of Hungary was mentioned. Another recorded gift exchange further illustrates how common gift recycling was, and that not only the Habsburgs were informed about the passions of the Ottoman dignitaries, but the Ottoman dignitaries themselves also knew what pleased the Habsburgs. Knowing about Maximilian's II interest in the natural sciences, the Grand Vizier Rüstem Pasha (c. 1500–1561) sent two bezoar stones, a medicinal substance comparable in effect to the *terra sigillata* objects, used against poisoning and other ills, which he had received from the Safavid Shah. The gift came in 1569 with an imperial emissary who had mediated the selection of the present.[96] In 1605 the later Emperor Mathias was presented with coral stones and other *curiosa* by an Ottoman dignitary in Hungary, reportedly selected by the giver to illustrate the country's beauty.[97] The Safavid embassy of 1610 brought among other things a golden cross encrusted with jewels, purported to come from the Temple of Solomon, deemed fit for a Christian sovereign. There was also a piece of jewelry with precious stones, four large topaz and amethyst stones, and a topaz vase. Marianna Shreve Simpson has referred to precisely this gift exchange to propose that in the Safavid context religious items were occasionally recycled or redistributed gifts.[98]

from the 16th to the 17th Century and Their Counterparts in Europe and the New World," in *Thirteenth International Congress of Turkish Art, Proceedings*, ed. Géza David and Ibolya Gerelyes (Budapest, 2009), 309–22.

96 Bart Sveri, "Representation and Self-Consciousness in 16th Century Habsburg Diplomacy in the Ottoman Empire," in *Das osmanische Reich*, ed. Kurz, Scheuz and Vocelka, 292.

97 Ibid., 292.

98 They are listed as a group in the *Kunstkammerinventar* of Rudolf II; the vase was identified with one in the *Kunstkammer* of the Kunsthistorisches Museum: KK 1346. Bauer and Haupt, *Das Kunstkammerinventar Kaiser Rudolfs II.*, 30, entries 504, 505, 507–10 and 72, entry 1330. On Safavid-European gift exchange: Marianna Shreve Simpson, "The Morgan Bible and the Giving of Religious Gifts between Iran and Europe: Europe and Iran during the Time of Shah Abbas," in *Between the Picture and the Word: Manuscript Studies from the Index of Christian Art*, ed. Colum Hourihane and John Plummer (Princeton: Index of Christian Art, Dept. of Art and Archaeology, Princeton University, 2005), 141–50, esp. 146.

This shows that redistributing gifts was common well beyond the Ottoman remit and was widely practiced within European courtly circles.[99]

The exchange of grand embassies (*Großbotschaften*) after the treaty of Zsitvatorok in 1606 brought ever more valuable objects of high quality to the imperial court, some of which survive today in the formerly imperial collections. From then onward the Habsburgs paid no tribute and received from the Porte gifts considered worthy of their imperial status. The inventory of Emperor Mathias already lists precious Ottoman pieces of jewelry explicitly attributed to such an embassy. These are, however, matters beyond the scope of this study.[100]

CONCLUSION

Focusing on objects of Ottoman manufacture entangled in the networks of gift exchange centered on the Habsburg court, this study has shed light not only on the asymmetric political relationship between the Habsburg and the Ottoman Empire during the second half of the sixteenth century, but also on the complexities of Habsburg collecting policies, the rise of a fashion for things Ottoman and – most importantly – imperial propaganda. The objects in discussion stem from different contexts: diplomatic gifts, booty or the marketplace. Many examples of gifts reveal the expressive and formative potential of objects within complex and shifting power structures, especially in connection with the often shifting or ambiguous conception of honor and prestige of giver and receiver. The power of objects is probably best illustrated by the gifts indicating submission, such as the kaftans given to the imperial emissaries as signs of their assumed vassalage, but also the Ottoman booty pieces sent to the emperor from the battlefield of Hungary as signs of his rising power.

There is certainly a case for arguing that continuity and transferability were key aspects in a world of objects circulating very easily across cultural divides even in a time of harsh military conflict. The gift-giving contexts studied here mirror the hierarchies of their time, with the Ottoman sultans standing at the top of the pyramid, but not going unchallenged. This was especially evident in the asymmetry of the value and quantity of gifts between the two courts. To the consolation of the emperors the booty items on the other end of the spectrum, dedications

[99] See: Reindl-Kiel, "Duft der Macht," 205–6.

[100] See, for instance, Voltelini, "Urkunden und Regesten," lxxxvii, entries 2037 and 2069; lxxxix, entries 2131 and 2133; Reindl-Kiel, "Duft der Macht," 245–49.

of spoils of war by their military officials, celebrated them as the superior defenders not only of the Holy Roman Empire but of the whole of Christianity. By turning them into commemorative materials used for propaganda purposes, the spoils of war were endowed with a high symbolic value, often contrasting with their relatively minor material value. Between these two poles Ottoman objects, new or reused, changed hands as presents by courtiers, relatives and foreign princes.

The perceived value and rarity of an object at the moment of its reception at a Habsburg court determined its future, which could be one of further movement or not. Immobilized objects were far from dead, too. Ottoman artifacts appear in a surprising number of key places for the production and representation of imperial power. Items deemed most precious and rare found their way into the noble nuclei of imperial collecting such as the *Kunstkammern*. Others, such as carpets, were used in palatial contexts. Yet others were put to propagandistic use, as permanent or ephemeral installations of imagined Habsburg superiority.

5

The Diplomatic Agency of Art between Goa and Persia

Archbishop Friar Aleixo de Meneses and Shah 'Abbās I in the Early Seventeenth Century

Carla Alferes Pinto

This chapter explores the social lives of artistic objects and their diplomatic agency in early seventeenth-century Asia.* It does so by focusing on the gift-giving activities of Friar Aleixo de Meneses, who served both as Archbishop of Goa (1595–1612) and as governor of the Portuguese empire in Asia (1607–9), with Shah 'Abbās I of Persia (1588–1629) (Figure 5.1). Toward the end of this study, a brief excursion further explores the gifts sent by Meneses to Fabio Biondi, an Italian noble who had served as the papal vice-legate in Portugal during the 1590s. This shall allow us to draw some comparisons between the various strategies of gifting involved.

Meneses's activity as a sophisticated gift-giver took off after his arrival in Goa in 1595. The capital of the Portuguese *Estado da Índia* was a particularly rich and diversified market with global connections facilitating a panoply of solutions in terms of gifting, many of which were used by Meneses in his diplomatic activities. Diplomatic exchange between the *Estado da Índia* and the Safavid empire was coordinated through missionaries of the Augustinian order, to which Meneses himself belonged. They pleaded for license to work with Christians in Persia, and indeed were hoping for some time to convert the Shah himself, while also pushing for commercial advantages at the Safavid court. The variety of goals thus pursued often required parallel lines of diplomatic management, with investments on more than one representational front. Material culture with a strong visual facet could sustain such challenges, but the

* This chapter has benefited from the support of CHAM (FCSH/NOVA-UAc), through the strategic project UID/HIS/04666/2013 sponsored by FCT.

FIGURE 5.1 Friar Aleixo de Meneses (1559–1617). *O lyvro de plantaforma das fortalezas da Índia da Biblioteca da Fortaleza de São Julião da Barra*, 1620.

codes were not always understood in equal manner by all. Between the Portuguese and Persia the potential for misunderstandings was as important as the prospects of successful exchange.

AUGUSTINIAN MISSIONS TO PERSIA

Shah ʿAbbās I rose to the throne of the Safavid empire in 1588 and, revealing exceptional leadership from early on, came to alter the geopolitical configuration of the entire region. Solidly organized as never before, the Persian empire under ʿAbbās confronted its nearest external opponents with confidence. The shah carried away important victories over the Uzbeks and the Ottomans, and soon also began to address the problems created by Portuguese interests in the Persian Gulf.[1] The main point of

[1] For an update on the relationship of Portugal with Persia, see Rui Manuel Loureiro and Vasco Resende, eds., *Estudos sobre Don García de Silva y Figueroa e os "Comentarios" da embaixada à Pérsia (1614–1624)*, 4 vols. (Lisbon: CHAM, 2010), vol. 4; and Luis Gil

contention was the island of Hormuz with its hugely profitable long-distance trade, including a customs house contributing substantially to the running of the *Estado*.[2] Hormuz controlled commercial transactions on grounds of its unique strategic location, at the mouth of the Persian Gulf, with important military and political implications for the entire region.

The diplomatic dialogue between the Portuguese and the Safavids was therefore crucial for the management of an inherently tense and unstable constellation of powers and commercial relations. As early as 1507, the Portuguese staked their claim to control over Hormuz, soon to be followed by the formal occupation of the island in 1515 and the construction of a fortress. The Safavids maintained in theory that Hormuz should pay them tribute, but in practice it was the Portuguese who used the existing networks of the virtually independent Gulf kingdom to consolidate their own power. For over a century, balance was maintained through the regular exchange of envoys and embassies between the two powers. On the Portuguese side, Lisbon (or Madrid during the Union of the Iberian crowns of 1580–1640) was a distant center often delegating its diplomacy in Asia to the viceroys in Goa. On the Persian side, the shah was ideally the figure around whom diplomatic activities converged, but his court often moved, thus complicating the task of foreign envoys. The Portuguese-Persian relationship remained a difficult one, its diplomatic history fraught by many vicissitudes including delays, intrigues, poisonings and suspicions of murder. It nonetheless allowed the two states to coexist for over a century, until the fall of Hormuz to the Anglo-Safavid alliance in 1622.[3]

The Augustinians played a key role in this story because Persia was, within the organizational framework of the Catholic missions, known as *Padroado Português do Oriente* (based on the legal rights conceded to the Portuguese Crown by the Holy See in matters of evangelization and ecclesiastical administration, stretching from the Cape of Good Hope to Japan), a

Fernandez, *El Imperio Luso-Español y la Persia Safavida*, 2 vols. (Madrid: Fundación Universitaria Española, 2006–9).

[2] On Hormuz, see Dejanirah Couto and Rui Manuel Loureiro, eds., *Ormuz, 1507 e 1622: Conquista e perda* (Lisbon: Tribuna da História, 2007), and Dejanirah Couto and Rui Manuel Loureiro, eds., *Revisiting Hormuz: Portuguese Interactions in the Persian Gulf Region in the Early Modern Period* (Wiesbaden: Harrassowitz Verlag/Calouste Gulbenkian Foundation, 2008).

[3] In the present text, and notwithstanding the different scopes of the words, "embassy" and "mission" are used indifferently, since Augustinian printed sources employed the term "embassy" when referring to the Order's missions to the Safavid court.

field they had the ambition to control and, in the late sixteenth century, came to hold firmly. There was a tacit agreement regarding the fields of action of the various missionary orders in the Padroado, and within this spatial order the Augustinians rose to prominence in East Africa, Hormuz and Persia. In fact, they gained their position in those places with considerable effort, having promptly answered, under Friar Agostinho de Jesus, a request in 1572 by King Sebastian (1557–78) for missionaries, sending twelve of their men to some of the most inhospitable and challenging places of the empire, including Mozambique and Hormuz.[4] In the early 1600s the Augustinian friar Félix de Jesus could thus safely state, in reference to his organization, that Hormuz was a "conquest of ours."[5]

The presence in Hormuz was only the first step toward the planned "spiritual conquest" of Persia inaugurated with a first official incursion in 1582. This mission took off in connection with two distinct sets of circumstances: first, the arrival in Goa of a new viceroy, Francisco Mascarenhas (1581–84), with letters from Philip II of Spain, now also king of Portugal, to the shah. This was evidently in connection with the Habsburgs' hope to consolidate what they saw as an important alliance against the Ottomans. Second, the entry of the Augustinians to Persia was facilitated by the temporary presence in Goa of an Armenian who had just completed an ambassadorial mission to Mohammad Khodabandeh (1577–87), the predecessor of Shah 'Abbās, in the service of the viceroy of Naples and could thus offer advice. Inspired perhaps by the Augustinians' presence in East Africa and Hormuz, Mascarenhas chose some members of that order for the task of visiting Persia. In addition, Friar Simão de Morais (also known as Friar Simão da Conceição) may have been chosen on grounds of his knowledge of Persian and Latin, the languages used in the missives.[6] As a consequence, Morais was given an

4 A recent pioneering study of the Augustine order in Persia is John M. Flannery, *The Mission of the Portuguese Augustinians to Persia and Beyond (1602–1747)* (Leiden: Brill, 2013). See also the letter that friar Agostinho de Jesus sent to Philip III (undated, but likely written in 1600), published in Carlos Alonso, "Nueva Documentación Inédita Sobre las Misiones Agustinianas en la India y en Persia (1571–1609)," *Analecta Augustiniana* 33 (1970): 345–47.

5 As stated in the "Primeira Parte da Chronica e Relação do Principio que teve a Comgregação da Ordem de S. Augostinho nas Indias Orientais," a manuscript from 1606 first published in Arnulf Hartmann, "The Augustinians in Golden Goa: A Manuscript by Felix of Jesus O.S.A.," *Analecta Augustiniana* 30 (1967): 83.

6 Roberto Gulbenkian and Carlos Alonso, "El P. Simón de Moraes, pioneiro de las misiones agustinianas em Persia," *Analecta Augustiniana* 62 (1979): 343–72, quoted in Flannery, *Mission of the Portuguese Augustinians*, 48.

audience with the shah and was able to deliver the gifts he was carrying. His presence at the Safavid court may be considered successful, since he was able to convert to Catholicism a number of Persians before his return to Goa in 1584. However, the official response of the shah to the king in Madrid was sent through an ambassador, not through the friar.[7]

Some years later, Phillip II sent instructions to the viceroy in Goa ordering a full-scale diplomatic mission to be launched under the leadership of a person of some rank. The solution found by the then archbishop Aleixo de Meneses fell somewhat short of the monarch's ambitions. For reasons that are not entirely clear, the viceroy Dom Francisco da Gama (1597–1600) delegated the organization of the diplomatic mission to Meneses, supporting the archbishop's plan to convince the Augustinian friar Nicolau de Melo to make a detour through Persia on his journey back from the Philippines to Europe. It is telling that the documentation about this mission is rather scarce, and that nothing is known about the gifts sent on this occasion. We do know, however, that the friar arrived in Isfahan in February 1599 shortly after the English tradesman and adventurer Anthony Shirley, who had already convinced the shah to enter into diplomatic negotiations with several other European courts.[8] Despite the difficult moment – with Shirley destabilizing the Goan mission – the interview between the Augustinian priest and the shah seems to have gone well. It was as a result of this meeting that the Augustinian residency in Persia was officially established. ʿAbbās had shown a desire of having near his court some Catholic priests with whom to converse, following examples of interreligious dialogue at the Ottoman and Mughal courts.[9] His attitude was, as one might expect, interpreted with excessive enthusiasm by the Augustinian friars who saw in it a sign of a possible inclination of the shah to convert to the Christian faith.[10]

Once in Persia, the Augustinians ventured to take part in ʿAbbās's own diplomatic missions to several European courts launched in April 1599.

[7] On further developments, see Flannery, *Mission of the Portuguese Augustinians*, 47–49.

[8] On this individual, see Richard Raiswell, "Sherley, Anthony, Count Sherley in the Nobility of the Holy Roman Empire (1565–1636?)," in *Oxford Dictionary of National Biography* (Oxford: Oxford University Press, 2004), online at www.oxforddnb.com/view/article/25423 (accessed 12 October 2016).

[9] Friar Agostinho de Jesus mentioned this matter in the letter he wrote to King Phillip III, probably in 1600. See Alonso, "Nueva Documentación Inédita," 346.

[10] Antonio de Gouveia, *Relaçam em que se tratam as guerras e grandes victorias que alcançou o grãde rey da Persia Xá Abbas do grão turco Mahometto* (Lisbon: Pedro Crasbeek, 1611).

Along with ambassador Husain Ali Beg and Anthony Shirley went Friar Nicolau de Melo; Nicolau de Santo Agostinho, an Augustinian lay brother of Japanese origin; and Friar Afonso Cordeiro, a Franciscan. The embassy has gained its place in the annals of history for the worst reasons. Problems began early on, with several intriguing attempts on the life of Friar Nicolau de Melo by Anthony Shirley, arguments between Ali Beg and, again, Shirley, and difficulties brought about by the chosen overland route to Georgia and to Russia.[11] The Augustinian friar ended up arrested in Moscow and, sixteen years later, burned at the stake. Shirley leisurely stole almost all of the gifts sent by the shah to the European princes. And in the end only Ali Beg made it to Rome and Madrid.[12]

CHRISTIAN VISUAL CULTURE FOR THE SHAH

The failure of the Shirley mission, along with alarming news about increased pressure on Portuguese interests in the region, was the background against which Philipp III (1598–1621) decided to have another emissary sent to the shah. The king's instructions arrived in Goa in 1601, where Viceroy Aires de Saldanha (1600–1605) soon prepared a mission. Its main goal was to inform the Persians about the transgressions of Husain Ali Beg and Anthony Shirley. The ultimate goal was to push for a reinvigorated alliance against the Ottomans. Again, Friar Aleixo de Meneses intervened as archbishop, demanding that the "enterprise and the embassy" be given to the Augustinians instead of the Jesuits, who purportedly had designs on entering Persia, too. Meneses prevailed. The Augustinians Jerónimo da Cruz and Cristóvão do Espírito Santo were chosen on grounds of their religious devotion and knowledge of the scriptures. To assist them with practical matters, the authorities appointed another Augustinian, António de Gouveia, a man said to have the necessary "maturity for business."[13]

[11] On Shirley, see most recently Vasco Resende, "'Un homme d'inventions et inconstant': Les fidélités politiques d'Anthony Shirley, entre l'ambassade safavide et la diplomatie européenne," in *Revisiting Hormuz*, ed. Couto and Loureiro, 235–60.

[12] Flannery, *Mission of the Portuguese Augustinians*, 52.

[13] As stated in the letter written by Aleixo to the archbishop of Braga, dated 23 December 1602, Biblioteca Nacional de Portugal, Lisbon, Cod. 3711, f. 58v; and Bernardino José de Senna Freitas, *Memorias de Braga contendo muitos e interessantes escriptos*, 3 vols. (Braga: Imprensa Catholica, 1890), 3: 59.

The incapacity shown by the Portuguese power structures to understand the importance of sending a credited embassy headed by an ambassador of high social rank, capable of proper political negotiation, probably hurt the commercial and strategic interests of the *Estado da Índia*. As was often the case, Goa did not quite do what Lisbon or Madrid intended. And while the use of more or less informal diplomatic missions composed by merchants was fairly common at the time, it remained important to value one's interlocutor by choosing highly dignified ambassadors in key moments at least. Theirs was the task of following rigorously the codes of etiquette and precedence practiced at foreign courts, building on their own high status in their motherland to gain credit in the host societies. None of this was the case with the chosen Augustinians, who were soon to attend audiences, rituals of representation and eloquence within a ceremonial framework that completely escaped them.[14]

The prospect of misunderstandings was thus written into the very nature of the embassy. In a well-known report of the events in Persia, Friar António de Gouveia paid much attention to the matters under discussion, and also dedicated long pages to the wondrous cities and customs he saw. However, his vision was strongly dominated by European and Christian ideals impeding his understanding of Persian court ritual. On being received by the Shah, for example, he described the place as being a "very large square veranda, similar to the cloisters of our convents."[15] Gouveia was on a mission of "teaching knowledge of the true God to pagans and idolaters." Driven by the belief that the shah might convert, the friar showed little sensibility to what went on around him. In one key moment of the reception, he went so far as to ignore the strict prohibition of kissing the shah's hand.

Most importantly for our purposes, the Augustinian envoy chosen by the archbishop of Goa proved incapable of understanding the ceremonial significance of performing a fully ritualized parade of gifts at the Persian court. To Gouveia, the ostentation was in scandalous contrast to Catholic ideals of modesty. As he observed the sumptuousness of some of the paraded objects, the bulk of which he described merely as "gilded things from China" ("*coisas da China douradas*") thus leaving us in the dark

[14] On this subject, see for example the Venetian narratives studied in Giorgio Rota, "Safavid Envoys in Venice," in *Diplomatisches Zeremoniell in Europa und Mittleren Osten in der Frühen Neuzeit*, ed. Ralph Kauz, Giorgio Rota and Jan Paul Niederkorn (Vienna: Verlag der Österreichischen Akademie der Wissenschaften, 2012), 213–49; on the relations between Persia, Venice and Rome, see 227–33.

[15] Gouveia, *Relaçam*, f. 46v.

regarding their exact nature, he wondered how it could be that all-important royal letters, the true signs of diplomatic reciprocity and respect, were relegated to the end. This seems particularly odd given that the profuse exchange of gifts was the diplomatic norm not only across Asia, but also in Europe.[16] Yet Gouveia's difficulty may have had its roots in tensions going back to Goa, where the gifts as such had been gathered.

While we do not have a list of objects, there were undoubtedly some from the Far East, probably gilded and/or lacquered pieces of small furniture or decorative objects, in conformity with the taste of the time. On the other hand, there was a book "lavishly bound with the whole life of Christ in prints" ("*riquissimamente encadernado, em que estava estampada toda a vida de Cristo*"), which had most likely come from Europe.[17] This book may have been the *Christi Jesu Vitae* of Benito Arias Montano (Antwerp, 1573), the *Evangelicae Historiae* of Jerónimo Nadal (Antwerp, 1593), the *Polyglot Bible* (Antwerp, 1567–72) or some other, more obscure title. Finally, there were "a few retables": mobile pieces of reduced dimensions. These must have been portable oratories with a wooden structure and side shutters enclosing a religious oil painting on wood or copper.[18] It is difficult to establish exactly how much attention the Augustinians placed on gifts in the making of this embassy. Aleixo de Meneses, it seems, did devise some sort of strategy. In a personal letter to his uncle Agostinho de Jesus, the Archbishop of Braga in Portugal, Aleixo explained how his dealings in Asia included diplomatic activities performed in parallel to those of the *Estado da Índia*.[19] In fact, some of what he did was in plain contradiction to the interests of the state, especially when Aleixo used Augustinian friars as agents of his own "external politics."[20] With regard to the grand embassy to Persia, then, we learn that Aleixo, while sending a letter (and probably

16 Annette Weiner states that "beliefs in the inherent morality of the norm of reciprocity had a long history in the West. The norm of reciprocity acted as the *modus vivendi*, authenticating the authority and autonomy of aristocrats, the Catholic church, and later, wealthy industrialists." Annette B. Weiner, *Inalienable Possessions: The Paradox of Keeping-While-Giving* (Berkeley: University of California Press, 1992), 29–30.

17 Gouveia, *Relaçam*, ff. 46 and 47, respectively. John Flannery considers that this may be a "copy in Portuguese of the work composed by the Jesuit Jerome Xavier at the court of Akbar, later translated into Persian as 'The Mirror of Holiness viz. the Life of the Lord Jesus.'" Flannery, *Mission of the Portuguese Augustinians*, 58.

18 Gouveia, *Relaçam*, f. 47v.

19 23 December 1602, Biblioteca Nacional de Portugal, Lisbon, Cod. 3711, f. 59.

20 As has already been pointed out in Sanjay Subrahmanyam, "Dom Frei Aleixo de Meneses (1559–1617) et l'échec des tentatives d'indigénisation du christianisme en Inde," *Archives de Sciences Sociales des Religions* 103 (1998): 39.

the referred "gilded things") to the shah, also targeted, with some of his gifts, a particular woman at the shah's court, who he believed was a Christian queen. From this "new Esther," the archbishop expected a personal commitment in the conversion to Catholicism of her husband and others in Persia.[21]

The belief in the existence of a Christian queen in Persia resulted from a complex religious, political and cultural misunderstanding sustained by the Portuguese ignorance of Safavid courtly structures. Once Gouveia was at 'Abbās's court, he realized the mistake, though he only briefly mentioned it in his *Relação*.[22] We thus do not quite know what happened to "all the fine retable pieces" that Aleixo de Meneses had found in Goa and sent to the nonexistent "Christian queen," though we shall come back to their possible fate. We can, however, affirm that painted retables and book prints would have stood squarely within the realm of post-Tridentine orthodoxy especially with regard to catechism. They also deserve attention at another level of analysis. In a letter dated December 1602, Meneses refers to the procurement of retables by using the verb "to find" ("*que achei*") – i.e., he had "found" them rather than commissioned them. Commissioning would naturally have taken much longer than acquiring images on the open market or getting them from a specialized workshop that may have had them in stock. In contrast with the illustrated printed books, which had to be imported from Europe, the paintings are very likely to have been bought and made in the capital of the *Estado*.

In all probability the retables were painted by Goan artisans, or possibly by members of a religious order in a convent workshop. Large numbers of such works were produced prior to the change in the iconographical schemes of the Goan churches in the second decade of the seventeenth century, when the old painted retables began to be replaced by others chiefly in woodwork (*talha dourada*, or gilt woodcarving) and by sculptures.[23] Although King John III of Portugal (r. 1521–57) had attempted to prohibit the manufacture of religious objects by non-Christian craftsmen in India in 1546,[24] and several edicts followed up

21 As narrated in the letter of 23 December 1602, Biblioteca Nacional de Portugal, Lisbon, Cod. 3711, f. 59; and Freitas, *Memorias de Braga*, 3: 60.

22 Gouveia, *Relaçam*, f. 56.

23 For a synthesis of gilt woodcarving works in Goan retables, and of painting in Goa, see Pedro Dias, *Arte de Portugal no Mundo: Índia. Artes decorativas e iconográficas* (Lisbon: Público, 2008), 13–34 and 49–80, respectively.

24 Jacinto Freire de Andrade, *Vida de Dom João de Castro quarto vizo-rei da Índia* [1651] (Lisbon: Agência Geral do Ultramar, 1968), 71.

on this, only few artists came to Goa from Portugal. It could thus be Indian as well as European painters who, in Goa, replicated some of Catholicism's most iconic images for diffusion across Asia, including Persia.[25]

Presumably, Friar Aleixo de Meneses would have engaged in a strategy of mounting an attractive visual program for his Persian "interlocutors," which would have been expected to elicit curiosity and the need for ensuing explanations – where, then, the Augustinian priests with their argumentative rhetoric would have unfolded their full potential as spearheads of the Catholic *Padroado*. In fact, the Augustinians were clearly very alert to the use of images and relics in Persia, as can be seen in António de Gouveia's report. In his description of the city of Yazd, for example, one notices not only an interest in the town's architecture, but the travelers' attention to the existence of countless looms in which several kinds of fabrics were woven. This was not on grounds of an interest in technology, but because there, in one of the workshops, the "image of Our Lady with her most blessed son in her arms" took shape, embroidered on a piece of crimson brocade, responding to an order from the shah – who himself had also, as Gouveia noticed, been seen wearing a dress with certain "Christian" images.[26]

It is very likely that the Augustinian friars already knew of 'Abbās's fondness for European painting in general.[27] Some years later, Gouveia came to mention how, during a visit to the church of the Augustinian convent of Isfahan, the shah had taken long minutes appreciating the paintings covering the walls – though in the end the main Goan image surviving in Isfahan today is not a painting, but a wood and ivory panel featuring St. Peter and St. Paul.[28] Again, the friars mistook this interest in images made "in the European manner" as a sign that their catechizing, further boosted by the inherently persuasive nature of Catholic

[25] George Kubler, *The Shape of Time: Remarks on the History of Things*, 6th ed. (New Haven and London: Yale University Press, 1970), esp. 71–77. See also the chapter "An Introduction to the Artistic Geography of the Americas: The Limits of Kubler's Legacy," in Thomas DaCosta Kaufmann, *Towards a Geography of Art* (Chicago and London: University of Chicago Press, 2004), 219–38.

[26] The passage reads "e eu o vi vestido em hum roupam com estas mesmas imagens, ou outras semelhantes" ("and I saw him [the Shah] dressed in an outfit with these same images [of the Virgin], or other similar [images]") Gouveia, *Relaçam*, f. 34 v. See also Flannery, *Mission of the Portuguese Augustinians*, 56.

[27] Gouveia mentions the taste "particularly of the Shah, who is most fond of painting," *Relaçam*, f. 176 v.

[28] Gouveia, *Relaçam*, f. 209.

iconography, was exerting its effect on their Muslim interlocutor. To Meneses, then, the gift was chiefly a vehicle for conversion – a conversion he strived for in his ecclesiastical capacity, as a sideline to the strictly political sphere of interstate diplomacy. Whether he also considered sending a painter rather than just paintings, we do not know.[29] Some years later, the Safavid court hosted a much-appreciated Flemish painter to satiate an interest in European-style portraiture.[30] By sending images rather than a producer of images, Meneses certainly did maintain a tight control on the iconographical range transmitted to the Shah (though this was also quite simply the easier option at the time).

The religious nature of the gifted paintings and other presents limited and inflected the very condition of these objects as diplomatic gifts. The priority of the Augustinian mission was to conquer "idolatrous and pagan" territories, and no particular attention was paid to the artistic features and materials used in the objects.[31] The gifts carried such a strong visual and textual component of religious nature that their ability to foment a political dialogue was infringed on.[32] In the context of an embassy understood as a part of the spiritual conquest of the East, these

[29] On the transformation of the services rendered by professionals, namely, painters, into diplomatic gifts, see Michael Auwers, "The Gift of Rubens: Rethinking the Concept of Gift-Giving in Early Modern Diplomacy," *European History Quarterly* 43, no. 421 (2013): 421–41.

[30] "At this audience [in June 1621, between the Shah, an English EIC agent and a Carmelite, friar Vicente of Saint Francis, sent to the court in 1604 by Pope Clement VIII] there was present a Flemish painter, whom the king was keeping in order to make use of him: and on this occasion he caused another painter, one of the best in Persia (but much inferior to the Fleming), to come and, to showcase his painter and his art, he drew out from a portfolio various designs on paper, among which was one of the Descent of Christ from the Cross, and another of Shah Tahmasp, great-grandfather of the king, which he kissed, making an inclination of his head." *A Chronicle of the Carmelites in Persia and the Papal Mission of the XVIIth and XVIIIth Centuries*, ed. Herbert Chick, 2 vols. (London: Eyre & Spottiswoode, 1939), 1: 254.

[31] See note 42 and Belchior dos Anjos's and Guilherme de Santo Agostinho's letter to the Order's provincial in Portugal (8 November 1604) in which they told the journey and events in Persia, with no mention of the subject. Note, however, that Luís Pereira de Lacerda (the ambassador sent to Persia by the king) gave up waiting for the shah and left the resolution of said embassy in the hands of the friars, with no allusion to the gift being made in any of the missives of the Augustinians or in the declaration that the ambassador left with them. See Alonso, "Nueva Documentación Inédita," 353–57.

[32] William Voelke, "Provenance and Place: The Morgan Picture Bible," and Marianna Shreve Simpson, "The Morgan Bible and the Giving of Religious Gifts between Iran and Europe/Europe and Iran during the Reign of Shah 'Abbas I," both in *Between the Picture and the World: Studies in Celebration of John Plummer*, ed. Colum Hourihane (Princeton: Princeton University Press, 2005), 12–23 and 141–50.

objects conveyed – as noted by Nicholas Thomas regarding gifts offered in other colonial contexts – a message inseparable from notions of authority, self-assertion and alterity, and were part of a larger tussle for political, cultural and economic control between colonizer and colonized.[33] At the end of the day, the persistent attempts of the Augustinians to catechize 'Abbās and the constant presence of the Christian religious images among their diplomatic gifts did not achieve the ruler's conversion but, despite the Shah's tolerational stance, produced tiresomeness.

All this being said, the materiality of the objects transacted with religious ambitions also came into connection with a wider process of globalization of forms, materials and artistic techniques. Contrarily to the Augustinian friars' wishes and beliefs, the artistic objects they carried were not intrinsically, objectively and exclusively carriers of a single religious truth. The mere act of looking at them would not prompt people in Persia to convert; yet they could be appreciated on other grounds. As artifacts, they were open to interpretation by whoever received them. Surely, the Persian court understood that these paintings were of a religious nature within the society and the cultural moment that created them, that is, an expanding Catholic empire. But for these non-Christian observers, the paintings did not necessarily carry the same narrow truth that the Augustinians believed they conveyed. The repositioning of these objects in the dynamic context of diplomatic relations between Catholics and Muslims implied a shift from their original use, a shift that occurred under the agency of the receiver rather than the giver.[34]

The complete story is, in fact, longer and more nuanced than seen so far. On the one hand, the shah did appreciate the religious dimension of these paintings, even though he did not feel compelled by them to convert to Catholicism. He observed these religious paintings as the cultural artifacts that they were, rightly classifying them as objects of devotion, but also maintaining a distance since in his view Islam succeeded to and hence also superseded the Christian tradition. He appreciated the artistry at stake and validated the artistic value of these objects, thus connecting with the process of "Iberian globalization" aesthetically, but without fully complying with

[33] Nicholas Thomas, *Entangled Objects: Exchange, Material Culture and Colonialism in the Pacific* (Cambridge and London: Harvard University Press, 1991), 185–208. See also Serge Gruzinski, *L'aigle et le dragon: démesure européenne et mondialisation au XVIe siècle* (Paris: Fayard, 2012), 111–62.

[34] Alfred Gell, *Art and Agency: An Anthropological Theory* (Oxford: Clarendon Press, 1998).

the Augustinians' ambitions.[35] On the other hand, he deemed it appropriate to put some of the gifts thus received to use by recycling them. On 4 October 1602 'Abbās informed the priests that he was himself preparing a gift to be sent to Alexander II (1574–1605) of Kakheti, the Christian king of Georgia, with whom the Safavids maintained a strategic relationship. Crucially, this gift was now to include some of the "pieces which the viceroy had sent him" from Goa, because they would be more adequate in Georgia than in Persia.[36] As noted by John Flannery 'Abbās sought with this gesture to make clear to the priests that renouncing Islam was not an option for him and that, therefore, the gifts would serve a better purpose at the court of a king who already shared the same religious ideas.[37]

This interpretation raises interesting questions pertaining to the anthropology of art. As Alfred Gell put it, "the nature of the art object is a function of the social-relational matrix in which it is embedded."[38] Once the Augustinians' gifts were seen as capable "social agents" that could play a role in the shah's relationship with the king of Georgia, their religious message could be rejected (locally) and maintained (through displacement) at the same time. A recognition of their artistic interest was also possible amid all this.

Interestingly, while the shah was probably unaware of the subtleties of the doctrinarian disputes between the different Christian currents, in forwarding the holy images to Georgia he also conformed to the universalist ambitions of the Holy See at the time. The Church worked hard to spread an ecumenical program of uniformization and submission of all Christian churches in Asia and Africa to the Roman rite. Concurrently, the recycling of the gift can be held to reveal the shah's appreciation for the artifacts and his own belief that he could participate in the circulation of Christian objects as a fully autonomous agent of interstate diplomacy in his own right.[39]

ART FROM ALL OVER ASIA ON THE WAY TO PERSIA

Let us come back briefly to the above-mentioned "gilded things from China," alluded to so disdainfully by Gouveia. Quite clearly, the

[35] Serge Gruzinski, *Les quatre parties du monde. Histoire d'une mondialisation* (Paris: Éditions de La Martinière, 2004).

[36] Gouveia, *Relaçam*, f. 53.

[37] Flannery, *Mission of the Portuguese Augustinians*, 59.

[38] Gell, *Art and Agency*, 7.

[39] On the practice of "gift recycling" in the Safavid court, see Simpson, "Morgan Bible," 146.

Portuguese were sending objects brought not from Europe, but rather gathered on the huge marketplace that was Goa. These are likely to have included artifacts that we now describe as "hybrids," often employing visual motifs of European origin in objects made with Asian techniques, materials and labor. The production of such objects was often inherently ambiguous, allowing for a blending of religious, commercial and political aspects.[40] But Aleixo's list of purchases also included *naturalia* such as animal calculi, namely, bezoar stones that could come from northwest India, Vijayanagar or, ironically, Persia (the latter, coming from the stomachs of Khurassan goats, being very highly valued) or from the Malayan Peninsula – indicating access to a global bazaar of commodities.[41]

Evidence regarding another Augustinian diplomatic mission, launched in 1607–8, confirms the interpretation presented so far.[42] Concerned with the Catholic monarchy's relations with Persia, and convinced by his advisers, diplomats and spies that the shah might be willing to convert, Phillip III requested Goa to send two more Augustinian priests to Isfahan. When the orders arrived in September 1607, Aleixo de Meneses was acting as governor following the unexpected death of his predecessor, Martim Afonso de Castro (1605–7). For the first time, Meneses held all the reins in his hands. He requested the Order's Provincial to name two friars and approved the dispatch of António de Gouveia and Guilherme de Jesus to Persia. There were several months to prepare the mission, but composing the diplomatic gift proved no easy task. The city's treasury

[40] Gruzinski, *L'aigle et le dragon.*

[41] Jorge M. dos Santos Alves, "A pedra-bezoar – realidade e mito em torno de um antídoto," in *Mirabilia Asiatica. Produtos raros no comércio marítimo / Produits rares dans le commerce maritime / Seltene Waren im Seehandel*, ed. Jorge M. dos Santos Alves, Claude Guillot and Roderich Ptak (Wiesbaden/Lisbon: Harrassowitz Verlag/Fundação Oriente, 2003), 122–23.

[42] In spite of there having been another embassy to Persia in the year of 1604, and one for which the presence of Augustinians was requested, I have no knowledge of any documentation in which Friar Aleixo makes mention of gifts. In the letter to his uncle on 20 December 1603, he mentions that he would send three friars (Belchior [or Melchior] dos Anjos, Guilherme de Santo Agostinho [or de Jesus] and Diogo de Santa Ana) to accompany the ambassador sent from Portugal, Luís Pereira de Lacerda. Focusing on the religious mission, he aimed to provide whatever was necessary to the functioning of the convent of Saint Augustine "in the court of the Persian" in Isfahan, and thus create the conditions for the shah's conversion. Biblioteca National de Portugal, Lisbon, Cod. 3711, f. 23; Freitas, *Memorias de Braga*, 3: 70; and Arthur Beylerian, *Cinq lettres inédites de D. Frei Aleixo de Meneses, Archevèque de Goa*, Separatas dos Arquivos do Centro Cultural Português, VIII (Paris: Fundação Calouste Gulbenkian, 1974), 591.

was depleted as a result of the countless battlefronts that had to be attended to, and in the end Meneses was forced to "augment the gift with some pieces found in his home."[43]

For the first time, we do possess a fairly detailed list of items chosen in Goa for the shah. This included "a silver tableware with work in relief, and the complete remaining service, all gilded, [this being something] that they did not use in Persia because they do not know how to do it; a number of bottles and jars of the same matter, but crafted in China, with reliefs, and of notable design. A number of screens from China and Japan, which were the first to have ever entered Persia and, as such, much esteemed, particularly by the Shah, who is very fond of painting; a silver cabinet, of no lesser curiosity than price, with the drawers filled with ambergris and a few gold jewels, garnered with emeralds and small rubies. A cup of *Abada* [i.e., a receptacle carved from a rhinoceros's horn] garnered with gemstones. Many other things from the Iberian Peninsula, as well as from China, of greater curiosity than price, but which I had procured because I understood that even if they had little worth among us they would be much appreciated by the Shah."[44]

The events surrounding the assembling process of this diplomatic gift suggest that we need to take a situational approach to the objects, emphasizing how things were transformed as they circulated. In Goa diplomatic gifts were exposed to thoughts about their relative value and role in different places. To follow Appadurai, we are compelled to "approach commodities as things in a certain situation, a situation that can characterize many different kinds of thing, at different points in their social lives."[45] Within the Portuguese narrative of the gift, the ambergris appeared as a part of the role of precious metals and stones. They were

[43] Gouveia, *Relaçam*, f. 171.

[44] "uma baixela de prata lavrada de bastiões, com todo o mais serviço, tudo dourado, coisa que na Pérsia não usam por não o saberem fazer; algumas garrafas e frascos da mesma matéria, mas lavrados todos na China, em obra de relevo, e de muito feitio. Alguns biombos da China e Japão, que foram os primeiros que tinham entrado na Pérsia e, como tais, muito estimados, particularmente do Xá, que é mui afeiçoado à pintura; um escritório de prata de não menos curiosidade que preço, com as gavetas cheias de âmbar e de algumas jóias de ouro, guarnecidas de esmeraldas e rubis pequenos. Um copo de guarnecido de pedraria. Muitos outros brincos assim de Hespanha como da China, de mais curiosidade que preço, mas que eu tinha buscado porque entendia, que ainda que valiam pouco entre nós não haviam de ser pouco estimados do Xá." In Gouveia, *Relaçam*, ff. 176v–7 (spelling updated).

[45] Arjun Appadurai, "Introduction: Commodities and the Politics of Value," in *The Social Life of Things: Commodities in Cultural Perspective*, ed. Arjun Appadurai (Cambridge: Cambridge University Press, 1986), 13.

seen as *matter*, a raw material of which some pieces had been placed in the drawers of a little cabinet, along with some jewelry (made of precious stones and metal), but in contrast to other precious materials that were mentioned as parts of more elaborate objects (for example, the mounting of a carved rhinoceros horn). The ambergris also assumed a hybrid role between precious stone and *materia medica*, as had been the case for a blood-stanching calculus, which Meneses, years earlier, had mounted on a beautiful ring and sent as a gift to Fabio Biondi.[46] It seems to be assumed here that *materia medica* was valued in Persia as in Goa on grounds of its health-giving properties. In contrast, other objects such as the "things ... of greater curiosity than price" mentioned at the end of the list were added to the pool following an expectation that they would be of greater value (or appreciation) in Persia than in Goa, or wherever they originally came from. This points to a difference between gifts that changed their value when moving across cultural borders (as most items of trade) and others that maintained it.[47]

Even though the 1608 list of gifts is far from detailed, it does allow us to point out some characteristics. On the one hand, there is the apparent omission of objects with religious contents, which may be accounted for by the more official and secular nature of the mission – Meneses now represented the *Estado da Índia* as governor, in the first place, and the city of Goa as its archbishop, in the second. Less tied up by the catechetic aspects of the gift, Meneses and Gouveia could develop some concern for the pleasure that it might bring to the Shah, especially on grounds of novelty (as with the screens from Japan) and technological exclusivity. In fact, they may have been inspired by a passage from Friar Félix de Jesus's narrative in the *Crónica* of 1606, where the author reports the delivery of the single named object taken to Persia by the secular ambassador Luís Pereira de Lacerda, in 1604. Lacerda ended up not meeting the shah, but when Friar Belchior dos Anjos came into the ruler's presence, he handed over a "chair of enamelled gold that the ambassador sent him, of which, taking it in his hand, he ['Abbās] asked the Priest if it was a Venetian work, and the Priest answered that it was Portuguese."[48] The most interesting aspect of this episode is the weight carried by a single object originating from Europe as opposed to several other, Asian artifacts that remained anonymous. The chair's technological exclusivity and

46 This was in 1595. On Meneses and Biondi, see below.

47 As explored in Zoltán Biedermann's chapter in this volume.

48 Hartmann, "The Augustinians," 117.

diplomatic agency was achieved on grounds of a combination, indeed a blending, of geographical, technological and aesthetic factors. According to the chronicler, the Augustinian envoy told 'Abbās that the chair had been sent "so that his goldsmiths could see such design and craft"[49] – an argument strengthened by the fact that, according to António de Gouveia, in 1608 the shah again manifested a desire to obtain some artisans capable of making objects similar to those sent from Goa that year.[50]

The variety of materials, forms and functions within the corpus of gifts transacted in 1608 is remarkable, as is their geographical diversity. As mentioned before, the Goan market provided a vast selection of pieces from all over Asia, thus participating in a wider commercial logic established long before the arrival of the Portuguese (Chinese crafts had a longstanding presence in Persia), and in processes that were under way regardless of whatever religion the Catholic archbishop may have fostered. Japanese (*namban*) screens (variations on a genre that was originally destined not for export, but rather for internal consumption by the military, political and economic elites of seventeenth-century Japan) could thus circulate successfully as diplomatic gifts precisely on grounds of the secularization of the arts that they resulted from.[51]

SOME GIFTS FROM GOA TO EUROPE: MENESES AND FABIO BIONDI

Before we conclude, it may be worth mentioning briefly how Meneses labored to find appropriate gifts not only for the shah of Persia (and other Asian rulers), but also for prominent figures in Europe. This is of some interest because it throws additional light on the complex relational nature of diplomatic gifting in such dispersed geographical settings. While in his contacts with Persia Meneses had peppered larger bodies of Asian gifts with select European objects, in his contacts with Europe he learned to gain symbolic capital from certain Eastern *exotica*. This is the case with the gifts that Meneses repeatedly sent to Fabio Biondi, the Holy Seat's vice-legate in Portugal, a man who had played an important role in his nomination as archbishop. Shortly after his arrival in Goa in 1595, Aleixo

[49] Ibid., 117. [50] Gouveia, *Relaçam*, f. 177.

[51] On this matter, see Alexandra Curvelo da Silva Campos, "Nuvens douradas e paisagens habitadas. A arte namban e a sua circulação entre a Ásia e a América: Japão, China e Nova-Espanha (c. 1550–c. 1700)," unpublished PhD thesis, Universidade Nova de Lisboa, 2007, 145–348.

chose to send a cross chiseled from a semi-precious stone and some calculi of animal excretions that, according to the tradition and knowledge of the time, had almost universal healing properties.[52] The miraculous powers of substances such as bezoar stones were known and famed in Europe, in the Middle East and in Asia, but such *materia medica* was much easier to come by in the East than in the West.[53]

That sending such substances involved certain risks was clear: Meneses himself wrote to Biondi that he felt "*affrontato*" ("challenged") by the magical properties that were attributed to them. Yet he finally embraced the risk ("*m'arrischei*") because the products in question might contribute to the prelate's good health. The inner conflict thus described reveals the complex personality of Meneses, a post-Tridentine dignitary of the Church Triumphant, but also a man of curiosity, alert to the knowledge of his time, erudite and meditative, and an avid reader and writer.[54] His careful formulation mirrored the tension between the diligence of wanting to know and becoming familiar with everything, the fascination for what was novel and eccentric and the ever-present self-restraint that resulted from his education and doctrine. At the same time that Aleixo sent substances that he did not completely understand and to which people attributed magical properties, he also drew attention to a cross made of rock crystal that was of comparatively minor monetary value, but above any possible suspicions as a religious object.

In addition to this, Meneses felt compelled to expound his certainty regarding the genuine provenance of the stones – an important aspect at a time when fakes were frequent.[55] And it is their genuine quality that makes such stones into individualized gifts, allowing for an accumulation

[52] Bezoar and porcupine stones were a topic of interest to Garcia de Orta (1499?–1568), who dedicated to them the forty-fifth and the fifty-eighth dialogue of his *Colóquios dos simples, e das drogas* printed in Goa in 1563 (ff. 170–71 and 225–6v).

[53] On the origin, history and effects of these stomach calculi, see Alves, "A pedra-bezoar," 121–34.

[54] A list of the known works by Friar Aleixo de Meneses is in Carla Alferes Pinto, "Traz à memória a excelência de suas obras e virtudes'. D. frei Aleixo de Meneses (1559–1617), mecenas e patrono," *Anais de História de Além-Mar* 12 (2011): 153–80.

[55] On the subjects of trading, pricing and falsifying stones, see Peter Borschberg, "The Trade, Use and Forgery of Porcupine Bezoars in the Early Modern Period (ca. 1500–1750)," *Oriente* 14 (2006): 60–78; and id., "The Euro-Asian Trade in Bezoar Stones (Approx. 1500–1700)," in *Artistic and Cultural Exchanges between Europe and Asia, 1400–1900: Rethinking Markets, Workshops and Collections*, ed. Michael North (Aldershot: Ashgate, 2010), 29–43.

of monetary and symbolic value.[56] The stones' authenticity was grounded exclusively in the archbishop's words, who based his belief in turn essentially on the fact that the stones were acquired in Goa. No reference was made to any sort of technical examination, medical validation, or record of provenance. What is particularly interesting, however, is how these gifts were destined to disappear from the start. While being the focus of discursive strategies conferring on them singular characteristics that made them inalienable in the sense proposed by Annette B. Weiner, they were also meant to be eaten by someone else.[57] By accepting and ingesting what was given to him, in turn, Biondi would place himself in Meneses's debt. Or, if we take into account Biondi's high status, we might also argue that this allowed Meneses to express the amplitude of his obligations. The edible gifts placed the idea of reciprocity on a platform of biological *servitude* (*to serve* is the verb Meneses and Biondi used in the letters they exchanged). In a way, from afar, Meneses acted like a doctor prescribing miraculous drugs to a patient who, pressed by ill health, might wish to believe in their powers.[58] And while the gift never arrived (the ship carrying it was lost), Biondi duly admitted in a letter dated 8 March 1597 that it "would bring much health and greatest enjoyment" merely for having been sent by Aleixo, concluding that "he was as obliged to him as he knew to be his duty."[59]

Aleixo made two further attempts at sending Biondi gifts from Goa. The first of these ended in the robbing and killing of a Franciscan emissary carrying the goods. The last time around, Meneses instructed a priest called Alberto Laércio to carry an exquisite object of art to Rome, where Biondi now resided: a Maldivian coconut shell with a mounting in silver that reproduced the shape of an eagle and had rubies set in the place of the eyes. Inside the object, a piece of the kernel of the coconut itself was held by a metal chain. This piece was meant to be ground and drunk with wine, counteracting every kind of poison or illness. Along with it also went two more stones, as well as two cups carved from the horns of a rhinoceros (which Meneses called a unicorn)

56 Natasha Eaton, "Between Mimesis and Alterity: Art, Gift, and Diplomacy in Colonial India, 1770–1800," *Comparative Studies in Society and History* 46, no. 4 (2004): 817.

57 "the motivation for reciprocity is centered not in the gift per se, but in the authority vested in keeping inalienable possessions. Ownership of these possessions makes the authentication of difference rather than the balance of equivalence the fundamental feature of exchange," Weiner, *Inalienable Possessions*, 39–40.

58 Susan Reynolds Whyte, Sjaak van der Geest and Anita Hardon, eds., *Social Lives of Medicines* (Cambridge: Cambridge University Press, 2002), 3–19 and 117–29.

59 Carlos Alonso, "Elección y consagración de Alejo de Meneses, O.S.A. como arzobispo de Goa," *Analecta Augustiniana* 49 (1986): 133–34.

and a few sticks of "*pau de Malaca*," a substance deemed to be of great advantage in the fight against fever.[60]

Friar Aleixo clearly remained attached to making Biondi's health the main focus of his gift-giving, but in his last attempt he also added an exquisitely crafted artifact to the *materia medica*. The stakes were high. By this time, Meneses was lobbying the Holy See to become a cardinal, an ambition that in such a distant corner of the world amounted to a considerable challenge. We do not know whether Biondi eventually received the Maldivian coconut or how he may have reacted to it, but the combination of sumptuous art and wondrous nature, risky in principle, was certainly easier for him to digest than the Catholic retables were for Shah 'Abbās.

CONCLUSION

The examples of material culture mentioned throughout this text reflect a multiplicity of geographical provenances in Portuguese gift diplomacy and afford a glimpse of Friar Aleixo de Meneses's complex diplomatic agency at the intersection of political, religious and personal plans. But while European and Christian dominance may appear to have been expressed on the senders' side, one also notices a fair deal of flexibility, and possibly some sort of apprenticeship and adaptation to the pragmatics of interstate diplomacy in Asia. At the end of the day, there seems not to have been too much discomfort toward the possible alterity that the artistic forms executed in Goa (or elsewhere in Asia) might express. Art historians have come to emphasize the hybrid nature of much of the art produced and circulated in and through Goa, including not just secular but also religious art. As proposed by Homi Bhabha, it has become possible to recognize the production of identity and alterity through discourses that unfold dialectically rather than by compliance and/or plain confrontation between colonizer and colonized.[61]

60 Carlos Alonso, "Documentación inédita para una biografia de Fr. Alejo de Meneses, O.S.A., arzobispo de Goa (1596–1612)," *Analecta Augustiniana* 27 (1964): 299–300. Note that João de Barros (c. 1496–1570) registered in his *Década III* (book 7, ch. 3) that the antidote proprieties of the Maldives' coconut shell were far superior to those of the bezoars. See Alves, "A pedra-bezoar," 130 and note 42.

61 For Bhabha, hybridity "becomes the moment in which the discourse of colonial authority loses its univocal grip on meaning and finds itself open to the trace of language of the other, enabling the critic to trace complex movements of disarming alterity in the colonial text." Homi Bhabha, "Signs Taken for Wonders: Questions of Ambivalence and Authority under a Tree Outside Delhi, May, 1817," *Critical Inquiry* 12, no. 1 (1985): 5–23. Cited in Robert J. C. Young, *Colonial Desire: Hybridity in Theory, Culture and Race* (London and New York: Routledge, 1995), 22.

We can only wish that further research might bring to the fore documents illustrating the impact of such hybrid artifacts at the Safavid court, and the manner in which they were perceived in comparison with objects brought from Europe by, for instance, the Carmelite missions or the English and Dutch embassies. Within the remit of what we may consider as the impact caused by the Iberian globalization on artistic forms, there is the wooden panel inlaid with ivory, dedicated to the cult of the Holiest Sacrament and representing an altar flanked by St. Peter and St. Paul. This image is still kept today in the Christian Museum at Julfa, the Armenian Christian neighborhood of Isfahan. It would be interesting to trace the biography of the object and determine whether the piece reached the Armenian community coming from the Safavid court or rather from the Augustinian convent.[62] Any future analysis of objects taken by the Portuguese to Persia will have to operate on two fronts: on the one hand, the study of their impact on Christian communities, and, on the other, the possible developments of technologies associated with the production of artistic objects by the Safavids themselves. For the time being, we are still confronted with much uncertainty regarding the latter.

62 Roberto Gulbenkian, *L'Ambassade en Perse de Luís Pereira de Lacerda et des Pères Portugais de l'Ordre de Saint-Augustin, Belchior dos Anjos et Guilherme de Santo Agostinho. 1604–1605* (Lisbon: Fundação Calouste Gulbenkian, 1972), picture between 36 and 37.

6

Dutch Diplomacy and Trade in *Rariteyten*

Episodes in the History of Material Culture of the Dutch Republic

Claudia Swan

The Dutch Republic, recognized as a sovereign nation in 1648, was built on a foundation of trade, and throughout the seventeenth century its mercantile and political interests were deeply enmeshed. Most historical accounts of the tiny republic on the North Sea emphasize Dutch interest in trade, and trade in spices in particular, as the motivation for establishing the Dutch East India Company, the Vereenigde Oostindische Compagnie (VOC).[1] The VOC was officially established in 1602 with the support of the States General of the United Provinces of the Netherlands, the governing body of the nascent republic, and the Stadholder Prince Maurits; around the time that the company became profitable several decades later, the republic was recognized as a sovereign nation. The fates of these two institutions, mercantile and political, were codependent. Indeed, trade in the early years of the struggle for independence from Spain, from whose dominion the seven United Provinces of the Netherlands broke free during the Eighty Years' War, was almost entirely focused on competition with the Spanish and Portuguese Crowns – first in the East Indies and later, with the establishment of the West-Indische Compagnie (WIC), in the West Indies.

In the early years of the VOC, commerce was as likely to require diplomacy as to give rise to acts of war. The majority of diplomatic efforts

[1] Jonathan I. Israel, *The Dutch Republic: Its Rise, Greatness, and Fall, 1477–1806* (Oxford: Clarendon Press, 1995); Maarten R. Prak, *The Dutch Republic in the Seventeenth Century: The Golden Age*, trans. Diane Webb (Cambridge: Cambridge University Press, 2005); Femme S. Gaastra, *The Dutch East India Company: Expansion and Decline*, trans. Peter Daniels (Zutphen: Walburg Press, 2003).

made by and on behalf of the United Provinces and its Stadholders in the early decades of the seventeenth century were intended to secure trade rights and privileges with nations and states and empires affiliated, for commercial purposes at least, with Portugal and Spain. The various Sultanates of the Strait of Malacca, which included Malacca, Johor and Aceh; the Sinhalese Kingdom; the Siamese Kingdom; the Moroccan kingdom; the Ottoman Empire: these and other foreign powers were all courted by the Dutch for the purposes of securing trading rights. In some cases, securing access to trade hubs and/or trade goods themselves involved military aggression against the Portuguese. The Dutch captured numerous Portuguese trade vessels in the years prior to and following the establishment of the VOC, seizing valuable goods sufficient to fund the efforts of the trading company – albeit by way of loot rather than anything approximating fair trade.[2]

Diplomacy was another means of securing a foothold in the competition with the Portuguese for trade in the East Indies, and with the French, English and Venetians in the Ottoman territories. Emissaries and missions traveled from and to the East Indies and from and to the Levant in the early decades of the Dutch Republic bearing missives and gifts – in the interest of trade. The emergence of the Dutch state as a global trading power resulted from military strategies and, simultaneously, by way of diplomatic and mercantile exchanges. Recent scholarship on early modern Dutch cultural exchange with and diplomacy in Asia by Adam Clulow, Mia Mochizuki, Cynthia Viallé and Kees Zandvliet demonstrates the complexities of diplomatic practices and political exchanges over the long term, to as late as the dissolution of the VOC at the close of the eighteenth century.[3] Dutch negotiations with Eastern powers often involved *rariteyten*, or rarities, mercantile access to which was one of the distinguishing qualities of the Republic in formation. In what follows, I take inspiration from these scholarly models and offer an account of the

[2] See, inter alia, Peter Borschberg, *Hugo Grotius, the Portuguese and Free Trade in the Indies* (Singapore: NUS Press, 2011).

[3] See Adam Clulow's chapter in this volume; Mia Mochizuki, "Deciphering the Dutch in Deshima," in *Boundaries and Their Meanings in the History of the Netherlands*, ed. Benjamin J. Kaplan, Marybeth Carlson and Laura Cruz (Leiden: Brill, 2009), 63–94; Cynthia Viallé, "'To Capture Their Favour': On Gift-Giving by the VOC," in *Mediating Netherlandish Art and Material Culture in Asia*, ed. Thomas DaCosta Kaufmann and Michael North (Amsterdam: Amsterdam University Press, 2014), 291–319; Kees Zandvliet and Leonard Blussé, *The Dutch Encounter with Asia 1600–1950* (Amsterdam and Zwolle: Rijksmuseum and Waanders, 2002).

role of curious, rare, exotic objects (*rariteyten*) in Dutch diplomatic relations across the map in the first decades of the seventeenth century, when the emergent nation was taking shape. Gifts and trade goods were, I suggest, interchangeable in early modern Dutch negotiations – negotiations that also pertained more broadly, outside the scope of Dutch encounters, in the early modern world. Broadly speaking, this chapter traces the role of material culture – the goods exchanged in the context of Dutch diplomacy – in the making of a new political entity.[4] While geographically the focal point of my account is The Hague, and the scope is limited chronologically to the opening decades of the seventeenth century, this chapter follows the centripetal mobilization of *rariteyten* by the Dutch for political ends into the middle of the seventeenth century and around the globe.

DUTCH-OTTOMAN DIPLOMACY

The early decades of the seventeenth century, the formative years of the Dutch Republic, were turbulent. The ongoing Netherlandish war of independence from the Spanish Crown reverberated across Europe and into North Africa and the Levant. Alliances negotiated in the first decades of the seventeenth century between, on the one hand, the northern European confederation of provinces that would be united as the Dutch Republic and, on the other, the immense and powerful Ottoman Empire may come as something of a surprise, but these affiliations came naturally given the mutual hatred of Spain.[5] The motto of leaders of the Dutch Revolt (the so-called sea beggars), "*Liever Turks dan Paaps*" or "*Liever Turks dan Paus*", declared it preferable to be Turkish (Muslim) than papal (Catholic). Insignia based on the motto, which the "sea beggars" wore, could be understood to reflect a positive conflation of interests: the crescent moon of Islam gains a face, a figuration inconceivable to Islam,

4 See Kees Zandvliet, *Maurits, Prins van Oranje* (Amsterdam and Zwolle: Rijksmuseum and Waanders, 2000), "Het Internationale Podium," 336–81, for an important account of the role of material culture in the Dutch presence on the global stage to 1625. On early modern diplomacy and material culture, see most recently Nancy Um and Leah R. Clark, eds., *The Art of Embassy: Objects and Images of Early Modern Diplomacy*, special issue, *Journal of Early Modern History* 20, no. 1 (2016).

5 See Abdelkader Benali and Herman Obdeijn, *Marokko door Nederlandse Ogen 1605–2005* (Amsterdam and Antwerp: De Arbeidspers, 2005), "1595–1625: Een waardevol bondgenootschap," 16–51; A. H. de Groot, *The Ottoman Empire and the Dutch Republic: A History of the Earliest Diplomatic Relations 1610–1630* (Leiden/Constantinople: Nederlands Historisch-Archaeologisch Instituut, 1978).

FIGURE 6.1 Anonymous, crescent moon pendant (*Geuzenpenning*) worn under Admiral Louis de Boisot during the Siege of Leiden, silver, 1574, Rijksmuseum, Amsterdam, 3.5 cm × 3.1 cm × 2.7 cm. Amsterdam: Rijksprentenkabinet, Rijksmuseum.

with its proscription against representing animate things (Figure 6.1).[6] The emblem signaled a deep compatibility between anti-Habsburg, anti-Spanish and anti-Catholic leaders of the United Provinces and the Islamic world, rendered in European terms.

Already in the final years of the sixteenth century, Dutch merchants sought access to North African Ottoman ports independent of English protection; and Ottoman envoys are recorded in the Netherlands as early as 1565 and again in the early 1580s.[7] In the course of the Dutch Revolt the city of Sluis in the southernmost province of Zeeland was won from the Spanish in 1604, and 1400 Muslim "galley slaves" were freed from Spanish captivity; 135 of them were returned to Morocco in 1605.[8] Freeing the captive Muslims increased the reputation of the lands of the Christian Prince Maurits among Muslim rulers and brought the United

[6] See R. van Luttervelt, "Liever Turks dan Paaps," *De Gids* 124 (October 1961): 150–63; K. F. Kerrebijn, "Zilveren halve manen," *De Beeldenaar* 25 (2001): 173–75.

[7] Willem Baudartius, *Emanuelis van Meteren Historie der Nederlandscher Gheschiedenissen* (Amsterdam: Jan. Evertsz. Cloppenburch, 1618), Book 31 introduces the 1612 treaty with the Ottoman court by reference to Murad III's sympathies for William of Orange. See also de Groot, *The Ottoman Empire and the Dutch Republic*, 83–85.

[8] Henry de Castries, *Les sources inédites de l'histoire du Maroc, Sér. 1 Dynastie saadienne* (The Hague and Paris: Martinus Nijhoff and Leroux, 1907), 65–67. See also Bülent Arı, "The First Dutch Ambassador in Constantinople: Cornelis Haga and the Dutch Capitulations of 1612," PhD diss., University of Ankara, 2003, 80; de Groot, *The Ottoman Empire and the Dutch Republic*, 92.

Provinces into contact with the Moroccan Sultan Mulay Zidan/Zaidan el Nasir (d. 1627; r. 1603–1627). The young Ottoman Sultan Ahmed I (1590–1617; r. 1603–1617), whose control extended to the westernmost terrain of North Africa, was also appreciative of Christians who freed captive Muslims. In the same decade, the States General supplied the Moroccan ruler with warships – an act that registered with King Philip III of Spain as acute aggression; it was mentioned in his Edict of Expulsion of the Moriscos from Spain in 1609. By 1612, an alliance between the United Provinces and Moroccan and Ottoman rulers appeared to promise the mutually beneficial defeat of Spain. Religious and humanist scholarship in the Netherlandish provinces and in the Maghreb advanced a complementary critique of Catholicism, and offered the possibility of actual communication – where scholars such as Thomas Erpenius (1584–1624) hosted the Moroccan envoy Ahmad ibn Qasim Al-Hajarī (c. 1570–c.1640) in Paris and again in Leiden, and missives to the States General in Arabic were promptly translated by the Leiden Arabist and Erpenius's mentor Joseph Justus Scaliger (1540–1609), for example.[9] Respective positioning of Prince Maurits and the Moroccan sultan vis-à-vis their shared enemy Spain was very much at issue in the opening decades of the seventeenth century and, likewise, in the exchange of diplomatic gifts.

In 1609, Hammu ben Bashir, the Moroccan emissary of King Mulay Zidan, arrived in the Netherlands and, together with the Jewish merchant Samuel Pallache (1550–1616), negotiated on behalf of the Moroccan king the first alliance between the Christian United Provinces and an Islamic power.[10] The agreement to pursue an alliance that "will be advantageous, useful, and profitable for [all] these lands" was sealed with gifts from the Moroccan king. A list provided by King Zidan itemizes "Two '*retal*' of ambergris; four '*retal*' of civet musk [or perfume]; four tapestries ['*haïthi*']

[9] On scholars of Hebrew and Arabic in the Netherlands, see Alastair Hamilton, *William Bedwell the Arabist, 1563–1632* (Leiden: Leiden University Press, 1985), esp. ch. 2, "Holland and After," 31–54; G. J. Toomer, *Eastern Wisdom and Learning: The Study of Arabic in Seventeenth-Century England* (Oxford: Oxford University Press, 1996), "The Netherlands," 41–52; G. A. Wiegers, "The Andalusî Heritage in the Maghrib: The Polemical Work of Muhammad Alguazir (fl. 1610)," in *Poetry, Politics and Polemics: Cultural Transfer between the Iberian Peninsula and North Africa*, ed. Ed de Moor, Otto Zwartjes and G. J. H. van Gelder (Amsterdam and Atlanta: Rodopi, 1996), 107–32, esp. 107–10.

[10] *Resolutiën der Staten Generaal van 1567 tot 1609*, vol. 14 (1607–9), ed. H. P. Rijperman ('s-Gravenhage: Martinus Nijhoff, 1970), 784–90. The full treaty is printed in Emanuel van Meteren, *Historie der Nederlandscher ende haerder na-buren oorlogen ende geschiedenissen* ('s-Gravenhage: [widow and heirs of] Hillebrant Jacobszn. Wouw, 1614), 660r–661r.

of satin made in the sultan's palace; two tapestries of Persian silk; a bed covering."[11] The records of the States General reflect receipt from the Moroccan emissary of a locked chest containing gifts and "amber and civet [musk]," which were distributed among representatives to the States General.[12] Precious spices and *naturalia* such as ambergris and civet musk may have been intended to recommend Morocco as a source for the wares the VOC sought in the East Indies; as for the gift of precious fabrics, fine textiles were the lingua franca of early modern diplomacy.[13] Indeed, these very wall hangings would soon be presented *by* the Dutch – to the English court, as we shall see.

Negotiations with Ottoman Sultan Ahmed I followed swiftly on the Moroccan exchange. In late October 1610, the States General received an entreaty from Constantinople to enter into a formal alliance with the "Turkish emperor" that would guarantee safe passage for citizens (merchants, in particular) of the United Provinces. The letter played on the insecurity of Mediterranean trade for the Dutch, who had not negotiated safe passage with the Ottoman sultan. If an ambassador were sent to Constantinople to secure alliances and trade capitulations, the letter assured its readers, the citizens of the United Provinces would "be privileged above other nations and able to conduct commerce more safely."[14] The Admiral of the Ottoman Navy, Khalil Pasha (d. 1629, later grand vizier of the Ottoman Empire), was prepared, the letter further specified, to submit letters from the sultan to the States General to this effect as soon as Prince Maurits and the States General gave indication of their interest.[15] The October letter was written not by the sultan or a member of his court, but by Jacob Gijsbrechtszn (Giacomo Gisbrechti), a jeweler from Antwerp who lived in Pera in Constantinople – an enterprising

[11] De Castries, *Les sources inédites de l'histoire du Maroc*, 175. De Castries notes that a "*retal*" is a pound of 19 ounces.

[12] On the Dutch record of the Moroccan gift and its local distribution, see *Resolutiën der Staten Generaal van 1567 tot 1609*, vol. 14 (1607–9), 786. The letter from King Mulay Zidan (dated 31 December 1612) is reprinted in de Castries, *Les sources inédites de l'histoire du Maroc*, 172–74.

[13] See Carrie Anderson, "Material Mediators: Johan Maurits, Textiles, and the Art of Diplomatic Exchange," *Journal of Early Modern History* 20, no. 1 (2016): 63–85.

[14] Klaas Heeringa and Jan Garbrand Nanninga, *Bronnen tot de geschiedenis van den Levantschen handel 1590–1826*, 4 vols. (Martinus Nijhoff: The Hague, 1910–66), vol. 1 (1590–1660), ed. K. Heeringa, 179–80 and 155–56 for general discussion. See also Van Meteren, *Historie der Nederlandscher*, 667v.

[15] Khalil Pasha was three times grand admiral and twice grand vizier; see *Encyclopedia of Islam* (Leiden: Brill, 1960–93), vol. 4 (1978), 970–72.

merchant who set his sights on mediating a most promising alliance.[16] Gijsbrechtszn had access to Khalil Pasha, the sultan's falconer and arguably the most influential member at Sultan Ahmed I's court, and was also well informed regarding the state of Dutch trade.[17]

By 1610 Dutch merchants had traded in Ottoman ports for as long as a decade in the absence of any official relations between the United Provinces and the Ottoman Empire under the protection of the French and English, nations in possession of trade agreements. With the 1610 treaty with Barbary (North Africa) in place, it must have seemed an excellent moment to secure relations between The Hague and Constantinople as well. A chronicle written within a decade of these events prefaces its account of diplomatic relations with the Ottoman Empire with a clear reference to trade: "Given that the States General of the United Netherlands seek ardently to improve trade, commerce, and traffic by ship, and that they received in 1610 a letter from Constantinople ..."[18] The Ottoman court, for its part, was keen on an alliance with a renowned anti-Spanish power; the Dutch victory at Gibraltar, in combination with their success at keeping the Spanish Crown at bay in the East Indies, amplified their interest. Gijzbrechtszn's letter seems to have reflected local interests in Constantinople, and Khalil Pasha's ambitions to form an anti-papal league meshed well with Dutch commercial ambitions. In November 1610 the States General met to deliberate on a letter they received from Khalil Pasha, which followed on Gijzbrechtszn's. The result was the first diplomatic mission from the United Provinces to Constantinople. The States General was certainly interested in the freedom of Dutch captives, but also foresaw how profitable unrestricted access could be to trade through Constantinople and ports in Algiers, Syria, Tripoli and Alexandria, among other places. Speaking on behalf of the sultan, the Ottoman admiral wrote that "this mighty portal [the Porte Sublime] is open to all

[16] In 2005 Antiquariaat van der Steur The Hague, listed for sale a 1605 passport issued to Gijsbrechtszn by Prince Maurits; he must by that time already have been resident in the Netherlands. His letters (in Dutch) to the State General are signed Giacomo Gisbrechti, presumably in accordance with diplomatic use of Italian.

[17] The receipt of the letter and resulting deliberations are recounted in Van Meteren, *Historie der Nederlandscher*, fol. 667r. See de Groot, *The Ottoman Empire and the Dutch Republic*, 48–52, 99, 163, 167. See also Ingrid van der Vlis and Hans van der Sloot, *Cornelis Haga 1578–1654: Diplomat and Pioneer in Constantinople* (Amsterdam: Boom, 2012), 69–74, and M. van der Boogert and J. J. Roelants, *De Nederlands-Turkse betrekkingen. Portretten van een vierhonderdjarige geschiedenis* (Hilversum: Verloren, 2012).

[18] Van Meteren, *Historie*, 667r.

friends such as you . . . who are in agreement with us, and their friends and ours; and to our enemies and those who are in agreement with them, such as the Spanish and the Duke of Tuscany, the Porte Sublime is inimical." Once official letters had been exchanged, Khalil Pasha wrote, the sultan "wished to celebrate them, and they shall be celebrated with greater honor than you could imagine."[19]

"RARITEYTEN VAN DESE LANDEN"

"Rare or unusual or curious objects from these lands" ("*rariteyten van dese landen*"): this phrase, borrowed from Dutch state documents, aptly describes the vast array of costly, elaborate, exceptional and locally produced objects and items presented by the first ambassador of the emerging Dutch Republic to the Ottoman Sultan Ahmed I in Constantinople.[20] The story of the 1612 Dutch gift – a story told more extensively elsewhere – concerns material culture in the context of Dutch trade, politics, science and visual culture in the seventeenth century.[21] The 1612 Dutch gift was a bounty of goods: woven, painted, printed, lacquered and mounted things; worked and traced and carved and bound things; lavishly crafted and otherwise wondrous things, some of them natural, some of them edible, some scientific, all of them expensive. Many were locally produced – by artisans and printers in Amsterdam and Haarlem, by noblewomen in Gelderland and by painters and harness-makers in The Hague – and many were brought to the Netherlands from the East, obtained along the trade routes that by 1612 had for a decade already been effectively controlled by the Dutch by means of the VOC. By conversion into a present, these became diplomatic things. Ninety-three crates were carefully packed and their contents listed before being loaded

[19] Heeringa, *Bronnen tot de geschiedenis van den Levantschen handel*, 1, 180–81; See de Groot, *The Ottoman Empire and the Dutch Republic*, 94–95.

[20] 13 August 1611, *Resolutiën der Staten-Generaal, Nieuwe reeks 1610–1670*, vol. 1, *1610–12*, ed. A. Th. Van Deursen ('s-Gravenhage: M. Nijhoff, 1971), 455.

[21] Claudia Swan, "Birds of Paradise for the Sultan: Early Seventeenth-Century Dutch-Turkish Encounters and the Uses of Wonder," *De Zeventiende Eeuw* 29 (2013): 49–63 with previous literature. The *locus classicus* is Nicolas de Roever, "Een Vorstelijk Geschenk. Een blik op de vaderlandsche nijverheid in den aanvang der zeventiende eeuw," *Oud Holland* 1 (1883): 169–88. Over the course of time, more attention has been paid to the diplomatic relations that motivated the presentation than to the gift itself; and the specialization within the fields of (diplomatic) history, art history and history of the decorative arts has blunted the impact of de Roever's study, which cuts across those fields.

on to a ship, the *Zwarte Beer*, which departed Enkhuizen in December 1612. Sixteen contained chairs; four contained porcelain; four more contained two salted oxen; and 3,138 pounds of Edam cheese were divided into 406 pieces and packed in seven packets.[22] Thirteen chainmail vests filled one container; forty-two packets contained butter. Two globes were packed in one chest; a lantern made in Amsterdam and intended for the Blue Mosque, under construction at that time, filled another; and each of two additional containers held two further candelabra. Masses of fabrics, embroidered gloves, birds of paradise, turned ivory objects and a number of other items were packed in one large case; forty-seven pieces of lacquer were packed in a container that also held a box containing 200 tulip bulbs.[23] The state gift presented to Sultan Ahmed I is but one example, among many, of the uses of material culture by the Dutch in the world. In addition, it exemplifies the crucial role rarities played in trade and diplomacy alike.

In March 1612 Cornelis Haga arrived in Constantinople with a limited retinue and a complex brief from the States General. There, in the early years of the Dutch Truce with Spain, he rapidly secured the favor of trade capitulations for the Dutch – that is, permission from the Sultan to trade legally and without penalty in Ottoman territories. In addition, he initiated negotiations on behalf of Dutch prisoners in North Africa. Haga was granted an initial audience with the young Sultan Ahmet at Topkapı Palace on 1 May 1612, on the occasion of his arrival. This elaborate ceremonial occasion is described at length in a Dutch pamphlet printed the same year, which declares that "all Turks were very pleased by the friendship and alliance secured between the Sultan and our lands." An alliance is declared, a friendship that in turn will unlock valuable trade routes, and one that guarantees freedoms that, as per the pamphlet, are "the best and most secure," never before granted anyone else, and that "far exceed those enjoyed by the French, the English, and the Venetians."[24] Hereby the Dutch were able to establish factors and consuls

[22] On Italian gifts of hard cheese to the Ottoman Porte, see Antonia Gatward Cevizli's chapter in this volume.

[23] See Heeringa, *Bronnen tot de geschiedenis van den Levantschen handel*, 1, 273–74.

[24] *VVaerachtich verhael, belanghende de aenkomste tot Constantinoplen, van den ambassadeur der … Staten Generael van de Vereenighde Nederlanden* (Alkmaar: Jacob Harmanszn Verblack, 1612), fol. 5r. The pamphlet also appeared in English, one year later, as *A True Declaration of the arrival of Cornelius Haga; (with others that accompanied him) Ambassadour for the generall States of the united Netherlands, at the great Citie of Constantinople* (London, 1613).

in the Levant and the Mediterranean, from Aleppo to Tunis. Haga presented gifts to the sultan during the initial audience, and, having secured trade concessions, he arranged to have another, massive presentation delivered to Constantinople. In spring 1613, the Dutch gift in the *Zwarte Beer* arrived. This shipload of objects comprised an expression of gratitude to a "friend" and ally, while the presentation of a lavish gift also complied with the expectations of the Ottoman court. An official record of the Dutch gift, "Inventory of the Goods and Presents Sent on Behalf of Their High Mightinesses [of the States General] to Constantinople, to Present to the Sultan and His Pashas, in the Year 1612," is preserved in the National Archive in The Hague. This list describes the objects presented to Sultan Ahmed and his court as "goods and presents" and "goods and delights"; in other state documents they are referred to as "rarities of these lands."[25]

The Dutch gift to Sultan Ahmed I was strategically assembled and the items presented were purchased over the course of roughly six months in 1612. Following the States General's acquiescence to requests from members of the imperial Ottoman court to engage in diplomatic relations, a Flemish jeweler resident in Constantinople, Lambert Verhaer, offered his expertise and service in purchasing appropriate items. In a letter to the States General dated September 1612, Verhaer recommended that the sultan be supplied with "*einige rarieteyten van desse landen*" ("some rarities of these lands"). Specifically, he proposes "that a great lantern be made for use in the new mosque which the Great Lord [the sultan] is now having built." Verhaer also proposed that fine chairs, upholstered in velvet, would go over well at the court, as would some "of those tapestries that are made in Delft" along with "several large pieces of porcelain, also some quartz crystal vases, some fine linen cloths costing six to eight guilders per *ell*, some fine brass candelabras such as are used here in the churches and in grand homes, some harnesses, some turned ivory works, some beautiful shells, and other such things." Verhaer's letter concludes with the specification that "also in favor there are all beautiful colors of

[25] *Inventaris van de goederen ende presenten, die van wege H.H.M. sijn gesonden naer Constantipolen, om te presenteern aen den grooten heer ende de Bassas, Anno 1612.* Nationaal Archief 1.01.02, 12593.9 Secrete kas Turkije: "*Stukken betreffende de afrekeningen terzake van de geschenken vanwege de Staten-Generaal in 1612 naar Turkije gezonden.*" "Goods and delights" is my translation of "*goederen ende fraeyicheden.*" Also published in Heeringa, *Bronnen tot de geschiedenis van den Levantschen handel*, 1, 266–74.

velvet, and satin – damask or plain are both desired."[26] When the *Zwarte Beer* – carrying Verhaer as well as the objects – set sail in December 1612, it carried all of the items he had recommended purchasing and then some. Verhaer was crucial in translating political need and will into material form, by negotiating the selection and the production of the gifts purchased in Amsterdam and in Haarlem in late 1612.[27]

In an official instruction from the States General dated 8 December 1612, Haga was reminded of the value of his negotiations to date and of the nature of Dutch expectations for continued contact and commerce with the Ottomans. The trade capitulations were said to be of great import, as was the liberation of slaves and the establishment of consuls in the Levant. The States General acknowledged "the fine success of [Haga's] legation" and "the fine work, diligence, and dexterity that he had shown, in the service of our country." As for the gift under way at the time this letter was written, it is specified that the States General intended and desired that Haga "should share and distribute all of the gifts [itemized in the included inventory] in such a way as to honor our land and that we may receive thanks for them."[28]

What made *rariteyten* appropriate or compelling gifts to present to foreign powers, especially of territories whence exotica came? The spectacular nature of many of the individual items and the extent of the gift, on which the States General spent roughly 25,000 guilders, attest to awareness of the splendor of Ottoman ritual and Ottoman gift exchange of the time. A crucial additional factor, in my view, is that the *rariteyten* the Dutch presented to the Ottoman sultan were prized items of the East Indian trade they had recently come to exploit and, indeed, in which they had begun to outstrip their rivals, the Spanish and Portuguese. Porcelain and lacquerware and birds of paradise were highly prized, exotic items newly available on the Amsterdam market. Their availability via the Dutch market was a development the Dutch celebrated publicly – in the form of printed images and local histories and paintings alike.[29] In view

[26] Heeringa, *Bronnen tot de geschiedenis van den Levantschen handel*, 1, 260–61.

[27] Verhaer is a fascinating figure, about which much remains to be said. He is described as "*commis*" in Resolutions of the States General dated 29 October and 17 November 1612; see Heeringa, *Bronnen tot de geschiedenis van den Levantschen handel*, 1, 262.

[28] Heeringa, *Bronnen tot de geschiedenis van den Levantschen handel*, 1, 264, citing N.A. Staten Generaal 7075.

[29] See, inter alia, Elmer Kolfin, "*Omphalos Mundi*: The Pictorial Tradition of the Theme of Amsterdam and the Four Continents, circa 1600–1665," in *Aemulatio: Imitation, Emulation and Invention in Netherlandish Art from 1500 to 1800. Essays in Honor of Eric*

of Dutch interest in trade with the Ottoman Empire, the gifts presented to the Ottoman court in 1613 require an analytic framework distinct from established accounts of interpersonal gift exchange. Michael Harbsmeier's account of early modern gift-giving recounts numerous instances from early travelogues of gifts exchanged in advance of trade relations, where donations or gifts were given in order to obtain trust and friendship, but endowed with a force or awe that was geared to dominance or at the very least competition in a trade economy.[30] Likewise, the Dutch gift to the sultan seems to have been intended to satisfy local requirements for imperial presentations (it was appreciably vast and contained numerous splendid items). At the same time, it demonstrated Dutch access to valuable merchandise; it represented Dutch trade might.

Baudartius's 1620 account of the Dutch gift contains two essential qualifications for our present purposes. He introduces a list of gifts as those presented on behalf of the States General and by Prince Maurits – the Netherlandish provinces were thus represented to the Ottoman sultan; and his list is immediately followed by the statement: "These presents were very welcome and greatly appreciated and were considered much more valuable than if they had just been so many vessels and beakers of gold and silver. Because silver and gold beakers and cups that the Turks receive, they bring straight to the Mint and make money of them."[31] Prior accounts of gifts to the Ottomans – Habsburg accounts in particular – bemoaned the incommensurability of the systems of value in play and the Ottoman tendency to melt down gifts of precious metals.[32] The Dutch gift extended well beyond currency (one chest was filled with 5000 "*Hollandse daelders*") and vessels (897 pieces of porcelain, in addition to numerous lacquerware vessels and drinking vessels made of shells and horns) to include butter and cheese. It may have fulfilled standard

Jan Sluijter, ed. Anton W. A. Boschloo (Zwolle: Waanders, 2011), 382–92; and Claudia Swan, "Lost in Translation: Exoticism in Early Modern Holland," in *The Fascination of Persia: The Persian-European Dialogue in Seventeenth-Century Art and Contemporary Art of Teheran*, ed. Axel Langer (Zürich: Scheidegger and Spiess, 2013), 100–16.

30 Michael Harbsmeier, "Gifts and Discoveries: Gift Exchange in Early Modern Narratives of Exploration and Discovery," in *Negotiating the Gift: Pre-Modern Figurations of Exchange*, ed. Gadi Algazi, Valentin Groebner and Bernhard Jussen (Göttingen: Vandenhoeck and Ruprecht, 2003), 381–410. Harbsmeier cites numerous instances from early travelogues of gifts exchanged in advance of trade relations.

31 Willem Baudartius, *Memorien, ofte Kort verhael der gedenckuveerdighste geschiedenissen van Nederlandt ende Vranckrijck* (Arnhem: Ian Iansz, 1620), fol. 18v.

32 Notably, Salomon Schweigger, *Ein Newe Reyßbeschreibung auß Teutschland nach Constantinopel und Jerusalem* … (Nürnberg: Johan Lanßenberger, 1608).

expectations that numerous valuable items be presented; it also contained local products of Dutch industry and agriculture (textiles, furniture, butter, cheese). The Dutch gift represented more than local production: it included such highly sought-after exotica as birds of paradise (eight in all) and a large Chinese chest. The "*rariteyten van dese landen*" also included hybrid works such as lacquerware vessels made by Willem Kick in Amsterdam in the manner of East Indian lacquerware, presented alongside lacquerware from the East.[33] By and large the Dutch gift was not fungible, although elements of it were edible (cheese, butter, meat) or intended for dispersal and use (fabric) or to be spent (currency). While it represented Dutch trade might, it could not readily be exchanged; the presentation of these goods took them out of market circulation. The *rariteyten* exemplify this dynamic. Procured by the Dutch in East Asia, they were highly valuable merchandise, the porcelain and other vessels and the birds of paradise, for example. Presented as gifts and enlisted in the show of Dutch trade might, they became priceless.[34]

While staggering in its proportions and scope, the Dutch gift adheres to the model of the diplomatic gift, intended to negotiate or to broker political relationships – in this case trade relationships controlled by the sultan. The gift is further characterized by two qualities. Firstly, the goods presented by the Dutch were mercantile goods, objects they mobilized on a market they were coming to dominate. (And in this sense, these objects were "*rariteyten van dese landen*," locally available foreign goods, or domesticated exotica.) They were market goods off the market, though. The other key quality has to do with display, and what Anthony Cutler calls the "ritual technology of display." In the case of diplomatic gifts, spectacle was key.[35] Contemporary accounts suggest that Haga's presentation gratified local expectations concerning display. Haga, Baudartius wrote, "honored the Turkish Emperor with some lovely presents all of which were exhibited publicly and for all the world to see, under a

33 See Reinier Baarsen, "Kistjes van Kick? Hollands lakwerk uit de vroege 17de eeuw," *Bulletin van het Rijksmuseum* 56 (2008): 12–27.

34 On rarity and gift-giving, see Anne Goldgar, *Tulipmania, Money, Honor and Knowledge in the Dutch Golden Age* (Chicago: University of Chicago Press, 2007), 56–57; and Florike Egmond, "Precious Nature: Rare Naturalia as Collector's Items and Gifts in Early Modern Europe," in *Luxury in the Low Countries: Miscellaneous Reflections on Netherlandish Material Culture 1500 to the Present*, ed. Rengenier Rittersma (Brussels: ASP Editions, 2010), 47–65.

35 Anthony Cutler, "Significant Gifts: Patterns of Exchange in Late Antique, Byzantine, and Early Islamic Diplomacy," *Journal of Medieval and Early Modern Studies* 38 (winter 2008): 79–101, 92–93.

long gallery, and they were all individually carried by attendants, from the smallest to the largest of them, according to the custom of these lands in order to amplify the display . . ."[36]

The matter of value and the crucial role display played for all parties to the Dutch gift are borne out by the birds of paradise – *rariteyten* that were certainly not fungible. Eight specimens were sold by Amsterdam merchants of Chinese porcelain to the purchasing agent for the States General, and in turn presented to the sultan in Constantinople. Although the birds transported to Constantinople did not fly there, they did ascend in value. The invoice of the Amsterdam merchants who sold birds to the purchasing agent for the States General shows that they cost thirty-one guilders each.[37] Baudartius's account of the gifts describes "three birds of paradise, valued at two thousand *daalders*, which the Sultan regarded with amazement."[38] As we know that three such birds actually cost just under a 100 guilders, the Sultan's amazement seems to have increased the value exponentially – to thirty-five times the current market value. It is worth noting that the arc of the projection follows the pattern of actual profits rendered, in these very years, in Amsterdam, on such goods as pepper and cloves.[39] While Baudartius's valuation of the birds of paradise might seem on par with calling an extremely valuable item "priceless," he does in fact name a price, and a very high one at that, for these *rariteyten*. The form of exchange – the presentation of a diplomatic gift on behalf of the States General to the Ottoman sultan – ostensibly departs from mercantile exchange, but in Baudartius's description it becomes clear that these highly valued objects derived their value from the market. They could be removed from the market, but the market values could not be removed from them.

GIFTS AND/OR GOODS

Early modern encounters among foreign potentates and their emissaries almost always involved the exchange of valuable goods as gifts. Most

[36] Baudartius, *Memorien, ofte korte verhael*, 13r.

[37] The receipts are preserved in the "Secrete Kas Turkije," N.A. 12593.9; see also de Roever, "Een Vorstelijk Geschenk," and Swan, "Birds of Paradise for the Sultan."

[38] Baudartius, *Memorien, ofte korte verhael*, 13r. This list, of the initial presentation to Sulthan Ahmed I, opens with: "*Voor eerst drie Paradys voghels, die-men schatte op twee duysent Daelders, die de Keyser met groote verwonderinghe aenghesien heeft.*"

[39] See Douglas A. Irwin, "Mercantilism as Strategic Trade Policy: The Anglo-Dutch Rivalry for the East India Trade," *Journal of Political Economy* 99, no. 6 (1991): 1296–314.

of these presentations were aligned with trade interests or practices: these gifts were nearly always related to negotiations concerning trade, which in turn were the negotiations by which international relations were forged. The first time birds of paradise were sent to Europe from the East Indies, their point of origin in trade circuits, it was in the form of a gift – to the Holy Roman Emperor and King of Spain Charles V – conveyed to him by the voyagers who had sailed with Magellan. A contemporary account specifies that when in 1522 Spanish ships were loaded at Tidore with cloves for the return to Spain, the Moluccan rulers presented letters and gifts for the emperor. "The gifts were Indian swords, etc. The most remarkable curiosities were some of the birds called *Mamuco Diata*, that is, the Bird of God, with which [the kings] think themselves safe and invincible in battle. Five of these were sent ..."[40] The birds were gifts, not commodities; they were in surplus to the merchandise supplied to the Europeans and, as such, integrally associated with while distinct from wares. The status of the bird of paradise as an object of a particular form of exchange (gift exchange), performed in the immediate context of trade, is noteworthy – and consistent with the later instance of the Dutch gift to Sultan Ahmed I. Like many other travel accounts written throughout the sixteenth and seventeenth centuries, the one cited here narrates the direct connection between gifts and trade along the Eastern routes. The birds of paradise given to Charles V are emblematic of trade and power relations alike. Their presentation, above and beyond the mercantile goods shipped back to Spain, was also made with political intent.

It was part and parcel of standard preparation among early modern European voyagers to assemble goods that could be and were presented as gifts in order to open negotiations and establish alliances that would result in trade; and many travelers' accounts record gifts presented to bring back to European rulers. The English ambassador Thomas Roe (c. 1581–1644) served at the court of the fourth Mughal emperor Jahangir at Agra, India, in 1615–1618 on behalf of the merchants of the East India Company. The published account *The Embassy of Sir Thomas Roe to the Court of the Great Mogul* contains several references to gifts – which Roe presented in an effort to secure trading rights. Roe represented both the English Crown and the merchants of the East India Company at

[40] Maximiliano Transylvanus, *De Moluccis insulis, itemque aliis pluribus mirandis quae nouissima Castellanorum nauigatio* (Cologne, 1523), fol. B6v.

the Mughal court. His accounts of gift transactions are as informative as they are poignant: Roe records many a skewed interaction. In a lengthy, occasionally despairing account written to the East India Company in February 1617, Roe explains his efforts on behalf of the merchants in a changing climate: "You can neuer expect," he writes, "to trade here vpon Capitulations that shalbe permanent. Wee must serue the tyme … appetite only gouerns the lordes of the kingdome." As regards how to procure the goods in which the East India Company wished to trade, Roe writes, "I haue propounded to you a New course, and will here Practise it."[41] The following paragraph opens with his report that gifts intended for the King [Akbar] had been seized by the Prince Jahangir and given by him to his father. Gifts were integral to trade negotiations, and these negotiations were anything but stable – or permanent.

In what I take to be a crucial passage, tucked in among a series of complaints some pages further along, Roe avers that it is the very trade on behalf of which he was acting that has spoiled the potency of gift-giving practices:

> The Presents you sent are in their kynds some good, others ordinarie. Noe man can tell what to aduise for; they change euery yeare their fancy … Your shipps haue made all things Common … and yearly ther Comes as many toyes of all kyndes as yours, which sould in hast by Marriners or others bound to the Sowthward hath made all Cheape and Common. They imitate euery thing wee bring, and embroder now as well as wee.[42]

An appendix to this report, "The Aduise from Sir Thomas Roe of Goodes and Presents for Surratt, 1617," lists a number of trade goods suitable for commercial exchange – textile in various colors, which he specifies; coral, vermilion; various precious and semi-precious stones from pearls and rubies to cat's eyes and agates; gold lace; and "Quivers for bowes and arrows, Indian fashion." Roe specifies that these arms, and clothing as well, be provided in the local sort and manner: "And generally I give you this rule: whatsoeuer you send in this kinde must be made by Indian

[41] Thomas Roe, *The Embassy of Sir Thomas Roe to the Court of the Great Mogul, 1615–1619, as Narrated in His Journal and Correspondence*, ed. William Foster, 2 vols. (London: Hakluyt Society, 1899), vol. 2, 469. See also Ania Loomba, "Of Gifts, Ambassadors, and Copy-Cats: Diplomacy, Exchange, and Difference in Early Modern India," in *Emissaries in Early Modern Literature and Culture: Mediation, Transmission, Traffic, 1550–1700*, ed. Brinda Charry and Gitanjali Shahani (Surrey and Burlington: Ashgate, 2009), 41–76.

[42] Roe, *The Embassy of Sir Thomas Roe*, vol. 2, 478.

patternes, for then they are of vse and euery bodies monie."[43] Nestled in among the gems listed as valued merchandise is a passage in which Roe declares that royal favor can be gained by way of just these goods, and indeed can spare the necessity of presenting gifts:

If you would finde anie rich stone to the value of 20,000*li.* to equall the Portugall, would give you great proffit and Credit ... By this meanes only you can compas a stocke and make your trade desired; vpon such a rare peece you maie get anie Conditions, for their Coveteousnes of them is vnsatiable. If you can send yerely in great stones of theis kindes or pearles 100 v 000*li.* ... it would vent [sell] to proffitt and make you highly requested. Without this the Kinge wilbe wearie; and it will save you presents.

Roe declares that the finest of wares will trump all other manner of negotiations. "All other things will faile you and with theis you may putt of anie thing." He even hazards the opinion that the English Crown might offload some of its less essential baubles in the interest of securing such favor. "The Towre, I ame perswaded, could furnish you with many great olde stones that are vseles."[44]

The subsequent section of Roe's 1617 report lists gifts suitable for presentation to the Mughal emperor on behalf of the English king, which are almost entirely consistent with the trade goods just enumerated.[45] Roe specifies that gifts such as he lists should be presented once in three years, and then only four or five of what he lists, "with one of good value."

"Fitt presentes from the King. Some good stone for once, or some rich peece of Arras, silke and gould, but one or two at most. A rich peece of Tissue or Cloathe of gould. A fine Crowne, sett with small stones. A faire bed feild, with lace or some worke. A rich feild Caparason and Sadle, the patterne from hence. A Coate of Sattin imbrodered, the paterne from hence. With theis: Some Cushions, Cabbennetts, glasses, Standishes and toyes of vse for others. Pictuers of all sortes, if good, in constant request; Some large storie; Diana this yere gave great content."[46]

Much more might be said of his recommendations, and of the pictures he did present in the event, and of the sorts of misunderstandings his negotiations appear to have elicited. For the present purposes, however, it will have to suffice to point to the relative interchangeability, as per Roe's recommendations and in the case of the Dutch gift to the Ottoman court alike, of gifts and goods – in substance and in presentation.

[43] Ibid., vol. 2, 486–87. [44] Ibid., vol. 2, 487. [45] Ibid., vol. 2, 488.
[46] Ibid., vol. 2, 488.

PRESENTS AND POLITICAL RECOGNITION

Early seventeenth-century Dutch images of trade and trade goods convey a similar fusion of the processes and products of gift-giving and of trade. This is aptly illustrated by a 1611 wall print by Claes Janszn Visscher after Pieter Bast that combines a profile view of Amsterdam and its harbor with a lengthy explanatory text and individual woodcut vignettes of specific landmarks (Figure 6.2).[47]

The extensive, anonymous text is a paean to a city still in formation. Amsterdam is already characterized as a global trade hub: "*De wijtvermaerde Hooft-Coop-stadt des gantschen Weerelts Amsterdam*," or "the world famous trade capital of the world." People from all parts of the world feel compelled, the text declares, to "send or present in person their priceless wares to Amsterdam, as if to a world-renowned empress." The presentation of gifts to the maid of Amsterdam pictured above the text that embodies these transactions represents a powerful rewriting of actual trade dynamics. The crowned, personification of the global entrepôt sits atop a throne of poles, the piles on which the city is built in the morass it occupies. She holds a ship in her right hand and the crest of the city in the other, as she receives delegations of what the text describes as "all the principle peoples of the world." The text revels in itemizing the fruits of current trade. The litany of goods from the East Indies is extensive: "the abundance of silk, precious gems, pepper, ginger, cinnamon, cassia, nutmeg, and other spices along with countless herbs and roots that is shipped from Java to Amsterdam is so great that one can hardly articulate it or describe it credibly." This verbal cornucopia extends to imports from Africa and Brazil as well Madeira and elsewhere in Spain and the Mediterranean and Turkey: "silk, damask, velvets, Caffa and other such artfully woven cloths ... fine bombazine, glass drinking cups, Venetian mirrors, bezoars etc. come here from Turkey, Italy, and other southern lands." In addition, the "Tartar and the Persian with a laden camel bring gemstones, Oriental pearls, the medicinal bezoar stone, many silks, balsam oil, and incense." The list also includes tin and lead and other goods from England, Prussian items, milk and cheese and eggs from more local regions; it is as replete with data as the image it qualifies, where a wide variety of local representatives embody the trade described. Amsterdam is a city made of goods, many of them exotic. Crucially, in neither the

[47] Boudewijn Bakker et al., *Het Aanzien van Amsterdam: Panorama's, Plattegronden en Profielen uit de Gouden Eeuw* (Bussum, 2007), plate 1.

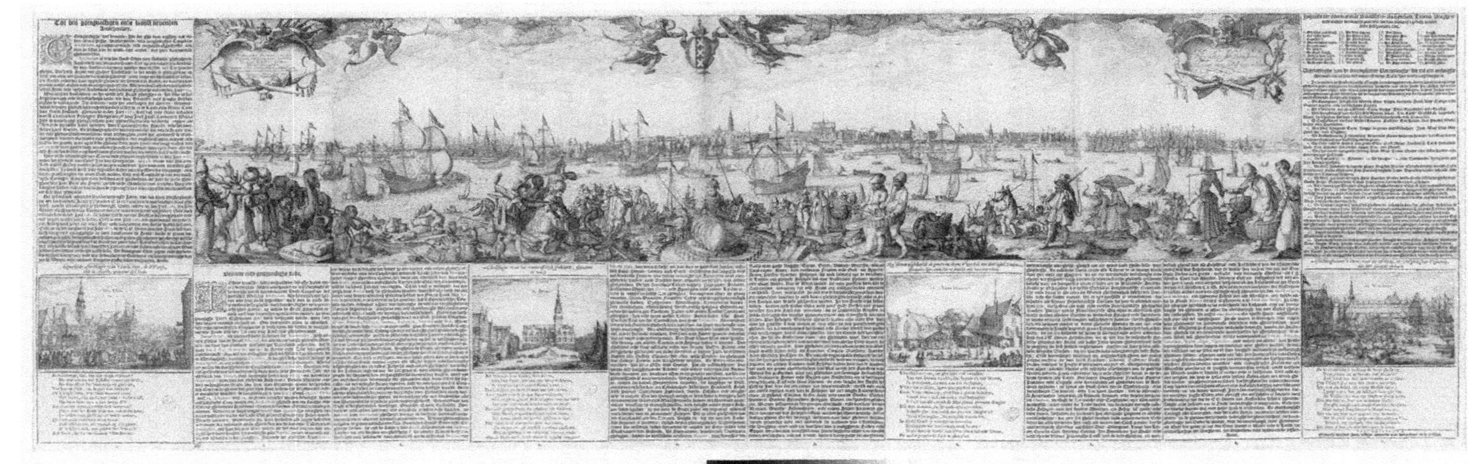

FIGURE 6.2 Claes Janszn Visscher, *Profile of Amsterdam from the IJ*, etching and engraving, with text, 1611, 44.1 cm × 147.4 cm. Amsterdam: Rijksprentenkabinet, Rijksmuseum.

text nor the image do intermediaries or agents mediate the transfer of goods: trade is represented as a direct function of the desire of the various peoples and nations depicted to present their goods and wares: the maid of Amsterdam sits among the various goods like an idol among remains of devotional rites. The text concludes, "In sum, everything that is necessary for the maintenance of the body and for the amusement of the spirit is here so abundant that you could say that God's merciful blessing, the very cornucopia or horn of plenty, is being poured down on us."[48] Here, trade goods are converted, rhetorically, into gifts or homage – and even into providential blessing.

By the time that the extraordinary iconographical program of the Oranjezaal at Huis ten Bosch, the residence of Amalia van Solms and Stadholder Frederick Hendrik in The Hague, was completed, the association of Dutch power with exotic goods was all but a commonplace. Jacob van Campen's 1648 *Triumphal Procession with Gifts from East and West* (Figure 6.3) forms part of the substantial, stunning pictorial cycle in the Oranjezaal commissioned by Amalia von Solms to commemorate her husband in the late 1640s.[49]

The larger-than-life composition features a wide range of artful, colorful, rare and valuable goods in combination with allegorical figures whose role seems merely to present or offer the luxuries: they are figures of abundance, of the copia of exotica. These are not the intermediaries via whom such goods made their way into the collection of the Stadholders – which, by the time this was painted, contained a vast array of comparable exotic goods.[50] Their collection, usually cited as a Northern Netherlandish outpost of Flemish baroque taste in painting, contained myriad exotica, described as "*Indisch*" and "*Oostindisch*" objects – from crystal, agate, serpentine, amber and coral to porcelain and lacquerwork, and from objects decorated

[48] The text is lengthy and anonymous and all citations are from it; translations are my own. See Boudewijn Bakker, ed., *Het Aanzien van Amsterdam. Panorama's, Plattegronden en Profielen uit de Gouden Eeuw* (Amsterdam: Thoth, 2007), 259–60.

[49] Margriet Eikema Hommes and Elmer Kolfin, *De Oranjezaal in Huis ten Bosch. Een zaal uit louter liefde* (Zwolle: Waanders, 2013).

[50] S. W. A. Drossaers and Th. H. Lunsingh Scheurleer, eds., *Inventarissen van de inboedels in de verblijven van de Oranjes en daarmee gelijk te stellen stukken 1567–1795*, 3 vols. ('s-Gravenhage: Martinus Nijhoff, 1974–76), vol. 1, 239–96 (*Inventaris van kostbaarheden, meubelen, schilderijen van Amalia van Solms 1654–1668*). See also Peter van der Ploeg and Carola Vermeeren, *Vorstelijk Verzameld. De Kunstcollectie van Frederik Hendrik en Amalia* (Zwolle: Waanders, 1997), esp. C. Willemijn Fock, "Frederik Hendrik en Amalia's appartementen: Vorstelijk vertoon naast de triomf van het porselein," 76–86.

FIGURE 6.3 Jacob van Campen, *Triumphal Procession with Gifts from East and West*, oil on canvas, 1648, Oranjezaal, Huis ten Bosch, The Hague. Koninklijke Verzamelingen, Den Haag/Staat der Nederlanden. Photo Margareta Svensson.

or made with tortoise-shell to coconuts, ivory and mother of pearl. Like the Bast-Visscher print, the larger-than-life painting of exotic goods by van Campen also features the colonialist trope of gifting as a means of institutionalizing the dominance of the recipient and naturalizing the processes by which such goods and stuffs were procured and transported and bought and sold. In the van Campen Oranjezaal painting, porcelain and feather parasols and parrots and Japanese armor are of a piece in a collage of exotica. Both of these images render exotic goods with a high degree of specificity (the parrot, the featherwork of the New World, the weave of the Japanese armor, the glaze and figuration of the porcelain vessel are highly individuated – and indeed, the fact that a set of human eyes peers out of the armor's mask at the apex of the composition conveys the unmistakable impression that each object is a stand-in for a people, a land even) at the same time that they, the print and the painting alike, render these goods as all equally subject to the forces and conditions of trade.

The visual rhetoric of the Bast-Visscher profile view of Amsterdam and the Oranjezaal composition of goods from the East and West Indies help to illustrate that gifts and trade goods were interchangeable in early modern Dutch negotiations – negotiations based on expectations that, as Roe's account of his embassy to India attests, pertained more broadly, outside the scope of Dutch encounters. Many of the precious or valuable goods depicted in either the wall print or the painting circulated by way of trade, and several were certainly presented as gifts. The collection of Amalia van Solms and Frederick Hendrik was densely populated with diplomatic or state gifts. A contemporary witness testified to the provenance of the very valuable goods belonging to Amalia as follows: "Nearly all foreign kings, princes, and potentates, the Indian companies, cities and wealthy societies of Holland sent her presents, which she received openly and graciously without subjugation or secretly."[51] Such gifts were tokens of recognition, much as the baubles Roe suggested be presented to

[51] "Presque tous les rois, les princes et les potentats étrangers, les compagnies des Indes, les villes et les riches sociétés de Hollande lui envoyaient des présents qu'elle recevait ouvertement et de bonne grâce sans bassesse ni en cachette." The quotation continues: "Ainsi elle possédait en peu de temps une prodigieuse quantité de vaisselle d'or massif pour tous les usages de la vie, des meubles pompeux de toutes sortes, des cabinets lambrissés de laque de la Chine, des vases de porcelaine d'une grandeur d'une forme et d'une abondance extra ordinaire, des coffres et des vases d'ambre, d'agate, de cristal de roche garnis de pierres précieuses sans nombre où les perles et diamants n'étaient point oubliés." Les mémoires du borgrave et comte Frederic de Dohna 1621–1688, ed. H. Borkowski (Königsberg, 1898), 27. Quoted in Drossaers and Lunsingh Scheurleer, *Inventarissen*, vol. 1, GS 147, 239.

the Mughal emperor. The suit of Japanese armor, for example, that occupies the upper portion of the canvas was likely a gift from the emperor to the Stadholder Maurits, given around the same time that James I of England received his own, in 1613.[52] Numerous other instances of gifts to the Dutch state come to mind here as well: when envoys of the sultan of Aceh arrived in the Netherlands in 1602, they came bearing gifts for their nominal host, Prince Maurits, Stadholder of the United Provinces, that included several spears and other armor as well as a talking parrot that spoke Malay.[53] The cassowary bird in Maurits's collection, of which two engravings survive, was one among many exotic creatures and items presented to the Dutch state in the early years of its development.[54] Other gifts include those brought by the Moroccan embassy to the Hague in 1605, sent by the Shogun Tokugawa Ieyasu to Maurits in 1609, and exchanged with the Siamese king in 1608 and 1609, as well as the presentations to the Ottoman Sultan made by the Dutch to the court in Constantinople. Diplomatic efforts were mobilized to secure recognition for the emergent statehood of the United Provinces outside the Netherlands – and simultaneously, the States General and its representatives received goods and presents that accorded them political recognition.[55]

MOBILIZING ALLIANCES

A signal instance of the Dutch mobilization of curious goods for political purposes is a state gift presented to King James I's son Henry Stuart,

[52] Glenn Adamson and Giorgio Riello, "Global Objects: Contention and Entanglement," in *Writing the History of the Global: Challenges for the Twenty-First Century*, ed. Maxine Berg (Oxford: Oxford University Press, 2013), who discuss the gift of suits of armor from the shogun; Mia Mochizuki discusses several instances of gifts in "Idolatry and Western-inspired Painting in Japan," in *Idols in the Age of Art: Objects, Devotions and the Early Modern World*, ed. Michael W. Cole and Rebecca Zorach (Surrey and Burlington: Ashgate, 2009), 239–66.

[53] In 1601, Sultan Alau'd-din Ri'ayat Shah of Aceh sent emissaries and gifts to Maurits; the gifts included "a small jewel and a ring with four big stones and some smaller stones, a dagger with a gold and copper sheath wrapped in a silver cloth, a golden cup and saucer and a gold-plated silver pot and two Malay speaking parrots with silver chains." Ingrid Saroda Mitrasing, "The Age of Aceh and the Evolution of Kingship 1599–1641," PhD diss., Leiden University, 2011, 88.

[54] Zandvliet, *Maurits, Prins van Oranje*, 318–19.

[55] Cardinal-Duke of Richelieu is reported to have given earrings to Amalia van Solms on behalf of the King of France, Louis XIII, "so that she would close her ears to their enemies' whispers." See also A. Arthur Kleinschmidt, *Amalia von Oranien, geborene Gräfin zu Solms-Braunfels. Ein Lebensbild* (Berlin: Räde, 1905), 26.

Prince of Wales in 1610. This presentation, orchestrated by the Dutch ambassador in London, Noel Caron, and assembled over the course of several months in early 1610, was motivated by a desire on the part of the States General to ingratiate itself with the presumed heir to the English throne. The Dutch were grateful for English support in the formulation of the Twelve Years' Truce (1609–21) with Spain and hopeful of future support. In the state documents relating to this gift, purchases are described as motivated by the ability "to thereby honor the Prince of Wales, whose succession is secure and whose friendship is necessary to these lands." Prince Henry is described as being "certain to succeed [his father as king]," and his friendship with the United Provinces is necessary. To Henry and his court the Dutch state presented a very fine array of objects, which included a series of tapestries, woven by François Spiering of Delft; two large West Indian bezoar stones and two East Indian bezoar stones; a painting by Hendrik Cornelisz Vroom of the Battle of Gibraltar and another painting of a storm at sea. The Dutch also gave four tapestries woven with gold that were presented, as we have seen, in The Hague in 1605 by Hammu ben Bashir, the ambassador of the King Mulay Zidan of Morocco, and an ivory fan "very subtly and artfully wrought" that had also been a gift, from the King of Siam to Captain Joris Spilbergen.[56] The 1610 Dutch gift occupies the margins of current historical and art historical work, but is another crucial record in the history of early modern global exchange – and of exchange in which cultural artifacts, *rariteyten* among them, played a crucial role.[57]

A final instance of the role cultural artifacts played in the transcultural exchanges staged by the Dutch in the early seventeenth century is from the accounts of Jacob van Heemskerck (1567–1607), one of the early Dutch

[56] J. J. Dodt van Flensburg, "Resolutiën der Generale Staten uit de XVII eeuw. Meer onmiddelijk betreffende de geschiedenis der beschaving," in *Archief voor kerkelijke en wereldsche geschiedenissen, inzonderheid van Utrecht*, 7 vols. (Utrecht: Bosch, 1838–48), vol. 5 (1846), 19.

[57] On the Dutch gift, see J. G. van Gelder, "Notes on the Royal Collection – IV: The "Dutch Gift" of 1610 to Henry, Prince of 'Whalis,' and Some Other Presents," *The Burlington Magazine* 105 (1963); 541–45, and Inge Broekman and Helmer Helmers, "Het Hart des Offraers: The Dutch Gift as an Act of Self-Representation," *Dutch Crossing* 31 (2007): 223–52. On Henry and his collection, see Roy Strong, *Henry Prince of Wales* (London: Thames and Hudson, 1986), 188; for an account of his collecting interests in the context of London collecting practices, see Stephen Orgel, "Idols of the Gallery: Becoming a Connoisseur in Renaissance England," in *Early Modern Visual Culture: Representation, Race, and Empire in Renaissance England*, ed. Peter Erickson and Clark Hulse (Philadelphia: University of Pennsylvania Press, 2000), 251–78, esp. 253–55. Neither of these accounts emphasizes the exotic objects in his possession.

Republic's great seafaring heroes. Van Heemskerck was involved in the earliest voyages to the East Indies, survived a winter on Nova Zembla and led the Dutch against the Spanish in the Siege of Gibraltar. As vice-admiral of the second Dutch East Indies Expedition, undertaken prior to the foundation of the VOC and a major source of inspiration for its founding, van Heemskerck maintained a journal, a "*Memorye*," from 1598 until 1600, the year in which the fleet returned to Amsterdam. In an entry on conducting trade along the Javanese coast and in the Moluccan Islands, van Heemskerck makes several useful recommendations, among them where to buy the best wines (Bantam) and meats (Bali) for provisioning. More immediately pertinent, if slightly delirious, are his directives for the conduct of trade in Asian goods:

> In order to trade most favorably in Banda and Ternate it is necessary to purchase in Bantam various sorts of porcelain, cottons, Bengalese and other linens, which are brought there by the Chinese, the Portuguese, and the Gujarati along with many other diverse sorts of wares which may be acquired there; so that when one travels from there to Jurtan and buys Madura and other sorts of cloths which the Portuguese bring there, and from there to Bali to buy Balinese cloths and rice on Timor and in other places . . .[58]

Such valuable goods as the Dutch brought back to the Netherlands – pepper and spices, porcelain, textiles – were extracted from a longstanding, dense network of trade relations. The back and forth of valuable goods is punctuated in van Heemskerck's account by reference to gifts, which greased the wheels of this market machinery. Gifts presented to the King of Bantam included, for example, "a gilt drinking vessel, certain velvet and silk textiles, some beautiful glasses, and gilt mirrors." From discussion of gifts exchanged between Prince Maurits and the King of Toeban it appears that the latter presented Maurits with a gilded kris and two beautiful ("*fraaye*") spears. Van Heemskerck recommends further transmission of letters and such objects ("*eenighe frayheyt*") to secure the relationship that he characterizes as one of trust and goodwill. The king is a lover of dogs, and shows the vice-admiral fifteen of them in his personal quarters, which van Heemskerck however deemed "ugly," writing that the Dutch will also therefore send a "beautiful and well-trained water

[58] Jacob van Heemskerck, "*Memorie, door Jacob van Heemskerck opgesteld over de wijze waarop, naar zijne bevinding op de kustplaatsen van Java en in de Molukken, den handel moet gedreven worden*," in *De Opkomst van het Nederlandsch Gezag in Oost-Indie (1595–1610)*, ed. J. K. J. de Jonge, 18 vols. ('s-Gravenhage: M. Nijhoff, 1864), vol. 2 (1864), 448–54.

dog."[59] Van Heemskerck adds that "if there is any cloth of a beautifully colored flower velvet and some other beautiful wares, that would bring about improvement." Van Heemskerck is referring to trade relations. He specifies that the Dutch do not trade with the Toebanese, but that things might in the future change. Later, he recommends that gifts be presented at Jurtan, also to the governor, and that Jurtan is "the finest port in all of Java where the bulk of trade in spices such as nutmeg, mace, and cloves takes place." Like the goods presented to Ottoman Sultan Ahmed I and exchanged in these decades among potentates around the globe, state or diplomatic gifts played a critical role in enabling commerce: wondrous wares guaranteed the circulation of valuable goods; and awe-inspiring gifts ensured the ebb and flow of valuable trade.

CONCLUSION: THE ECONOMY OF THE EARLY MODERN GIFT

This chapter analyzes a number of gifts made on behalf of the States General of the United Provinces of the Netherlands and Prince Maurits, Stadholder, in the early decades of the seventeenth century, the formative years of the Dutch Republic, which would gain full recognition in 1648. One of the primary claims I make is that the Dutch saw and represented themselves as merchants in exotic, foreign, curious and rare goods par excellence. Likewise, gifts presented on behalf of the United Provinces featured these sorts of objects, also frequently referred to as *rariteyten*, or rarities. In examining the role of exotic merchandise in Dutch negotiations with foreign powers during the first decades of the seventeenth century, I have considered the relationship between the objects presented as gifts and the value of those same objects as merchandise in an emergent market. Negotiations between the States General of the Netherlands and/or Dutch merchants and foreign rulers are here represented by case studies, the first of which concerns gifts presented by the States General in the course of securing trade agreements with the Ottoman sultan. Dutch presents were made in the spirit of affirming diplomatic and political relations – and specifically, in the case of the Netherlands, relations bearing on trade.

In an essay on late antique, Byzantine and early Islamic diplomacy and exchange, Anthony Cutler has observed that diplomatic gifts have been "consigned by historians to that special *oubliette* where they keep the

[59] Van Heemskerck, "*Memorie*," 450.

evidence they consider unhelpful to the understanding of political and economic events." Cutler calls attention to what we might think of as the specific gravity of diplomatic gifts. Recent studies in diplomatic history and on the agents of diplomatic negotiations offer new ways of thinking about the exchange of information and goods and, for example, *negozio* as the dynamic of early modern diplomacy and trade alike.[60] Marika Keblusek, for example, has proposed a deeply compelling model for the study of early modern agents who negotiated policy, goods and knowledge alike. Pointing out that "the commercial aspects of brokerage – the *trade* in art and news and services – have mostly been overlooked in scholarship on agents and agency," Keblusek asserts that "agent" be understood as a function rather than a profession.[61] She has demonstrated the great potential and historical pertinence of considering cultural and political brokerage or negotiations as integrally linked: agents obtained access via either political or cultural endeavors, or both, and used each in close association with the other. By extension, as this chapter proposes, diplomatic gifts can fruitfully be understood as agents of political and cultural negotiations alike. In some instances, these aims were inseparable.[62] Overall, what seems of signal importance is to acknowledge the intersection of political and mercantile interests in the economy of the early modern diplomatic gift. Gifts presented in the early decades of the seventeenth century by the Dutch – whether by or on behalf of the VOC, the States General or the stadholder himself – were more often than not exemplary mercantile goods, many of them *rariteyten*. These curious, exotic, luxury goods represented Dutch trade might and, in turn, their political reach. As the foregoing episodes in the history of material culture of the Dutch Republic demonstrate, mobilizing *rariteyten* was a crucial means by which the Dutch sought to identify themselves politically and commercially on the global stage.

[60] See, for example, Marika Keblusek and Badeloch Noldus, eds., *Double Agents: Cultural and Political Brokerage in Early Modern Europe* (Brill: Leiden, 2011).

[61] Marika Keblusek, "Introduction: Double Agents in Early Modern Europe," in Keblusek and Noldus, *Double Agents*, 1–9, 4.

[62] A fascinating instance that lies beyond the scope of this chapter is the so-called "coronation casket" sent from Ceylon to Catherine of Portugal in 1541–42; see Annemarie Jordan Gschwend and Johannes Beltz, *Elfenbeine aus Ceylon. Luxusgüter für Katharina von Habsburg (1507–1578)* (Zürich: Museum Rietberg, 2010), 35–40 and Biedermann in this volume. See also Marika Keblusek, "The Embassy of Art: Diplomats as Cultural Brokers," in Keblusek and Noldus, *Double Agents*, 11–25.

7

Gifts for the Shogun

The Dutch East India Company, Global Networks and Tokugawa Japan

Adam Clulow

Gift-giving was a vital component of global exchange in the early modern world. As such, it became a feature of "European expansion" in the sixteenth and seventeenth centuries. Arriving in distant lands, Europeans stepped ashore clutching a bewildering array of gifts that were deployed for varied purposes, to garner favor, win trading concessions or secure territorial footholds. The items in question ranged from tiny trinkets – that could be transported in large quantities – to massive manufactured items that required the services of specialist craftsmen, and exotic animals such as elephants, camels and cassowaries. In the Americas, gift-giving seemed, from the very outset, capable of securing far-reaching results for minimal outlays. Columbus famously presented cheap gifts – "some red caps and some glass beads ... and many other things of little value" – and used the subsequent reception as a key part of his justification for Spanish dominion.[1] In other instances, the presentation of small quantities of gifts underpinned territorial expansion, most notably on the island of Manhattes (Manhattan), which the Dutch claimed to have acquired for just 60 guilders' worth of goods. Stephen Greenblatt writes of the "European dream, endlessly reiterated in the literature of exploration ... of the grossly unequal gift exchange: I give you a glass bead and you give me a pearl worth half your tribe."[2] In Asia, by contrast, gift-giving frequently proved more treacherous. In 1498, Vasco da Gama

[1] Clements Markham, ed., *The Journal of Christopher Columbus (during His First Voyage, 1492–93)* (London: Hakluyt Society, 1893), 37.

[2] Stephen Greenblatt, *Marvelous Possessions: The Wonder of the New World* (Chicago: University of Chicago Press, 1991), 110.

famously stumbled at the first hurdle by presenting a set of clearly inadequate gifts that prompted court officials at Calicut (now Kozhikode) to complain that even the poorest of merchants would not offer such gifts.[3] In Asia, as Europeans came into contact with well-established states with a long history of diplomatic interaction, it required an extended learning process lasting for years or sometimes even decades to master the basics of gift-giving.

This chapter examines gift exchange in early modern Asia with a particular focus on the long interaction between the Dutch East India Company (Vereenigde Oost-Indische Compagnie, or VOC) and Tokugawa Japan (1600–1868). Over the course of close to two centuries, from 1609 to the collapse of the VOC in the late eighteenth century, the organization established itself as a prolific gift-giver as its representatives handed over hundreds of thousands of guilders' worth of objects on annual trips to the shogun's headquarters in Edo. The sheer quantity of these gifts has drawn the attention of a number of scholars, including Cynthia Viallé, Michael Laver and Martha Chaiklin, who have contributed a series of important studies examining VOC gift-giving practices and the tremendous diversity of items brought to the archipelago by the Company.[4] While the VOC ultimately emerged as a highly proficient gift-giver that was capable of using its offerings to smooth its way through the turbulent arena of Tokugawa politics, it had a rocky start in Japan where Dutch agents presented meager gifts that came attached to problematic diplomatic credentials. How then did the Company overcome these problems? This chapter focuses on three developments – the reengineering of the status of VOC agents in Japan, the creation of a highly effective regional gift

[3] E. G. Ravenstein, ed., *The Journal of the First Voyage of Vasco da Gama, 1497–99* (London: The Hakluyt Society, 1898), 62.

[4] The most recent is Viallé's brilliant survey of VOC gift-giving across Asia. Cynthia Viallé, "'To Capture their Favor': On Gift-Giving by the VOC," in *Mediating Netherlandish Art and Material Culture in Asia*, ed. Thomas DaCosta Kaufmann and Michael North (Amsterdam: Amsterdam University Press, 2014), 291–319. See also Cynthia Viallé, "In Aid of Trade: Dutch Gift-Giving in Tokugawa Japan," *Tokyo Daigaku Shiryō Hensanjo kenkyū kiyō* 16 (2006): 57–78; Martha Chaiklin, *Cultural Commerce and Dutch Commercial Culture: The Influence of European Material Culture on Japan, 1700–1850* (Leiden: CNWS, 2003); id., "The Merchant's Ark: Live Animal Gifts in Early Modern Dutch-Japanese Relations," *World History Connected* February 2012: http://worldhistoryconnected.press.illinois.edu/9.1/chaiklin.html (accessed 20 September 2016); Michael Laver, "Most Exquisite Curiosities of Nature and Art: The Dutch East India Company, Objets d'Art and Gift Giving in Early Modern Japan," *World History Connected* (June 2013), http://worldhistoryconnected.press.illinois.edu/10.2/laver.html (accessed 20 September 2016).

network in Asia and the increasing involvement of Tokugawa officials – that combined to transform the nature of the Company's gift-giving practices in Japan. The Company was, in other words, a successful gift-giver in part because it ceded control to its Japanese interlocutors, who drew up long lists of demands that were presented annually to the VOC.[5]

ENCOUNTERING JAPAN

The Dutch East India Company was established in 1602, and, from the beginning, VOC officials struggled to find the right kind of gifts to present to local rulers. This was especially the case in Japan, which was situated at the furthest edges of the Company's trading circuits in Asia. In 1608, one year before the first VOC expedition reached Japan, Victor Sprinckel, the newly installed VOC chief merchant of the factory at Patani on the Malay peninsula, decided to send a letter to Tokugawa Ieyasu, the first Tokugawa shogun, explaining why the Company had as yet failed to establish trading relations with Japan.[6] In addition to his letter, which provided a long account of the difficulties faced by the Dutch in overcoming Portuguese resistance to their presence in Asia, Sprinckel enclosed a set of gifts intended for Ieyasu, who, although officially retired, remained the dominant power in the archipelago. Isolated in Patani and without access to the kind of luxury goods that were conventionally presented in such situations, Sprinckel was compelled to improvise. His list of gifts consisted of an odd assortment of items worth just 112 guilders and included six large bowls, twelve dishes, three frosted glass cups, three French drinking goblets, five clear crystal cups, four striped cups, seven French wine glasses, ten yards of black cloth, thirteen Danzig bottles, six blue round bottles and seven small porcelain bowls.

That such gifts failed to meet acceptable standards was clear in Sprinckel's letter, in which he explained that these items should not be seen as "gifts but should be accepted by way of congratulations, that is not considering the present but the will behind the deed."[7] Although the

[5] I am by no means the first to note the key role played by Japanese officials in the VOC gift-giving process. See in particular Viallé, "In Aid of Trade," 68; and Chaiklin, *Cultural Commerce and Dutch Commercial Culture*, ch. 4.

[6] F. C. Weider, *De Reis van Mahu en De Cordes door de Straat van Magalhães naar Zuid-America en Japan, 1598–1600* (The Hague: M. Nijhoff, 1923), 3: 81–84.

[7] "... niet voor een present en mach bestaen, maer alleenlijck tot een congratulatie niet aansiende de gifte, dan taccepteren de wijlle voor de dat ...". Ibid., 3: 83–84.

precise distinction between gifts and congratulatory offerings is far from obvious, it is clear that Sprinckel believed it had to be made in order to properly distinguish the items he had enclosed and the kind of gifts the shogun could expect from the Dutch in the future. It was a familiar strategy that was adopted by other European representatives in equally tricky circumstances. In 1498, for example, Da Gama had explained that his offering "was his own [private gift] and not the king's; and that if the King of Portugal ordered him to return he would entrust him with far richer presents."[8]

In 1609 when the first VOC expedition finally reached Japanese shores, it encountered a similar problem. As they prepared to dispatch an embassy to seek an audience with the retired shogun, the leaders of the expedition discovered that they had few items in the holds of their ships suitable for being handed over to Tokugawa officials. They did, however, have access to a bustling trading entrepôt, albeit one dominated by the Company's Portuguese rivals, in the form of Nagasaki, which was located just a few hours' sailing time down the coast of Kyushu. Determined to secure appropriate items, they decided to dispatch an agent with 200 reals to purchase "second or third hand in Nagasaki some silk which would be useful to honor some of the nobles here as there is nothing in these ships that can be used for gifts but these are essential."[9] These regular shopping trips to stock up on gifts became a feature of early VOC gift-giving in Japan. In 1615, for example, the Dutch factory again sent an agent down the coast of Kyushu to purchase some more presentable goods from Portuguese merchants, although their envoy was given strict instructions to do so the most discreet way possible through multiple intermediaries in order to prevent news leaking out.[10]

As the Company struggled with the issue of inappropriate gifts, it also contended with a second, potentially more serious problem. The first

8 Ravenstein, ed., *The Journal of the First Voyage of Vasco da Gama*, 61. See also Robert S. Wolff, "Da Gama's Blundering: Trade Encounters in Africa and Asia during the European 'Age of Discovery,' 1450–1520," *The History Teacher* 31, no. 3 (1998): 297–318.

9 "Mede is goet gevonden dat ditto Specx mede sal gegeven werden twee hondert realen van achten omme deselve mogelijck sijnde in Langesacke voor de 2 ofte derde hant te besteeden inne sijde waren dienstich omme aen d'ene ende d'andere van de edelen alhier te vereren, alsoo in de schepen gants nijet en is omme enich schenkagie te doen ende nochtans necessaerlijck moet geschieden." Tokyo daigaku shiryō hensanjo, ed., *Dai Nihon Shiryō* (Tokyo Daigaku Shuppankai, 1901–), series 12, 6: 465. This massive compendium includes a selection of Dutch documents related to this first expedition.

10 Resolutions of the Japan factory, 10 September 1615, VOC 1061: 249v.

Dutch representatives to reach Japan presented themselves as ambassadors and offered diplomatic gifts and letters in the name of an external power. This was not, as we might expect, the directors of the Company, the so-called *Heeren* or Gentlemen 17, or even the States-General in The Hague, which held sovereign authority over the United Provinces. Rather, VOC representatives offered gifts in the name of a fictive monarch, the "king of Holland," who was introduced into diplomatic negotiations across Asia in order to smooth out the Company's rough edges and present a readily recognizable diplomatic figurehead.[11] The "king of Holland" was in fact Prince Maurits, the *Stadhouder* (literally State Holder) of a number of Dutch provinces and the highest-ranking aristocrat in the United Provinces. Despite their republican background, VOC agents such as Viktor Sprinckel routinely identified Maurits as "our King," or "*onsen Coninck*," and used his distant presence to structure subsequent exchanges.[12] When VOC agents offered gifts during the first years of the Japan factory they did so, therefore, not on behalf of a mercantile company but in the name of a figure presented as the shogun's brother ruler, the sovereign of Holland.

Pushing the *Stadhouder* forward in this way resolved a number of potentially problematic issues by transforming VOC agents from unfamiliar characters on the diplomatic scene into the representatives of just another monarch. This strategy had, however, the added effect of raising a slew of new issues for Dutch gift-givers. One obvious problem was that the Dutch were not the only Europeans present at the shogun's court. When one VOC agent "began to extoll their kinge of Holland to be the greatest king in Christendom & one that held all the others under," an English merchant also present at the shogun's court declared that he "needed not to lie soe loude, for that they hadd no king at all in Holland but were governed by a conte [count], or rather they governed him."[13] A second issue centered on the question of ownership of the gifts. When the shogun accepted gifts from the Dutch and offered items in return he did so according to a straightforward formula that assumed reciprocity between the "sovereign of Japan (*Nihon kokushu*)" and the "sovereign of

[11] As discussed in more detail in Adam Clulow, *The Company and the Shogun: The Dutch Encounter with Tokugawa Japan* (New York: Columbia University Press, 2014), ch. 1.

[12] Weider, *De Reis van Mahu en De Cordes*, 3: 81–84.

[13] Anthony Farrington, ed., *The English Factory in Japan, 1613–1623* (London: British Library, 1991), 1: 778–79. The English factory in Japan was established in 1613 and lasted for roughly a decade until it was closed down for economic reasons in 1623.

Holland (*Oranda kokushu*)."[14] Thus Ieyasu wrote to Maurits acknowledging the items he had received and offered gifts, usually swords or suits of armor, in return.[15] But of course the Dutch representatives who received these gifts did not in fact represent the "king of Holland" but were rather the employees of an independent mercantile organization.

Who then did the gifts received from the shogun actually belong to? The answer seems to have been that no one really knew. Jacques Specx, the head of the VOC factory in Japan from 1609 to 1613 and then again from 1614 to 1621, held onto two swords and two suits of armor for a number of years before eventually deciding they should be sent on to his superiors. He did so reluctantly, however, and in a 1613 letter indicated that he expected to be rewarded for surrendering items that he felt he had at least some claim to.[16] Back in the United Provinces, the Amsterdam Chamber, which eventually took possession of the gifts, was equally unsure as to who they belonged, and in a resolution dated February 1615 its members resolved to pass the troublesome items over to the Gentlemen 17 to render a final decision.[17]

The more serious problem was that the Company decided over time to abandon its reliance on the "king of Holland" as a prerequisite for diplomatic interaction and hence gift-giving. This was in part because the need to obtain letters from the *Stadhouder* as a first step before initiating new missions imposed an unacceptable delay on the dispatch of embassies, many of which were needed precisely because there was an urgent crisis that required averting. As a result, the VOC switched to a new strategy centered around the Governor-General in Batavia as the crucial figurehead for VOC diplomacy. Thus in 1627 when the Company dispatched a new mission to meet with the shogun in Edo, it carried letters and gifts to be presented not from the "king of Holland" but in the Governor-General's name. When the ambassador arrived in Edo, he dutifully explained that he had come from the Governor-General in

[14] For another example of the usage of *Nihon kokushu* in a different context, see John Hall, ed., *The Cambridge History of Japan: Early Modern Japan* (Cambridge: Cambridge University Press, 1991), 297.

[15] Konchiin Sūden, *Ikoku nikki shō*, ed. Murakami Naojirō (Tokyo: Sankūsha, 1911), 17–20.

[16] Letter from Jacques Specx, August 2, 1613, VOC 1056. For a discussion of these gifts, see Kees Zandvliet, ed., *The Dutch Encounter with Asia, 1600–1950* (Zwolle: Waanders, 2002), 102. Viallé notes that a number of VOC agents did end up keeping gifts presented in Japan despite clear regulations to the contrary. Viallé, "'To Capture their Favor,'" 309.

[17] Viallé, "In Aid of Trade," 74. What happened to the items in the end is unclear.

Batavia to thank the shogun for the friendship the Dutch had received in the years since the establishment of the Company's trading outpost in Japan.[18] Tokugawa officials, however, refused to recognize the status of the Governor-General, who they dismissed as nothing more than a local official, "a servant or servant of a servant," and a figure that was clearly not qualified to dispatch ambassadors or present gifts to the shogun. Because the embassy did not come from a sovereign actor, it was forbidden from even offering its gifts to the shogun and ordered to depart immediately.[19] In this way, issues of diplomatic status fatally compromised the presentation of gifts.

FINDING THE FORMULA

Over time, the VOC found solutions to both problems, settling on an effective formula that started to yield predictable results year after year. The question of the underlying logic of VOC gift exchange proved the more difficult to resolve and it required the complete reorientation of the nature of the Company's relationship with the shogun. This commenced in 1630 when Dutch representatives started to drop any reference to an external power, either the "king of Holland" or the Governor-General in Batavia, and to emphasize instead their desired role as humble vassals of the shogun.[20] An important letter sent to Japan in this year explained that "the Netherlanders shall display such faithful service to his Majesty [the shogun] in all matters just as his Majesty expects from the Japanese that are his own vassals."[21] On later occasions, Company agents declared that

[18] 4 October 1627: Daghregister van de reijse gedaen bij Pieter Nuijts ende Pieter Muijser, oppercoopman, als ambassadeurs aen den keijser ende rijcxraden van Japan van 24 Julij 1627 tot 18 Februarij 1628, VOC 1095; 456–458v.

[19] 5 November 1627, Nuijts/Muijser *Dagregister*, 484.

[20] Nagazumi Yōko was the first to identify the Company's use of this terminology in her landmark translation of some of the early diaries kept by the VOC opperhoofd in Japan. Nagazumi Yōko, *Hirado Oranda shōkan nikki*, 4 vols. (Tokyo Iwanami Shoten, 1969–70), 2: 6. For a more detailed examination, see Nagazumi Yōko, "Orandajin no uketa goon to hōkō," in *Sakoku o hiraku*, ed. Kawakatsu Heita (Tokyo: Dōbunkan, 2000). Katō Eiichi has described Tokugawa/VOC relations as a "fictive master–servant relationship." Katō Eiichi, *Bakuhansei kokka no seiritsu to taigai kankei* (Kyoto: Shibunkaku Shuppan, 1998), 155.

[21] "... de Nederlanderen haere Maij. bij alle occurenten wederom in alles sulcken getrouwen diensten sullen bethoonen als haere Maij. van Jappanders haere Maij. eygen vasalen souden moghen verwachten." Remonstrantie aen de heeren rijcxraden van Sijne Keyserlijcke Mayesteyt in Japan pr. den E. Willem Janssen derwaerts gesonden, 24 July 1630, VOC 855, unfoliated.

they wished "to be like vassals of His Majesty [the shogun]," and that they stood ready to spill "their last drop of blood in service of His Majesty and preservation of the Japanese realm."[22] Concealed within this obviously hyperbolic language was a key shift, a move out of a sovereign category in which Dutch agents claimed the same status as conventional state ambassadors, into a new subsovereign category in which they deliberately positioned themselves as loyal subordinates intent on taking up their place alongside the shogun's domestic vassals.

The result of this shift was that the nature of VOC gift-giving also changed from diplomatic offerings presented by a foreign power to tribute offered up by a domestic subordinate. The vehicle for doing this was the famous *hofreis*, or visit to the court by the chief merchant (*opperhoofd*) of the factory, which assumed a routinized form in 1634 and lasted essentially unchanged until 1790.[23] The post-1634 *hofreis* can best be seen as a combined product of the Company's insistence on its new role as loyal vassal and Tokugawa willingness to accommodate this. If the Dutch wished to present themselves as vassals defined only by their connection to the shogun, the regime, which had its own interests in keeping its relationship with the Company functioning, was quite clearly ready to consent.

As it developed, the *hofreis* assumed some features that looked very similar to the visit of a domainal lord (*daimyo*), including a fixed calendar and a ritualistic performance of submission in Edo.[24] The link between the two was readily apparent to VOC observers, who noted that "all daimyo and shomyo, that is, all greater and lesser territorial lords, appear annually at the shogun's court. They pay homage by offering their respects and presenting gifts … This custom is also enforced upon the

[22] "… wij trachten als vassalen van [sij]ne Maj. te sijn …" and "… trouwe dienaren, wiens laetste druppelbloets, ten dienste van de May. ende behoudenisse des Japansen rijcx geresolveert blijven te spenderen." Tokyo daigaku shiryō hensanjo, ed., *Dagregisters gehouden door de Opperhoofden van de Nederlandse Faktorij in Japan* (Tokyo: University of Tokyo Press, 1974–), 3: 302; 6: 204 (hereafter *Dagregisters Japan*).

[23] Kanai Madoka, *Nichiran kōshōshi no kenkyū* (Kyoto: Shibunkaku, 1986), 172–92. As Viallé points out, the *hofreis* could be said to have commenced in 1609 and there were sporadic visits from 1609 to 1634 whenever VOC ships arrived in Japan. Cynthia Viallé, "Zingen voor de shogun. VOC-dienaren aan het Japanse hof," in *Aan de overkant. Ontmoetingen in dienst van de VOC en WIC (1600–1800)*, ed. Lodewijk Wagenaar (Leiden: Sidestone Press, 2015), 39.

[24] For a discussion of the domestic system of daimyo visits, see Constantine Vaporis, *Tour of Duty: Samurai, Military Service in Edo, and the Culture of Early Modern Japan* (Honolulu: University of Hawai'i Press, 2008).

servants of our illustrious Dutch company."[25] The switch from high-level diplomatic missions into the subsovereign category had the twin effect of both simplifying and routinizing VOC gift-giving. Vassals did not need to pair their gifts with diplomatic letters and there was no need to prove the ambassador's credentials as the proxy of a recognized sovereign. This eliminated the pitfalls that had claimed the 1627 embassy and smoothed out the gift-giving landscape by rendering the *opperhoofd* as just another domestic subordinate traveling up to Edo to offer tribute to his lord.

The second problem, that of meager or inadequate gifts, was initially resolved by taking advantage of an area of technology in which the VOC held an unquestioned advantage over the Tokugawa regime, that of artillery production.[26] In 1615, the Company presented the retired shogun with an iron cannon weighing 3000 pounds at an estimated value of 420 guilders.[27] To make it immediately functional, it came with all the necessary accessories, including fifty rounds of cannon balls and a large quantity of gunpowder. The Dutch did not generally ship over unused cannon to Asia for use as gifts and such items were usually stripped, as in this case, from VOC vessels. This strategy carried its own risks but even though the Company did possess the capacity to forge cannon in its Japan factory, these were deemed insufficiently appealing for the shogun, who would, according to one observer, rather have one European cannon than ten cast in Japan.[28] Lesser officials were, however, regularly presented with cannon made in Japan, including a 600-pound falconet worth 192 guilders. In addition to the cannon, the Bakufu also displayed a sustained interest in the specialists required to operate them and made regular requests for master gunners prepared to enter "the service of His Imperial Majesty [the shogun]."[29]

Despite their obvious appeal, such gifts were not without their problems. They were, for example, extremely heavy and hence difficult to

[25] Engelbert Kaempfer, *Kaempfer's Japan: Tokugawa Culture Observed*, ed. and trans. Beatrice Bodart-Bailey (Honolulu: University of Hawai'i Press, 1999), 280.

[26] If Japanese muskets and musketeers were a match for their European equivalent, then the same could not be said of heavy ordnance, a technology in which Japan lagged both behind Europe and other East Asian powers like China. Adam Clulow, "Finding the Balance: European Military Power in Early Modern Asia," *History Compass* 13 (2015): 148–57.

[27] Resolutions of the Japan factory, 28 October 1615, VOC 1061: 250v–250.

[28] Charles Boxer, *The Christian Century in Japan, 1549–1650* (Berkeley: University of California Press, 1951), 207.

[29] Resolutions, 26 September 1615, Japan factory, VOC 1061: 252.

transport from Hirado on the edges of western Kyushu all the way to Edo in the center. The cannon presented in 1615 weighed 3,000 pounds, while another set of two cannon from Holland that were offered to the shogun topped the scales at 3,358 pounds.[30] There were also some concerns within the organization that the VOC was giving away valuable military technology. The issue came up in relation to the shogun's request for heavy mortars, which were shipped to Edo for a demonstration in 1639. Although the event itself was not entirely successful, with a misfiring mortar injuring the gunners and some of the spectators, it received a rapturous response from the shogun, who informed the Dutch that he was delighted with weapons that he described as a "jewel of [your] land" (*een cleijnnodie van t lant*).[31] The result was continued requests for new mortars but also a backlash within the Company, with one official writing that the organization should not so readily share its advanced military technology.[32] Despite this, the Company continued to present artillery pieces, and in 1649 it offered the shogun two "fine metal cannon."[33]

In addition to military items, the Company also became increasingly proficient in securing luxury objects capable of appealing to Tokugawa officials. These came initially from the United Provinces, but VOC officials gradually developed a highly efficient intra-Asian gift network capable of transporting a vast range of items within the organization's trading area. The most famous, and arguably the most successful, gift from Europe was a huge brass chandelier that was presented to Tokugawa Iemitsu, the third Tokugawa shogun, in 1636. The item first appears in the opperhoofd's diary from 21 March 1636, in which it is described as a brass chandelier with thirty arms.[34] The reference provides no sense of the monumental nature of the item, which weighed almost 800 pounds and was erected for display on a special nine-foot wooden frame.[35] Beautifully crafted by Joost Gerritzoon, who had produced similar items for the famous Oude Kerk in Amsterdam, its size meant that it had to be disassembled for transport and each piece individually marked with Japanese characters so that they could be put together correctly in

30 Provisionele raminge van schenckagien voor haere keyserlijcke Mayesteit rijcxraden ende andere grooten in Japan, VOC 854: 72–75.

31 *Dagregisters Japan*, 4: 82.

32 Charles Boxer, "Notes on Early European Military Influence in Japan (1543–1853)," *Transactions of the Asiatic Society of Japan* 8 (1931): 84.

33 Instructie voor den Pieter Blockhovius, gaende van hier per T'jacht den robijn naer Japan, VOC 873.

34 *Dagregisters Japan*, 2: 18.

35 Ibid., 2: 48.

the shogun's castle.[36] In Edo, the chandelier was warmly received and quickly shipped over to decorate the great mausoleum at Nikkō, the construction of which was about to be concluded.[37] There it remains on display today, still in a prominent position near the Yōmeimon, the famous "sun-bright gatehouse" that marked the entrance to the sacred inner precinct (Figure 7.1).[38] Dutch writers were well aware of the powerful symbolism involved in displaying the gift in such a charged environment, writing that the "Lustre" of "the Emperors Tomb in *Niko* ... was made the greater, by the Branch'd Candlestick given by the *East India* Company, to the *Japan* emperor, as being Cast of Copper, and brought from *Holland*."[39]

Such was the success of the chandelier, which arrived just in time to feature in the opening celebrations for the new complex, that the Dutch continued to present such items for a number of years thereafter. In 1640, for example, they offered a standing copper chandelier valued at 2,700 guilders; 3 years later this was followed up by an enormous lantern, a monumental piece of brasswork that stood 3 meters high, weighed 4,523 pounds and cost 16,053 guilders.[40] Not surprisingly for an object of this size and value, it came accompanied by a special craftsman, Carel Jonassen of Amsterdam, who was brought over to Japan to take charge of the gift. The lantern, which was specially marked with Tokugawa cartouches, was also dispatched to Nikkō to be placed on display (Figure 7.2).

Not all luxury items from Europe were quite so large or so grand, and the VOC was also content to present a range of more practical

[36] Ibid., 2: 58. [37] Ibid., 2: 23.

[38] William Coaldrake, *Architecture and Authority in Japan* (London: Routledge Curzon, 1996), 186. Gerhart, who has analyzed the iconography of this structure, describes the Yōmeimon as the "focal point of Tokugawa efforts to create divine authority." Karen Gerhart, *The Eyes of Power: Art and Early Tokugawa Authority* (Honolulu: University of Hawai'i Press, 1999), 74.

[39] Arnoldus Montanus, *Atlas Japanensis: Being Remarkable Addresses by Way of Embassy from the East-India Company of the United Provinces to the Emperor of Japan*, trans. John Ogilby (London: 1670), 152. Emphasis in this translation.

[40] These items are treated in detail in Th. H. Lunsingh Scheurleer, "Koperen kronen en waskaarsen voor Japan," *Oud Holland* 93 (1979): 69–74. Mia Mochizuki has produced two important articles that reference the chandelier: Mia Mochizuki, "Deciphering the Dutch in Deshima," in *The Boundaries of the Netherlands: Real and Imagined*, ed. Marybeth Carlson, Laura Cruz and Benjamin J. Kaplan (Leiden: Brill, 2009), and Mia Mochizuki, "Idolatry and Western-Inspired Painting in Japan," in *Idols in the Age of Art. Objects, Devotions and the Early Modern World*, ed. Michael Cole and Rebecca Zorach (Aldershot, UK: Ashgate, 2009).

FIGURE 7.1 Chandelier presented by the Dutch East India Company in 1636.
© Author's photograph.

FIGURE 7.2 Lantern presented by the Dutch in 1643.
© Author's photograph.

gifts including large quantities of wine, cloth and even a featherbed in 1652.[41] While gifts from Europe could prove highly successful, such items required years to transit from the United Provinces and were not always assured of the desired reception. The enormous 1643 brass lantern was publicly praised by Tokugawa officials but it secured no dramatic improvement in the Company's position. As a result, the Dutch came to depend more and more on their intra-Asian trade network to supply appropriate items. This shift brought VOC gift-giving in Japan more

[41] Cynthia Viallé and Leonard Blussé, *The Deshima Dagregisters* (Leiden: Universiteit Leiden, 2001–2010), 12: 41.

in line with the organization's overall trade strategy; as a rule, the Company's fortunes depended more on shipping goods from one part of Asia to another than on the simple importation of European wares. The potential of such a system was famously described by an early Governor-General who wrote that "Piece goods from Gujarat we can barter for pepper and gold on the coast of Sumatra; rials [silver currency] and cottons from the [Coromandel] coast for the pepper in Bantam; sandalwood, pepper and rials we can barter for Chinese goods and Chinese gold; we can extract silver from Japan with Chinese goods."[42] The Dutch developed a similarly elaborate network designed to move exotic gift items from one part of its trading empire to another.

The range of gifts brought to Japan from other parts of Asia is staggering and includes, to name just a handful, carpets from Surat; iron rockets from Tuticorin on the Coromandel coast; Bengal *tafficila* or *taffechelas*, a mixed silk and cotton cloth; and Tonkin *peling*, a fine silk.[43] Persia was a particularly active hub in the Company's sprawling Asian gift network and carpets and cloth from this part of the world were regularly presented to Tokugawa officials. Some of these could be extremely lavish. A particularly magnificent gold and silver carpet, fully 6.5 yards long and 3.5 yards wide, valued at 510 guilders, was presented in Edo in 1634.[44] The Company's capacity to move gifts between different parts of Asia depended on a constant flow of letters between the individual factories and Batavia providing information on the availability of exotic items and the desirability of particular imports.[45] Thus the Governor-General instructed the opperhoofd in Japan to assess the impact of "2 carpets and 12 pieces of gold and silver laken [a rich cloth] that have been received from Persia" and if they pleased Tokugawa officials to "advise President Geleynsz in Gamron and request [them] again."[46] For its part, the Japan factory was not simply a recipient of gifts; rather, it was another hub in the Company's gift network and

42 Michal Pearson, *The Indian Ocean* (London and New York: Routledge, 2003), 151. For an examination of the Company's fully developed trading system, see Els M. Jacobs, *Merchant in Asia: The Trade of the Dutch East India Company during the Eighteenth Century* (Leiden: CNWS, 2006).

43 For details of these various cloths, see Giorgio Riello and Tirthankar Roy, eds., *How India Clothed the World: The World of South Asian Textiles, 1500–1850* (Leiden; Boston: Brill, 2009).

44 *Dagregisters Japan*, 1: 34.

45 Viallé, "'To Capture their Favor,'" 296.

46 "Soo de overgaende 2 pees alcatijven ende 12 pees goude en silvere laeckenen nu uyt Persia ontfangen near de Japanse maniere gemaect ende aangenaem sijn, sal UE.'tselve aen den president Geleynse in Gamron adviseren …" *Dagregisters Japan*, 9: 219.

Japanese lacquerware was frequently carried by VOC ambassadors to the great courts of Southeast and South Asia. One particularly rich mission dispatched to Mughal India in 1711 carried with it 256 pieces of Japanese lacquerware for presentation to the emperor.[47]

Perhaps the most striking gifts from other parts of Asia were exotic animals, which were regularly transported from one part of the Company's trading area to another.[48] In the 1650s for example, the VOC presented a Javanese deer, a cassowary we presume from New Guinea, two Bengali oxen that were "beautifully caparisoned and harnessed to the carriage" and an ostrich picked up in its South African outpost.[49] The last was particularly well received, prompting a series of questions concerning its geographical origin, gender, manner of capture, age and future growth. In addition to securing exotic animals from the lands under its control, the VOC was also quite willing to take advantage of its Asian network to essentially regift items. In 1675, the king of Abyssinia presented the Governor-General with "2 rare wild donkeys (*woutesels*)" that were subsequently exported to Japan and presented to the shogun.[50] But although they invariably piqued Tokugawa interest, presenting live animals created a range of additional problems. One official remarked of the importation of live birds that these "are useless too and none should be brought here by the Company ... for apart from the problems of transporting them, they are subject to a sudden death here and the Company is forced to keep them till the journey to the Court in the middle of winter, when it is very cold and hazardous."[51]

Its capacity to draw an array of exotic items from its Asian outposts gave the Company a significant advantage as a gift-giving organization, but this does not fully account for its overall success in Japan. A further explanation lies in the fact that during the heyday of VOC gift-giving, control over part of the process was in fact wrested from the Dutch and placed in the hands of the intended recipients. The explanation for this development lies in the changing nature of the VOC gift-giving process after 1634 when the *hofreis* was set on an annual basis. In other parts of

[47] For details of this mission, see J. Ph. Vogel, ed., *Journaal van J. J. Ketelaar's hofreis naar den Groot Mogol te Lahore: 1711–1713* (The Hague: Martinus Nijhoff, 1937).

[48] As discussed in Chaiklin, "The Merchant's Ark."

[49] Viallé and Blussé, *Deshima Dagregisters*, 12: 101, 290, 382 and 340.

[50] J. A. Van der Chijs, H. T. Colenbrander and J. de Hullu, eds., *Dagh-register gehouden int Casteel Batavia vant passerende daer ter plaetse als over geheel Nederlandts-India, 1675* (Batavia and The Hague: Landsdrukkerij/Martinus Nijhoff, 1887–1931), 60.

[51] Viallé and Blussé, *Deshima Dagregisters*, 11: 275.

Asia, the Company gave gifts periodically to local rulers and officials, but the schedule was either unpredictable – depending for example on the succession of a new monarch – or determined by VOC agents, who were free to decide when the next mission should depart. Japan is set apart in that the Company lost control over the timeline, which stipulated that VOC agents must travel to Edo every year without fail to present gifts.[52] In fact, the Bakufu fixed precise annual dates, as it did for individual daimyo, for the *opperhoofd* to depart from Nagasaki on his way to Edo. The rigid nature of these regulations is summed up by Engelbert Kaempfer, who wrote that just as "the shogun gives every prince and vassal in the empire a day on which he has to set out and begin his annual journey to court, so the Dutch too are assigned a day for their departure. This is the fifteenth or the sixteenth day of the Japanese first month, which corresponds to February in our calendar."[53]

Fixing the *hofreis* to such a rigid timeline opened the gift-giving process to manipulation. The result was that initiative passed from the Dutch to the recipients, who were free to dictate which gifts they wished to receive with the expectation that a regular cycle of visits to the court would eventually bring these items directly into their hands. One of the first officials to grasp the possibilities for doing this was Matsura Takanobu, the lord of Hirado, a maritime domain in which the Dutch were based from 1609 until they were moved to Nagasaki in 1641. In 1636 he presented the opperhoofd with a detailed list of demands that included two statues of Hollanders carved out of wood, one master and one servant, two of the largest dogs that could be found, five or ten pheasants from the Cabo Verde archipelago in the Atlantic, eight or ten birds from Siam, ten beautiful peacocks, a quantity of telescopes and spectacles, an extremely large mirror, colored captain's plumes that were worn by soldiers in battle and green or blue parakeets.[54] As soon as these items arrived in Japan, they were to be handed over to the daimyo either for his personal pleasure or to be offered to the shogun. The list forms an early example of a distinctive genre, the *eisen*, or demands, that were issued to the factory's opperhoofd every year.[55] The scale of the eisen gradually expanded, morphing from Matsura Takanobu's relatively short list to

[52] Viallé, "In Aid of Trade," 62. [53] Kaempfer, *Kaempfer's Japan*, 280.

[54] *Dagregisters Japan*, 2: 161.

[55] For an excellent discussion of the *eisen*, see Martha Chaiklin, *Cultural Commerce and Dutch Commercial Culture*. Viallé cites an earlier example of a demand by the lord of Hirado from 1620 for some sheep. Viallé, "In Aid of Trade," 66.

far more expansive documents that detailed individual demands for the shogun as well as a range of Tokugawa officials, all of whom were interested in acquiring specific items. One important milestone was 1641 when, as a result of the factory's forced relocation from Hirado to Nagasaki, control over these lists passed from the hands of Hirado domain to Bakufu officials such as the Ōmetsuke (inspector general) Inoue Masashige.[56]

A good example of a mature *eisen* comes from 1652 when Inoue handed over a meticulous listing of "various rarities and goods" that were demanded by the shogun and six additional officials, including the shogun's great uncle and a number of trusted advisors.[57] The demands are remarkably detailed: the gifts for the shogun include more than forty specific demands, ranging from exotic curiosities to scientific items. The former category included unicorn horn, mermaids' teeth, battle plumes and specially made iron contraptions designed to replace a (presumably amputated) hand and to enable the wearer to wield either a sword or a pen. The scientific component of the list was equally precise and included an anatomy book with detailed illustrations of human dissections, and "a complete anatomy of a human body, the body being fashioned in copper, wood or another material so that one can perfectly see all the details of the human parts."[58] Such documents were strikingly global, treating the VOC trading area as an emporium from which exotic goods and items could be drawn at will. They reveal a precise understanding of the geographical extent of the Company's area of operations, including demands, for example, for the feathers of Sumatran birds, mats from modern-day Sri Lanka and an array of Persian goods. Although many of these items were extremely difficult to procure, the *opperhoofd* was required to sign onto a written promise stipulating that he would ensure their arrival in Japan.

The 1652 list reveals a gift-giving process that had become essentially collaborative. In addition to providing a precise list of gifts, Tokugawa officials also vetted what the Company had brought in, accepting the goods they were happy with and (to the great irritation of VOC agents) discarding those that did not meet the cut. One particularly irksome exchange took place over a copy of Dodonaeus' *Cruydt-boek*, a famous

[56] For Inoue, see Timon Screech, "A 17th-Century Japanese Minister's Acquisition of Western Pictures: Inoue Masashige (1585–1661) and His European Objects," in *Transforming Knowledge Orders: Museums, Collections and Exhibitions*, ed. Larissa Förster (Paderborn: Willem Fink, 2014), 72–106.

[57] Viallé and Blussé, *Deshima Dagregisters*, 12: 64–65. Viallé, "In Aid of Trade," 68.

[58] Ibid., 65.

herbal that had been requested years earlier by one official.[59] When it was at last handed over, the recipient expressed his unhappiness with the gift, complaining that the illustrations were too small and poorly drawn. Because of this, he requested that the Company procure a larger book with more substantial illustrations. This back and forth over an item that had not been easy to procure in the first place caused the opperhoofd to lament that such texts did not come in various sizes like shoes in the store of shoemaker to be ordered according to individual whims.[60]

THE GIFT AND EUROPEAN EXPANSION

The scale of VOC gift-giving in Japan was vast. For over 150 years, the Company's representatives made the long trip to Edo bearing large quantities of gifts that would have totaled over this period hundreds of thousands or more likely millions of guilders. In many ways, the history of VOC gift-giving is one marked by successful adaptation in which the organization overcame the twin problems that had confronted the first generation of VOC envoys in Japan. The question of status was resolved by discarding past attachments in favor of a simplified presentation that pictured the Dutch as the shogun's loyal vassals while the Company also developed a highly sophisticated network capable of moving goods around Asia to meet the peculiar demands of individual courts. But part of this adaptation came in the form of surrendering control over the process itself as Tokugawa officials came to play an increasingly prominent role in VOC gift-giving in Japan. The result was that the Company's gift-giving operations became visibly collaborative.

In the New World, the arrival of European envoys bearing gifts often came with momentous consequences. Gifts formed an indispensable part of the claiming process, proving a mechanism to exert influence over territories and people. In many places, the gift functioned as little more than a Trojan horse, opening up avenues for conquest and possession that were quickly exploited. In Japan, by contrast, the dynamic underpinning of European gift-giving was very different. Here VOC gift-giving was part of a wider settlement that saw the Company accept a subordinate position in its relationship with the shogun. When they turned to the topic of

[59] For a study of this important work, see W. F. Vande Walle and Kazuhiko Kasaya, eds., *Dodonæus in Japan: Translation and the Scientific Mind in the Tokugawa Period* (Kyoto: International Research Center for Japanese Studies and Leuven University Press, 2001).

[60] 24 April 1659, Dagregister Zacharias Wagenaer, NFJ 72, unfoliated.

Japan, the Company's directors observed that "we can give our officers no other instructions than to satisfy this arrogant, grand and punctilious nation in everything." Dutch agents in Japan should, they suggested, "go armed with modesty, humility, courteousness and friendship, see never to dictate to the regime but always to bend to its wishes."[61] The gift may have been a vital part of VOC operations in Japan, but it was one that functioned according to the rhythms imposed by Japanese officials.

[61] P. Mijer, *Verzameling van Instructiën, Ordonnanciën en Reglementen voor de Regering van Nederlandsch Indië* (Batavia, 1848), 99.

8

"From His Holiness to the King of China"

Gifts, Diplomacy and Jesuit Evangelization

Mary Laven

In February 1582, four Japanese teenagers left Nagasaki on a journey to Rome. They were accompanied by the Italian Jesuit Alessandro Valignano, "Visitor to the East Indies." The East Indies was an enormous jurisdiction that stretched from Goa on the west coast of India to Macao and Nagasaki in the Far East. The "ambassadors" were all boys, the dependants of three *daimyo* (territorial lords) who had converted to Christianity (Figure 8.1). Their mission was twofold: to promote the evangelization of East Asia and to learn more about European civilization. Escorted by priests and attendants, the foursome traveled to Europe via Macao, Melaka and India. They arrived in Lisbon in August 1584, two and a half years after bidding farewell to their parents in Japan, having also left their spiritual father Valignano (at his superiors' orders) in Goa.[1] In March 1585, the boys were received in Rome by Pope Gregory XIII, to whom they presented a series of gifts: a folding screen, a bamboo desk, examples of Japanese varnish and lacquerwork, and suits of armor. The Japanese embassy was carefully controlled by the Jesuits, who insisted that the boys stay only in houses belonging to the Society. That way they could be protected from contamination with the religious controversies that beset Europe in the late sixteenth century. As publicity stunts go, this one was a major success. The boys, who communicated in Latin and wore clothes cut in the European style, attracted benign curiosity

[1] For details of Valignano's career, see M. Antoni J. Üçerler, "Alessandro Valignano: Man, Missionary, and Writer," *Renaissance Studies* 17, no. 3 (2003): 337–66.

FIGURE 8.1 Portrait of the young men and royal ambassadors from Japan. Hand-colored engraving on paper. Augsburg, 1586. Kyoto University, Kyoto.

wherever they went. Their visit was the subject of much talk, a vast amount of correspondence, some portraits and no fewer than fifty-five publications.[2]

This chapter concerns another diplomatic initiative of Alessandro Valignano – one that is far less well known, mostly (we may suppose) because it never happened. The non-event is recorded for posterity in a document held in the Jesuit archive in Rome, entitled "Memorial of the Things to Be Sent as a Present by His Holiness to the King of

[2] On the Japanese envoys and their gifts, see Donald Lach, *Asia in the Making of Europe*, 3 vols. (Chicago: University of Chicago Press, 1965–93), 1: 688–706; J. F. Moran, *The Japanese and the Jesuits: Alessandro Valignano in Sixteenth-Century Japan* (London: Routledge, 1993), 6–19; Luís Fróis, *La première ambassade du Japon en Europe, 1582–1592*, ed. J. A. Abranches Pinto et al. (Tokyo: Sophia University, 1942); and Greg Irvine, "Japanese Diplomatic Relations with Europe," in *Encounters: The Meeting of Asia and Europe, 1500–1800*, ed. Anna Jackson and Amin Jaffer (London: V&A Publications, 2004), 100–101.

China."[3] We can date the "Memorial" to 1588, when Valignano sent Michele Ruggieri – one of a handful of Jesuits who had been operating as a missionary in China since 1579 – back to Europe to garner support for a papal embassy to Beijing. The document, which is signed by Valignano, consists of fifteen densely written pages providing detailed descriptions in Spanish of the twenty-one gifts that should accompany the papal delegation. It is written as an itemized list. While numbers 1 to 4 describe the presentation of the gifts and number 26 estimates the total cost of the gifts, the majority of the entries (items 5 to 25) list the presents, either singly or in groups. The twenty-six points may be summarized as follows:

1. Importance attached to the arrangement and display of gifts by the Chinese.
2. Media in which the pope's letter to the Chinese emperor should be written.
3. Presentation of the pope's letter.
4. Media and presentation of the letter given to the *dutang* or provincial viceroy.
5. [Gifts commence here.] An illuminated manuscript New Testament on parchment, covered in crimson velvet and richly worked with gold thread.
6. Three belts of the sort that the Emperor of China is accustomed to; Michele Ruggieri to advise.
7. Three helmets to match.
8. Three strings of coral.
9. A reading desk richly decorated in stones of various colours, such as they are accustomed to have in Rome.
10. Twenty-five pieces of brocade; decoration specified.
11. *Byobu* or screens, of the kind brought to Rome by the Japanese Knights.
12. Two mirrors made of Venetian glass.
13. Five pieces of triangular glass, made in Venice.
14. 200 pieces of Venetian stained glass, including representations of lions, serpents, and dragons.
15. Two boxes, made in the Venetian fashion.

[3] Archivum Romanum Societatis Iesu, Fondo Gesuitico, 722, no. 2, fols. 1–9. See also my discussion in Mary Laven, *Mission to China: Matteo Ricci and the Jesuit Encounter with the East* (London: Faber, 2011), 69–72, 85–99.

16. A dozen sandglass clocks.
17. A mechanical clock.
18. Two globes: one celestial and one terrestrial.
19. Some architecture books.
20. More picture books, representing beautiful figures, such as popes or emperors.
21. Paintings of Christ in Glory and of the Assumption; images of the Virgin and Child.
22. Images of Rome, ancient and modern.
23. A box with five or six dozen feathers of various colors.
24. Flemish locks.
25. An organ and a harpsichord, Flemish.
26. Total cost: five to six thousand ducats.

While the jumble of assorted objects defies easy categorization, four main strategies emerge from Valignano's wish list. The first is what the Jesuits themselves would have referred to as the *modo soave*: the gentle approach. Be sensitive to the mores of the host culture. When in Rome do as the Romans do. The second strategy is to impress by means of the demonstration of skill and technology from the Christian world: the virtuoso approach. The third is the attempt to forge human contacts through material mélanges, hence the conspicuous inclusion of European-made artifacts that seek to emulate Asian culture: we might call this the connective approach. The fourth strategy is to import objects of doctrinal significance, whose meanings are either unknown to the Chinese or deliberately concealed from them: this last approach I am going to describe as evangelical smuggling.[4]

Valignano's *modo soave* is instantly apparent in the opening paragraphs of this document, which attend to matters of presentation. "First of all," he says, "one has to understand that, for this people, the arrangement and display of things matters no less than the things themselves."[5] The Memorial therefore describes not only "the things that will be highly esteemed and well adapted to the use of the Chinese," but also the manner

[4] For more general discussion of the Society of Jesus, its approach to mission and its engagement with science and the arts, see John W. O'Malley, *The First Jesuits* (Cambridge, MA: Harvard University Press, 1993); John W. O'Malley et al., eds., *The Jesuits, Cultures, Sciences and the Arts, 1543–1773* (Toronto: University of Toronto Press, 1999); John W. O'Malley and Gauvin Alexander Bailey, eds., *The Jesuits and the Arts, 1540–1773* (Philadelphia: St Joseph's University Press, 2005).

[5] Archivum Romanum Societatis Iesu, Fondo Gesuitico, 722, no. 2, fol. 1.

in which they are presented.[6] Thus, the pope's letter to the Chinese emperor, accompanying the embassy, must be written in gold on the finest and most delicate parchment (*not* paper), with gold cords and a gold seal (*not* lead). It should also be illuminated, and surrounded by rich and beautiful pictures, including images of lions and serpents, the insignia of the emperor. On one side, the pope's message must be written in Latin; on the other, in Chinese. The carefully crafted letter should then be rolled, tied with the cords, and placed in a box lined in crimson velvet. The Memorial also offered precise instructions as to the writing of a letter addressed to the provincial governor in Canton (whose cooperation would be required if a papal embassy were to be allowed to proceed north to Beijing) and of two letters patent designed to ease the passage of the envoys. Here it was important to make sure that the decoration of the letter for the *dutang* was scaled down to fit his rank. The writing on these documents need not be in gold letters nor should the illumination be so rich; as for the cords, it was sufficient that these be made of silk and that the seal be of silver.

These considerations testified to the sharpness of the Jesuit ethnographical eye. Valignano had written extensively about the cultures in which he lived and worked (Mozambique, India, Japan), and was at pains to note how customs varied across the world.[7] In particular, in his *Observations on the Habits and Particular Customs of Japan*, written in 1581, he explored food, dress, table manners, cleanliness and the use of honorific forms; one section touches directly on the importance of finding appropriate gifts.[8] Small wonder, therefore, that he was keen to spell out the significance of presentation and of observing rank when offering gifts to the emperor and his viceroys. When, in item 1 of the list, Valignano spoke of the things that were "highly esteemed and well adapted to the use of the Chinese" ("muy estimadas y acomodadas al uso delos Chinas") he was explicitly deploying the concept of "accommodation" – the famous Jesuit tendency to compromise that was to win the Order notoriety in China in the later seventeenth and eighteenth centuries.[9] Within the diplomatic context, however, one might see accommodation as

[6] Ibid. [7] Üçerler, "Alessandro Valignano," 352–59.

[8] Josef Franz Schütte, *Valignano's Mission Principles for Japan*, trans. John J. Coyne, 2 vols. (St. Louis: Institute of Jesuit Sources, 1980–85), 1, part 2: 155–90; on gifts in particular, see 184–87.

[9] Nicolas Standaert, "Jesuits in China," in *The Cambridge Companion to the Jesuits*, ed. Thomas Worcester (Cambridge: Cambridge University Press, 2008), 172–73; David Mungello, "An Introduction to the Chinese Rites Controversy," in *The Chinese Rites*

fundamental to the success of global gifts. These were of course designed to sweeten, not to sour relations, and the evidence suggests that early modern ambassadors at least tried to respect the tastes and values of their hosts in selecting appropriate presents.[10]

The appeal of virtuosity has been eloquently discussed by the anthropologist Alfred Gell, who perceives "the technology of enchantment" as key to our desire for art. According to Gell, the admiration we feel for works of art results from the difficulty we have in "mentally encompassing their coming-to-being as objects." Since the technical process by which they have been created transcends our understanding, we are forced to construe it as "magical."[11] This is a theory that is perhaps especially applicable to the reception of foreign artifacts: because the technical processes of production are all the more obscure to the beholder, so the sense of enchantment may be expected to be correspondingly greater. Gell's argument may help to explain the attraction of exotica to elite Chinese in the late Ming period, and the particular fascination that Europeans had for that most unfathomable Chinese product: porcelain.[12]

Valignano sought to demonstrate the virtuosity of European material culture through a rich assortment of high-quality objects. At the heart of the list is a clutch of luxury commodities made in the Visitor's native Italy. Three items (numbered 12–14) represent the renowned achievements of the Venetian glass industry: two mirrors, five "triangular pieces of glass"

Controversy: Its History and Meaning, ed. David Mungello (Sankt Augustin: Institut Monumenta Serica, 1994), 3–14.

[10] On early modern diplomatic gifts, protocol and occasional faux pas, see Olga Dmitrieva, "From Whitehall to the Kremlin: The Diplomacy and Political Culture of the English and Russian Courts," in *Treasures of the Royal Courts: Tudors, Stuarts and the Russian Tsars*, ed. Olga Dmitrieva and Tessa Murdoch (London: V&A Publications, 2013), 18–24; Maija Jansson, "Measured Reciprocity: English Ambassadorial Gift Exchange in the Seventeenth and Eighteenth Centuries," *Journal of Early Modern History* 9, no. 3 (2005): 348–70; Diana Carrió-Invernizzi, "Gift and Diplomacy in Seventeenth-Century Spanish Italy," *Historical Journal* 51, no. 4 (2008): 881–99; *Journal of Early Modern History* 20, no. 4 (2016), special issue on early modern diplomacy. For a more general discussion of "gifts gone wrong," see Natalie Zemon Davis, *The Gift in Sixteenth-Century France* (Oxford: Oxford University Press, 2000), 110–41.

[11] Alfred Gell, "The Technology of Enchantment and the Enchantment of Technology," in *Anthropology, Art and Aesthetics*, ed. Jeremy Coote and Anthony Shelton (Oxford: Clarendon Press, 1992), 40–66, esp. 46–49, on "the halo-effect" of technical difficulty.

[12] On Chinese enthusiasm for exotica, see Craig Clunas, *Superfluous Things: Material Culture and Social Status in Early Modern China* (Cambridge: Polity, 1991), 58. On European fascination with Chinese porcelain, see, for example, Jackson and Jaffer, *Encounters*, 224–31.

and 200 pieces of stained glass.[13] Of these, perhaps the most obvious luxury good is the looking-glass. Mirror-making took off in the early sixteenth century in Venice, as is indicated by the establishment in 1570 of a specific guild, *l'arte degli specchieri*.[14] "Triangular pieces of glass" may seem less appealing gifts. However, the refraction of light through prisms was already a well-known party-trick of the Jesuits in China by the time that the Memorial was written; as early as 1584, the Portuguese Jesuit Francisco Cabral had cited "triangular crystals" among the exotica that delighted Chinese guests to the Zhaoqing residence.[15] The request for a large consignment of stained glass is less explicable, since the glass-blowers of Murano (unlike their colleagues in northern Europe) were not renowned for producing colored glazing. Venetian churches are famous for their floors, not for their windows, and the nobility used lightly tinted "bottle glass" in their palaces.[16] However, Venice did produce enormous quantities of colored glass for the Ottoman market and it was perhaps this connection that prompted Valignano to consider glass depicting "lions, serpents, and dragons" to be an ideal gift for the Chinese.[17]

Valignano also requested "two boxes" (item 15) in the Venetian fashion, clearly not intended as humble pieces of storage equipment but as intensely decorated works of artistry.[18] Meanwhile, from Rome, a reading desk richly decorated in stones of various colors (item 9) was to

[13] On Chinese enthusiasm for imported glass, see Emily Byrne Curtis, *Glass Exchange between Europe and China, 1550–1800: Diplomatic, Mercantile and Technological Interactions* (Aldershot: Ashgate, 2009).

[14] Francesca Trivellato, *Fondamenta dei vetrai: lavoro, tecnologia e mercato a Venezia tra Sei e Settecento* (Rome: Donzelli Editore, 2000), 137; id., "Murano Glass, Continuity and Transformation (1400–1800)," in *At the Centre of the Old World: Trade and Manufacturing in Venice and the Venetian Mainland, 1400–1800*, ed. Paola Lanaro (Toronto: CRRS Publications, 2006), 159.

[15] M. Howard Rienstra, ed., *Jesuit Letters from China, 1583–4* (Minneapolis: University of Minnesota Press, 1986), 28.

[16] Paul Hills, *Venetian Colour: Marble, Mosaic, Painting and Glass, 1250–1550* (New Haven: Yale University Press, 1999), 109; Deborah Howard, *Venice and the East: The Impact of the Islamic World on Venetian Architecture, 1100–1500* (New Haven: Yale University Press, 2000), 154–55.

[17] On the manufacture of colored glass for export to the Ottoman market, see Deborah Howard, "Cultural Transfer between Venice and the Ottomans," in *Cultural Exchange in Early Modern Europe, vol. 4: Forging European Identities, 1400–1700*, ed. Herman Roodenburg (Cambridge: Cambridge University Press, 2013), 157–59.

[18] See, for example, a Venetian chest (c. 1500), made of walnut and rosewood inlaid with ivory, in Elizabeth Currie, *Inside the Renaissance House* (London: V&A Publications, 2006), 49.

be commissioned.[19] Renaissance depictions of St. Jerome in his study provide a reminder that the Italian *studiolo* was a very showy space and that the paraphernalia of reading and writing encapsulated important aspects of masculinity in this period.[20] Given that learning and literacy were equally central to Chinese models of manhood, this was an obvious area in which bookish Jesuits and highly educated mandarins might bond.[21]

Brocade (item 10) was another classic Italian luxury product, of substantial economic worth.[22] The Jesuits' list specified twenty-five pieces of brocade of the finest quality, divided into five categories. Five pieces should be "rich and lustrous," light in weight, including one of gold cloth, another of silver. The next five should be of the finest floral design with "golden flowers, as they have in Italy" – these should be crimson, rose, white, green and yellow. The next five pieces should be of silk interwoven with gold, of the same colors (although the white may be changed for another "fresher" hue). The next five should be of the finest velvet (same colors). And the final five should be of the finest cloth of diverse colors, including green and yellow. They should be transported in a well-made gilded trunk, lined with satin of vermilion or yellow, and laid down in such a manner that they would not suffer from the long voyage.

Global travelers were used to weighing civilizations according to the quality of their textile products. The Italian merchant Francesco Carletti, who was in China in the 1590s, took detailed notes on the cloth that he saw in the Cantonese markets: "They weave those cloths of gold in very varied and beautiful and showy patterns, and instead of the silver and gold that go into them, they place there a certain thread of silvered and

[19] For relevant examples, see Bertrand Jestaz, "Jean Ménard et les tables de marbres romaines d'après un document nouveau," *Mélanges de l' École Française de Rome: Italie et Méditerranée modernes et contemporaines* 124 (2012): 2–23.

[20] On male sociability and display in the study, see Dora Thornton, *The Scholar in His Study: Ownership and Experience in Renaissance Italy* (New Haven: Yale University Press, 1997).

[21] Benjamin Elman, *A Cultural History of Civil Examinations in Late Imperial China* (Berkeley: University of California Press, 2000); and Kai-Wing Chow, *Publishing, Culture and Power in Early Modern China* (Stanford: Stanford University Press, 2004), esp. 90–148.

[22] Renata Ago, *Gusto for Things: A History of Objects in Seventeenth-Century Rome*, trans. Bradford Bouley and Corey Tazzara with Paula Findlen (Chicago: University of Chicago Press, 2013), 115 and 120.

gilded paper which, cut very thin, they spin in the way that we make spun gold and silver."[23] However, the ostentatious beauty of Chinese cloth hid its ephemeral nature: "instead of silk they use another thread that seems the same and has the same quality except that it must be protected from water and dust, because water will destroy it and dust tarnish it."[24] During a late fifteenth-century Venetian embassy to Persia, the Sultan had told the Venetian ambassador: "Your cloths are beautiful but they are a bit too heavy."[25] This kind of mutual observation and competition was part and parcel of the exchange of global gifts, though Valignano no doubt hoped that his twenty-five brocades, so carefully selected, would attract only admiration from the Chinese emperor.

Scientific instruments presented another facet of European technical excellence drawn on to impress the Chinese. It was unsurprising that the Visitor's list of desiderata should include several timepieces: both sand-glass clocks and a mechanical table clock (items 16 and 17). These state-of-the art objects – often produced in Augsburg – were, in the latter half of the sixteenth century, a standard feature of the diplomatic gift package designed for rulers in the Ottoman lands.[26] While Valignano does not specify the preferred origin of the clocks for the Chinese emperor, he provides detailed instructions regarding matters of size, materials and design.[27] The Jesuits' clocks had already caused quite a stir in southern China, and Pope Gregory had sent the four Japanese ambassadors home with a clock. However, Valignano thought there was room for improvement and that the proposed table clock should be "better" and "bigger" than that which had been recently acquired. The wonder aroused by European clocks seems not to have owed so much to their reliability as keepers of time as to the magic of the automaton. As Matteo Ricci put it in a letter of 1583, the Chinese "marvel more to see a machine that

[23] Francesco Carletti, *My Voyage around the World* (Italian ed., 1701; London: Methuen, 1965), 148.

[24] Ibid., 148. Carletti spoke more favorably of the durability of Indian textiles. See Barbara Karl, "'Marvellous Things Are Made with Needles': Bengal Colchas in European Inventories, c. 1580–1630," *Journal of the History of Collections* 23, no. 2 (2011): 306.

[25] Howard, *Venice and the East*, 60, on Giosafat Barbaro's mission to Tabriz, 1473.

[26] Carina L. Johnson, *Cultural Hierarchy in Sixteenth-Century Europe: The Ottomans and Mexicans* (Cambridge: Cambridge University Press, 2011), 224–26.

[27] See Barbara Burn, ed., *Masterpieces of the Metropolitan Museum of Art* (Boston: Bullfinch Press, rev. ed. 1997), 132–33, for an illustration and analysis of an astronomical table clock dating from 1568.

moves by itself and sounds the hours, than at its skill at telling the time."[28]

Equally one might question just how functional were the globes and other astronomical devices that the Jesuits brought into China.[29] But they clearly worked well to generate curiosity and to start conversations. Moreover, they reassured the donors of their claims to cultural and technological superiority. They were the material counterpart to the boastful remarks of Matteo Ricci: "If China were the whole world, there is no doubt that I could call myself the greatest mathematician and natural philosopher, for what they say is laughable, and it is a marvel how little they know."[30] In terms of diplomacy, one might think this approach left something to be desired. But if the pope's envoys were to enjoy due status in China, it was important that they should demonstrate their cultural credit.

The architecture books requested by Valignano (item 19) functioned in much the same way. Of relatively small value in themselves – at least compared with finest brocades or bejeweled chests – their worth lay in their capacity to convey Western culture: to show the Chinese European buildings and urban spaces in all their glory. This intention again chimed with Ricci's written observations: Chinese buildings, constructed without foundations, were – he said – "inferior to ours," in terms of both their "beauty and their strength."[31] When Valignano demanded architectural books, he was almost certainly thinking of Sebastiano Serlio's *Treatise on Architecture*, published in Venice in 1537, a book that was at once learned, practical and highly visual – and so accessible to some degree

[28] Matteo Ricci, *Lettere (1580–1609)*, ed. Francesco d'Arelli (Macerata: Quodlibet, 2001), 52; the significance of clocks to the Jesuits' China mission is further discussed in Laven, *Mission to China*, esp. 151–52.

[29] On the significance of cartographic gifts, see Peter Barber, "'Procure as many as You Can and Send Them Over': Cartographic Espionage and Cartographic Gifts in International Relations, 1460–1760," in *Diplomacy and Early Modern Culture*, ed. Robyn Adams and Rosanna Cox (New York: Palgrave Macmillan, 2011), 13–29. Matteo Ricci's famous redrawing of the map of the world, with Asia at its center, has been the subject of much scholarly discussion; for a seminal contribution, see Walter Mignolo, "The Movable Center: Geographical Discourses and Territoriality during the Expansion of the Spanish Empire," in *Coded Encounters: Writing, Gender and Ethnicity in Colonial Latin America*, ed. Francisco Cevallos-Candau et al. (Amherst: University of Massachusetts Press, 1994), 15–45; reissued in Walter Mignolo, *The Darker Side of the Renaissance: Literacy, Territoriality, and Colonization* (Ann Arbor: University of Michigan Press, 1995), 219–58.

[30] Ricci, *Lettere*, 316.

[31] Pasquale d'Elia, ed., *Fonti ricciane* (Rome: La libreria dello stato, 1942–49), 1: 29.

to a sinophone "reader." The images of Rome were thought to be similarly instructive regarding European civilization, past and present.[32]

Though focused on the artisanal products of Italy, center of the Catholic world, the ornate and luxury goods on Valignano's list also gesture toward the global reach of the Roman Church. The Jesuits planned to make the most of their contacts, and Valignano knew how to exploit the Society's connections in Northern Europe, especially the Catholic stronghold of Antwerp, in order to source the most magnificent gifts. The Chinese, who had been much struck by the Jesuits' locking doors and chests, were bound to be impressed by a dozen and a half or more Flemish locks, both large and small, gilded and engraved with Chinese script.[33] As for the request for a Flemish harpsichord, Valignano once again had his finger on the pulse. A major innovation in harpsichord construction had taken place in Antwerp around 1580 with the work of Hans Ruckers and his descendants. The new Flemish harpsichords were more solidly built than their Italian equivalents, and the use of iron strings for the treble ensured a more sustained note. Elaborately painted and decorated and often bearing Latin mottoes, these beautiful instruments extend the list into a new sensory domain and aspire to assert the sophistication of Western music.[34]

The request for a box of feathers reminds us of the expansion of European domination into new worlds. Contacts between the Jesuits in East Asia and their brothers in New Spain were continually refreshed via communication with the Philippines. Earlier discussions among the Jesuits in China had suggested that the Emperor might like a live ostrich, but Valignano obviously judged this suggestion to be impractical; the feathers therefore served as an iridescent token of the Jesuits' access to exotica.[35]

[32] See the engravings of Rome, ancient and modern, by Antonio Lafreri; http://speculum.lib.uchicago.edu (accessed 12 October 2017).

[33] On the wonder occasioned by the "doors, windows, keys and chests" at the Jesuit residence in Zhaoqing, see Ricci's letter of 20 October 1585 to Claudio Acquaviva; *Lettere*, p. 100. For examples of highly ornate Flemish locks from this period, see two illuminating catalogues: *La Fidèle Ouverture ou l'Art du Serrurier* (Rouen: Musée le Secq des Tournelles, 2007), and *Open Slot. Sluitwerk en slotemakers in Nederland uit de 15e tot de 19e eeuw* (Delft: Stedelijk Museum Het Prinsenhof, 1986).

[34] For a technical comparison of Italian and Flemish keyboard instruments and on the early contribution of the Ruckers family, see Frank Hubbard, *Three Centuries of Harpsichord Making: Makers of the Harpsichord and Clavichord* (Cambridge, MA: Harvard University Press, 1965), 45–60.

[35] Laven, *Mission to China*, 85.

Italy, Flanders, New Spain – the provenance of the gifts, where stated, charts the connections available to sixteenth-century Jesuits, while also mapping the parameters of the Catholic world. Maija Jansson has observed that "the gifts exchanged in early modern Europe, for the most part, reflected a country's resources and the particular skills of its artisans." (Thus the French offered tapestries and embroidery, the Russians distributed furs and the English gave silverware.)[36] The Venetian glass and Roman carpentry on Valignano's list fit this model well enough. But Jesuits in East Asia (who happened to come disproportionately from Italy) wanted to do more than show off the artisanal talents of their fatherland. They were equally keen to advertise the reach of the Catholic Church, and the wealth and quality of the goods produced within it.

While many of the gifts on the list served to broadcast the merits of European civilization to a Chinese audience, others apparently attempted to emulate Asian culture. The most obvious examples of these "connective" gifts appear near the start of our list (items 6 and 7): "3 belts of the sort that the Emperor of China is accustomed to wear (Michele Ruggieri to advise); 3 helmets to match." It is extraordinary that Valignano was instructing the pope (and his men on the ground in Europe) to try to recreate these imperial accessories in the workshops of Rome in order to ship them back as presents for the Emperor. No wonder Ruggieri would be called on "to advise." But the curious requests for pseudo-Asian goods did not end there. The most bizarre proposal of all (item 11) was for the pope to commission a set of Japanese-style screens – or byobu – to give to the Chinese emperor. We can only begin to imagine what such a hybrid object – conceived by an Italian, in Macao, based on Japanese design principles, executed in Italy – might have looked like.[37]

The idea evidently came from the celebrated byobu that the Japanese Knights had given Pope Gregory. (This was when this exotic term first made its way into European documents.) This example depicted Oda Nobunaga's magnificent castle at Azuchi. Nobunaga, the most powerful man in Japan, had presented the screen to Valignano, despite the fact that the emperor of Japan had himself beseeched Nobunaga for the screen (or so the Jesuit mythology went). The mystique of this artifact was doubtless increased by the fact that Nobunaga was assassinated and his castle

[36] Jansson, "Measured Reciprocity," 349.

[37] Oliver Impey, *The Art of the Japanese Folding Screen* (Oxford: Ashmolean Museum, 1997).

totally destroyed in 1582, the very year that the Japanese ambassadors set out for Europe.

Presumably, what appealed to Valignano about the byobu was not only its value and beauty – such that emperors might fight over it – but its role in conveying Japanese culture across the seas. By the same token, the byobu that Valignano encouraged the pope to commission would tell the Chinese emperor all about Europe. Byobu were already associated with the role of representing "other cultures," and a new craze for *namban* (literally, "southern barbarian") screens that depicted Western figures and adopted a Western style of painting had seized the Japanese elite in the 1580s, at the very point that Valignano was drafting the Memorial.[38]

The decorative themes requested by Valignano for the Roman byobu would encapsulate many different aspects of European culture: images of the months of the year, of men and women in European dress, of horses and other animals, of palaces and churches. The description ends: "The panels themselves must be well made and elegant . . . ; I believe that this will be one of the most esteemed things that will be presented to the King of China." The proposed byobu was the ultimate connective object: a stunning piece of artistry that deployed Western visual idioms on an Asian form in order to illustrate aspects of European life (seasons, customs, architecture) of potential interest to the Chinese. At the same time, this versatile piece of furniture – light, portable and capable of reconfiguring interior spaces in an instant – adapted itself equally well to the function of Jesuit evangelism. To Valignano, the proposed screen was a physical manifestation of the way in which Catholic Universalism might accommodate variety: its capacity to convey the single indivisible religious truth through many languages and cultural forms.

The final aspect of Valignano's list that demands attention is the (not exactly conspicuous) place of religion. How did the gifts specified by the Jesuits aim to advance the Society's mission? Amid the glass, clocks and

[38] On namban screens, see Grace A. H. Vlam, "Kings and Heroes: Western-Style Painting in Momoyama Japan," *Artibus Asiae* 39, nos. 3–4 (1977): 220–50; Charles R. Boxer, *Fidalgos in the Far East, 1550–1770* (Hong Kong: Oxford University Press, 1968), 20–26; and Yukio Lippit, "Japan's Southern Barbarian Screens," in *Encompassing the Globe: Portugal and the World in the Sixteenth and Seventeenth Centuries*, ed. Jay Levenson, 3 vols. (Washington, DC: Freer & Sackler, 2007), 2: 244–53. See also Olivia Meehan, "The European Presence in Japanese Screen Painting of the Late Sixteenth and Early Seventeenth Centuries," PhD dissertation, University of Cambridge, 2011, and Giovanni Raneri, "Folding Screens, Cartography and the Jesuit Mission in Japan, 1580–1614," PhD dissertation, University of Manchester, 2015.

luxury goods, just two items were of explicit religious significance. The first was an illuminated manuscript New Testament (item 5), which Valignano suggested it might be possible to acquire from an Italian monastery. Failing this, he added, a missal or prayer-book would do just as well; after all, "the Chinese will not be able to understand what is written." This telling aside reminds us of the difficulties of evangelizing across a language barrier, but also suggests how invested the Jesuits were in the visual rhetoric of their gifts. It was the aesthetic impact of the Christian books that mattered, rather than their doctrinal content. Moreover, the Jesuits were well aware that some aspects of Christian teaching could do more harm than good. Thus, in the other explicit reference to artifacts of Christian significance, Valignano carefully vetted which religious images might and might not be given to the Emperor. In item 20, he requested "more picture books, representing beautiful figures; not martyrs, not wars, not the passion of Christ; a book of popes would be good; and a book of emperors." And in item 21, Valignano specified the guises in which Christ and the Virgin Mary might be depicted: again, images of the crucifixion were to be avoided, but paintings of Christ in Glory, the Assumption, and the Virgin "with her baby in her arms" were deemed appropriate. (Christian iconography of the Virgin and Child was to catch on in China, as can be seen in seventeenth-century representations of the Buddhist deity Guanyin, which appear to owe something to the influence of Christian art.)[39] The catch-all phrase repeated in Valignano's specifications for Venetian stained glass (14) as well as for picture-books (20) was "cosas alegres." The pope was on no account to send the Emperor images of suffering; only representations of "happy things."

Valignano's concern with display and ostentation was therefore coupled with an awareness of the importance of concealment: the Memorial detailed texts whose meanings would not be spelled out and images that would not be shown. Other objects may have been intended to convey more or less secret meanings. Take the "pieces of triangular glass" requested by the Jesuits. It is tempting to translate these as prisms, but to do so risks investing the objects with a scientific significance that they would not have until the later seventeenth century.[40] The Jesuit

[39] Derek Gillman, "Ming and Qing Ivories: Figure Carving," in *Chinese Ivories from the Shang to the Qing*, ed. William Watson (London: British Museum Publications, 1984), 35–50; Craig Clunas, *Art in China* (Oxford: Oxford University Press, 1997), 128–29.

[40] Simon Schaffer, "Glass Works: Newton's Prisms and the Uses of Experiment," in *The Uses of Experiment: Studies in the Natural Sciences*, ed. David Gooding et al. (Cambridge: Cambridge University Press, 1989), 67–104.

missionaries in China had already deployed these gifts in their dealings with provincial officials, and they had gone down a storm. But we must ask why the missionaries had decided to take triangular pieces of glass with them to China in the first place. It is possible that the Jesuits viewed them as valuable props in rituals of healing and exorcism.[41] Perhaps the glass triangles also appealed to the Jesuits as symbols of the Trinity. If this *was* the Jesuits' idea, they would have taken care to keep it quiet since the Trinity (along with the crucifixion) was off the list of approved doctrines for propagation in China at this time.[42]

I am more confident in proposing a hidden religious significance behind the request for strings of finest-quality coral (item 8). Together with gold, silver, lapis lazuli and other precious metals and stones, coral was esteemed in China as one of the seven Buddhist treasures. Valued for its fine veins and glossy surface, it was frequently used by craftsmen in the creation of religious artifacts and other decorative objects.[43] In Europe, meanwhile, as every good Catholic knew, coral symbolized the blood of Christ. The coral necklace that the baby Jesus was often depicted wearing was meant to prefigure the suffering of the adult Christ. In Europe, coral beads were also commonly used to make rosaries.[44] Ever attentive to the *modo soave*, Valignano would not have offered the Chinese emperor an explicitly Christian devotional object; instead, he smuggled Christian truths into beautiful objects that would play to Chinese tastes.

Valignano's gift list – as carefully crafted as the objects it described – was the creation of a very particular moment. In the spring of 1588, the Visitor to the East Indies arrived back in Macao from Goa in company with his charges, the four Japanese youths. The return of the boys was celebrated, as was the eclectic array of presents that they brought with them from European princes, prelates and civic dignitaries. These included portraits of the Spanish royal family, atlases and city plans, jewelry and musical instruments.[45] But the celebration of the global

41 Laven, *Mission to China*, 154–57.

42 The selection of doctrines that Matteo Ricci deemed appropriate for Chinese consumption was crystallized in his Chinese catechism, published in Beijing in 1603. Ricci, *The True Meaning of the Lord of Heaven*, ed. D. Lancashire and P. Hu Kuo-chen (St. Louis: The Institute of Jesuit Sources, 1985).

43 Jessica Rawson, ed., *The British Museum Book of Chinese Art* (London: British Museum Press, 1992), 182–83.

44 Giovanni Tescione, *Il corallo nella storia e nell'arte* (Naples: Montanino, 1965).

45 For details of the European gifts and their impact on Japanese elite tastes, see Vlam, "Kings and Heroes."

exchanges that had taken place in Lisbon, Madrid and Rome contrasted with the mood of despair that was taking hold of the Jesuits in response to their encounters on East Asian soil. In July 1587, the Japanese regent Toyotomi Hideyoshi had formally banned all public Catholic missionary activity, while early in 1588 the first Jesuit residence established in mainland China at Zhaoqing was stoned by angry locals – a dramatic prelude to the missionaries' expulsion from the city the following year.[46]

In two contemporary letters sent from Macao, both long and urgent in tone, Valignano wrote to Claudio Acquaviva, the General of the Society of Jesus, to insist on the necessity of the papal embassy and accompanying gifts.[47] The first letter, which was dated 10 November 1588, dwelled on the difficulties facing the China mission: the arrogance and ignorance of the mandarins, the lack of respect shown to the European priests, the exhausting demands made on the Jesuits to offer hospitality to officials, and the all-pervasive xenophobia that afflicted China. This was the context in which Valignano deemed the proposed papal delegation to be essential: if an embassy of this kind were to be sent from Rome with all the gifts enumerated in the Memorial, Valignano was confident that, "with the favour and help of Our Lord," the mandarins of the Province of Canton would allow the Jesuits who would accompany the delegation to continue northward to Beijing in order to meet with the emperor. By this means, the "great door to the conversion of China" would be opened.[48] Eleven days later, Valignano wrote a second letter to Acquaviva "regarding the embassy." This time, he dealt more directly with the question of the gifts, again referring to the Memorial, which (he emphasized) should be followed to the letter. The utmost care should be taken in sourcing the gifts – the coral should be the finest available, and only the best painters and jewelers should be employed to produce the other objects – since deficiencies in quality could risk the whole enterprise. Any doubts about the extent of the expenditure should be brushed aside:

[46] On Hideyoshi's anti-Christian measures, see Üçerler, "Alessandro Valignano," 348, and Timon Screech, "The English and the Control of Christianity in the Early Edo Period," *Japan Review* 24 (2012): 6. For an account of the Jesuits' stay in Zhaoqing, see Laven, *Mission to China*, 31–67.

[47] J. L. Alvarez-Taladriz, "El proyecto de embajada del papa al la China y el padre Alejandro Valignano, S.J. (1588)," *Tenri Daigaku Gakuho* 89 (1973): 60–94; and id., "El proyecto de embajada del papa al la China y el padre Alejandro Valignano, S.J. (Conclusion) (1588–1603)," *Tenri Daigaku Gakuho* 91 (1974): 167–82.

[48] Alvarez-Taladriz, "El proyecto" (1973), 81.

five to six thousand ducats would be money well spent.[49] After four frustrating years spent in Goa, when Valignano had missed out on the unsurpassed possibilities for networking occasioned by the Japanese embassy to Europe, the Visitor to the East Indies was clearly itching to make his mark on the mission, and here at last was the opportunity. A great deal hung on Valignano's decision to send the veteran missionary Michele Ruggieri back to Europe with the Memorial.

The failure of Ruggieri's efforts to persuade the pope to sponsor an embassy to China seems to have resulted from chance events and pressures closer to home. Pope Gregory XIV, whom Ruggieri met in Rome in 1590, died in the following year, and the papal curia was more preoccupied with the religious wars raging through Europe than with the conversion of the Chinese. There was to be no papal embassy to China until the disastrous envoy of 1705 when the Pope's representative, Bishop Maillard de Tournon, fell into deep disagreement with the Kangxi Emperor over the matter of papal supremacy. But while Valignano's global gifts never materialized, the textual record of the Memorial does survive, offering a verbalized feast of objects, replete with detail, and transforming the often mundane mode of the inventory into a baroque showcase.[50]

Valignano's list reinforces much of what we have come to expect of diplomatic gifts, insofar as they attempt to render in compressed material form the culture of the donors.[51] Far from being a diplomatic faux pas, the gifts that celebrated Western civilization were intended to vindicate the position of the papal envoys at the Chinese imperial court. Indeed, it was imperative that the Jesuits demonstrate to their hosts the high levels of civility and sophistication that obtained in Europe, in order to give credibility to the Christian religion.[52]

[49] Alvarez-Taladriz, "El proyecto" (1974), esp. 169–70. Note that Alvarez-Taladriz was apparently unaware of the survival of the "Memorial."

[50] On early modern inventories, see Giorgio Riello, "'Things Seen and Unseen': The Material Culture of Early Modern Inventories and Their Representation of Domestic Interiors," in *Early Modern Things: Objects and Their Histories, 1500–1800*, ed. Paula Findlen (London: Routledge, 2013), 125–50; and Renata Ago, *Gusto for Things*.

[51] Christian Windler, "Tributes and Presents in Franco-Tunisian Diplomacy," *Journal of Early Modern History* 4, no. 2 (2000): 168–99.

[52] The same concerns are evident in Valignano's earlier "Instructions" for the delegation of Japanese boys: J. A. Abranches-Pinto and H. Bernard, "Les instructions du Père Valignano pour l'ambassade japonaise en Europe (Goa, 12 décembre, 1583)," *Monumenta Nipponica* 6 (1943): 391–403. See esp. 396–97 where Valignano extols the need to "make the Japanese understand the glory and greatness of Christian law and the majesty of the Princes and Lords who follow that law, and the grandeur and wealth of our kingdoms and cities, and the honor in which our religion is held."

But Valignano's list also exceeds our expectations, in its surprising inclusion of imitation Eastern goods such as Chinese helmets and Japanese screens. This complex second-guessing of the Chinese emperor's tastes might be seen as a form of tact, taking the Jesuit principle of accommodation to a new level, or it might represent yet more spiky one-upmanship ("anything you can do, we can do better"). It certainly testifies to the fluidity and responsiveness of global material culture in this period. Just as the potters of Jingdezhen were commissioned to mass-produce bowls and plates for European and Islamic markets, so the carpenters and painters of Rome might be expected to turn their hands to making byobu.

Like the triangular glasses that Valignano proposed to convey to China, the gifts on his list are prismatic, scattering colors in many directions. My attempt to divide them into the softly-softly, the brashly virtuosic, the hybridizing and those that smuggle religion as the Trojan Horse smuggled Greeks cannot withstand the complexity of the Memorial, in which each object condenses multiple meanings and opens up a variety of perspectives. Indeed, the cultural complexity of these objects may be part of their perceived value as luxury goods and objects of exchange. A key part of their variousness lies in the ways in which they create relationships of equilibrium and disequilibrium between donor and recipient – relationships that complicate inequalities of status, reminding the Chinese that their Jesuit visitors were representatives of their own mighty empire. Simultaneously boastful and subservient, the gifts shuttle between the assertion of difference and the fabrication of sameness. And they rely fundamentally on the perception that Chinese culture, like the culture of the Catholic West, was deeply invested in things and the innumerable conversations they might prompt.

9

"With Great Pomp and Magnificence"

*Royal Gifts and the Embassies between Siam and France in the Late Seventeenth Century**

Giorgio Riello

On 1 September 1686, the ambassadors of the King of Siam Phra Narai were received with great honor by Louis XIV of France at Versailles. More than 1500 courtiers were in attendance when the three ambassadors and their retinue entered the Hall of Mirrors escorted by some of France's most illustrious courtiers, administrators and servants of the Crown. Louis XIV sat on a throne more than two meters high wearing a gold-background suit with large diamonds; he was accompanied by the Dauphin, Monsieur (the king's brother), the Prince de Condé, Monsieur de Chartres, the Duke of Bourbon and other prominent members of the royal family.[1] The Siamese ambassadors made quite an entrance into a room decorated for the occasion with a large Persian carpet and magnificent silver candelabra. The ambassadors' tall pointed hats, their daggers and muslin robes did not escape attention. The scene was completed by Siamese music as was the custom in royal ceremonies in Siam.[2]

* I would like to thank Olivier Raveux for his archival help and Claire Tang for her assistance. Research for this chapter has been financially supported by the Leverhulme Trust (Philip Leverhulme Prize). Earlier versions of this chapter were presented at the University of Warwick, the Institute of Historical Research - University of London, Columbia University and the University of New South Wales. I am grateful for all the comments received, in particular, from Maxine Berg, Zoltán Biedermann, Anne Gerritsen and Charles Walton.

[1] Louis-François du Bouchet Sourches, *Mémoires du marquis de Sourches sur le règne de Louis XIV*, 13 vols. (Paris: Librairie Hachette, 1882–93), 1: 438. See also Ronald S. Love, "Rituals of Majesty: France, Siam, and Court Spectacle in Royal Image-Building at Versailles in 1685 and 1686," *Canadian Journal of History* 31, no. 2 (1996): 194–95.

[2] David R. M. Irving, "Lully in Siam: Music and Diplomacy in French–Siamese Cultural Exchanges, 1680–1690," *Early Music* 40, no. 3 (2012): 400; and M. Benoît, *Versailles et*

They made a speech in Siamese that was translated into French.[3] Philippe Dangeau, present at the ceremony, recounted that the Siamese ambassadors remained at the foot of the large throne and presented the letter from the King of Siam to Louis XIV. Courtiers were impressed by the fact that "the Siamese show the deepest respect in all their actions, and they returned to the entry of the Hall of Mirrors, walking backwards, as they did not want to turn their back to the King."[4]

This was one of the most extravagant ceremonies during the entire reign of the Sun King (r. 1643–1715). It was not the first time that the King of France received ambassadors from Asia but pomp was well above any previous embassy.[5] Since their arrival at Brest the previous June, the Siamese ambassadors had received a triumphal welcome in every town and city on their way to Paris. A decree had been issued on how best to welcome the Siamese ambassadors in an attempt to restrain people's enthusiasm and curiosity.[6] Several printed portraits of the ambassadors and their exotic costumes were produced; artists of the caliber of Charles Le Brun were commissioned to produce sketches of the embassy, the ambassadors and their presents.[7] Almanacs were printed of "The solemn embassy of the King of Siam to the King [of France] for the establishment of commerce with these people of the Orient" showing the audience with

les musiciens du roi 1661–1733. Étude institutionelle et sociale, 2 vols. (Paris: Picard, 1971), 1: 62–63.

3 On the audience granted to the Ambassadors of the King of Siam, 1686, see Bibliothèque nationale de France (hereafter BnF), Département des manuscrits, Français 16633: "Cérémonies du règne de Louis XIV, recueil formé, au moins en partie, d'après le Journal de Mr De Sainct (1666–1671 et 1682–1691)," which includes five portraits of the Siamese ambassadors.

4 Philippe Dangeau, *Journal du marquis de Dangeau*, 19 vols. (Paris: Firmin Didot Frères, 1854–60), 1: 377–78.

5 Stéphane Castelluccio, "La galerie des glaces: les réceptions d'ambassadeurs," *Versalia* 9 (2006) : 24–27. This was not the case of other courts in Europe. For instance, the Pope had already received several embassies from Asia. See, for instance, Opher Mansour, "Picturing Global Conversion: Art and Diplomacy at the Court of Paul V," *Journal of Early Modern History* 17, no. 5 (2013): 525–59.

6 *Les ambassadeurs de Siam, à Saint-Quentin, en 1686*, ed. Georges Lecoq (Paris: Rouveyre, 1874).

7 See, for instance, Charles Le Brun (1619–90), "Louis XIV recevant les ambassadeurs de Siam dans la galerie des Glaces, le 1er septembre 1686, entre 1686 et 1690," Paris, École nationale supérieure des beaux-arts, inv. PM2533; "Portrait du premier ambassadeur de Siam," Paris, Musée du Louvre, Départment des Arts graphiques, inv. 28866; "Louis XIV donne audience aux ambassadeurs des nations éloignées," Paris, Musée du Louvre, Départment des Arts graphiques, inv. 29758. See also Antoine Maës, "L'ameublement du salon d'Apollon, XVIIe-XVIIIe siècle," *Bulletin du Centre de recherche du château de Versailles*, https://crcv.revues.org/12144 (accessed 24 September 2016).

Louis XIV (Figure 9.1), the allegorical alliance between France and Siam as embodied by their respective rulers, and other views of the diplomatic triumph of the King of France. Donneau de Visé published four supplements of his *Mercure Galant* totaling nearly two thousand pages between July 1686 and January 1687 minutely describing the Siamese ambassadors' eight-month residence in France.[8] At their departure in March 1687, a medal was struck in their honor and a bronze bas-relief was produced.[9] The Siamese embassy sparked a fashion for *siamoiserie* in France and across Europe and a variety of works on the Kingdom of Siam were published.[10] Its splendor and publicity made it such a well-known event that even a generation later the ambassador of Spain to England would recount his 1712 entrance into London by saying, "The people followed me as though I were an ambassador from Siam."[11]

The 1686 Siamese embassy to France produced a trail of visual, material and documentary evidence that in turn generated a large body of studies that began as early as the mid-nineteenth century.[12] The gifts that the Siamese ambassadors brought to Louis XIV played a central role in the success of the embassy and its enduring fame. These gifts have been interpreted as indicators of both the high cultural value of Asian goods

[8] *Voyage des ambassadeurs de Siam en France ...* (1686); *Suite du Voyage des ambassadeurs de Siam en France ...* (1686); *Troisième partie du Voyage des ambassadeurs de Siam en France ...* (1687); *IV. et dernière partie du Voyage des ambassadeurs de Siam en France ...* (1687). For a general analysis, see Thomas Hedin, "Versailles and the *Mercure Galant*: The Promenade of the Siamese Ambassadors," *Gazette des Beaux-Arts* 119 (1992), esp. 149–56. On the visual culture of the embassies, see the excellent aricle by Meredith Martin, "Mirror Reflections: Louis XIV, Phra Narai, and the Material Culture of Kingship," *Art History* 4, no. 3 (2015): 653–67.

[9] Michel Jacq-Hergoualc'h, "Les ambassadeurs siamois à Versailles le 1er septembre 1686 dans un bas-relief en bronze," *Journal of the Siam Society* 72 (1984): 19–35. The medal is reproduced in Martin, "Mirror Reflections," 657.

[10] Donald F. Lach and Edwin J. Van Kley, *Asia in the Making of Europe, vol. 3: A Century of Advance* (Chicago and London: University of Chicago Press, 1977), 1189. This has prompted Sarah Benson to argue that "The major commodity coming out of Siam was information" through what she calls a "collectible paper museum of Siamese wonders." Sarah Benson, "European Wonders at the Court of Siam," in *Collecting Across Cultures: Material Exchanges in the Early Modern Atlantic World*, ed. Daniela Bleichmar and Peter C. Mancall (Philadelphia: University of Pennsylvania Press, 2011), 160.

[11] Cited in Dirk van der Cruysse, *Siam and the West, 1500–1700*, trans. Michael Smithies (Chiang Mai, Thailand: Silkworm Books, 2002), 381.

[12] Early works include Auguste-Alphonse Étienne-Gallois, *L'ambassade de Siam au XVIIe siècle* (Paris: Typographie E. Panckoucke et Cie., 1862); Lucien Lanier, *Étude historique sur les relations des la France et du Royaume de Siam* (Versailles: Aubert, 1883), 73–86; A. Lounay, *Histoire de la Mission de Siam 1662–1811*, 2 vols. (Paris: Téqui, 1920), 1: 51–55.

FIGURE 9.1 "L'audience donnée par le roy aux ambassadeurs du roy de Siam à Versailles le premier septembre 1686" (Hearing given by the king to the ambassadors of the King of Siam at Versailles), print. Published by Nicolas L'Anglois, Paris, 1687. Bibliothèque nationale de France, Reserve QB-201 (171)-FT 5 [Hennin, 5551].

and the influence and power that the French king had not just among European but also Asian rulers. They were at the core of a fashion for things Oriental that swept Europe in the late seventeenth century. Yet while Oriental commodities and gifts were much appreciated in Europe, historians underline the limited standing of European goods in Asia and the cultural impenetrability of Asian royal courts. The analysis of the gifts sent by Phra Narai to the French court and, in turn, the gifts that Louis XIV sent to Siam challenge the idea that European commodities were less appreciated in Asia than Asian goods in Europe. Beyond the veneer of the publicity and pomp of the Siamese embassy, the Siamese gifts were underappreciated and the understanding of Siam and its politics at the French court remained superficial. By contrast, Phra Narai had a much more cosmopolitan understanding of his kingdom's position in global affairs and was a connoisseur of European culture, art, science and material culture. This finding becomes apparent once we contextualize the arrival of the Siamese ambassadors at Versailles in September 1686 within a series of mutual embassies between France and Siam over the course of the early 1680s. Moving away from national perspectives, we are able to see the entanglements of events and people surrounding the ambassadorial relationship between the two kingdoms. The exchange of gifts reveals not just the cultural attitudes of France and Siam toward each another but also the expectations – sometimes misconceived – of what these embassies were supposed to achieve.

This chapter starts therefore by considering the 1686 embassy and the role played by Siamese gifts. It then moves toward a contextualization of this embassy and shows how it was just one of a series of mutual exchanges of embassies and gifts. An equal, if not more important, role was played by the gifts sent by Louis XIV to the King of Siam. Carefully chosen by the King of Siam's ambassadors, the conspicuous gifts sent by Louis to Siam contributed to what I propose to call the "cosmopolitan making" of Siamese kingship. In a context of interaction over several embassies, royal gifts clearly acted as a way to overcome what Subrahmanyam calls "incommensurabilities."[13] Gifts responded to a shared language of appropriate long-distance royal relationships, though they

[13] On the concept of incommensurability, see Sanjay Subrahmanyam, *Courtly Encounters: Translating Courtliness and Violence in Early Modern Eurasia* (Cambridge, MA: Harvard University Press, 2012), 155. See also id., "Par-delà l'incommensurabilité: pour une histoire connectée des empires aux temps modernes," *Revue d'Histoire Moderne et Contemporaine* 54, no. 4-bis (2007): 34–53.

also revealed the many misapprehensions implicit in diplomatic exchange across continents. As noticed by Meredith Martin, the gifts at the core of Franco-Siamese relations in the 1680s allow us to adopt a mirror perspective that helps us relativize Euro-centered narratives.[14] Moreover, the Franco-Siamese gift exchange alerts us to the pitfalls of diplomacy and the eventual failure of France to develop a sphere of influence in Siam. Notwithstanding the publicity that this diplomatic exchange received at Versailles and in France, it ended with a dramatic cessation of diplomacy between the two countries that lasted for nearly two centuries.

THE SIAMESE GIFTS TO THE KING OF FRANCE: THE CREATION OF A PUBLIC SPECTACLE

The enormous quantities of gifts presented and their legacy were key to the success of the Siamese embassy to the court of France in 1686. The harangues by the Siamese ambassadors, published soon after their reception at Versailles, included detailed lists of the gifts: 54 items from the King of Siam to the King of France; 59 items from the Siamese Prime Minister – the Greek-born Constance Phaulkon[15] – sent to the King of France; 53 items from the King of Siam to the Dauphin of France; 47 items from the Princess of Siam to Madame la Dauphine; and several other presents to the Duke of Burgundy, the Duke of Anjou, the Marquis de Seignelay (Minister of the Marine) and the Marquis de Croissy (Secretary of State). This simple listing does not capture, however, the vastness and value of the gifts. The final item on the king's list, for instance, included "1500 pieces of Porcelains, the best and most curious of all the Indies

[14] Martin, "Mirror Reflections."

[15] Constance Phaulkon (1647–88) was a Greek adventurer who became prime counselor to King Narai in the late 1670s. He was born in northern Cephalonia and traveled as a sailor in Europe and Asia. He arrived in Siam in 1675 after working for the English East India Company. Phaulkon, an Anglican, converted to Catholicism in 1682 and married a Catholic woman of mixed Japanese-Portuguese descent. When the foster brother of Phra Narai staged a coup d'état in 1688, Phaulkon was arrested and beheaded. See Henri Bernard, ed., *Mémoire du P. de Bèze sur la vie de Constance Phaulkon* (Tokyo: Presses salésiennes, 1947). On Phaulkon's career, see E. W. Hutchinson, *Adventures in Siam in the Seventeenth Century* (London: Royal Asiatic Society, 1940), 69–91; Alain Forest, *Falcon: l'imposeur de Siam. Commerce, politique et religion dans la Thaïlande du XVIIe siècle* (Paris: Les Indes Savantes, 2010); Bhawan Ruangsilp, *Dutch East India Company Merchants at the Court of Ayutthaya: Dutch Perceptions of the Thai Kingdom, ca. 1604–1765* (Leiden: Brill, 2007), 125–28; and Maurice Collis, *Siamese White* (London: Faber & Faber, 1936), on Phaulkon's relationship with Samuel and George White.

(more than 250 being very fine, and comprising many cups, plates, small dishes, and big vases of all shapes and sizes)."[16]

The volume of the gifts was so large that it was decided to send them by frigate from Brest via Le Havre to Rouen, from where they were moved to Paris on barges along the Seine.[17] According to the *Mercure Galant*, there were as many as 132 bales, so many that the ambassadorial delegation had to wait in Berny for the gifts to arrive before proceeding to Paris.[18] The presents had created a great deal of problems already in Siam where it had taken days to pack and load them on two French vessels. Two elephants for the King of France's grandson had to be unloaded at the last minute, much to the relief of the captain of the French vessel.[19]

The gifts included a variety of items familiar to seventeenth-century European elites, such as porcelain cups and vases, ewers, trunks, cabinets, coffers and Japanese screens. Some of them were made of tambac, an alloy of copper and gold, several were made of silver and pure gold, others were lacquered. What is distinctive is that the majority of such gifts did not originate in Siam. Siam was not a manufacturer of luxury items but had extensive diplomatic and commercial ties with political entities throughout East Asia.[20] It was seen as appropriate for the King of Siam to gift artifacts of Chinese or Japanese manufacture, though it is unknown whether these were acquired through diplomacy or trade, categories that, as we will see, were not always distinct in the case of Siam and other Asian countries as underlined by Adam Clulow in this volume.

[16] Archives Nationales de France (hereafter AN), Colonies (Aix en Provence), C[1]23 ff. 21–34: *Harangues faites à Sa Majesté et aux princes et princesses de la maison royale par les ambassadeurs du roi de Siam, à leur première audience (1er septembre 1686), et à leur audience de congé (14 janvier 1687)* (Paris: S. Mabre-Cramoisy, 1687), partly reproduced in Michael Smithies, ed., *The Discourses at Versailles of the First Siamese Ambassadors to France, 1686–7* (Bangkok: Siam Society, 1986). See also AN, Colonies, C[1]23 ff. 260–64: "Mémoire des présents envoyés par le roi de Siam, par Phaulkon et la princesse, au roi de France et à la famille royale (1687?)."

[17] Van der Cruysse, *Siam and the West*, 364; *Étude historique et critique du Journal du Voyage de Siam de Claude Céberet, envoyé extraordinaire du Roi en 1687 et 1688*, ed. Michel Jacq-Hergoualc'h (Paris: l'Harmattan, 1992), 45.

[18] Michael Smithies, "The Travels in France of the Siamese Ambassadors 1686–7," *Journal of the Siam Society* 77, no. 2 (1989): 61.

[19] François-Timoléon de Choisy, *Journal du Voyage de Siam*, ed. Dirk van der Cruysse (Paris: Fayard, 1995), 279; Claude de Forbin, *The Siamese Memoirs of Count Claude de Forbin 1685–1688*, ed. Michael Smithies (Chiangmai: Silkworm Books, 1997), 61.

[20] On Siam's diplomatic relations, see Stefan Halikowski Smith, *Creolization and Diaspora in the Portuguese Indies: The Social World of Ayutthaya, 1640–1720* (Leiden: Brill, 2011), 101–7.

The gifts received by Louis XIV are difficult to assess in their origin and value because none of them has reached us: no single artifact in French or international collections can be confidently attributed to the 1686 or other embassies between Siam and France.[21] We rely instead on detailed lists as well as visual sources. A print like "The Presents of the King of Siam to the King [of France] in 1686" (Figure 9.2) had clearly a celebratory function, though it illustrates items whose presence is known from documentary sources. One can identify the "coffers full of Japanese lacquered objects decorated in tambac," "two pieces of cannon six feet long" with silver finishing, "a small golden bottle from Japan," "nine pieces of bezoar stone," "a ship made of gold with all its tools," "a Chinese *chevalier* that turns" and a selection of the 1500 pieces of porcelain mentioned above, all listed in the print's cartouche.[22]

The gifts were so many that they started being displayed at Versailles on Wednesday in preparation for the Sunday formal audience.[23] They were as much at the center of discussion and the curiosity of courtiers as the Siamese ambassadors themselves. The series of prints commemorating the event positioned the gifts at the very center of the audience, although contemporary accounts make it clear they were not displayed in the Hall of Mirrors but remained in the nearby salon de la Guerre.[24] This was partially the result of the fact that central to the ceremony was the

[21] Two exhibitions held in 1986 and 2014 attributed the artifacts to the Franco-Siamese embassies. See *Phra Narai roi de Siam et Louis XIV* (Paris: Association Française d'Action Artistique, 1986); Marie-Laure de Rochebrune, ed., *La Chine à Versailles: art et diplomatie au XVIIIe siècle* (Paris: Somogy Éditions d'art, 2014).

[22] They coincide with the following items: (1) Two pieces of Cannon six foot long cast, hammered cold, set out with Silver, mounted on their carriages, garnished also with Silver, made at Siam; (4) A Golden Ship, (called a Sommer) after the Chinoise fashion, with all its Tacklings; (5) 2 Flagons of Gold embost, of Japon, to stand on a Cupboard, which may be put upon occasion into a Japon Trunk where their places are marked; (11) Two Silver Trunks, (finest) Japon work (some parts of steel). (no. 1); Two Chinoise Horsemen carrying in their hands 2 small Cups, who have a motion by springs, all of Silver in the Chinese manner; (51) Nine pieces of Bezoar of several animals; (54) Fifteen thousand and fifty pieces (in fact, one thousand five hundred or one thousand five hundred and fifty) of porcelains, the best (and most curious) of all the Indies (more than two hundred and fifty being very fine, and comprising many cups, plates, small dishes and big vases of all shapes and sizes). For the entire list of presents shown in the almanac, see Maxine Preaud, *Les effects du soleil. Almanacs du regne de Louis XIV* (Paris: Réunion des Musées Nationaux, 1995), 84–87.

[23] Dangeau, *Journal*, 1: 375.

[24] Stéphane Castelluccio, ed., *Les fastes de la galerie des glaces. Recueil d'articles du Mercure Galant (1681–1773)* (Paris: Payot, 2007), 81–84 on the description of Versailles, and 114–25 on the Siamese embassy.

FIGURE 9.2 "Louis XIV reçoit à Versailles les ambassadeurs du roi de Siam 1 septembre 1686" (Louis XIV receiving the ambassadors of the King of Siam at Versailles), engraving 0.82 m × 0.52 m. Musée du Louvre, collection Rothschild. Photo © RMN-Grand Palais (Musée du Louvre)/Jean-Gilles Berizzi.

presentation of the letter from the King of Siam, a gold-leaf document that was treated with utmost veneration by the foreign ambassadors.[25]

The Siamese gifts and the 1686 embassy were appropriated by Louis XIV in an attempt to elevate himself to the rank of an Asian despot. Such magnificence had been carefully staged: the entire protocol had been set after the debacle that had characterized embassies received in previous years at Versailles when the events had turned into chaos. The gifts themselves were no surprise as they had been selected by the abbé de Choisy, the embassy's co-adjutant in Siam, perhaps – as we will see – not with the greatest success.[26] No expense was spared to entertain the Siamese ambassadors. Mr. Torf, in charge of their stay in France, recounts that the food bill alone – meat, roosters, pigeons, roast beef, chickens, rabbits, turkeys, as well as fruit, salads, wines and spirits – cost an enormous 262 livres per day.[27] In its procession to Paris and Versailles, the embassy was given status that far outstripped the honors of any other previous embassy. They entered Paris on 12 August 1686 with a procession of more than sixty carriages; the crowds were so great that the procession had to be halted several times.[28]

The chief ambassador, Ok-phra Wisut Sunthorn, most commonly known as Kosa Pan, made a great impression on everyone. He was at the center of court life during his stay at Versailles where he was received by the Dauphine and the princesses of the royal household.[29] After the ceremony, the Siamese ambassadors were then sent on a tour of Flanders and on their return were received by the Dauphin and Dauphine. The French gazette and literary magazine *Mercure Galant* detailed the process of the embassy that included sixteen formal receptions and visits to the Royal Academy of Painting and Sculpture, the Royal Printers, the Sorbonne, the College of Louis-le-Grand, the Comédie Française, the Comédie Italienne and several churches.[30] This was a great spectacle in which the presents constituted the pinnacle. It was also a triumph for Louis XIV with the embassy being presented as the alliance between two great kingdoms and an act of respect and submission to Louis. It was supposed to seal a commercial agreement securing France privileged

[25] Kosa Pan, *The Diary of Kosa Pan (Ok-Phra Wisut Sunthon) Thai Ambassador to France, June–July 1686*, ed. Dirk Van der Cruysse and Michael Smithies (Bangkok: Silkworm Books, 2002), passim.

[26] Castelluccio, "La galerie des glaces," 33.

[27] Étienne-Gallois, *L'ambassade de Siam*, 97.

[28] Smithies, "Travels in France," 68.

[29] Dangeau, *Journal*, 1: 378.

[30] Smithies, "Travels in France," 62–69.

access to the Siamese ports to establish bases from which to trade with China and Japan. There was also a rumor that the King of Siam was considering converting to Catholicism, a fact some perceived was well attested by the valuable gifts sent to the very Catholic king of France.[31]

Amid such bold claims of how much France had achieved diplomatically, commercially and faith-wise in Siam, it is no surprise that the gifts were subjected to a great deal of scrutiny. Choisy – perhaps not untouched by personal interest as he had himself selected the gifts in Siam – estimated that the gifts were valued at the equivalent of 20,000 gold écus "without including the value of work; and I won't say anything of [the value] of the Japanese cabinets, the screens and the porcelain."[32] The value of the gifts was key to convince France that Siam was one of the richest kingdoms in Asia and therefore a priority for France to secure trade with. The Comte de Bussy reports that the Abbé de Choisy "recounts of the marvels of that kingdom, among which the fact that the houses of the city of Siam are golden. He stayed in a room with purple velvet tapestries embroidered in gold. The ambassadors have carried back for the King and the Dauphin presents of inestimable value."[33]

Those for whom – like the artist Le Brun – the spectacle rather than diplomatic claims was central recorded the lure of exotic costumes and objects. One of his drawings conveys the French fascination with the Siamese gifts: a porcelain vase on an octagonal base and different views of a dagger and its holder (Figure 9.3).[34] Yet not everyone was so impressed. Some argued that the presents were very fine but that Siam was not a kingdom of fabled richness. This would explain why the Siamese king – unlike Louis – had to get hold of the gifts from abroad, namely, from China and Japan. The Count of Sourches disagreed with those who thought the gifts to be fine and expensive: "The gifts which the King [of Siam], their master, sent to the king and to the Dauphin ... consisted of a great number of rather ugly porcelain pieces, a few Chinese

31 Lanier, *Étude*, 85.

32 François-Timoléon de Choisy, *Mémoires pour servir à l'histoire de Louis XIV* (Clermont-Ferrand: Éditions Paleo, 2008), 54.

33 *Correspondance de Roger de Rabutin, comte de Bussy*, ed. L. Lalanne, 6 vols. (Paris: Charpentier, 1858–59), 5: 570.

34 L. Beauvais, *Musée du Louvre, Départment des Arts graphiques, Inventaire general des dessins, école française, Charles Le Brun (1619–1690)*, 2 vols. (Paris: Réunion des Musées Nationaux, 2000), 1: no. 3036, 852. It is probable that Le Brun was present at the audience given by Louis XIV on 1 September 1686. The other sketch is of the ambassador's dress, especially their pointed shoes and hats and their sabers.

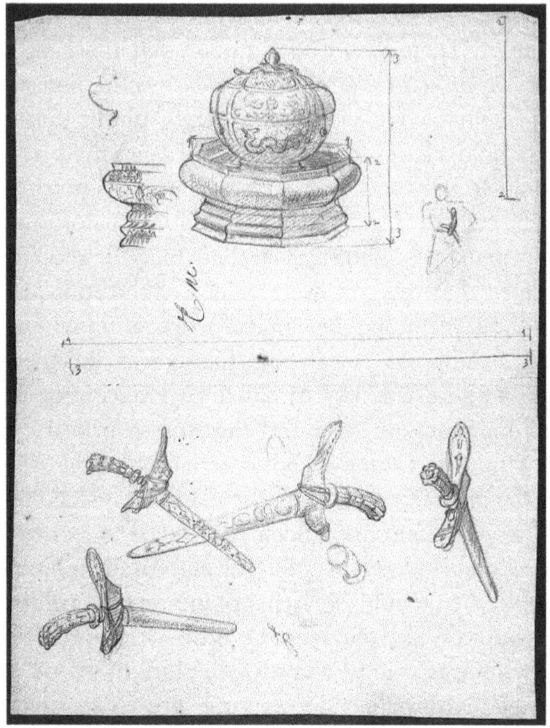

FIGURE 9.3 "Vase, poignards," drawing by Charles Le Brun (1619–90), 1686. INV 30337-recto.
© Musée du Louvre département des Arts graphiques, © Photo RMN-Grand Palais (musée du Louvre)/Michel Urtado.

cabinets, and screens, rather fine, and a few gold and tambac vases, rather indifferent."[35] Another courtier, Mr. de Louvois, was even more caustic when he said to the Abbé de Choisy that he thought the presents to be worth less than 1500 pistoles, a trivial amount.[36]

The royal family seems to have had a more pragmatic approach to the issue of the gifts. The lists show a large amount of what by the 1680s were well-known Asian artifacts in noble and royal interiors. Clearly problematic in their sheer quantity and size, already on the Monday, one day after

[35] Sourches, *Memoires du marquis de Sourches*, 1: 438.

[36] To which Choisy replied: "I know for a fact that there is more than twenty thousand crowns of solid gold there, not counting the workmanship and that is leaving out the japanned cabinets, the screens, and the porcelain." Lanier, *Étude*, 83.

the audience, at a grand dinner in honor of the Princess of Conti, the Dauphin organized a lottery in which part of the Siamese gifts were distributed among the courtiers.[37] Yet this was not necessarily a dismissal of the Siamese gifts, as regifting among courtiers was common practice. In fact Dangeau claimed in his diary that on Thursday the same week "the King found the gifts that the Siamese gave to the Dauphine very agreeable, and he is very happy also with the gifts that he received from M. Constance [Phaulkon], the King of Siam's favorite, that are both delightful and magnificent."[38] The gifts had clearly performed a public function but in private they might have fulfilled less the expectations of the king and royal family. Louis was less interested in porcelain and lacquered chests and more interested in items that could be included in his cabinet of curiosities.[39] The French embassies that preceded and that followed the 1686 Siamese embassy to France served in fact to replenish his library and print room (*cabinet du roi*) with Oriental books, manuscripts and engravings that can be glimpsed in the extensive correspondence that the monarch exchanged with Colbert in his capacity as head of the *bâtiments du roi*.[40]

GIFTING IN CONTEXT: THE SIAMESE AND FRENCH EMBASSIES OF THE 1680S

The gifts brought from Siam to Louis XIV in 1686 might have been more important from the point of view of courtly appearances than for the true appreciation that they produced. Yet one of the problems of interpreting both the gifts and the 1686 embassy is that they tell us only part of the story, one set in France and linked to the politics of Versailles and the image-making strategies of its ruler. Some "lateral thinking" comes from a short diary left by Kosa Pan, the chief Siamese ambassador, of the first two months spent in France. This is a rare seventeenth-century personal account of a non-European traveler to France. Alas, the fragment – apparently left behind by mistake on departure – does not include the reception at Versailles.[41] There are, however, other

[37] Dangeau, *Journal*, 1: 378. [38] Ibid.

[39] Ronald S. Love, "Royal Protocol and Cultural Synthesis in the Preparations for the Chevalier de Chaumont's Embassy to Siam in 1685," *Proceedings of the Western Society for French History* 34 (2006): 17.

[40] Nicholas Dew, *Orientalism in Louis XIV's France* (Oxford: Oxford University Press, 2009), 20–21.

[41] Kosa Pan, *Diary of Kosa Pan*.

sources, both manuscript and printed, that help us to contextualize the 1686 Siamese embassy within a set of mutual exchanges between Siam and France.

Diplomatic relations between Siam and the West had started well before Louis XIV showed any interest in the Asian kingdom. The Portuguese had been present in Siam since 1511 and were the main European commercial partners throughout the century, trading in cardamom, black lacquer, rayskins and wax. As for other parts of the Indian Ocean, the Dutch acquired substantial influence over the first half of the seventeenth century and by 1634 had signed a treaty giving them the monopoly of the trade in deerskins between Siam and Japan, renewed thirty years later when the Dutch influence in Siam was at its highest.[42]

It was probably the increasing influence of the Protestant Dutch, much to the detriment of the Catholic Portuguese, that had prompted Pope Clement IX to send a diplomatic letter to Phra Narai in 1673 (Table 9.1).[43] The Pope's message was accompanied by a letter and presents from Louis XIV.[44] Under the insistence of the Apostolic Vicar in Siam, Phra Narai had thought of sending an embassy to France the same year, but the war between France and Holland had prevented it.[45] An embassy was eventually sent from Siam to France in December 1680 with fifty large crates of gifts and two elephants.[46] However, the ship sank on the coast of Madagascar the following year.[47] Therefore the ambassadorial relationship between France and Siam started when two Siamese noblemen arrived at Calais in 1684 sent by their king to inquire about the fate of the previous embassy. Though they were not received formally by Louis XIV (as they were not ambassadors), it was

[42] Maria da Conceição Flores, "A Embaixada de Pedro Vaz de Siqueira ao Sião em 1684," *Anais de História de Além-Mar* 3, no. 3 (2002): 354–56.

[43] Michael Smithies and L. Bressan, *Siam and the Vatican in the Seventeenth Century* (Bangkok: River Books, 2001), 55.

[44] AN, Colonies, C[1]22 ff. 17–18: "Liste des curiosités que le roi de Siam souhaiterait recevoir en présent du roi de France (1673?)."

[45] Lounay, *Histoire de la Mission de Siam*, 51.

[46] Dirk Van der Cruysse, "Aspects of Siamese-French Relations During the Seventeenth Century," *Journal of the Siam Society* 80, no. 1 (1992): 66; Kosa Pan, *Diary of Kosa Pan*, 3; Michel Jacq-Hergoualc'h, *L'Europe et le Siam du XVIe au XVIIIe siècle: apports culturels* (Paris: Harmattan, 1993), 62.

[47] Ronald S. Love, "Lost at Sea: The Tragedy of the Soleil d'Orient and the First Siamese Embassy to France, 1680–1684," *Proceedings of the Western Society for French History* 29 (2001): 60–71; Michael Smithies, "Siamese Mandarins on the Grand Tour, 1688–1690," *Journal of the Siam Society* 86, nos. 1–2 (1998): 107.

TABLE 9.1 *The Ambassadorial Relationships between France and Siam, 1673–1688*

Date	Embassy/event	Key people who wrote about it
1673	**Letters sent by Pope Clement IX and King Louis XIV** of France to Phra Narai, King of Siam	
1680, Jan.	**Siamese embassy** sent to France.	
	Shipwrecked 1681	
1684, Jan.	**Two Siamese emissaries** sent to France	
1684, Nov.	Arrival in France	
	Received by Louis XIV	
1685, Mar.	**First embassy to Siam** departs France	Chevalier de Chaumont (ambassador) (1)
1685, Sep.	Arrival in Siam	Abbé de Choisy (co-adjutant) (2)
1685, Dec.	Departure from Siam with the Siamese Embassy	Père Tachard (3)
		Claude de Forbin (4)
1685, Dec.	**First embassy to France** departs Siam	Kosa Pan (5) and two co-ambassadors
1686, Jun.	Arrival in France	
1686, Sep.	Audience at Versailles	
1687, Mar.	Departure from France with the new French Embassy	
1687, Mar.	**Second embassy to Siam** departs France	La Loubère (ambassador) (6)
1687, Sep.	Arrival in Siam	Claude Céberet (co-adjutant) (7)

(*continued*)

TABLE 9.1 (*continued*)

Date	Embassy/event	Key people who wrote about it
1687, Nov.	Audience by Phra Narai	Père Tachard (8)
1688, Jan.	Departure from Siam with the second Siamese embassy	
1688, Jan.	**Second embassy to France** departs Siam	Père Tachard (8)
1688, Jul.	Arrival in France	
1688, Jun.–Jul.	Coup d'état in Siam and death of Phoulkon	
1688, Dec.	and Phra Narai	
1690, Feb.	Louis XIV cancels the audience at Versailles	
	Departure of the Siamese ambassadors	

Key published texts (original French editions or modern editions):

(1) Alexandre de Chaumont, *Relation de l'ambassade de Mr le Chevalier de Chaumont à la cour du roi de Siam* ... (Paris: Seneuze et Horthemels, 1686).

(2) Abbé François-timoleon de Choisy, *Journal du voyage de Siam fait en 1685 et 1686 par Monsieur d'abbé de Choisy* (Paris: S. Mabre-Cramoisy, 1687).

(3) Guy Tachard, *Voyage de Siam, des peres Jesuites* ... (Paris: Seneuze et Horthemels, 1686).

(4) Claude de Forbin, *Voyage du comte de Forbin à Siam, suivi de quelques détails extraits des mémoires de l'abbé de Choisy* (Paris: Bibl. des chemins de fer sér, 1853).

(5) Kosa Pan, *The Diary of Kosa Pan (Ok-Phra Wisut Sunthon) Thai Ambassador to France, June-July 1686*, eds. Dirk Van der Cruysse and Michael Smithies (Bangkok: Silkworm Books, 2002).

(6) Simon de La Loubère, *Du Royaume de Siam*, 2 vols. (Paris: Jean-Baptiste Coignard, 1691).

(7) *Étude historique et critique du Journal du Voyage de Siam de Claude Céberet, envoyé extraordinaire du Roi en 1687 et 1688*, ed. Michel Jacq-Hergoualc'h (Paris: l'Harmattan, 1992).

(8) Guy Tachard, *Second Voyage du Père Tachard et des Jésuits envoys par le Roi au Royaume de Siam* (Paris: Horthemels, 1689).

decided that the two emissaries would be escorted back to Siam by a French embassy.[48]

What is commonly referred to as the first French embassy to Siam therefore preceded the 1686 Siamese embassy. It was headed by the chevalier de Chaumont as ambassador extraordinary, aided by François-Timoléon de Choisy, titular abbot of Saint-Seine in Burgundy as co-adjutant.[49] The embassy accompanied back the two Siamese envoys and encompassed also six Jesuits on their way to China and several missionaries to Siam, including the Jesuit Guy Tachard, who was to have a prominent role in both the first and second French embassy to Siam.[50] This was a relatively large embassy comprising 265 men. As only two vessels were made available, the entourage had to be kept to a minimum to allow space for a large cargo of gifts. It was estimated that the gifts from Louis to the King of Siam were valued at 300,000 écus.[51]

The great importance given to the gifts presented at Versailles in 1686 had little to do with the glorification of Louis XIV but was an act of reciprocal respect after what the French ambassadors had learned in Siam the previous year. The French were quite surprised with the treatment given to the presents they carried for the King of Siam, despite the fact that they had been instructed about Siamese royal protocol.[52] Part of the issue was that while Europeans saw the gifts as expensive commodities, the Siamese treated them as emanations of the very persona of the king. The Jesuit father Guy Tachard had spent several years in Siam, yet he was surprised by the reverence shown to the gifts on barges: "So soon as they were loaded, they put out with great silence, and took their station in the middle of the Channel. All the while that they lay there, there was

[48] Jules Sottas, *Une Escadre française aux Indes en 1690. Histoire de la Compagnie royale des Indes Orientales, 1664–1719* (Paris: Plon-Nourrit et Cie, 1905), 137–39. See also AN, Colonies, C[1]22 ff. 173–74: "Lettre du barcalon à Colbert annonçant l'envoi en France d'ambassadeurs siamois ... Lettre expédiée par Phaulkon (1685)."

[49] Key texts of the First French Embassy to Siam are Alexandre de Chaumont, *Relation de l'ambassade de Mr le Chevalier de Chaumont à la cour du roi de Siam ...* (Paris: Seneuze et Horthemels, 1686); Abbé François-Timoleon de Choisy, *Journal du voyage de Siam fait en 1685 et 1686 par Monsieur d'abbé de Choisy* (Paris: S. Mabre-Cramoisy, 1687); Guy Tachard, *Voyage de Siam, des pères Jésuites ...* (Paris: Seneuze et Horthemels, 1686); Claude de Forbin, *Voyage du comte de Forbin à Siam, suivi de quelques détails extraits des mémoires de l'abbé de Choisy* (Paris: Bibl. des chemins de fer sér, 1853).

[50] Raphaël Vongsuravatana, "New Investigations on Franco-Siamese Relations in the 17th Century: For a Rehabilitation of Father Tachard," *Journal of the Siam Society* 82, no. 1 (1994): 97–100, and id., *Un Jésuite à la Cour de Siam* (Paris: France-Empire, 1992).

[51] Love, "Rituals of Majesty," 171–89, esp. 180.

[52] Love, "Royal Protocol," 4.

not the least Noise to be heard upon the Shore, and no Balon [vessel] was then suffered to come up or down the River, lest they might fail in the Respect that is due to the Balons of State, and to the Presents they carried" (Figure 9.4).[53]

Yet the French were also perplexed that in Siam the French royal gifts were scrutinized in detail. "Before that the King's Presents went out of our hands," recounted Simon de la Loubère on the second embassy to Siam, "some of the King of Siam's Officers came to take an exact description thereof in writing, even to the counting all the Stones of every sort which were interspers'd in the Embroideries."[54] He proposed a negative interpretation claiming that the Siamese "are really concern'd only for the Profit" and that by thoroughly checking the gifts they wanted to ensure that their king received more than he was giving. Yet La Loubère himself admitted that the situation was more complex than it might appear at first sight: "'Tis a trafficking under an honourable Title, and from King to King," he wrote. Reciprocity was greatly valued in Siamese culture and as such the King of Siam had to evaluate what he received in order to reciprocate on at least an equal footing. This had indeed been an issue just a few years earlier when Monseigneur Pallu arrived at Ayutthaya in July 1682 with letters from Louis XIV and Innocent XI and obtained an audience with the King of Siam. He carried with him gifts of glass flowers, paintings of the adoration of the Magi, the ascension of Jesus Christ, and the apparition of the cross to Constantine. However, under the insistence of Phaulkon, he offered Louis XIV's presents as personal gifts and not on behalf of the king, as "the presents did not seem proportionate to the grandeur of the one and of the other king."[55]

The 1686 profusion of gifts at the Versailles ceremony thus assumes a different meaning, one of necessary reciprocity among "brothers" as many of the harangues underlined. Yet the Siamese ambassadors must have been mortified by the way in which Louis and his court remained comparatively indifferent to their gifts. La Loubère, once again, explains that in Siamese culture what was expected was a true appreciation of the gifts as a sign of respect for the ruler who sent them:

[53] Guy Tachard, *A Relation of the Voyage to Siam*, 160–61.

[54] Simon de La Loubère, *A New Historical Relation of the Kingdom of Siam by Monsieur de La Loubere* ... (London: Printed by F.L. for Tho. Horne, 1693), 110. See also *Étude historique et critique du Journal du Voyage de Siam de Claude Céberet*, 93–94.

[55] Lounay, *Histoire de la Mission de Siam*, 52.

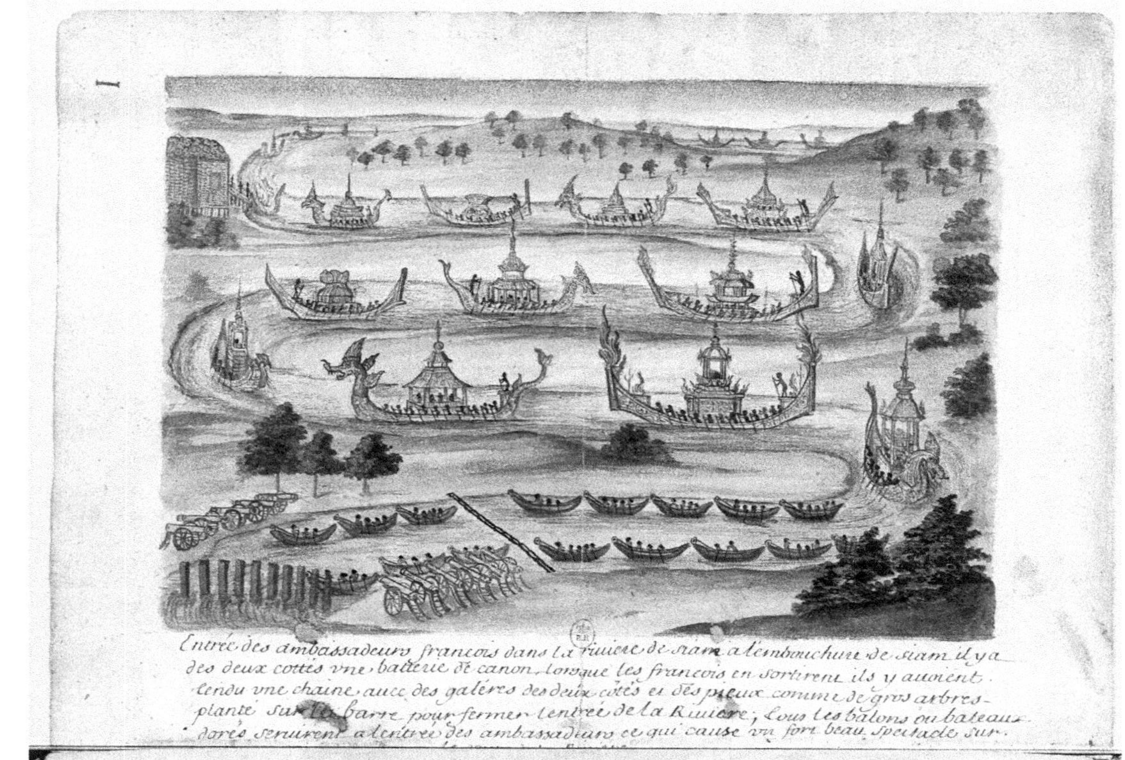

FIGURE 9.4 “Arrival of the French ambassador in Siam,” drawing from the volume Usages du Royaume de Siam, en 1688, c. 1688.

If it is any thing of use, tho' it be not for their use, they publickly prepare whatever shall be necessary to use it, as if they had a real desire thereof. If it is any thing to wear, they will adorn themselves therewith in your presence. If they are Horses, they will build a Stable on purpose to lodge them. Was it only a Telescope, they would build a Tower to see with this Glass. And so they will seem to make an high account of all sorts of Presents, to honour the Prince which sends them, unless he has received Presents from their part with less demonstrations of Esteem.[56]

Louis XIV might have been somewhat careless in his behavior at home, but the quantity of gifts previously sent to Siam made it clear that the French knew what was expected of them. In fact, the French were very much at a disadvantage in Siam, compared at least with the position enjoyed by the Portuguese, English, Dutch and indeed the Persians.[57] Although they had the support of Constantin Phaulkon, magnificent gifts were a necessity to gain the favor of the king. It was all important to convince the king of the benefit of an alliance with France, as all trade in cotton, tin, ivory, lead, sappan-wood, sulfur, saltpeter and various Chinese commodities and luxuries was a royal monopoly from which the king received substantial revenues in taxation.[58]

Part of the munificence of Louis XIV might have also been the result of the rather optimistic assessment made by the French priest Bénigne Vachet, who having spent several years in Siam acted as the official interpreter for the emissaries of the King of Siam, who reached Versailles in 1684. He convinced the French king that a large embassy was required as there was the potential to convert Phra Narai to Catholicism.[59] Vachet, as a member of the French Missions étrangères present in Siam since 1662, was keen to receive the support of the King of France and a large embassy would legitimize his position.[60] The French mission in Siam was not in good relations with either the Dutch or the Portuguese. They were

[56] La Loubère, *A New Historical Relation*, 110

[57] This was the case not just commercially but also diplomatically. See Stefan Halikowski-Smith, "'The Friendship of Kings Was in the Ambassadors': Portuguese Diplomatic Embassies in Asia and Africa during the Sixteenth and Seventeenth Centuries," *Portuguese Studies* 22, no. 1 (2006): 101–34; Adam Clulow, *The Company and the Shogun: The Dutch Encounter with Tokugawa Japan* (New York: Columbia University Press, 2014), esp. ch. 1; Zoltán Biedermann, *The Portuguese in Sri Lanka and South India: Studies in the History of Diplomacy, Empire and Trade, 1500–1650* (Wiesbaden: Harrassowitz, 2014), esp. ch. 2.

[58] Smithies and Bressan, *Siam and the Vatican*, 20; Benson, "European Wonders," 158–59; Manich Jumsai, *History of Anglo-Thai Relations* (Bangkok: Chalermnit, 1970), 19; Vongsuravatana, *Un Jésuite à la Cour de Siam*, 98–103.

[59] Van der Cruysse, "Aspects of Siamese-French Relations," 66–67.

[60] The *Société des Missions étrangères de Paris* (MEP) was founded in 1658 as a Catholic missionary organization of secular priests and lay persons.

in commercial and political competition with the Dutch, while the French laymen of the Missions étrangères were seen as an encroachment on the power of the Portuguese Jesuits.[61]

For his part, the King of Siam was all too aware that he needed to please the French. He had not opposed the establishment of the Jesuits in his kingdom. Indeed, Narai's closest adviser, the Greek Phaulkon, converted to Catholicism after his marriage to a Japanese woman, herself a convert.[62] Phra Narai had politely acknowledged the many invitations to embrace the Catholic faith and accepted several presents of crucifixes and religious-themed paintings. However, it remains unknown how much the King of Siam might have appreciated the meaning of these gifts or if, on the other hand, they remained for him a sign of the religious identity of their giver. For sure he understood that he was in need of a European ally against the increasing power of the Dutch East India Company.[63]

Encouraged by the prospect of commercial gains and a possible conversion of the King of Siam, Louis XIV decided to send a second embassy to Siam with the return voyage of Kosa Pan and the other Siamese ambassadors. This was an even larger affair compared with the first one, leaving France in March 1687 and arriving in Siam in September.[64] The second embassy comprised 1,361 men – troops, officers, ambassadors and priests – onboard six vessels, which again carried magnificent presents. This time, however, Père Tachard, much to the annoyance of both the chief ambassador La Loubère and his co-adjutant Claude Céberet, was secretly instructed to provide military help to Phaulkon and the king.[65]

THE FRENCH GIFTS TO THE KING OF SIAM: THE CREATION OF A PRIVATE SPECTACLE

So far I have detailed the great spectacle of the 1686 Siamese embassy to Versailles and the role played by gifts. I have also contextualized it within a mutual relationship, explaining how the gifts received by Louis reflected the

[61] Lach, *Asia in the Making of Europe*, 3: 420–34; Ruangsilp, *Dutch East India Company Merchants*, 122–25.

[62] Flores, "A Embaixada de Pedro Vaz de Siqueira," 355.

[63] Hans ten Brummelhuis, *Merchant, Courtier and Diplomat: A History of the Contacts between the Netherlands and Thailand* (Lochem: De Tijdstroom, 1987), 33.

[64] Key texts on the Second French Embassy to Siam are Simon de La Loubère, *Du Royaume de Siam*, 2 vols. (Paris: Jean-Baptiste Coignard, 1691); *Étude historique et critique du Journal du Voyage de Siam de Claude Céberet*; and Guy Tachard, *Second Voyage du Père Tachard et des Jésuits envoys par le Roi au Royaume de Siam* (Paris: Horthemels, 1689).

[65] Smithies, "Siamese Mandarins," 108.

political and economic conditions in Siam rather than France. But what did the King of Siam make of the gifts sent by Louis XIV? As we have seen, the principle of reciprocity was fundamental in governing the relationship between the two monarchs. Yet the literature is replete with stories of how Asian rulers and their subjects scorned European artifacts, often seeing them as devoid of any charm, material worth or cultural value.

Detailed records of the goods sent by Louis and the royal family as ambassadorial gifts to Siam were kept by the French court, especially for the second embassy. Among the commodities "the most singular of the Kingdom," the French sent five clocks (two of which pendulum), furniture, crystal-ware, gold watches, a gold crown of diamonds (worth 13,500 livres), clothing, saddles and harnesses, court swords, twelve muskets, eight pairs of ornate pistols, two miniatures of Louis XIV painted on enamel and garnished with diamonds, a chest-full of medallions bearing the French monarch's profile, and an equestrian portrait of the Sun King.[66] A selection of luxury French fabrics and gold brocades was acquired from Marcellin Chartier, "marchand et fabricant de draps d'or, d'argent et soie à Paris": 15 meters (12 *aunes*) of gold brocade at 90 livres per *aune*; 7 aune of green, gold and silver brocade at 80 livres per *aune*; 9 *aunes* of violet brocade, etc. for a total of more than 28,000 livres.[67]

The gifts to Phra Narai from Louis were worth an astonishing 175,431 livres without including the personal gifts sent by other courtiers.[68] These were procured from the royal repository and from several Crown suppliers and included also two large mirrors; two sedan chairs; crystal mirrors decorated with precious stones; crystal candelabra and chandeliers; wall-brackets in white, red and jasper marble, with gold feet; Savonnerie carpets; Gobelins tapestries; marble tables; an organ; porcelain vases of Sèvres; and "all sorts of exquisite furnishings." The latter gifts were no random selection of goods. They served to furnish the new audience hall at the Palace at Lophuri (Louvo). Tachard in his second embassy recounts: "The Audience hall of the palace in Louvo is

[66] AN, Colonies, B[2] 52: "Passeport pour les presens que le Roy envoy au Roy de Siam, 23 Janvier 1685," ff. 53r and 53v. Cit. in Love, "Royal Protocol," 16.

[67] These are for the second embassy. AN, Colonies, C[I]23, ff. 38–46: "État des présents envoyés par le roi, la famille royale, les ministres et le père de La Chaise au roi de Siam, à sa famille, à Constance Phaulkon et aux ambassadeurs (1687)"; C[I]23, ff. 52–54: "Fournitures pour les ambassadeurs et leur suite (interprète cochinchinois, le sieur François, interprète) (1687)"; and Étienne-Gallois, *L'ambassade de Siam*, 121.

[68] AN, Colonies, C[I]23, ff. 47–51: "État général des présents, avec leur prix (1687)."

completely covered in huge mirrors which the King of Siam has caused to be brought from France" (Figure 9.5).[69] This was not the only space that the King of Siam was building in European style. He had also planned accommodation for the ambassadors in Western style. It appears that such building was not completed when the final French delegation sojourned in Siam. However, the place where the ambassadors stayed was part furnished "à la française," with chairs with blue and red velvet and gold fringes to complement Japanese screens, painted cotton hangings and divans.[70]

Phra Narai was an avid collector not just of Asian luxuries but also the best that could be found in Europe.[71] He seemed to like to surround himself with a mixture of luxury items from Europe, Japan, China and Persia to form a rather eclectic style. In the 1670s, he had ruled that all courtiers should dress in the Persian fashion donning long robes, large trousers, and pointed shoes, but he replaced Islamic turbans with the pointed hats that so much charmed the French.[72] Part of the royal palace was indeed built in Iranian style, though by the early 1680s the king seemed to be more interested in "European exotica". The Dutch (VOC) and English East India companies were well aware of the king's many passions and furnished him with jewelry, coral, amber, diamonds, glass, perfumes, horses, cockatoos, birds of paradise and rich cloth.[73] In 1682 the Dutch – the rivals of the French in Siam – contributed to the construction of the hall at Lophuri by supplying as many as 162 "very elegantly coloured glass panes (or panels), ordered specifically from Holland by His Majesty, consisting of 52 pieces with varied flower designs, 56 with all sorts of birds, 53 with ships" accompanied by white marble, gold cloth and lace procured from Holland.[74]

The French East India Company learned that in order to receive the King's favor suitable gifts were required. When André Deslandres-Boureau

69 Michael Smithies, *Mission Made Impossible: The Second French Embassy to Siam, 1687* (Chiang Mai: Silkworm Books 2002), 35.

70 Choisy, *Journal du Voyage de Siam*, 192; *A Relation of the Voyage to Siam ... in the Year 1685* (Paris: White Lotus Press, 1999), 127.

71 Benson, "European Wonders," 156.

72 Jean Aubin, "Les Persans au Siam sous le regne de Narai (1656–1688)," *Mare Luso-Indicum* 4 (1980): 100.

73 Dhiravat na Pombejra, *Siamese Court Life in the Seventeenth Century as Depicted in European Sources* (Bangkok: Department of History, Faculty of Arts, Chulalongkorn University, 2001), 122–67; Jacq-Hergoualc'h, *L'Europe et le Siam*, 54–55.

74 Cited in Pombejra, *Siamese Court Life*, 130. On the VOC gifts, see also Ruangsilp, *Dutch East India Company Merchants*, ch. 5.

FIGURE 9.5 "Audience solennelle donnée par le roi de Siam au chevalier de Chaumont et à l'abbé de Choisy le 18 octobre 1685" (Solemn hearing by the King of Siam to the knight of Chaumont and the abbot of Choisy, 18 October 1685), print, A Paris ches Nolin, rue St. Jacques, à la place de la Victoire C. pr. Regis. Bibliothèque nationale de France, département Estampes et photographie, Reserve FOL-QB-201 (61).

arrived in Siam in September 1680 to establish commerce on behalf of the French company, his gifts "were found most beautiful," reports François Martin.[75] The gifts presented by the VOC and the French company were often requested. In fact the difference between a gift and a purchased item was often difficult to establish as the King of Siam would let the Europeans have lists of what he required as "gifts." As the king controlled all international trade, so trade with the king was subsumed into a form of gifting for which in return the Companies received the kind of commodities that they needed for the intra-Asian and the trade to Europe.[76]

The murkiness of the boundary between gift and purchased commodity was present also in the more rarefied ambassadorial relations between states. Part of the job of Kosa Pan and the first Siamese embassy to France was to procure sufficient quantities of goods to furnish the palace in Lophuri. Dangeau explains that the Siamese ambassadors visiting Versailles in 1686 did not just receive gifts to bring back to Siam but "also bought several curious products of France for the King of Siam."[77] He adds that this was the reason why "they have been so curious about glass and enamels. They bring back a large number of excellent glass for a gallery that the king has built."[78] The quantity of goods that they acquired in France was absolutely prodigious. They often asked for goods that were technically impossible such as mirrors 20 feet high and cannons that could hold balls of 300 pounds in weight.[79] They had to content themselves with 4,263 mirrors of different dimensions from the factory at St. Gobain for both the palaces at Ayutthaya and Lophuri; 4,300 pieces of crystal fruit and flowers for Siamese-style chandeliers and candelabra. These were accompanied by no fewer than seven Savonnerie carpets as well as large quantities of textiles such as velvets and linens.[80]

[75] *Mémoires de François Martin, fondateur de Pondichéry (1665–1696)*, ed. Alfred Martineau, 3 vols. (Paris: Société d'éditions géographiques, maritimes et coloniales, 1931–34), 2: 206 (December 1680).

[76] E. W. Hutchinson, "Les premières relations de la Compagnie française des Indes et du Suam au XVIIe siècle," *Bulletin de la Société des Etudes Indochinoises* 17, no. 1 (1942): 1–24, esp. p. 8.

[77] Dangeau, *Journal du marquis de Dangeau*, 1: 115.

[78] Ibid., 1: 116.

[79] Jacq-Hergoualc'h, *L'Europe et le Siam*, 86.

[80] AN, Colonies, C[I]23, ff. 249–58: "Mémoire général de tout ce que le roy de Siam a ordonné à ses ambassadeurs de lui faire faire ou acheter en France" (1687). There was also an assortment of other commodities including lace jackets and beaver hats of different colors; 160 cannons, 200 blunderbusses, and 20 quivers; and elephants' marks and several harnesses for male and female elephants. It remains unclear who actually paid

This large quantity of artifacts was clearly awaited in Siam, as Tachard tells us that on the arrival of the second French embassy in 1687 "some parts here and there [of the palace at Lophuri] were not decorated; [but that] since the most recent pieces which were awaited from France have arrived, work is being carried out non-stop, and soon it will be complete."[81] He was expressing some anxiety as already at embankment in Brest it was noticed that several of the commissioned objects were in a very poor state due to faulty packaging and careless handling.[82] Probably because of the need for repairs and also with the idea of producing locally what was needed for the hall, the Siamese instructed Father Vachet to hire the services of five Parisian artisans, three glassmakers, a clock-maker and a goldsmith.[83] This would have allowed the Siamese king to speed up the acquisition of the necessary luxury goods without relying entirely on either gifts or commissions to be delivered from Europe.

The difference between gifts and "purchases" was further complicated by the fact that Louis had sent similar items during the previous embassy that – although once again damaged during the journey – must have pleased the King enough to order more to be brought back by the following embassy. These included two large Savonnerie carpets costing 4,000 livres each that had been made to fit exactly the audience hall (and arrived undamaged), the best pieces of brocades and Holland linen that could be found (which were instead very damaged), glass for a total value of 18,000 livres, several watches and a pendulum clock produced by M. Martineau, a well-known horologist, that chimed the hours "à la manière de Siam."[84] Overall five boats had to be used to move the presents into the Siamese capital.[85]

Both French embassies carried a variety of weapons, swords and other blades whose cases were decorated with precious stones, and small mirrors of various shapes with golden and silver borders. The most appreciated items were optical instruments such as telescopes and magnifying glasses. An example of such an item was a binocular that could distinguish objects at two leagues of distance, made of gold and

for these items. Surely the French East India Company was involved in financing the purchase and it is probable that it simply paid for them in exchange for favors and goods (return gifts) for their Asian trade. Jacq-Hergoualc'h, *L'Europe et le Siam*, 93. Jacq-Hergoualc'h also provides a full transcription of the order lists. Ibid., 87–100.

81 Smithies, *Mission Made Impossible*, 35.

82 Van der Cruysse, *Siam and the West*, 382.

83 Pombejra, *Siamese Court Life*, 162.

84 "Voyage et séjour des envoyés Siamois en France. Mémoire de Bénigne Vachet," in *Histoire de la mission de Siam, 1662–1811: documents historiques*, ed. Adrien Launay, 2 vols. (Paris: Douniol and Retaux, 1920), 1: 149.

85 Choisy, *Journal du Voyage de Siam*, 190.

enameled,[86] and two large globes – one celestial and one terrestrial (of which the Siamese had actually provided the model).[87] The King of Siam had a keen interest in astronomy and requested as diplomatic gifts a variety of globes, telescopes, clocks and lenses by both the French and the Dutch.[88] The French mixed their religion and diplomacy and in an attempt to please Phra Narai, six Jesuits with excellent knowledge of astronomy were sent as part of the second embassy in order to assist the king with the observation of a solar eclipse (Figure 9.6).[89]

What is striking in reading the lists of gifts received by Phra Narai is that they were carefully chosen (and indeed supplemented through purchases) to fulfill the king's ambitions and passions. In this sense, they were very dissimilar from the rather "indifferent" gifts that Louis received, of great effect and value but rather unwanted. Phra Narai expressed instead his personality and ambitions through the gifts he received. They made it clear that he was a man of great culture. It is said that he frequented the Persian community in Siam when still a prince and, on ascending to the throne in 1657, named a Persian as his chief minister and was taught by another learned Persian about the wider world.[90] The king was well informed and extremely inquisitive, questioning the French ambassadors about European politics and showing great knowledge of the topic.

The presents to King Narai therefore acted as a reminder of the cosmopolitan horizons of the Siamese ruler and his erudition. If Louis XIV had used the Siamese gifts to give body to his claims to Oriental-like power, Phra Narai's gifts and associated ambassadorial receptions showed not just an appreciation of Western goods and protocol but also the king's ability to interact with different cultures. In 1685, the very year in which the first French embassy arrived in Siam, for instance, Phra Narai gave a solemn audience to Pero Vaz de Siqueira, who represented Portuguese mercantile

[86] "Voyage et séjour," 150.

[87] AN, Colonies, C¹24 ff. 90–92: "Lettre de M. de Lagny sur la fabrication, par Martineau, de deux globes terrestres destinés au roi de Siam (13 octobre 1686)." The celestial was decorated with the zodiac, the constellations and the seven planets, all made of stones of different colors. And the entire system moved, "so that by giving the year, month, day and hour, as chosen, one could see all the movements of the skies in that date ... This small wonder was sufficient to have pride of place in the palaces of the grandest of princes." The second was a terrestrial globe of the same dimension. It showed the flux and reflux of the sea at any time of the year. "One had to see it to believe it." Ibid.

[88] Benson, "European Wonders," 157.

[89] Jacq-Hergoualc'h, *L'Europe et le Siam*, 80–81.

[90] Van der Cruysse, *Siam and the West*, 282.

FIGURE 9.6 "The Sun Eclipse," drawing from the volume *Usages du Royaume de Siam, en 1688*, planche 7, c. 1688.

interests in Asia.[91] Just a few years earlier, in 1682, Narai had sent an embassy to the Safavid ruler Shah Sulaiman "accompanied by the finest gifts the Siamese king could produce" and had received a Persian embassy carrying equally magnificent gifts in return a few years later.[92]

[91] Differently from the French embassies that represented the King of France, those sent by the Portuguese and the Dutch were in the name of the Portuguese viceroy and the governors of the Dutch East Indian Company, respectively. David K. Wyatt, *Thailand: A Short History* (New Haven and London: Yale University Press, 1984), 114.

[92] Ibn Muhammad Ibrāhīm, *The Ship of Sulaimān*, trans. John O'Kane (London: Routledge & Kegan Paul, 1972), 77. See also David Wyatt, "A Persian Mission to Siam in the Reign of King Narai,"*Journal of the Siam Society* 62, no. 1 (1974): 151–57; Muhammad Ismail Marcinkowski, "Persian Religious and Cultural Influences in Siam/Thailand and Maritime Southeast Asia in Historical Perspective: A Plea for a Concerted Interdisciplinary Approach," *Journal of the Siam Society* 88, nos. 1–2 (2000): 186–94.

The Franco-Siamese relationship established in the 1680s through mutual embassies looks different when seen from a Siamese point of view. This is not just because Narai was better informed, more cosmopolitan and had a better sense of the science, culture and material culture of distant lands than Louis XIV. The selection of gifts makes clear that from Narai's point of view this was not necessarily a relationship between equals: the French had much to gain from an alliance with Siam and access to the country's ports. Louis XIV, even if referred to as a "brother" and a ruler of equal status, was no equal in any sense. His ambassadors received exemptions from the usual prostration that much annoyed European ambassadors in Asia in the early modern period and were treated with utmost care; no expense was spared.[93] However, Narai's requests, and indeed insistence on the importance of gifts, acted as a signifier of a gap between the expectations of the two rulers.

EPILOGUE: SURPLUS GIFTING AND THE EMBASSY THAT NEVER HAPPENED

If in 1686 the Siamese ambassadors had received an unprecedented welcome to France, by the summer of 1688 little remained of Louis XIV's enthusiasm. When in July that year the second embassy returned to France, the king was not pleased to receive contrasting reports. The ambassadors made it clear that Phra Narai would never convert to Christianity and that the value of trade in Siam was perhaps not worth the game. None of them had any idea that both Phra Narai and Phaulkon were dead and that the French position in Siam had been effectively annihilated.[94]

Louis faced a second problem, the fact that a third embassy had been sent by the late King of Siam with the returning second French embassy. He had attempted to stop the reciprocation of expensive gifts. On the previous embassy Cèberet said that "on regards the presents that Mons. Phaulkon sent to France last year, that these continuous presents are tiring the court and that we have the order to do whatever is possible to stop this sending of ambassadorial and envoys' presents."[95] Yet this had

[93] Love, "Rituals of Majesty," 182. See also the detailed description of the treatment of the first embassy: BnF, Département des manuscrits, Français 17239 (Mélanges sur la Chine), ff. 98–114: "Relation anonyme du voyage de l'un des Jésuites, qui accompagnaient les ambassadeurs du roi de France à Siam en 1687, par Jean Richaud (?)."

[94] The death of the king followed a revolution supported by the Dutch. Phaulkon was arrested and later beheaded. Lounay, *Histoire de la Mission de Siam*, 1: 204.

[95] *Étude historique et critique du Journal du Voyage de Siam de Claude Céberet*, 92.

led to nothing as according to Tachard at the farewell audience in Siam, "work was still going on wrapping the presents which the King of Siam and M. Constance [Phaulkon] were sending to France, for this prince, having received for the second time most magnificent gifts from our king, desired to send some which were still more precious and numerous than those sent on the first voyage."[96]

Louis XIV, having obtained the publicity that he wanted, now considered how best to untangle himself and stop future embassies. He unwillingly consented to receive the Siamese ambassadors, but later reconsidered his decision and sent the ambassadors to Rome instead for an audience with the pope. This allowed Louis to withdraw from granting more concessions or investing further resources into what looked like a rather unpromising initiative. Some of the presents for the King of France were therefore "recycled" for the pope. Three boxes of about 300 kilograms each were sent to Rome and included an octagonal gold casket worked in filigree weighing 15 pounds from Phra Narai and a silver casket and tray weighing 13 pounds from Phaulkon, though it is said that most of the presents were distributed among members of the pope's family, the powerful Odescalchi.[97] After having fruitlessly waited for months to be received by Louis, the ambassadors went back to Siam in February 1690, but not before they had been converted to Catholicism by the pope.

Undelivered gifts and an embassy that was never received effectively ended the Franco-Siamese relationships of the 1680s. The presents that in 1686 had been so much celebrated were now perceived as an embarrassment and a reminder of a failed mission. They were also presented with connotations negative enough to convince Louis XIV that it was unwise to receive the new delegation and the presents altogether. He had inquired about the new presents, only to be told that they were not tokens of affection and friendship from another powerful ruler, but tools of the scheming Phaulkon and that "the magnificence of the presents intended for the king [of France] and the court could contribute to the designs that the minister had in mind."[98] This is why according to Chevalier de Forbin, who spent two years in Siam, when he was asked to stay behind as the first embassy left for France, Phaulkon had "drained the Kingdom [of Siam] to produce something magnificent ... and that not satisfied in

[96] Smithies, *Mission Made Impossible*, 57.

[97] Smithies and Bressan, *Siam and the Vatican*, 70; Smithies, "Siamese Mandarins," 112–14.

[98] De Forbin, *Voyage du comte de Forbin à Siam*, 38.

having taken everything that could be found in Siam, he also sent to China and Japan to carry back everything that is most rare and curious, things that he continued loading on the King's ships until there was no space for more."[99]

The gifts exchanged between the kingdoms of France and Siam were an integral part of one of the most celebrated Eurasian embassies of the early modern period. Yet they fulfilled different functions in France and in Siam. By going beyond the great Versailles event and decentering the narrative away from France, I have shown how in Siam gifts assumed a rather different meaning, one that was governed by a genuine interest in things European. Early modern embassies were also large and complex events that involved sometimes hundreds of people. Gifting practices served as much to represent their rulers and nations as they represented individual interests, thus making us alert to the perils of constructing narratives that are all-encompassing and give little space to the understanding of specific individuals.

The exchange of embassies between France and Siam was also a short one and ended in failure rather than the establishment of cultural or economic connections between these two parts of Eurasia. Louis had never fully appreciated the gifts from Siam, while Phra Narai had treasured them. Yet none of the gifts survive or are traceable. Those in France were partly distributed among courtiers and partly dispersed with the French Revolution. Those in Siam mostly ended in the large funerary pyre of Phra Narai, a pyramid "40 feet high" that included not just the many religious objects accepted by the Siamese king but also many of the presents from Louis, including the portrait "of our good King and those of the major seigniors of the court." And all "was burned with great pomp and magnificence."[100]

[99] Ibid., 38. [100] Lounay, *Histoire de la Mission de Siam*, 1: 203, note 1.

10

Coercion and the Gift

Art, Jewels and the Body in British Diplomacy in Colonial India

Natasha Eaton

INTRODUCTION: CHARISMA OF THE GIVER?

Frustrated by the long-delayed reply to his proposed treaty with the English East India Company, the Persian Qajar envoy Mirza Ab'l Hasan Ilchi Shirazi (1745–1825) had plenty of time to record the details of his quotidian life in London in the *Hayrat-nāma-ye sofarā – Book of Wonders* (1809–10).[1] During this stint of "ennui," Ab'l Hasan was invited to the home of the Chairman of the Company's Court of Directors, Charles Grant:

> He took my arm and led me upstairs to a room where the portrait of the Qibleh of the Universe – 'Fath Ali Shah – was displayed on an easel at the entrance of the room . . . Then the Chairman took me to another place where the portraits of Shah Abbas's ambassador were hanging. He told me he wished to have my portrait painted to hang beside that of the ambassador of Shah Abbas.[2]

On this occasion the Company gave 250 guineas for Ab'l Hasan's full-length likeness by the reasonably well-known painter William Beechey (Figure 10.1), which they showcased at the Royal Academy exhibition before finding it a permanent home in the chamber of the Finance Committee of East India House – the headquarters of the English East India Company. A rare act of generosity – as we shall see – on the part of the

[1] The British Library holds a manuscript copy of Ab'l Hasan's diary, "Khayaratnamah-yi sufara," British Library (hereafter BL), Add Ms 23,546. Ab'l Hasan traveled as an ambassador working extensively in Asia and Europe. He spent 1809 and 1810 in England.

[2] Ab'l Hasan, *The Heirat Nameh, or Book of Wonders of Ab'l Hasan* (London: Bloomsbury, 1990), 34.

FIGURE 10.1 William Beechey, *Ab'l Hasan, Envoy Extraordinary from the King of Persia to the Court of King George III*, 1810. Oil painting. 92 in × 56 in (234 cm × 142.5 cm).

Company, this recourse to portraiture may have been an acknowledgment of the public use of likenesses by the Qajar rulers. The Shahs used portraits in public processions while their court chroniclers record miracles performed by such images, which scholars have suggested to be termed icons.[3]

Adhering to the kind of portraiture favored for the depiction of kings, judges and ambassadors – a style that fitted into the monumental décor at East India House – Beechey features Ab'l Hasan full length and resplendent in fine gold-thread dress standing in a fantasy/studio setting that features the usual classical column and swathe of scarlet fabric. This type of portraiture, this chapter argues, had been common in Anglo-Indian relations since at least the 1760s. As one of the purposes of Ab'l Hasan's visit had been to promote the Anglo-Persian silk trade, two fine, intertwined fabrics adorn the table represented in the picture. More ambiguously, the sitter rests his right hand on a fold of white. Is this yet more cloth (given its rough edge) or rather a promissory "note" from the English East India Company? Ab'l Hasan's left thumb and first finger barely touch the jeweled hilt of his prized ceremonial sword, while the right hand poises more decidedly on the fold of white.

Painted with reasonably decent European pigments, the materiality of the portrait was probably no match for the glittering gold leaf that adorned the Qajar-painted portrait of the ruler 'Fath Ali Shah (179–1834) later gifted to the Company. In Beechey's portrait of Ab'l Hasan there was a lack of "continuum" between the materiality of the objects depicted and that of the image itself (i.e., no gold or gilt-laden pigment used to depict his dress or sword) and that this may not have been irrelevant at the time is suggested by a posterior episode from the same diplomatic context. Several months later, when no treaty had in fact materialized, George III received Ab'l Hasan in his private chamber in order to offer the Qajar ruler 'Fath Ali Shah expressions of his satisfaction that he derived from the "friendship" that he expressed now existed between Britain and Persia: "With his own hand, the king fixed to my waist an old and enamelled dagger set with diamonds which he asked me to keep as a memento of him."[4] After enduring the tedium of multiple sittings for a painted portrait so as to please the Company, here finally

[3] Layla S. Diba, "Images of Power and the Power of Images," in *Royal Persian Paintings: The Qajar, 1785–1925* , ed. Layla S. Diba and Maryam Ekhtiyar (New York: Brooklyn Art Museum, 1998), 30–49.

[4] Ab'l Hasan, *Heirat Nameh, or Book of Wonders*, 34.

was a gift of which to boast: perhaps this beautiful dagger could itself become a powerful symbol of cross-cultural allegiance in another painted likeness.[5] The next morning, however, Ab'l Hasan wrote to his host Sir Gore Ouseley: "the diamond in the king's gift of the dagger is glass! It is a very unpleasant situation."[6]

Was this merely George III's negligence, naïveté about an alternative regime of value, or a sly cultural snub that attempted to assert British authority through the imitation of Indian customs? Here seemingly was a gift of no or at least of different "value," but how shall we read it? Ab'l Hasan's relationship with the Company remained ambivalent.[7] I would like to suggest that such ambivalence resonates in British colonial portraiture right from its first implementation in later eighteenth-century India. Hasan's case regarding the diamond suggests that we may seek to unravel the complex role not just of power but also of value and desire in early modern transcontinental diplomacy. What I mean by this is that "talking up the gift" was a critical strategy in colonial practices at this time. There was a strong desire for portraiture to do the work of diplomacy.

In this chapter I seek to analyze the agency of British portraits as gifts at Indian courts in the later eighteenth century and the controversy they generated. I look to the value, desire and uncertainty of how things operate within such a context. As is well known, along with the term "commodity," the term "gift" has long been a much debated anthropological topic. What Arjun Appadurai has called "methodological fetishism" has become the byword for a new type of inquiry into the ontology of possession and circulation of things.[8] When commodity, following Appadurai, is defined in terms of a "situation," a state from which things can flow in and out in the course of their "social" lives, the categorical bipolarity of gift versus commodity becomes difficult to hold on to. This allows us to complicate regimes of value; perhaps that is indeed what was

[5] It is known that Ab'l Hasan sat for several European artists during this visit to London, including Beechey and Thomas Lawrence. See "The Persian Ambassador, Mirza Abul Hasan Shirazi (born 1776)" at the Fogg Art Museum, Harvard University. See also C. W. Millard, "A Diplomatic Portrait: Lawrence's 'The Persian Ambassador,'" *Apollo* (February 1967): 115–21.

[6] Ab'l Hasan, *Heirat Nameh, or Book of Wonders*, 67.

[7] A'bl Hasan would return to London for further diplomatic negotiations in 1820.

[8] Arjun Appadurai, "Introduction: Commodities and the Politics of Value," in id., ed., *The Social Life of Things: Commodities in Cultural Perspective* (Cambridge: Cambridge University Press, 1986), 3–63.

meant by the gifter's use of glass in the dagger presented by George III to Ab'l Hasan and its devastating recognition by the recipient. But while Appadurai has dealt considerably with the lives of things and how they move in and out of cultural situations, it also seems to me that the most effective way of grappling with these variable cultural strategies in terms of singularization is the distinction between alienable and inalienable possessions proposed by the anthropologist Annette Weiner. Her argument is that highly prized things are valued more if they are "suspended" from circulation: they are imbued with the charisma of the giver that is hard to return, difficult to give away, even hazardous to receive.[9] Inalienable possessions acquire their force and scarcity-value from the fact that they are heritable within a closed descent group. They have an exclusive and cumulative identity, first, from their association with a particular series of owners and, second, from their ties to cosmological forces – the dead, ancestors, gods or sacred places. The crucial fact about such possessions is that they cannot, under most circumstances, be freely exchanged: their authority makes them a key source of social and political prestige and hence of social hierarchy. This is why these are objects of intense competition.

Bearing this in mind, here I would like to examine the intercultural negotiations around the "gift" in early colonial India. The contexts I explore are those Indian courts targeted most intensely by the British in the later eighteenth century – Lucknow (in Awadh), Hyderabad (in the Deccan) and Arcot (in the Carnatic). Examining this interface between Mughal and British "regimes of inalienability," I want to see what role was played by the "image-gift" in Anglo-Indian diplomacy – did it function both as gift and as tribute, and if so did this incite both conflict and a new agency for the portraiture?

GIFTS IN LATE MUGHAL INDIA

The *nawabs* (rulers) of the eighteenth-century courts of India borrowed heavily from Mughal ideas of gifting and its relationship with artistic practice. Kai Kā'ūs Ibn Iskander (1021 to after 1082), author of the famed *Mirror for Princes* – the *Qābūs Nama* – advised rulers not to send out or to gift their body or their image too often: "Expose yourself to the general gaze only rarely and so prevent yourself from becoming a spectacle

[9] See Annette Weiner, *Inalienable Possessions: The Paradox of Keeping-While-Giving* (Berkeley: University of California, 1992).

commonplace."[10] Celebrated by their court chroniclers as the earthly mirrors or shadows of Allah, the Mughal emperors were, as the emperor Akbar's chief historian Ab'l Fazl ibn Mubarak (1551–1602) claimed, also linked by genealogy to the Islamic notion of the divine as the unrepresentable.[11] Mughal rulers devised multivalent strategies for projecting ideas of divine presence to their subjects and rivals. They incorporated the Hindu idea of contact with the divine – *darshan* (seeing and being seen by the divine) into their daily appearances before their subjects as well as appropriating Timurid and Mongol myths of genealogy that were heavily invested in Islamic neo-illuminist philosophy, which stressed a divine mode of kingship; they also claimed through their use of Sufism that they had direct communication with Allah.[12]

Even European, particularly Catholic, art could be incorporated into allegories of the mystical and devotional significance of Mughal sovereignty.[13] Here in his bust-length portrait Emperor Jahangir (r. 1605–27) shimmers with an aura of religiosity as can be seen by his halo illuminating the darkness; it can be conjectured that by presenting himself in a window frame he is commanding the artist to depict *darshan* (the emperor appeared twice daily at an open window in his palace to receive crowd adulation). Jahangir is positioned above Isa (Jesus) whose torn clothes and white marble *jail* provide another worldly humility indicative of the emperor's inner contemplation. In terms of Hashim and Ab'l Hasan's courtly representation he simultaneously assumes the role of Christian saint/ascetic, Hindu holy man and emperor – all of which center on what appears to be a Jesuit image gift.[14] At least in terms of pre-eighteenth-century artistic production there was space for such confident eclecticism.

Conveying the charisma of their presence to subjects and rivals also necessitated the Mughal agency of gift. In Mughal domestic policy, subordinates offered valuable tributes or *nazr* (offering) and received in

10 Kai Kā'ūs Ibn Iskander, *The Nasihat-nama Known as Qābūs Nama*, ed. Ruben Levey (London: Luzac, 1951), 223.

11 See Ab'l Fazl, *A'in-i Akbari: Institutes of Akbar, or the Akbarnama*, 2 vols. (Delhi: Oriental Books, 1978), vol. 1.

12 See John F. Richards, *The Mughal Empire* (Cambridge: Cambridge University Press, 1993).

13 Jahangir commissioned a series of "Dream Images" that frequently depict him in a devotional pose and/or receiving gifts.

14 On their three missions to the Mughal court the Jesuits offered numerous images including the Polyglot Bible and a couple of copies of the "St. Luke Madonna" from Rome.

return *khil'at* (robes of honor) minutely graded in terms of rank and occasion from the wardrobe of the ruler. The gifting of these robes and their acceptance signified a symbolic incorporation into the king's body and a literal incorporation into the Mughal body politic. This is but one instance whereby Mughal rulers styled themselves as the "embodiment of hospitality" – which also became a major subject of Indian court art.[15] Jahangir and his father Akbar only very occasionally gifted images of themselves to devoted followers in ceremonies that conflated the worship of the Mughal Emperor with that of the sun: here was another reading of the halo and in relationship with the divine. Recipients of these minuscule portraits were expected to wear them either in their turban or around their necks on a gold chain as markers of their devotion to the emperor.[16]

Although Europeans had attempted to introduce portraits into Mughal India from the mid-sixteenth century, this was a limited success. This might be partly due to James I's ambassador Sir Thomas Roe's presentation of a print of Jahangir to the emperor that Jahangir saw to be a crude, materially unworthy and *unlike* likeness of the emperor.[17] But art, especially portraiture, could carry a kind of inalienable value which the Company sought to use especially in times of duress. By the 1760s the Company's directors were condemning colonial *and* Indian gifting practices as bribery and extortion inherent to the common stereotype of "Oriental despotism."[18] They were highly suspicious of what they perceived to be the extravagance of Mughal gifting practices, so they sought out alternatives.[19]

Given the growing controversies at this time surrounding the corruption of British "nabobs," colonial officials did pay heed to the Company's and parliamentary demands. The Regulating Act of 1773 prohibited British officials from accepting or soliciting land, money and jewels from

[15] These acts of charity extended into the kingdom as emperors built rest-houses, wells, roads, alms houses. The third pillar of Islam is alms and gifting is carefully graded by the Sharia – gift is inward submission not outward ostentation that will assist in the purification of the soul.

[16] Richards, *Mughal Empire*, 45.

[17] England's envoy Sir Thomas Roe noted the lack of success of Jahangir's likeness at the Mughal court. It would appear as if portraits were far more inalienable in Mughal India than in Britain. I discuss this below.

[18] John R. McLane, *Land and Local Kingship in Eighteenth-Century Bengal* (Cambridge: Cambridge University Press, 1993), 43.

[19] N. K. Sinha, ed., *Fort William–East India House Correspondence and Other Contemporary Papers Relating Thereto (Public Series). V. 1767–1769* (Delhi: National Archives, 1949), entries for 4 March 1767; my emphasis.

Indians.[20] The Company sought to redefine what constituted gifts with legal validity. Gifts were allowed, in the words of historian Nicholas B. Dirks, "only if they were given for reasons deemed satisfactory in British courts of law, which proposed new taxonomies of gifts and new ideas of political expediency."[21] With this in mind, Governor-General Warren Hastings commissioned the translation of *Forms of Herkern* ("Letters to Foreign Princes," 1782), which describes in detail Islamic giving and receiving of "varieties of rarities of your country."[22] At the same time he tried to replace or at times to supplement Mughal gifts of land grants, jewels and money with a British, but still symbolic and highly personal form of gift: the painted portrait.

In eighteenth-century Britain portraits were increasingly used to strengthen bonds of sociability so as to convey a certain presence of the absent friend/ally through the mediation of likeness.[23] Public men exchanged likenesses (whether oil paintings or prints) to extend kinship networks; they hoped these gifts would also remain "market inalienable."[24] George III used his portraits to promote his cult of sovereignty in the American Colonies, West Indies, Minorca and the colonial trading posts in India. The portrait stood in for the absent monarch – in ways that alluded to the status of portraits as sovereign substitutes used by the rulers of France.[25]

Strategically located close to the French settlement of Pondicherry and the British city of Madras, and staking a claim over the neighboring

[20] At the same date, the Company abolished the annual *Puniyah* ceremony at the prince (*nawab*) of Murshidabad's court at Murshidabad. This had been a highly symbolic occasion when all the important land rentiers in the kingdom of Bengal offered tribute money in return for robes.

[21] Nicholas Dirks, "From Little King to Landlord: Colonial Discourse and Colonial Rule," in *Colonialism and Culture*, ed. Nicholas B. Dirks (Ann Arbor: University of Michigan Press, 1992), 184. See BL, Add Ms 29,092: "Warren Hastings, Durbar Accounts, 1780–85, Hastings Papers."

[22] Francis Balfour, *Forms of Herkern: The Insha-yi Harkhana Corrected from a Variety of Manuscripts* (Calcutta: Erdwin, 1781), 12.

[23] For the exchange of likenesses between public men in Britain, see Louise Lippincott, "Expanding on Portraiture: The Market, the Public and the Hierarchy of Genres in Eighteenth-Century Britain," in *The Consumption of Culture, 1600–1800: Image, Object, Text*, ed. Ann Bermingham and John Brewer (London: Routledge, 1995), 75–88.

[24] What I mean by "market inalienable" are those objects that cannot easily be alienated/transformed into commodities by their sale in the market.

[25] For Louis XIV's portraits as substitutes for the ruler, see Thomas Crow, *Painters and Public Life in Eighteenth-Century Paris* (New Haven: Yale University Press, 1985); Gunter Gebauer and Christoph Wulf, *Mimesis, Art, Culture, Society*, trans. Don Reneau (Berkeley: University of California Press, 1998).

territory of Tanjore, the successor state of the Carnatic played a critical role in South Asian politics. After annexing key territories in the Carnatic the Company provided the defeated nawab with troops, while attempting to coerce other political favors from him. Nawab Muhammad Ali has become known for his shrewd political negotiations and military aggression – he attempted to annex the kingdom of Tanjore and maintained a lobby of supporters in the British Parliament. He employed the former Madras governor, the bankrupt Nicholas Morse, as his "interior designer," and Company engineer John Call as the architect of his 1760s Anglicized Chepauk Palace in Madras. In an attempt to compete with the growing number of French traders in the capital of Arcot, the Court of Directors sent Muhammad Ali gifts of a carriage, globes, a lion, card tables, engravings and two of the well-known artist George Stubbs's oils of *Lion and Tigers*. They told their envoys at the court of Arcot that these gifts should be presented to Muhammad Ali over a lengthy period of time so as to give the appearance of a "regular system" of colonial presence: "we think presents though of no great value, frequently presented may have a better effect than to send them all at once."[26]

George III also sent letters of "friendship" to Muhammad Ali. As we have seen above in the later case of Ab'l Hasan, George III stressed the rhetoric of "friendship" in his diplomatic dealings. Friendship has its own politics of rhetoric and mistrust.[27] In this case "friendship" was already beginning to stress an increasingly hierarchical relationship between the British king and Indian nawabs. Under pressure from the Governor of Madras, George Pigot (in post from 1755 to 1763), Muhammad Ali sent jewels to George III. In reciprocation, the British monarch dispatched one of his many stock-in-trade likenesses by the court painter Allan Ramsay and his studio of assistants, which was accompanied by a letter:

> We accept with satisfaction the white stone which you have sent to us as a mark of your attachment. We shall wear it ourself and deliver it down to Our successors in remembrance of you and in order that you may have before your eyes a memorial of Our regard and affection We send you Our picture and that of Our Queen.[28]

[26] Henry D. Love, *Vestiges of Old Madras, 1640–1800. Traced from the East India Company's Records at Fort St George and the India Office*, 4 vols. (Madras: Government Press, 1913), 3: 618–19.

[27] See Jacques Derrida, "The Politics of Friendship," *American Imago* 50, no. 3 (2003): 353–91.

[28] Love, *Vestiges of Old Madras*, 77. George Paterson also makes mention of "pictures of their Majesties of Britain as proof of friendship and regard," BL, Eur Ms 379/3, f. 247 (15 August 1772).

Swathed in ermine and in a slightly exaggerated swagger pose, Ramsay's likeness of the king is the kind of standard royal image sent out from the artist's extensive studio. As we see in the case of Ab'l Hasan's later portrait (Figure 10.1), it really set the tone for the portrayal of the sovereign/ambassador. On hearing of the arrival in Madras of the group of images, Muhammad Ali sent instructions via his agent:

> That the pictures if they were small and easy to be conveyed, should be sent with the letters to Vellore and there be lodged till he should desire and we should find a proper opportunity to send for and deliver them in such a manner with such ceremony and distinction of that kind mainlined and as would do him most honor on the eyes of the country people.[29]

It seems that the nawab was expecting the pictures to be small scale, perhaps even to be miniatures within the tradition of Mughal diplomacy. His expectations are dressed up in a diplomatic language heavy with ritualistic expectations and a rhetoric of reverence.

A few weeks later, his English agent reported the nawab's response: "I have received the eight pictures of the king, princes etc., which you are pleased to send me out of friendship and am very glad to receive them. I never saw such pictures which are indeed of an exceeding good shape."[30] Possibly referring to the monumental size of these elaborately gilt-framed likenesses, Muhammad Ali's reaction is ambiguous. But in the months that followed, the nawab did sit for a portrait by the minor artist Tilly Kettle, who had just arrived in Madras, which was sent to George III (Figure 10.2).[31] The question of the payment of nawab's portraits is somewhat contentious – a point to which I shall return.

In addition to his gifts of portraits to Governor-General Warren Hastings, Lord Pigot, Governor of Madras, and George III, Muhammad Ali tried to put pressure on the British king and Company directors through his influential lobby of supporters in London who discussed his political situation in Parliament.[32] But beyond these traditional mechanisms of power brokerage, Nawab Muhammad Ali also attempted to insinuate complicity on grounds of the new portrait gifting praxis. Such

[29] BL, India Office Records (hereafter IOR), Home Miscellaneous Series H/30 (30 August 1768).

[30] Love, *Vestiges of Old Madras*, 2: 79.

[31] For Arcot, see John Gurney, "The Nawab of Arcot"s Debts," D.Phil dissertation, University of Oxford, 1964.

[32] Ibid., 67–78.

FIGURE 10.2 Tilly Kettle, *Muhammad Ali Khan, Nawab of Arcot*, 1768. Painted on paper. Victoria and Albert Museum, Bequeathed by Miss Charlotte Sulivan, IM.124–1911.

regulated projection of his royal person also tints his correspondence with George III:

I have Your Majesty's picture night and day before me, endeavoring to console myself by imagining that I have the honor of being ever in your Majesty's Presence. I was desirous of attending in person Your Majesty to return my grateful thanks for the favor of Your Majesty's picture ... I have sent Your Majesty the picture of myself and my children, together with some cloths and some rosewater, hoping that the picture may have that honor of being affixed in Your Majesty's royal sight.[33]

While George III stressed that jewels are, as anthropologist Annette Weiner would put it, inalienable ("we remember you by wearing your jewel," which will become an inalienable possession in our family), Muhammad Ali's letter establishes imitation-as-reciprocation at two levels. The visual idiom of his portrait pays compliment to Ramsay's likeness of George III while challenging the king to participate in his idea of reciprocal portrait appreciation: you look on my image night and day as I look on yours. It would seem then that at least at the level of diplomatic rhetoric the sovereign portrait gift had in this instance achieved some success. Ultimately bored by the increased presence of European artists at his court (to which I turn below), Muhammad Ali would however be coerced by the Company to entertain the presence of a number of European artists. And it would seem that he became the blueprint for colonial attitudes toward Indian rulers in relation to the image gift. Whether he wished these portraits to become inalienable possessions within his family is questionable. He seems to have cared little about the fate of his portraits, which after all were not aesthetically in tune with the artistic taste of his court.

THE FACIALITY OF CORRUPTION: WARREN HASTINGS AND THE IMAGE GIFT

On 11 May 1786 the famous British political satirist James Gillray published a caricature print entitled *The Political-Banditti Assailing the Saviour of India* (Figure 10.3). It is an amalgamation of high art and popular citations – including references to the actor David Garrick as Hamlet, physiognomic studies of anger by French theorist Charles Le Brun, the artist John Hamilton Mortimer's feted depictions of *banditti*

[33] Muhammad Ali quoted in Court Correspondence, vol. 18 (January 1770). Cited in Love, *Vestiges of Old Madras*, 2: 123 (my emphasis).

FIGURE 10.3 James Gillray, *The Political-Banditti Assailing the Saviour of India*, 1786.

in Italy attacking "innocent" and usually wealthy travelers on the open road and the by then usual vilification of the Whig politician and aesthetician of the Sublime and the Beautiful – Edmund Burke, who is depicted as a scrawny, armor-clad, bespectacled Jesuit who has "charged" his firearm with the impeachment charges marked on his bag. One of the best-known images of Hastings's governorship, the image foresaw a number of other prints concerned with India, pictorial likeness and jewels. Astride a camel laden with a celebratory account of conquest and at least four purses of gems meant for the Company, the Crown and, as suggested by its espied label marked "ditto," for himself, the Governor-General Warren Hastings combats the Whig "*banditti*" attack with a shield that bears the British crown and a motto. The motto promises that at least for now he can consider Hastings protected by the "SHIELD OF HONOUR." Unlike the three Whig politicians Burke, Lord North and Charles James Fox, Hastings's face is based on a portrait by the reputed artist Johann Zoffany, which had been published around this time as the frontispiece to Hastings's Indian memoirs. At first glance it appears that to avoid any excessive caricature of Hastings's visage would seem to be Gillray's sign of support for Hastings. The print was reissued two years later but this time by the publisher William Holland during Hastings's trial for impeachment. The very ambiguous, perhaps disparate meaning(s) of the image could then be reread as public opinion rose against Hastings.

Already aware that British satirists were turning against him in the early 1780s, Warren Hastings believed that the British rulers of Bengal must conduct a foreign policy within a diplomatic system comparable to that of Europe while simultaneously upholding at least some outward appearance of Indian diplomacy based on "face-to-face relations."[34] This belief in *presence as inalienability* determined how he attempted to regulate the circulation of his own likenesses. The reputed "success" of portrait exchange at Arcot may have prompted Hastings to incorporate the protocol of portrait gifting into his diplomatic repertoire. Due to Hastings's initial lack of contacts in London's royal circles, however, George III could not be called on to gift his portrait to those nawabs Hastings wished to undermine. These nawabs were primarily the rulers of Bengal, Hyderabad and Arcot where the East India Company had designs. In this case Hastings substituted his own locally painted likeness for that of the king. Here in another way to Gillray's satire is Hastings

[34] Peter J. Marshall, "The Making of a Political Icon: The Case of Warren Hastings," *Journal of Imperial and Commonwealth History* 27, no. 3 (1999): 6.

playing with, perhaps supplementing or usurping royal power. Throughout his trial for impeachment, George III is believed to have adopted a silent loyalty that visual satirists picked up on their attacks on Hastings, his relationship with the monarch and his wife as well as the Lord Chancellor Edward Thurlow.[35]

But Hastings's use of portraits also brings into even more acute focus the radical distinction between colonial and Mughal ideas of presence. The trope of Oriental ruler would be frequently used by Hastings's enemies, who called him "an Indian rajah with a white face – the most terrible creature in God's creation."[36] Even before his trial for impeachment (1788–95) when one political commentator claimed that the print shops formed the channels through which the enemies of Warren Hastings generally transmitted their accusations and insinuations, Hastings's portraits played a critical role in his self-projection in a range of political contexts.[37]

Certainly in the years before the trial it was widely believed that Charles Fox's efforts to reform the English East India Company had been undermined by the satirist James Sayers, who cast him as a fictitious oriental despot – Carlo Khan. As the satires from the time of Hastings's trial suggest, Sayers being an anti-Whig lawyer was certainly in Hastings's employment. Sayers had been instrumental in producing the critical satires that had brought down the Fox–North coalition and the India Bill in December 1783. While Sayers's satires attack Burke as a raving Irish man in many guises, he was careful not to include images of Hastings based on his painted portraits.[38] It would seem that portraiture's entanglement with inalienability and gift was a high, perhaps too sensitive matter for pro-Hastings supporters. This is because of the volatile nature of the public sphere and the political weight given to the agency of likenesses in Britain and India. Faciality, whether the

[35] See Marcia Pointon, *Brilliant Effects: A Cultural History of Gemstones and Jewellery* (New Haven: Yale University Press, 2009).

[36] Philip Lawson and Jim Phillips, "'Our Execrable Banditti': Perceptions of Nabobs in Mid-Eighteenth-Century Britain," *Albion* 16, no. 3 (1984): 239.

[37] This is according to E. K. Robinson's reading of Nathaniel Wraxhall, *Wraxall's History and Posthumous Memoirs*, 8 vols. (London: Richard Bentley, 1836), 4: 342–45; E. K. Robinson, *Edmund Burke: A Life in Caricature* (London: Yale University Press, 1996), 45.

[38] It is important to note that when Hastings was acquitted in 1795, James Sayers produced a print (probably paid for by Hastings) that shows the former governor-general as a marble bust emanating radiance in front of an exasperated Edmund Burke, who holds a paintbrush.

painted physiognomy or the caricature, acted as a critical tool for publicizing politics in the public sphere – hence its danger.

Thus the use of a portrait of Hastings in Gillray's *Political Banditti* is loaded with connotations of the former governor-general's attempts to reform gifting in India. But reforming the image gift in India meant negotiating land and jewels, which as we have seen were held in high esteem. Unlike the affective investment expected from Hastings's likenesses in personal kinship networks, his images became ensnared in networks of powerful nawabs Hastings had never met, in parts of India where he had political, often expansionist ambitions: portraiture then would in part have to do the work of the absent colonial ruler. In the 1780s Indian officials at the independent court of Hyderabad recorded that when the Company annexed Indian states its agents sent messages of friendship, accompanied by European novelties as gifts before requesting or coercing land grants to establish a factory, which would then be armed ready for strategic interventions into the kingdom's affairs.[39] Less than the artifacts themselves, the strategic *timing* of giving, obliging and receiving constituted their agency. What I mean by this is portraits became subsumed in the complex colonizing mechanisms that had little respect for aesthetic principles. But because portraits invoked presence then, they had powerful political weight as substitutes for personhood.

A magnificent Shia city, Hyderabad acted as the wealthy center of the Deccan. Its ruler, the *nizam* Ali Khan (r. 1762–1800), negotiated his strategic position between Mysore, the Carnatic and Maharashtra, and played off the British against the French, to the frustration of both.[40] On his arrival at Hyderabad in the summer of 1784, the Company's Resident Richard Johnson failed to assert Hastings's influence where the dominant external force was Nana Phadnavis, Prime Minister of the Marathas – the Company's enemy. Johnson's letters reveal his personal frustration and his isolation from politics, as he complained that "although I spare neither pains nor expense, authentic information is very difficult to be had

[39] Abd al-latif Shustari, *Tuhfat al 'Alam*, Pers. Ms. Elliot 382, Bodleian Library Oxford, ff. 167–76, cited in Gulfishan Khan, *Indo-Muslim Reactions to the West during the Eighteenth Century* (Karachi: Oxford University Press, 1998), 58–59.

[40] Ashwin Kumar Bakshi, "The Residency of Hyderabad, 1779–1857," PhD Thesis, Osmania University, 1990, 39, notes that from the mid-1770s the Nizam seems to have favored French men at his court over the English. Although the Company wanted to ban all French men, Nizam Ali Khan observed that they were hardly French: "those Europeans are vagrants and aliens to their native country, that they are not French but the refuse of various nations."

here ... it is occasioned by the extreme fear that every man of note suffers that he should be prospected of any intercourse with a foreign resident."[41] To gain favor, assisted by gifts, Johnson wanted Nizam Ali Khan to agree to far-reaching plans that would give him a dominant position in South India if he allied with the British. The nizam's authority would be extended to the Carnatic, which was at the time held by Muhammad Ali (who had been denied it in 1768, leading to his siding against the Company with Mysore). In return, he would make huge payments to the British, settle Muhammad Ali's debts and maintain a British brigade in the Carnatic at his own expense.[42]

Johnson was the first Company Resident to use intensive gifting in the Deccan – including art.[43] He compared the British portrait gift to the exchange of "inalienable" Indian objects. Writing to Hastings he commented:

> I presented your picture handsomely framed to the *soubah* [the nizam] as a peculiar mark of friendship requiring his in exchange, a mode which I said amongst us was familiar to your interchange of turbans. He accepted it as such and is making up a picture in return. You will see how much this pleased him by his particular mention of it in his letter as what he prized much above all the other valuable presents to be laid before him by me from you.[44]

Although a degree of iconographic and rhetorical reciprocity had been asserted in the case of the exchange of George III and Muhammad Ali's portraits, this equivalence would be disrupted by Hastings's likenesses. The best he could hope for was for mutual appreciation of artistic difference. Nizam Ali Khan styled himself as an art patron to rival the rulers of Arcot, Mysore and Lucknow. He collected rare Mughal images; he commissioned illuminated chronicles of his predecessors and of events from his own reign, which included images of conflict with the Company and his preference for French adventurers. If Nizam Ali Khan did reciprocate with a portrait for

[41] John Rylands Library, Manchester, Johnson Papers Eng Ms 195: "Richard Johnson to Warren Hastings July 4, 1784." This confirmed Johnson's previous intelligence: Eng Ms 195, March 5, 1784: "The Nizam seems to be one of those princes whose existence or power of existence depends on being the keystone of an arch up equal purpose from all sides."

[42] Peter J. Marshall, "Richard Johnson, Collector," unpublished paper. I am grateful to the author for a copy of this paper.

[43] Bakshi, "Residency of Hyderabad," 32, notes that a trickle of gifts had been used by previous residents.

[44] BL, Hastings Papers, Add Ms 29167, f. 253: "Richard Johnson to Hastings, December 20, 1784."

Hastings, it was not by a British artist. This indicates his refusal to participate in the colonial gift precedent set by his rival Muhammad Ali. Throughout his reign no colonial painter visited Hyderabad. Intent on remaining independent, Nizam Ali Khan did not want to entertain colonial painters, who as we shall see in the case of Lucknow, were ambitious and intrusive.[45] After receiving Hastings's portrait, he did entrust the governor-general through Johnson (Hastings was about to resign and return to London) with a diamond ring to be gifted to George III. Like Muhammad Ali (and Mughal rulers before them), Nizam Ali Khan believed that precious jewels not only possessed inherent magical, divinatory powers but also carried the charisma of the giver and their previous owners. But for the British public, this gift (lacking the element of inalienable presence of portraits) was not truly "singular." Hastings's enemies accused him of trying to bribe the English king, thus insisting on the purely commercial value of the gifted objects while British satirists as I have suggested above pictured him as a base, calculating official out only to seek royal favor through gifts. At Hyderabad at this time political relations between the Company and the nizam collapsed. Although recalled from Lucknow in 1782, much to his anger and disappointment, Johnson had already accumulated hundreds of Mughal images from this leading cultural city. And Hastings would try to do the same.

Johnson and Hastings competed for Mughal miniatures with those European traders Antoine de Polier, John Wombwell and Claude Martin, based in Lucknow. Many of these pictures came from the courts of former Mughal rulers and they would in turn be copied by contemporary Indian artists in Lucknow. European artists also began to appropriate stylistic elements from Mughal art at Lucknow as this city became the site of artistic experiment where an "Anglo-Indian *qalam*" (style) came into being precisely at this time.

On his accession to the throne in 1775, the nawab Asaf ud-daula (1775–97) moved the Awadhi capital from Faizabad to Lucknow, which he transformed into a Shia capital to rival Hyderabad. Like Arcot and Hyderabad, Lucknow became the hotbed of intrigue where French, Dutch, Armenian, Portuguese, British and other traders, soldiers, diplomats and later artists all sought to make their fortunes. Lucknow had

[45] As I have suggested above in the Carnatic Muhammad Ali seems to have had little time for European painters. His likenesses by them are remarkably similar, suggesting that after Tilly Kettle few artists could experiment with the designated form of likeness. Maybe they had limited or no access to the ruler himself.

been the target of Company expansion since the 1770s, when Hastings dispatched several Political Residents to implement the Company's agenda of territorial annexation. As early as 1775, the Company attempted to depose the new nawab, and for the rest of his life Asaf ud-daula continually contested British policies of expansion.[46]

In an attempt to improve Anglo-Indian relations, Hastings spent five months at Lucknow.[47] In the hope of impressing the court with European aesthetics, he invited one of George III's former favorites, Zoffany, as his official artist. Still free from Company control, the Lucknow court did not adhere to the gifting strictures of the Regulating Act. In the eyes of one of the court's poets, this had been a fabulous epoch characterized by lavish gifting: "At the time of his [Hastings's] departure, the exalted *nawab* gave gifts to Hastings' men in such large numbers that no one could ever imagine. Every person of any note was given a horse, an elephant and a fine robe."[48] Asaf wanted to project the image of an exalted ruler who gives to his subordinates and allies in dazzling, public displays of munificence.[49]

Hastings left Lucknow in late August 1784 having failed to reach a new agreement and feeling "horrified" (at least in his correspondence to the Company) by the lavish entertainments Asaf had organized for him – which incidentally had the effect of increasing Awadh's debts to the Company.[50] As a gesture of contempt for the Company's policy and perhaps also for that hybrid "Anglo-Indian style" developing in his capital, the nawab gave one of his portraits by Zoffany to a disgraced Company official about to be court-martialed, while ordering his artists to adjust the physiognomy, pose and setting to produce images more in line with his ideas of *firāsa* (physiognomy). Although Zoffany would spend three years at Lucknow in the patronage of the Martin circle, he had few commissions from the nawab. No British artist visited Hyderabad until the court came under indirect Company rule in 1798. But while both Hastings's and Johnson's political missions ultimately failed, the image gift was already making a devastating impact.

[46] Richard Barnett, *North India between Empires: Awadh, the Mughals and the British, 1720–1801* (Berkeley: University of California Press, 1980).

[47] *Calendar of Persian Correspondence Being Letters Mainly Relating to Affairs in Bengal*, 11 vols. (Calcutta: GPO, Imperial Archives Series, 1911), vol. 5 (May 20, 1781). Asaf ud-daula wanted the Resident Bristow to be recalled; if Hastings did not comply, he also threatened to write to the British Prime Minister.

[48] Mīr Taqī Mīr, *Zikr-i Mir: The Autobiography of the Eighteenth-Century Mughal Poet: Mir Muhammad Taqi Mir*, trans. C. M. Naim (Delhi: Oxford University Press, 1999), 124.

[49] Mir, *Zikr-i Mir*, 121–23.

[50] BL, Hastings Papers, Add Ms 29121 (3 May 1784).

While Hastings tried to deploy the exchange of portraits at still-independent Hyderabad as a means for negotiating cultural difference, at courts already coming under indirect Company control colonial likenesses began to subvert indigenous gifting and patterns of artistic patronage. Hastings's peculiar mimicry of Mughal and British gifting practices had a cutting edge: it operated as de facto tribute from the indigenous rulers for which no return gift was made. At Lucknow and Arcot, Hastings's successors dispatched British artists to take the likenesses of these nawabs, but did not reciprocate with their own portraits. Instead, they annulled or at least mystified the notion of art as gift, by anticipating that princes would send their likenesses to the governor-general and pay the British painter for this "privilege." Perhaps the portrait-gift became a species of "tribute"? By this I mean the idea of reciprocation broke down as the painted likeness became a coercive token. This is especially the case of the role of portraits at Arcot and Lucknow – those courts most set on by the British.

The difference between British and Indian ideas of inalienability and obligation now structured the image-gift. During a diplomatic mission to Lucknow in 1797, Governor-General Sir John Shore described these conflicting interests in a letter to his wife:

> This day I had a private audience with the nawab ... I have refused a fortune ... my answer ... was this; that a barleycorn from him was equal in my sight to a million rupees; but I could not but express my concern that he and his people were ignorant of our customs and my character to make such an offer ... I added that I had seen in his *shusha khana* [*sic*] ["mirror room"] – some pictures of his ... of which I begged to have one as a memorial of our friendship ... I took one about fifteen inches square done by Zoffany, not set in diamonds, which is a strong resemblance to the nawab and for which to say truth, I would not give two pence. It pleased him.[51]

While much literature on the gift argues that the donor acquires superiority over the receiver and in the process creates indebtedness, here the "recipient" solicited the gift through a covert exercise of his power over the giver, by forcing him to part with what Shore perceived to be an "inalienable possession."[52] Shore claimed that a single grain outstrips a million rupees, that this singular token alone could embody the nawab's

[51] Victoria Manners and George Williamson, *Johann Zoffany, R.A., His Life and Works, 1735–1810* (London: John Lane, 1920), 20.

[52] Marcel Mauss, *The Gift: Forms and Functions of Exchange in Archaic Societies*, trans. Ian Cunnison (London: Cohen and West, 1954), 45–67.

exalted presence – that it is gift enough. Yet his private correspondence deflates the "inalienable" image-gift into little more than a banal souvenir. His action also suggests his power to choose anything he desired. A painted likeness being tied to notions of inalienability made it rhetorically desirable – even if Shore had no interest in portraiture it would seem.

Against the grain of Muhammad Ali's staged iconicity Asaf had other plans for his colonial likenesses. That his portrait was "not set in diamonds" indicates that soliciting likenesses in jewel-encrusted frames was a common practice. Aware of the by now archaic ritual of *shast wa shabah* (introduced by Akbar, whereby a portrait is bestowed on the giver in the emperor-sun prostration) which involved setting imperial images in diamond or pearl frames (a practice he would later imitate, by giving his miniature image to devoted followers), Asaf intended to style himself as a successor to the Mughal rulers. But from a colonial perspective, to ask for a picture in a diamond frame (seemingly "legal" and reportable to the Company authorities) contained a crucial subtext. The nawab wanted to gift colonial pictures so as to foist a sense of personal obligation onto the recipient. Anticipating this colonial pressure to give and playing with their desire for what they perceived as inalienable possessions, Asaf invited British officials to the "anglicized" spaces of his palace or presented his colonial-painted likenesses to colonial governors. During the same period, Company officials voraciously "collected" rare illuminated Mughal manuscripts, which on return to Britain they frequently claimed were presents, or which they gifted to George III.[53] By denying the British access to his treasury, library and *karkhana* (studio), Asaf hoped to deflect the scopic drive of the Company from the inner lives of his court and from his preferred definition of "inalienable possessions" – Mughal and Persian art. He staged his British-painted portraits as objects for competition and possession, while keeping them at a suitable distance from his established iconography of kingship.

[53] For instance, in 1799 John Shore, again at Lucknow, was "gifted" the famous Padshahnama manuscript, now in Windsor Castle. Asaf ud-daula had died in 1797 and the politics of succession had been fiercely fought – the British pushing their candidate Saadat Ali Khan to accession. During this coup, the famous Padshahnama was "gifted" along with five other Mughal manuscripts: "this is the most splendid Persian manuscript I ever saw ... which was shown to me at Lucknow and I was there informed that the deceased Nabob Asophuddoulah purchased it for 12000 Rs., or about £1500". Milo C. Beach and Ebba Koch, *King of the World: The Padshahnama Manuscript* (Windsor: Windsor Castle Publications, 1997), 13.

This distance did however involve a politics of display, as it had been the case with Muhammad Ali's portraits. Writing to thank Muhammad Ali for his portrait, Hastings promised that "for want of a better place to put it, it will hang in the Court House along with the portraits of the King and Queen of England. As this is the room where all public ceremonies are held, as well as the court of justice, the portrait will become the object of attention."[54] Hastings "orientalizes" the Court House in Calcutta to project an "occidentalized" version of the Mughal hall of audience.

These display strategies became entangled with the difficult negotiations between artists, nawabs and governors. Toward the end of his stay at Arcot (fl. 1774–80), the Scottish portraitist George Willison complained to Hastings:

> I have ever since been soliciting the payment of this picture that was sent you and having now the space of four years been assured with repeated promises of the nawab ... but I find myself as distant from my reward as I was the first day and I am afraid it will be my hard fate to submit to the necessity of putting up with the loss ... even after repeated intentions that I have given him of the necessity that he had put me under of applying to you and repeated requests on his part that I would not do so, as he would pay me himself. You will easily see how unwilling I was to trouble you with this demand.[55]

Mildred Archer long ago suggested that Muhammad Ali, for "having the honor" of a British artist at his court, should have paid for the portrait and send it as gift to Hastings in Calcutta.[56] But in Britain, portraits were rarely paid for by their sitters; rather, the picture's recipient, eager to have the likeness of the person portrayed, paid the painter's fee.[57] The East India Company was demanding as much as half the annual revenue of kingdoms such as Awadh, and so it could well have afforded to pay for nawabs' portraits. Its refusal emphasizes the ambivalence of colonial foreign policy even in the domain of face painting.

The British portraitists such as Willison, Zoffany and Ozias Humphry were themselves caught up in a field of tension. They charged their Indian sitters as much as they could (Willison wanted "double at the durbar," while Humphry increased his prices by 100 percent, billing Asaf ud-daula

[54] Mildred Archer, *India and British Portraiture, 1770–1825* (London: Sotheby Parke Barnet, 1979), 123.

[55] BL, Hastings Papers, Add Ms 29145, f. 203: "George Willison to Hastings."

[56] Archer, *India and British Portraiture*, 45.

[57] Louise Lippincott, "Expanding on Portraiture: The Market, the Public and the Hierarchy of Genres in 18th-Century Britain," in *Consumption of Culture 1600–1800: Image, Object, Text*, ed. Ann Bermingham and John Brewer (London: Routledge, 1995).

£1000 for a miniature). Yet their position, caught between the Company and court, remained precarious. Although Hastings maneuvered British artists across India, his successors Sir John Macpherson (1785–86) and Lord Cornwallis (1786–93) maintained a far more ambivalent attitude toward these portraitists. Given this lack of official interest, the reforms of the Parliamentary India Act of 1784 and severe economic recession, by 1786 Calcutta's colonial portrait market had collapsed. Desperate painters left in search of either exotic landscapes as the inspiration for print schemes or portrait commissions at other independent Indian courts.[58]

Both the nawabs of the Carnatic and Awadh played on the greed of colonial traders – including British artists. By promising to meet their extravagant fees, but then delaying once the pictures were finished, Muhammad Ali and Asaf ud-daula used *deferral* as a strategy. But deferral had its own cost. Although colonial artists left these courts unpaid, they later tried to claim payment through Company intervention. Willison's bill at Arcot was eventually settled when incorporated with the nawab's debts, which the Company recuperated through *tankhwah* – the assignment of revenue on a tract of land or its annexation to the Company.[59] By the 1770s tankhwahs had been used by both the Company and private traders in their attempts to recover loans from the nawab of the Carnatic, as well as providing a means for paying those mercenary troops stationed in foreign kingdoms. At Arcot, the internal order of revenue collection and the unity of the nawab's court had been destroyed by this system, the result being the formation of a network of Company interests across the Carnatic.[60] Likewise in 1780s Awadh, the Resident at Lucknow initially promised the British miniaturist Ozias Humphry a tankhwah to the value of £4,830 for the following year at 12 percent interest, although Humphry, impatient to return to London, did not want to wait. At the same time, the Resident at Benares negotiated Humphry's rival – Charles Smith's fees through the promise of yet another tankhwah in exchange for the settlement of debts owed to Europeans.[61] Nine years after his return to London, the miniaturist John Smart, who worked for ten years at Arcot, complained that his bill of £1600 remained unpaid and

[58] See Natasha Eaton, *Mimesis across Empires: Artworks and Networks in India, 1765–1860* (Durham: Duke University Press, 2013), ch. 2.

[59] See Gurney, "Nawab of Arcot's Debts." [60] Ibid., 112–16.

[61] See Rosie Llewellyn-Jones, *A Very Ingenious Man: Claud Martin in Early Colonial India* (Delhi: Permanent Black, 1992), 125; Llewellyn-Jones, *A Man of the Enlightenment: Claud Martin in Eighteenth-Century India* (Delhi: Oxford University Press, 2003).

so he submitted several affidavits to the Company.[62] Zoffany applied to the Court of Directors to return to India in 1811 to recover his debts, which had once been promised through tankhwah. Although Smith and Willison were paid the money they were "owed," the fate of other artists indicates that the Company used tankhwahs to appropriate their fees for itself.[63] The demands of a few European artists may have been one among several motives for implementing land annexation, but their pleas were ultimately ignored by the Company's aggressive military and financial expansion into Indian kingdoms.

CONCLUSION: THE QUESTION OF LIKENESS

Likeness then had multivalent significations as an object, as coercive token, as an object that incited debt. Certainly artists were the pawns in this diplomatic game. If portraits can be deemed to be gifts by their invocation of likeness, the uneasy relationship between likeness and inalienability led to numerous diplomatic quandaries and acts of aggression, which this chapter has hoped to flag up.

As the last independent nawab of Awadh, and as a great patron of artists and civic town planning saving Awadh in time of famine, Asaf ud-daula became a mythical, heroic figure whose reputation was enhanced by his ambivalent approach toward British art.[64] Unlike Muhammad Ali, he had no interest in disseminating his portrait to Britain and although he encouraged later European artists to produce a series of views of Lucknow, he rejected their finished drawings; one of his ministers warned Cornwallis that the Lucknow regime would not tolerate printing presses. No British painter was satisfied with his treatment in Awadh, as the nawab favored his own court art to anything the British could do.[65]

62 BL, IOR, Home Miscellaneous Series, H/298, f. 1496; H/322, f. 469.

63 Both the Scottish artists Charles Smith and George Willison were well connected in London and Calcutta society. Their relatives were politicians and Company directors, which helped them to persuade high-ranking colonial officials to intervene on their behalf. Failing to settle issues of payment, Humphry, Smart and Zoffany returned to London, hoping that they would be able to continue their struggle for money by petitioning the directors or making contact with important Company officials such as Hastings.

64 See Eaton, *Mimesis across Empires*, esp. ch. 4, for discussion of this in more detail.

65 No portrait painter was swiftly paid and Ozias Humphry records that Asaf ud-daula sat three times "without any apparent impatience," which suggests expectations of the *nawab*'s aversion to British artists. Royal Academy of Art, London, HU/1–8: "Ozias Humphry's Diary," vol. 3, f. 6.

At this time princes maneuvered revenue away from Company surveillance or control. Instead of paying off British debts, nawabs built up commission networks with private traders whose relations with the Company were equivocal.[66] Images participated in the game of bluff and counterbluff as nawabs sought to exclude the British from surveillance, access or control of their resources, turning conspicuous consumption – mimicry of the elite collecting practices of the Other – into a specific form of control: an object-driven, obstinate resistance.[67]

But still, Ab'l Hasan had to write that a jewel has now only become a "likeness": it is a bit of glass! The colonial dialectic between jewels and portraits had come into being in and out of the colony, which opened up questions of inalienability, tribute and the gift. This from a colonial perspective is I think best encapsulated by Gillray's *Political Banditti* (Figure 10.3). Behind the irony of Gillray's SHIELD OF HONOUR, which ambiguously represented royal power, here is an ominous take of an emerging regime of colonial value that while it sought to appropriate, even to fetishize jewels, could not as yet decide what it wanted to do about the question of likeness – painted or otherwise. But there were also other ways of working with colonial images and jewels: to see through the colonial charade in the face of diplomacy, as my opening case of Ab'l Hasan suggests. Perhaps Ab'l Hasan as an international traveler in the Islamic world had a sense that even by the late eighteenth century coercion and recognition had come to characterize the British colonial gift, whether it be jewel, portrait, a bit of glass or otherwise.

[66] Llewellyn-Jones, *A Very Ingenious Man*, 126. This is especially the case with Tipu, who sent an envoy to Paris, receiving the favor of the French royals in 1789 and commissioning a French man – Cherry – to take his portrait and another to construct a mechanical tiger mauling a colonial official.

[67] Barnett, *North India between Empire*, 101.

Index

For EU product safety concerns, contact us at Calle de José Abascal, 56–1°, 28003 Madrid, Spain or eugpsr@cambridge.org.

www.ingramcontent.com/pod-product-compliance
Ingram Content Group UK Ltd.
Pitfield, Milton Keynes, MK11 3LW, UK
UKHW020338140625
459647UK00018B/2213
* 9 7 8 1 1 0 8 4 0 1 5 0 0 *